Sustainable Development Goals Series

The **Sustainable Development Goals Series** is Springer Nature's inaugural cross-imprint book series that addresses and supports the United Nations' seventeen Sustainable Development Goals. The series fosters comprehensive research focused on these global targets and endeavours to address some of society's greatest grand challenges. The SDGs are inherently multidisciplinary, and they bring people working across different fields together and working towards a common goal. In this spirit, the Sustainable Development Goals series is the first at Springer Nature to publish books under both the Springer and Palgrave Macmillan imprints, bringing the strengths of our imprints together.

The Sustainable Development Goals Series is organized into eighteen subseries: one subseries based around each of the seventeen respective Sustainable Development Goals, and an eighteenth subseries, "Connecting the Goals," which serves as a home for volumes addressing multiple goals or studying the SDGs as a whole. Each subseries is guided by an expert Subseries Advisor with years or decades of experience studying and addressing core components of their respective Goal.

The SDG Series has a remit as broad as the SDGs themselves, and contributions are welcome from scientists, academics, policymakers, and researchers working in fields related to any of the seventeen goals. If you are interested in contributing a monograph or curated volume to the series, please contact the Publishers: Zachary Romano [Springer; zachary.romano@springer.com] and Rachael Ballard [Palgrave Macmillan; rachael.ballard@palgrave.com].

Marco Tavanti

Developing Sustainability in Organizations

A Values-Based Approach

palgrave
macmillan

Marco Tavanti
School of Management
University of San Francisco
San Francisco, CA, USA

ISSN 2523-3084 ISSN 2523-3092 (electronic)
Sustainable Development Goals Series
ISBN 978-3-031-36906-3 ISBN 978-3-031-36907-0 (eBook)
https://doi.org/10.1007/978-3-031-36907-0

Cover illustration: Barbara Boensch/Alamy Stock Photo

This Palgrave Macmillan imprint is published by the registered company Springer Nature Switzerland AG
The registered company address is: Gewerbestrasse 11, 6330 Cham, Switzerland

To our current generation. That we may become conscious of the shared responsibilities for our common future. As an Oglala-Lakota Chief once told me: "we are the ancestors of future generations."

Foreword

In a rapidly evolving world, the fate of our planet, the prosperity of our societies, and the well-being of our species are inextricably linked to the values and practices we collectively embrace. The book you hold in your hands is more than a mere collection of ideas and concepts; it is an urgent call for action, a compelling manifesto for change, and a clarion call to revolutionize the way we think, act, and lead in the pursuit of sustainability.

As you embark on this transformative journey, you will be confronted with the complexity, the urgency, and the moral imperative of sustainability. The dimensions of this challenge encompass not only the ecological balance of our planet but also the social and economic ramifications of our choices. This book presents an integrated and holistic perspective on sustainability, one that transcends the traditional silos of academia and industry, and transcends borders and disciplines.

This is not a book for the faint of heart or the complacent. It is a provocative and inspiring invitation to examine your own values, beliefs, and actions and to challenge the status quo. It is an invitation to redefine success and to reimagine leadership, management, and innovation in organizations. It is a call to acknowledge the urgency of the sustainability crisis and to respond with courage, creativity, and determination.

The pages that follow are a treasure trove of cutting-edge insights, grounded in empirical research and illuminated by vivid case studies. You will meet pioneers and visionaries from around the world who are pushing the boundaries of what is possible and demonstrating the power of human ingenuity and collaboration. Through their stories and their wisdom, you will discover the transformative potential of sustainability as a guiding principle, a source of inspiration, and a catalyst for innovation.

As you delve into the depths of this book, you will be challenged to question your own assumptions and to reconsider the paradigms that have shaped your worldview. You will be equipped with the knowledge, the tools, and the motivation to become an agent of change in your own organization and in the world at large. The path to a sustainable future is not an easy one, but it is one that we must all walk together.

As you read the chapters and cases of this book, you will recognize the critical need for academia to integrate sustainability into the very fabric of their management, leadership, and innovation curricula. No longer can educational institutions afford to teach in silos; the next generation of leaders, managers, and innovators must be equipped with a deep understanding of sustainability principles and practices, and the ability to incorporate them into their decision-making processes. The world is rapidly changing, and academia must rise to the challenge, ensuring that future generations are prepared to tackle the sustainability crisis head-on.

In this spirit, I appeal to you, the reader, to embrace the profound potential of measurable impact for sustainability practices in organizations. By implementing evidence-based strategies and monitoring our progress, we can ensure that our actions not only serve our immediate goals but contribute to a net benefit for our common good and shared future. As you journey through this book, let the stories and insights inspire you to be a pioneer, to redefine your understanding of success, and to relentlessly pursue a sustainable legacy in your own organization.

The stakes are high, and the time for action is now. The future of our planet, the vitality of our ecosystems, and the very survival of our species depend on our collective willingness to embrace the values and principles of sustainability. This book is an essential guide for anyone who seeks to be a part of the solution and a catalyst for change. It is an invitation to join the vanguard of a new, sustainable era in human history—an era defined by compassion, wisdom, and a fierce commitment to the greater good.

The power of collective action cannot be understated. Each of us, individually and together, has the potential to change the trajectory of our world. By embracing sustainability, we can contribute to a brighter, more equitable, and more prosperous future for all. The choices we make today will resonate through generations, and the time to act is now. Let us unite in our shared commitment to sustainability and forge a path towards a world that flourishes in harmony with nature, ensuring the well-being of all its inhabitants.

The journey begins here, with you, as you open this book and take your first steps towards a deeper understanding of the dimensions and values of sustainability, and the implications for leaders, managers, and innovators in organizations. Together, let us rise to the occasion and transform our organizations, our institutions, and our world for the better, leaving an enduring legacy for the generations to come. Let us face the challenge together and create a future that is truly sustainable, equitable, and just.

Welcome to the sustainability revolution.

Santiago, Chile

Alfredo Sfeir-Younis, Ph.D.
President, Zambuling Institute for Human Transformation
Fmr. Director and First Environmental Economist at the World Bank

Preface

This book emerges from my work in sustainability with academic partners in Europe and the United States, Africa and Latin America, Southeast Asia, and the Middle East. It is written with YOU in mind. You who share a common passion and action to make the world a better place for all, including future generations. As an educator of leaders, managers, and entrepreneurs, this book is written from the perspective of a student of these disciplines. As a professional myself and a trainer for sustainable development competencies, I referenced initiatives and practices which help develop our professional capacity. As a fellow global citizen and student of the world, I have organized the parts and chapters of this book with the elements that are most needed in developing sustainability capacities worldwide and across sectors. I have attempted to bridge analytical perspectives with practical considerations. The selection of material is based on my 20+ years of experience teaching dedicated leaders and impactful entrepreneurs. I have included information about managers from diverse backgrounds and sectors to demonstrate these examples. I hope it inspires your interest and gives you the tools to navigate the complexities of developing and integrating sustainability into organizations.

I vividly remember in 2006 when I was sitting at a conference next to Ray C. Anderson, at that time the founder and chairman of Interface Inc. We began talking about sustainability values. He really impressed me as he shared my same passion and that of numerous NGO leaders who wanted to make the world a better place. He was not using a humanistic or philanthropic language, but was making a business case for poverty alleviation and sustainable development. We were at a gathering of academics and leaders connected to the United Nations Global Compact (UNGC). We were developing an initiative to educate leaders and managers for sustainability and global responsibility. Those conversations set the foundation of what became the Principles of Responsible Management Education (PRME). It was then that I realized my own responsibility as a leadership professor and sustainability practitioner was needed to contribute to the development of sustainability mindsets and skills of leaders, managers, entrepreneurs, and global citizens. It also confirmed my call to promote sustainable development and develop academic-community partnerships with social enterprise organizations in Chiapas, Mexico, and other remote communities worldwide.

We need competency and effective capacity to protect the term sustainability from becoming a jingoistic buzzword. While the field of sustainability is rapidly expanding across disciplines and sectors, one of the main challenges is educating sustainability leaders, managers, and practitioners with comprehensive mindsets and competent skill sets. The risk of expanding and applying "sustainability" or the "Sustainable Development Goals" as buzzwords for every situation without grasping its dimensions, pillars, implications, and specific implications is to create more citations of "green-washing" or "SDG-washing." That is why we share a responsibility to do good with higher purpose efforts and do it well through competent actions. Through this writing, I hope to connect with you who care about our common (shared) values, our common good (and well-being), and our common home (and common future). I hope you enjoy the book and together we can become more conscious of our interconnectedness and common future.

San Francisco, USA — Marco Tavanti

Acknowledgments

I am grateful to many people and organizations who have contributed to this book. My MBA and EMBA business students have given me useful insights in the selection and analysis of case studies of sustainability leaders and organizations that should be studied in business schools. My MPA and public service students have given me their perspectives on policy design and systems thinking which has been critical in the perspectives of this book. My MNA and nonprofit management students have given me their perspectives for multi-sector partnership and multi-stakeholders participation, and community well-being that have been included in this book.

My colleagues at University of San Francisco's School of Management and at DePaul University's School of Public Service have been crucial in the development of these perspectives and for identifying the challenges and opportunities to develop and integrate sustainability into higher education. The leaders, organizations, and institutions that have collaborated with me during the past 20+ years of global immersions, study abroad programs, and academic partnerships have been essential for identifying the principles, dimensions, and approaches for sustainable community and international development. I am grateful to The United Nations Ambassadors Club video conferences coordinated by Amb. Ahmad Kamal and Prof. Pat Szczerba, with the New York UN headquarter visits, conferences, partnerships, and projects. There I met with Dr. Alfredo Sfeir-Younis, George Kell of the UNGC, and Secretary-General Kofi Annan and Ban Ki Moon, Mary Robinson, Jeffrey Sachs, and many others. I am also grateful to partnerships with the UNDP, the World Bank, FAO, and IFAD that have provided some of the perspectives included in this book.

Specifically, I would like to acknowledge and express my deepest gratitude to Dr. Alfredo Sfeir-Younis for mentorship and coaching on sustainability leadership all these years. I also would like to thank Gen. (Ret.) Charles E. Tucker for his leadership, collaboration, and friendship in the World Engagement Institute (WEI). His insights on sustainable human security have been essential for instilling and integrating human rights-centered approaches to sustainable development. I am deeply grateful to my colleague and friends Dr. Larry Brewster and Noreen Barrington for their attentive and insightful editing. Finally, I also would like to express my gratitude to my life companion Liz Wilp who has accompanied the journey of the last 25 years and has inspired many perspectives on education, diversity, inclusion, and participation through her leadership in the Sustainable Capacity International Institute (SCII) and the consultations in the SDG-Services. I am also grateful to my daughter, my parents, and my family for their patience with me while dedicated to this book during my academic sabbatical.

About This Book

This book is designed to give an overview of the main aspects of sustainability in leadership values and mindsets, managerial practices in organizations across sectors, and through innovative solutions and impact measurements. The title of this book "*Developing Sustainability in Organizations*" emphasizes the connection between the educational aspects of sustainable development in organizations across sectors and industries. The subtitle "*A Values-based Approach*" indicates how values and principles are the foundation of every practice in sustainability leadership, management, innovation, and impact. It is written with a "*birds-eye view*" perspective that allows the reader to get a panoramic and long-range overview of the key elements for core sustainability subjects. It is not a theoretical or philosophical exercise on the notions of sustainability—which, although still important, could be discovered in other publications. It is not a detailed technical manual for specific sustainability practices which are continuously evolving and can be in other expert publications.

The purpose of this book is therefore to educate professionals and university students about the essential theories, core initiatives, and best practices to integrate sustainability into organizations. Sustainability leadership, management, innovation, and impact are reviewed from the perspective of shared values and core principles. The combination of theoretical and practical applications is designed to give the reader a deeper, scientific, and critical understanding of the urgent, complex, and necessary values for a sustainable future for all. The writing style is explanatory and pedagogical in nature, geared to self-taught professionals and graduate students in management programs such as MBAs (Business), MPAs (Public), or MNAs (Nonprofit). The cases are selected to be relevant for educational and development needs across sectors from private-corporate to public-governmental as well as NGO-civil society. The sections are organized in a way that the reader and an instructor can easily access and reference key elements to be considered for each topic. As illustrated in Figure 1, the book is organized in four parts focusing on the values connected to sustainability leadership, management, innovation, and impact. These core areas and their key components are identified as essential for developing sustainability in organizations through an integrated and values-based approach.

Part 1: Sustainability Leadership: This first part introduces the main elements of sustainability as relevant to the values and principles that make the foundation for sustainability leadership practices. It addresses the core principles and practices of sustainability as related to core values for social (people), environmental (planet), and economic (prosperity). It provides the reader with an integrated view of mindsets and the role of higher purpose with cases and examples of sustainability leaders and organizations leading the way. It provides an overview of core sustainability documents and declarations that are central for understanding the evolution of sustainability practices in organizations.

Part 2: Sustainability Management: This second part explores the managerial and practical elements of promoting sustainability in organizations and institutions. It follows the first part exploring leadership values as foundations for good leadership practices and focuses on management practices as relevant to organizational administration across sectors. It specifically focuses on integrating perspectives for economic, environmental, social, and governance (EESG). It provides a comprehensive overview of today's practices of sustainability management in organizations through tools and perspective including sustainable HR and sustainable impact investing. It offers numerous cases of key initiatives and leading organizational examples across diverse sectors.

Part 3: Sustainability Innovation: Part three illustrates how sustainability innovation is correlated with other practices such as social entrepreneurship, ecopreneurship, and frugal approaches. It presents the cases of emerging new forms of organizations that embed their sustainability mission into the core business activities. This part of the book presents examples of technological innovations and how they contribute

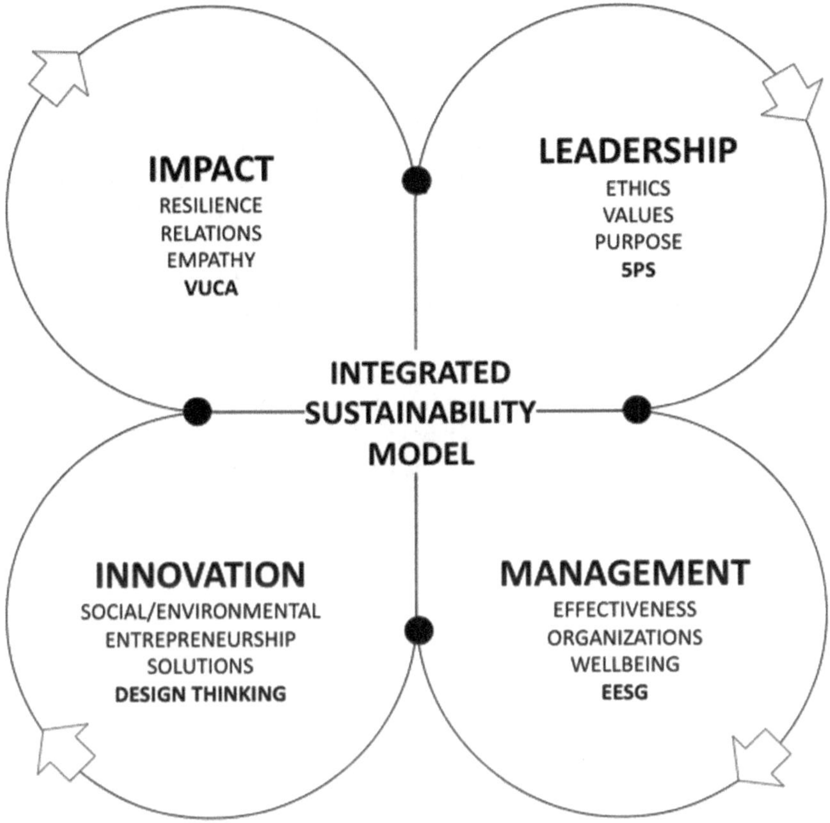

Fig. 1 Developing sustainability model

to achieve the SDGs. It also presents Design Thinking methods for creating sustainability innovative solutions along other frameworks, methods, and approaches.

Part 4: Sustainability Impact: The final part introduces the notion of sustainability impact in relation to policies and international normatives and commitments that can have a systemic impact on the future of society and the world. It provides frameworks connected to sustainability measurements and standards in sustainability reportings and certifications.

The book includes a number of cases and organizational examples to better understand how sustainability is integrated by organizations, leaders, and innovators. The cases are purposely descriptive in nature to allow the reader, students, and faculty to design their own case study analysis exercises where they can analyze the people and organizations with the focus area of their course or lessons. Students can use these cases to critically, comparatively, and constructively analyze them. The list of abbreviations gives you a chance to assess how well you know the different initiatives. You could also use the glossary at the end of the book to have a rapid overview of some essential subjects related to sustainability. I have included lists of some of the most known books, documents, initiatives, and tools used in sustainability organizational practices. These readings have inspired generations of sustainability leaders and the initiatives will hopefully help you collaborate with others in your own organization. These tools are known to sustainability managers and used by many Chief Sustainability Officers (CSOs). They can be useful to enhance your own competencies and career contributing to sustainability.

Contents

About the Author

Dr. **Marco Tavanti** is Professor for Sustainability Value Leadership at University of San Francisco's School of Management. In his 30 years teaching and professional experience, he has advanced and directed numerous international partnerships with academic institutions worldwide for the development of conscious leaders and sustainable communities. He has contributed to the establishment of the *United Nations Global Compact* and its *Principles of Responsible Management Education*. As President of the *Sustainable Capacity International Institute* and co-founder of the *World Engagement Institute*, he links teaching with professional development for sustainable human security in post-conflict and challenging contexts. He has published more than 100 studies in the area of sustainability, value leadership, and cross-cultural aspects of responsible management education. He serves on the Editorial Board of the Journal of Management for Global Sustainability and has recently published *Sustainability Ethics: Common Good Values for a Better World* and, with Dr. Alfredo Sfeir-Younis, *Conscious Sustainability Leadership: A New paradigm for Next Generation Leaders.*

Abbreviations

5Ps	People, Planet, Prosperity, Peace, Partnership
AACSB Int.	Association to Advance Collegiate Schools of Business
AASHE	The Association for the Advancement of Sustainability in Higher Education
AfCFTA	Africa Continental Free Trade Area
AIA	Appreciative Inquiry Approach
AMBA	Association of MBAs
BCtA	Business Call to Action
BIA	Benefit Impact Assessment
BII	Business Integrity Initiative
BRAC	Building Resources Across Communities
C2C	Cradle to Cradle
CARB	California Air Resources Board
CBD	Convention on Biological Diversity
CDP	Carbon Disclosure Project
CE	Circular Economy
CEAP	EU Circular Economy Action Plan
CEO	Chief Executive Officer
CICs	Community Interest Companies
CoICs	Community Innovation Centers
CPTPP	Comprehensive and Progressive Agreement for Trans-Pacific Partnership
CSO	Chief Sustainability Officer
CSR	Corporate Social Responsibility
CSV	Creating Shared Value
DEI	Diversity, Equity, and Inclusion

DESA	UN Department of Economic and Social Affairs
DJSI	Dow Jones Sustainability Indexes
DT	Design Thinking
ECLAC	Economic Commission for Latin America and the Caribbean
EESG	Economic, Environmental, Social, and Governance
EFMD	European Foundation for Management Development
EITI	Extractive Industries Transparency Initiative
ELIS	Environmental Labeling and Information Schemes
EMAS	EU Eco-Management and Audit Scheme
EMS	Environmental Management Systems
EPA	US Environmental Protection Agency
EPR	Extended Producer Responsibility
ESD	Education for Sustainable Development
ESG	Environmental Social Governance
ETFs	Exchange-Traded Funds
ETSs	Emissions Trading Systems
FPIC	Free, Prior and Informed Consent
FSC	Forest Stewardship Council
FSM	Financial Sustainability Management
GAP	Global Action Programme
GCF	Green Climate Fund
GDP	Gross Domestic Product
GHG	GreenHouse Gasses
GIFT	Global Initiative for Fiscal Transparency
GMO	Genetically Modified Organism
GNH	Gross National Happiness
GRI	Global Reporting Initiative
HESI	Higher Education for Sustainability Initiative
IDEA	Inclusion, Diversity, Equity, Accessibility
IMP	Impact Management Project
IR	Integrated Reporting
ISO	International Organization for Standardization
L3C	Limited Liability Company with Low Profit
LCA	Life Cycle Assessment
LCI	Life Cycle Inventory
LCIA	Life Cycle Impact Assessment
LEED	Leadership in Energy and Environmental Design
LGBTQ+	Lesbian, Gay, Bisexual, Transgender, Queer
MDG	Millennium Development Goal
MFIs	Microfinance Institutions
NGO	Non-Governmental Organization
NRDC	Natural Resources Defense Council
OECD	Organization for Economic Co-operation and Development

OGP	Open Government Partnership
PES	Payment for Ecosystem Services
PRME	Principles of Responsible Management Education
RAS	Robotics and Autonomous Systems
REDD+	Reducing Emissions from Deforestation and Forest Degradation
RME	Responsible Management Education
RSPO	Roundtable on Sustainable Palm Oil
SASB	Sustainability Accounting Standards Board
SDG	Sustainable Development Goal
SDSN	Sustainable Development Solutions Network
SEC	US Securities and Exchange Commission
SHRM	Sustainable Human Resource Management
SIA	Social Impact Assessment
SME	Small and Medium Enterprise
SMEd	Sustainable Management Education
SOI	Sustainability-Oriented Innovation
SPP	EU Sustainable Public Procurement
SRI	Socially Responsible Investing
SRM	Sustainable Risk Management
SROI	Social Return on Investment
STARS	Sustainability Tracking, Assessment & Rating System
SVC	Sustainable Value Creation
TBL	Triple Bottom Line
TCFD	Task Force on Climate-related Financial Disclosures
TI	Transparency International
UN	United Nations
UNAI	UN Academic Impact
UNCAC	United Nations Convention Against Corruption
UNDP	UN Development Programme
UNFCCC	UN Framework Convention on Climate Change
UNGC	UN Global Compact
UNGPs	UN Guiding Principles on Business and Human Rights
UNHCR	UN Human Rights Council
UNICEF	UN Children's Fund
VUCA(S)	Volatility, Uncertainty, Complexity, Ambiguity, and Unsustainable
WBCSD	World Business Council for Sustainable Development
WFP	UN World Food Programme
WHO	World Health Organization
WWF	World Wildlife Fund

List of Figures

List of Cases

CHAPTER 1

Introduction to the Era for Sustainability

Abstract This chapter introduces the main concepts of the sustainability movement and introduces the reader to recognized sustainability leaders and managers. It describes the challenges and opportunities of the Anthropocene geological era and the necessary tools that are needed to go from climate change to resilience using stakeholder engagement and developing multi-disciplinary mindsets. These global environmental and human security challenges create an opportunity for us all to come up with our own unique contributions to address these challenges. Sustainability is a paradigm that offers solutions to wicked, complex, and systemic problems. But it requires mindset shifts in individuals, organizations, and societies. This chapter highlights some of the core challenges and sustainability opportunities of our time.

Keywords Anthropocene · Climate change · Global challenges · Interconnectedness · Mindset shifts

> *There are opportunities even in the most difficult moments*
> —(Wangari Maathai, Founder of the Green Belt Movement, In *Unbowed*)

M. Tavanti, *Developing Sustainability in Organizations*, Sustainable Development Goals Series,
https://doi.org/10.1007/978-3-031-36907-0_1

The Global Challenges of the Anthropocene Epoch

We live in a time with enormous and complex global challenges. We call them "wicked problems." They are complex, systemic challenges that are difficult to define, understand, and solve due to their interconnectedness and the presence of conflicting perspectives and values. Some of the most urgent challenges have to do with unsustainable human activities. We call this "Anthropocene"—a proposed geological epoch that recognizes the profound impact that human activities are having on the Earth's systems and processes. Since the Industrial Revolution in the late eighteenth century, human activities have had a significant and widespread impact on the Earth's systems, altering its climate, altering land and ocean chemistry, and reducing biodiversity. These human-driven environmental changes are expected to have far-reaching and potentially disastrous consequences for the planet and its inhabitants. But the challenges are not only environmental. These are interlinked to social, economic, and peace and security issues and have made them even more complex for the lack of cooperation and partnership beyond borders. Wicked global problems require new leadership mindsets, integrated approaches for managing across sectors, and innovative and impactful solutions to steer the current direction and regenerative and resilient societies (Hull, 2020). Solutions to wicked problems also require coordinated solutions and proper policies also require proper public policies to foster more innovations and make significant impact (Head, 2022). The biggest problems of our current global-local (glocal) societies vary depending on geographic location, cultural context, and historical moment, but here are a few of the most urgent issues that are widely recognized as significant global challenges:

1. **Climate change**: Climate change is one of the biggest threats facing our planet, causing rising temperatures, more frequent and severe weather events, and significant impacts on biodiversity and human communities. Human activities, such as deforestation, agriculture, and climate change, are leading to the loss of species and habitats, reducing biodiversity, and the overall health of ecosystems (Thunberg, 2023). This is having a significant impact on the stability of ecosystems, their ability to provide services such as pollination and pest control, and the resilience of the planet to environmental changes. Since the industrial revolution, the widespread burning of

fossil fuels has increased the amount of greenhouse gasses (GHG) in the atmosphere, leading to global warming and climate change. This has resulted in rising sea levels, more frequent and intense heat waves, droughts, and storms, and the melting of polar ice caps. As the ocean absorbs about one-quarter of the carbon dioxide emitted into the atmosphere, it has led to a decrease in the pH of seawater, a process known as ocean acidification. This is changing the chemical balance of the ocean, making it more acidic and threatening marine life, especially those with calcium carbonate shells, such as mollusks and some species of plankton.

2. **Poverty and inequality**: Despite significant economic growth in recent decades, poverty and inequality remain widespread and persistent problems, with billions of people lacking access to basic needs such as food, water, and healthcare. Poverty and inequality are complex issues that are intertwined with many other global challenges, including economic development, health, education, and the environment. Poverty and inequality can have a significant impact on economic growth and socio-political stability. Poverty results in a lack of access to basic needs such as food, shelter, and healthcare, which leads to poor health, malnutrition, and early death. Inequality perpetuates poverty and can result in marginalized communities having less access to opportunities and resources, perpetuating the cycle of poverty and disadvantage. Addressing poverty and inequality is essential for building a more sustainable and equitable world for all people.
3. **Conflict and violence**: Political conflict, ethnic tensions, and violence continue to disrupt communities and undermine peace and stability in many parts of the world. Conflict and violence are complex issues that are often rooted in economic, political, and social inequalities. They can cause immense human suffering, particularly for civilians who are caught in the crossfire or who are forced to flee their homes. Conflict can also result in trauma, which can have long-lasting psychological and social consequences. Addressing these underlying factors requires new frameworks such as sustainable human security beyond national security, national borders, and nationalistic sentiments. Addressing root causes of conflicts, social injustice, discrimination, and resource access is essential for

reducing conflict and promoting peace and stability. The international community has a critical role to play in supporting efforts to resolve conflicts, reduce violence, and promote sustainable peace.

4. **Global migration**: Global migration is a wicked problem due to the political, social, and economic challenges it creates, the conflicting perspectives on the causes and solutions, and the need for coordinated international action. Global migration is increasingly becoming a "forced migration" as it is interconnected with many other issues, such as conflict, poverty, discrimination, and environmental degradation. Addressing migration requires a holistic approach that takes into account these interconnected issues. In relation to global forced migration, not only conflict but also economic and environmental factors can contribute to displace large numbers of people, who may cross borders and seek refuge in neighboring countries. This can result in increased pressure on neighboring countries and can lead to further instability in the region. Addressing migration requires a commitment to human rights and the protection of vulnerable populations, as well as a recognition of the contributions that migrants make to their host countries and the world at large.
5. **Racism and discrimination**: Racism, discrimination, and prejudice are still widespread in many societies and are a significant source of social, economic, and political strife. Racism and discrimination are serious global challenges that have far-reaching consequences for individuals, communities, and societies. They are considered to be "wicked problems" because they are deeply rooted and complex societal issues that are difficult to address and solve. Racism and discrimination are interconnected with many other social, economic, and political issues. For example, racism and discrimination can result in poverty and inequality, which can perpetuate further discrimination and division. Addressing racism and discrimination, therefore, requires a holistic approach that considers these interconnected issues. Solving these issues requires sustained efforts from individuals, communities, and governments to promote equity, inclusion, and understanding.
6. **Global Health**: Health pandemics such as COVID-19 have exposed and exacerbated existing health and social inequalities and have had far-reaching impacts on economies, societies, and individuals. In addition, the healthcare system itself is a wicked problem due to

its complexity, cost, and the challenges of balancing access, quality, and affordability. They can lead to increased poverty, decreased economic productivity, and decreased quality of life for those affected.

Poor health and pandemics can have significant human impact on individuals, communities, and societies. In spite of the many advancements in medical research and technology, there are significant disparities in access to healthcare and health outcomes across the world. For example, people living in low- and middle-income countries are more likely to die from preventable causes such as infectious diseases and maternal mortality.

Moreover, many countries and communities are not prepared for pandemics and other global health threats, such as the Ebola outbreak in West Africa in 2014. This highlights the need for increased investment in global health preparedness and response. In order to address these challenges, it is necessary to invest in global health and pandemic preparedness, improve access to healthcare and treatments, promote research and innovation in health, and increase collaboration and cooperation between countries and communities. These efforts will help to improve global health outcomes, reduce disparities in access to healthcare, and promote greater resilience in the face of pandemics and other global health threats (Nunes, 2022). The recent COVID-19 pandemic has highlighted the interconnectedness of global health, the need for coordinated international response, and the importance of investing in preventative research and universal access to care (Gates, 2022).

7. **Environmental degradation**: Rapid population growth and urbanization, along with unsustainable development practices, have led to widespread environmental degradation, including deforestation, habitat loss, and pollution (Rawson, 2021). In order to address these challenges, it is necessary to promote sustainable urbanization, improve access to resources and services, reduce inequality and poverty, and invest in infrastructure and services that are resilient and adaptable to changing populations and needs. These efforts will help to reduce the negative impacts of rapid population growth and urbanization and promote more sustainable and equitable cities and communities.

8. **Political polarization**: Political polarization and the increasing influence of special interests have made it difficult to address many of the most pressing problems facing society, such as climate change and inequality. Political polarization impedes governance and decision-making processes thus making it difficult for politicians and policymakers to reach consensus on important issues. It can undermine democratic institutions and processes by creating a toxic and divisive political environment that discourages participation and engagement. It can lead to increased conflict and violence, particularly when individuals or groups feel that their political views are not being represented or heard. This can result in protests, violence, and even civil war, causing significant harm to individuals, communities, and societies. It can widen social divides by creating an "us vs. them" mentality which can lead to increased prejudice and discrimination against individuals or groups with different political views.

   It can also undermine international cooperation by making it difficult for countries to work together to address global challenges, such as climate change, poverty, and inequality. In order to focus on these challenges, it is necessary to promote dialogue and collaboration across political divides, invest in democratic institutions and processes, and encourage political leaders and policymakers to work together to find common ground and solutions to important issues. Additionally, it is important to invest in education and public discourse which promotes critical thinking, empathy, and respect for different perspectives and opinions. These efforts will help reduce political polarization and promote greater social, political, and economic stability and cooperation.
9. **Cybersecurity**: Cybersecurity is a wicked problem due to the constantly evolving nature of technology, the global interconnectedness of networks, and the need to balance security with privacy and innovation. Cyberattacks can pose a threat to critical infrastructure, such as power grids, water supplies, and financial systems. This can result in widespread disruption and have serious consequences for individuals, communities, and entire nations. Cyberattacks can have a significant economic impact by compromising sensitive information, disrupting business operations, and leading to financial losses for individuals and organizations. Cybersecurity threats can also impact privacy and personal security by compromising sensitive

information, such as financial and personal data, and putting individuals at risk of identity theft and other forms of fraud. As the field of technology is rapidly evolving, it is very difficult to stay ahead of cybersecurity threats making it a never-ending challenge to keep systems and networks secure. Addressing cybersecurity requires a multifaceted approach that takes into account the unique context and circumstances of each individual case. It requires international cooperation and collaboration between governments, businesses, and individuals to effectively address cybersecurity challenges on a global scale.

Sustainability can help to solve wicked global problems by addressing root causes such as poverty, inequality, and environmental degradation, rather than just treating the symptoms. In addition, sustainability can help by approaching these problems from a systems perspective, taking into account the interconnectedness of social, economic, and environmental systems. By identifying and addressing the interrelated causes of wicked problems, more comprehensive solutions are developed.

It also helps by creating collaboration and partnerships between different actors, including governments, businesses, and communities, to address global challenges. This helps to leverage the resources and expertise of a wide range of stakeholders and create more effective solutions. Sustainability focuses on creating solutions that are not only effective in the short term, but also have long-term benefits and impact. This helps to ensure that solutions to wicked problems are sustainable and have lasting impact. In addition, sustainability can be the key to addressing these complex problems by supporting the principles of sustainable development, including economic growth, social inclusion, and environmental protection. This helps to balance economic, social, and environmental considerations and create solutions that are sustainable and equitable. By incorporating these principles, sustainability can help to address wicked global problems and create a more sustainable and equitable future. Additionally, by focusing on systemic solutions and encouraging collaboration, sustainability can help to promote lasting and comprehensive change in addressing complex global challenges.

These wicked global problems are complex and interrelated, and solving them will require coordinated and sustained efforts from individuals, organizations, and governments. Our current and future generations are charged to find solutions to address the main challenges related to the

Anthropocene epoch. Some of these challenges are intrinsically complex to understanding the extent of our human responsibility in relation to nature and how possibilities can be empowered through economic, social, political, and institutional coordinated solutions. Some of the important challenges inherent to the concept of Anthropocene include:

1. **Understanding the extent and impacts of human activities**: The Anthropocene represents a new and unprecedented stage in the Earth's history, and understanding the full extent and impacts of human activities is a major scientific and societal challenge.
2. **Addressing the root causes of environmental degradation**: Addressing the root causes of environmental degradation, such as unsustainable consumption patterns and the use of fossil fuels, is a major challenge for the Anthropocene, as it requires significant changes in the way we live and do business.
3. **Balancing economic growth and environmental protection**: The Anthropocene requires finding a new balance between economic growth and environmental protection, which can be difficult to achieve in the face of competing interests and conflicting priorities.
4. **Addressing global environmental challenges**: The Anthropocene requires addressing global environmental challenges such as climate change, biodiversity loss, and resource depletion, which have far-reaching impacts and require coordinated international action.
5. **Reconciling human interests with those of the natural world**: The Anthropocene requires reconciling human interests with those of the natural world, which can be difficult given the scale and complexity of the environmental challenges we face.
6. **Ensuring environmental justice and equity**: The Anthropocene requires ensuring environmental justice and equity, taking into account the needs and perspectives of marginalized communities which can be challenging in practice.

Addressing these challenges will require sustained effort and collaboration across sectors, as well as innovative solutions and new approaches to creating a more sustainable and equitable future. It will also require new sustainability mindsets and transformative paradigms for managing complexities across sectors, fields, and regions. Therefore, sustainability can no longer be a buzzword without aligned and integrated approaches for collective actions and systemic solutions. It can no longer be relegated to specialized fields and offices, but integrated and coordinated as the main priority. In education, sustainability can no longer be an elective simply related to environmental or financial courses only. It must be part of the core courses of every degree-seeking student.

An Age for Sustainability and Resilience

Sustainability is the main challenge and opportunity of our generation because it involves finding ways to meet the needs of the present without compromising the ability of future generations to meet their own needs. It is a complex and urgent issue that affects all aspects of human society, from the environment and economy to social equity and political stability. Addressing sustainability challenges requires a collective effort and innovative solutions, and presents an opportunity to create a more just, equitable, and prosperous future for all. Failure to address sustainability challenges could result in catastrophic consequences for human well-being and the planet.

Several authors have argued that we live in an age of sustainability. Back in the beginning of the movement, Donella Meadows (1972), with other leaders of the Club of Rome, wrote a provocative book entitled *Limits to Growth*, in which they argued that we are approaching the limits of our planet's capacity to support human activity and that sustainability is essential for human survival. Paul Hawken (2007), in his book *Blessed Unrest*, argues that there is a global movement for social and environmental justice that is working towards a sustainable future. Thomas Friedman (2008), in his book *Hot, Flat, and Crowded,* argues that the world is facing multiple sustainability challenges, including climate change, and that addressing these challenges presents an opportunity for innovation and economic growth. Jeremy Rifkin (2011), in his book *The Third Industrial Revolution*, argues that the convergence of new communication technologies, renewable energy, and decentralized energy systems will usher in a new era of sustainability. Jeffrey Sachs (2015), in his book *The Age of Sustainable Development*, argues that we live in an age where sustainability is both a moral imperative and an economic opportunity, and that achieving sustainable development is essential for global prosperity. These authors, among others, make the case that sustainability is a critical issue of our time, and that addressing sustainability challenges is necessary for a prosperous and equitable future.

Jeremy Rifkin (2022), in his more recent publication entitled *The Age of Resilience*, makes a compelling argument underlying how we are moving from an Age of Progress (characterized by the value maximization through efficiency) to an Age of Resilience (characterized by shared values solutions around adaptivity). He argues that we are transitioning from the Age of Progress and Efficiency, which was based on fossil fuels and centralized power structures, to the Age of Resilience, which is based on renewable energy and distributed power structures. Specifically, he argues that the Age of Resilience is characterized by the following resilient dynamics and sustainability priorities:

1. **Renewable Energy**: The Age of Resilience is defined by the development of a new energy infrastructure that is based on renewable energy sources, such as solar, wind, and geothermal power. This infrastructure will be more distributed and localized, with energy produced and consumed at the local level.
2. **Distributed Power**: The Age of Resilience will be characterized by a shift towards more distributed power structures, where individuals and communities have greater control over the production and consumption of energy. This will lead to greater energy independence and a more resilient energy system.
3. **Collaborative Economy**: The Age of Resilience will also be defined by a more collaborative economy, where sharing and cooperation are valued over competition and individualism. This will lead to greater social cohesion and a more resilient society.
4. **Internet of Things**: Rifkin argues that the Internet of Things (IoT) will play a critical role in the Age of Resilience, as it will allow for greater connectivity and efficiency in the use of energy and other resources.

Indeed, this vision for an Age of Resilience resonates with those who aspire to promote shared values around sustainability, equity, inclusion, and participation through participatory, collaborative, social, and circular economies. By embracing renewable energy, distributed power structures, and a more collaborative economy, Rifkin believes that we can create a more resilient and prosperous future for all. But can we do this in the international complexities of our often divided societies and selfish, often contradicting national, organizational, and personal interests? Fortunately, we have a blueprint for a sustainable future for all.

The Sustainable Development Goals as a Blueprint

The SDGs, also known as the Global Goals, adopted by 193 UN Member States in 2015 present the most comprehensive plan to address some of the world's most pressing challenges. The SDGs identify the most urgent priorities for a more sustainable future for all people and the planet. They are to be achieved by the year 2030, but while some progress has been made in achieving some of the goals, some goals are lagging behind. The COVID-19 pandemic has slowed the progress of most goals and revealed the systems challenges behind many of the goals and their targets. Here is a brief overview of the goals and their progress:

1. **No Poverty (SDG 1)**: This goal aims to eradicate poverty in all its forms and dimensions, including extreme poverty, by promoting sustainable economic growth, decent work for all, and social protection for those in need. Extreme poverty rates have declined in many regions of the world, but progress has been uneven. The COVID-19 pandemic has pushed millions into extreme poverty, reversing some of the gains made in recent years.
2. **Zero Hunger (SDG 2)**: This goal aims to end hunger and malnutrition by improving food security, promoting sustainable agriculture, and supporting small-scale food producers. Hunger rates have been declining globally, but progress has slowed in some regions due to conflicts and climate change. The pandemic has worsened food insecurity in many countries.
3. **Good Health and Well-being (SDG 3)**: This goal aims to ensure that everyone has access to quality healthcare and is able to lead healthy and fulfilling lives. Progress has been made in improving access to healthcare, reducing maternal and child mortality, and fighting infectious diseases. However, the pandemic has exposed weaknesses in healthcare systems and highlighted the need for more investment in health.
4. **Quality Education (SDG 4)**: This goal aims to provide inclusive and equitable quality education and promote lifelong learning opportunities for all. Enrollment rates in primary education have improved, but access to quality education remains a challenge in

many countries. The pandemic has disrupted education systems and widened inequalities in access to education.

5. **Gender Equality (SDG 5)**: This goal aims to eliminate all forms of discrimination and violence against women and girls and achieve gender equality and the empowerment of all women and girls. Progress has been made in improving gender equality in education and political participation, but women and girls still face discrimination and violence in many areas. The pandemic has worsened gender inequalities, with women bearing the brunt of the economic and social impacts.
6. **Clean Water and Sanitation (SDG 6)**: This goal aims to ensure availability and sustainable management of water and sanitation for all. Significant progress has been made in improving access to clean water and sanitation, but many people still lack access to these basic services. Climate change and water scarcity pose new challenges to achieving this goal.
7. **Affordable and Clean Energy (SDG 7)**: This goal aims to ensure access to affordable, reliable, sustainable, and modern energy for all. Renewable energy has become more affordable and accessible, but progress in expanding access to electricity and clean cooking fuels has been slow. The pandemic has also disrupted energy systems and slowed investments in renewable energy.
8. **Decent Work and Economic Growth (SDG 8)**: This goal aims to promote sustained, inclusive and sustainable economic growth, full and productive employment, and decent work for all. The global economy has grown, but progress in reducing unemployment and improving working conditions has been slow. The pandemic has caused job losses and economic downturns in many countries.
9. **Industry, Innovation and Infrastructure (SDG 9)**: This goal aims to build resilient infrastructure, promote inclusive and sustainable industrialization, and foster innovation. Investment in infrastructure and innovation has increased, but progress in expanding access to these resources has been uneven. The pandemic has also disrupted supply chains and slowed investments in infrastructure.
10. **Reduced Inequalities (SDG 10)**: This goal aims to reduce inequality within and among countries, and promote social, economic, and political inclusion for all. Progress has been made in reducing inequalities within and between countries, but many inequalities persist, particularly for marginalized groups. The

pandemic has worsened inequalities and highlighted the need for more equitable policies.

11. **Sustainable Cities and Communities (SDG 11)**: This goal aims to make cities and human settlements inclusive, safe, resilient, and sustainable. It seeks to address challenges such as urbanization, overcrowding, and inadequate housing, as well as improve air and water quality, reduce waste and greenhouse gas emissions, and increase access to green spaces and public transportation. Progress has been made in improving access to basic services and reducing urban pollution, but the rapid pace of urbanization poses new challenges to achieving this goal. The pandemic has also disrupted urban life and highlighted the need for more resilient and sustainable cities.
12. **Responsible Consumption and Production (SDG 12)**: This goal aims to ensure sustainable consumption and production patterns, reduce waste, and promote sustainable use of natural resources. It seeks to address challenges such as overconsumption, pollution, and the depletion of finite resources, and encourages businesses and individuals to adopt more sustainable practices. Progress has been made in promoting sustainable consumption and production practices, but more needs to be done to reduce waste and promote circular economies. The pandemic has also disrupted supply chains and highlighted the need for more sustainable and resilient production systems.
13. **Climate Action (SDG 13)**: This goal aims to take urgent action to combat climate change and its impacts. It seeks to address challenges such as rising global temperatures, increased frequency of extreme weather events, and the loss of biodiversity, by promoting the transition to a low-carbon economy, increasing access to clean energy, and reducing greenhouse gas emissions. Progress has been made in reducing greenhouse gas emissions and promoting renewable energy, but more needs to be done to address the urgent threat of climate change. The pandemic has also disrupted climate action efforts and highlighted the need for more ambitious climate policies.
14. **Life Below Water (SDG 14)**: This goal aims to conserve and sustainably use the oceans, seas, and marine resources for sustainable development. It seeks to address challenges such as overfishing, ocean acidification, and pollution and promotes sustainable

fishing practices, marine protected areas, and the restoration of degraded marine ecosystems. Progress has been made in reducing overfishing and protecting marine ecosystems, but more needs to be done to address the threats posed by climate change and pollution. The pandemic has also disrupted marine conservation efforts.

15. **Life on Land (SDG 15)**: This goal aims to protect, restore, and promote the sustainable use of terrestrial ecosystems, forests, wetlands, and deserts. It seeks to address challenges such as deforestation, land degradation, and loss of biodiversity and promotes reforestation, restoration of degraded lands, and sustainable agriculture practices. Progress has been made in reducing deforestation, protecting biodiversity, and promoting sustainable land use practices. However, many species are still at risk of extinction, and land degradation remains a significant challenge. The pandemic has also disrupted conservation efforts and highlighted the need for more resilient and sustainable land use practices.
16. **Peace, Justice and Strong Institutions (SDG 16)**: This goal aims to promote peaceful and inclusive societies for sustainable development, provide access to justice for all, and build effective, accountable, and transparent institutions at all levels. It seeks to address challenges such as conflict, violence, corruption, and discrimination and promotes the rule of law, human rights, and good governance. Progress has been made in reducing violence, promoting access to justice, and strengthening institutions. However, corruption, inequality, and human rights abuses remain significant challenges. The pandemic has also disrupted governance and justice systems and highlighted the need for more accountable and transparent institutions.
17. **Partnerships for the Goals (SDG 17)**: This goal aims to strengthen the means of implementation and revitalize the global partnership for sustainable development. It seeks to address challenges such as a lack of financing, technology, and capacity building and promotes collaboration and cooperation among countries, businesses, civil society, and other actors to achieve the SDGs. Progress has been made in promoting international cooperation and mobilizing resources for sustainable development. However, more needs to be done to strengthen partnerships and leverage the expertise and resources of different stakeholders. The pandemic has

also disrupted international cooperation and highlighted the need for more coordinated and effective partnerships to address global challenges.

These are just a few examples of how the SDGs are attempting to address some of the main global challenges of our generation. The common systems challenges and pandemic disruptions to these goals have slowed their progress and highlighted the need for new coordinated solutions. The SDGs are interdependent and interconnected, and addressing one goal will have a positive impact on others. By working together and committing to achieving the SDGs, the world can create a more sustainable, equitable, and peaceful future for all. Addressing these challenges is critical for achieving a more sustainable and equitable future for all people and the planet.

The SDG goals and targets serve as a blueprint for sustainability solutions. They require a personal and collective mindshift in order to succeed both locally and internationally. As we will consider in Chapter 2, mindsets are important for framing the necessary beliefs, attitudes, and assumptions towards sustainability leadership.

Mindsets are often deeply ingrained and can be difficult to change, but they are not necessarily static. I use the term mindshift to refer to the necessary, fundamental, and transformative changes in the way people think about sustainability and business. As we will explore later in detail, we need a mindshift in sustainability thinking involving shifts in perspectives, assumptions, and ways of approaching problems and challenges in new and innovative ways. As a way to introduce sustainability in leadership, management, innovation, and impact, I highlight eight core shifts necessary to understand and implement sustainability solutions (Fig. 1.1).

Shift 1: From Green Thinking to Whole Systems Thinking

The shift from green to whole systems thinking has had a significant influence on the development of sustainability in society. Green thinking, which emerged in the 1970s and 1980s, focused primarily on reducing environmental impacts through pollution control, resource efficiency, and

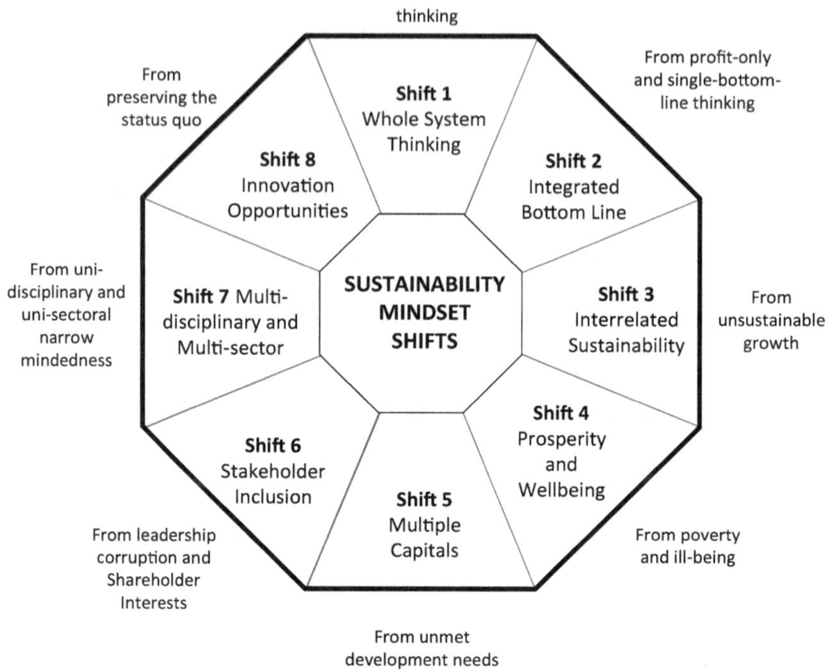

Fig. 1.1 Sustainability mindset shifts

the use of renewable energy. While important, this approach had limitations in that it often failed to consider the broader social, economic, and ecological contexts in which environmental issues arise.

Whole systems thinking, on the other hand, takes a more comprehensive and integrated approach to sustainability. It recognizes that environmental, social, and economic issues are interdependent and that sustainability cannot be achieved by focusing on any one of these issues in isolation. Instead, whole systems thinking emphasizes the need to address sustainability challenges in a holistic and integrated manner, considering the entire system of which they are a part. Figure 1.2 represents the core values associated with the dimensions of sustainability in concentric circles.

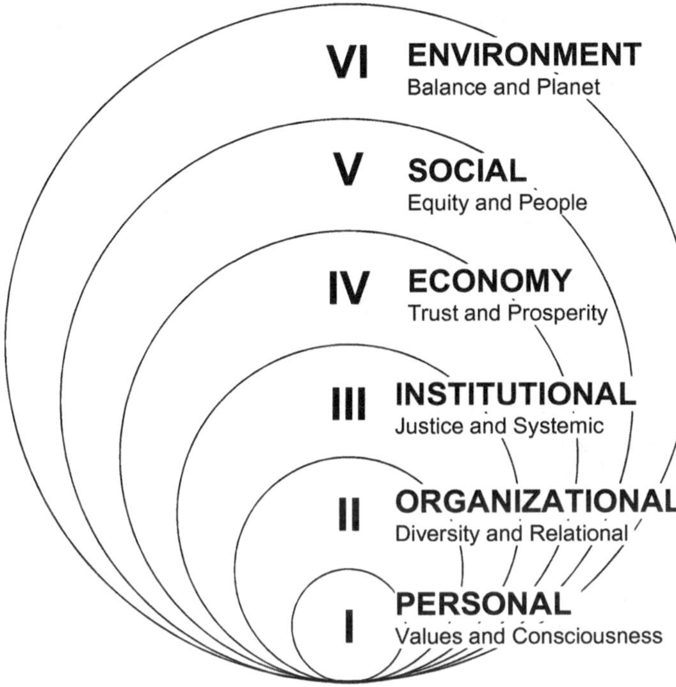

Fig. 1.2 Concentric values of whole systems thinking for sustainability

The concentric circles model of sustainability is considered a better representation than the Venn diagram for several reasons. First, it establishes a hierarchy of priorities, with the environment as the foundation, society in the middle, and the economy at the center. This model emphasizes the interdependence of the dimensions and their nested nature, reflecting the interconnected impacts of actions across the dimensions. Additionally, as in our representation, it allows for the integration of other aspects of sustainability, such as the individual, organizations, and systems-institutions. Other elements could be added such as governance, technology, and culture, creating a more inclusive representation. Lastly, the concentric circles model highlights the importance of maintaining the integrity of each dimension for the resilience and adaptability of the whole system.

The shift to whole systems thinking has influenced the development of sustainability in society in several ways. First, whole systems thinking places a greater emphasis on systems thinking, which involves understanding the interconnections and interdependencies among different components of a system. This has led to the development of more complex and integrated sustainability frameworks that take into account the multiple dimensions of sustainability. Second, whole systems thinking recognizes that environmental sustainability cannot be achieved without addressing social and economic issues. This has led to a greater emphasis on social and economic sustainability, including issues such as poverty reduction, social justice, and economic prosperity. More recently, it has influenced advanced development such as integrated reporting where financial and diversity elements are integrated in the organizational sustainability reporting. Third, whole systems thinking recognizes that sustainability challenges require the engagement of multiple stakeholders, including governments, civil society, and the private sector. This has led to the development of more participatory and inclusive approaches to sustainability, which involve engaging stakeholders in the design, implementation, and evaluation of sustainability policies and initiatives.

The whole systems thinking recognizes the interdependence of various sustainability dimensions including the concentric values for the individual, organizations, institutions, the economy, society, and the environment. The shift from green to whole systems thinking has had a profound influence on the development of sustainability in society by promoting a more integrated and comprehensive approach to sustainability that recognizes the interconnections and interdependencies among different dimensions of sustainability. Sustainability trends in society emphasize the global interconnectedness of economic, environmental, and social systems and the need to consider them holistically. This can help stakeholders generate integrated responses that take into account the interdependence of our global supply chains and the interdependencies between different bottom lines.

Shift 2: From Pillars to Integrated Bottom Line

The concept of sustainability with its integrated values has also been evolving. Sustainability has traditionally been viewed through the lens of the three pillars of sustainability. These pillars are economic growth, environmental protection, and social equity.

1. **Economic Sustainability**: Economic sustainability refers to the ability of an economy to function effectively and efficiently over the long term, with a focus on economic growth, job creation, and the elimination of poverty.
2. **Social sustainability**: Social sustainability refers to the well-being of people, communities, and society as a whole. This includes access to education, healthcare, housing, and employment opportunities, as well as the promotion of social equity, diversity, and human rights.
3. **Environmental sustainability**: Environmental sustainability refers to the preservation of natural resources and ecosystems for future generations. This includes reducing greenhouse gas emissions, conserving biodiversity, and managing natural resources in a sustainable manner. These dimensions are interrelated and equally important for ensuring a sustainable future.

There are several models that implement more integrated models of sustainability, including the Triple Bottom Line (TBL) which recognizes the interdependence of economic, social, and environmental sustainability and seeks to balance these three dimensions in decision-making. This balance, which could be a tension in many cases, indicates the interrelated identities of economic, environmental, and social factors in our organizations and societies. Here is how the circles of the TBL can be connected:

1. **Economic Bottom Line**: The economic circle of the TBL refers to the financial impact of business decisions on the organization and its stakeholders. It encompasses aspects such as profits, revenue, cost savings, and return on investment. The economic circle is related to the other two circles because it affects the organization's ability to invest in sustainability initiatives and in creating economic value in a way that is environmentally and socially responsible.
2. **Environmental Bottom Line**: The environmental circle of the TBL refers to the impact of business decisions on the natural environment, including aspects such as resource use, pollution, and greenhouse gas emissions. The environmental circle is related to the other two circles because it affects the organization's ability to operate sustainably over the long term and to ensure that its economic and social activities do not degrade the environment.

3. **Social Bottom Line**: The social circle of the TBL refers to the impact of business decisions on people and society, including aspects such as employee well-being, community development, and human rights. The social circle is related to the other two circles because it affects the organization's ability to operate sustainably over the long term and to ensure that its economic and environmental activities do not harm people or society.

While the TBL model is a useful framework for sustainability, it also has limitations. For example, the TBL model can be complex and difficult to implement, as it requires organizations to balance and integrate three different dimensions of sustainability. This can be challenging, especially for small businesses with limited resources. The TBL model can be interpreted as subjective, since it requires organizations to make judgments about what is economically, environmentally, and socially sustainable. These judgments can be influenced by factors such as cultural values, personal beliefs, and stakeholder priorities. Despite these limitations, the TBL model remains a valuable tool for promoting sustainability, because it encourages organizations to consider the interconnectedness of economic, environmental, and social factors in their decision-making.

The risks of not considering sustainability as an integrated model are not just conceptually problematic. Separating financial, social, and environmental concerns can have serious implications for companies and leaders, possibly resulting in risks for the company's reputation and legal compliance, as well as financial, social, and environmental risks. For instance, if organizations do not take sustainability seriously and fail to integrate social, environmental, and financial concerns, they risk damage to their reputation with consumers, investors, and other stakeholders. Negative publicity, such as accusations of environmental damage, human rights violations, or unethical business practices, can harm a company's brand and result in lost customers and revenue. They can be exposed to legal risks, such as fines, lawsuits, or regulatory penalties, as a result of non-compliance with environmental, labor, or other regulations.

In some cases, non-compliance can result in criminal charges or imprisonment for senior executives. If organizations do not consider social sustainability issues, they may encounter social risks, such as negative impact on local communities, worker exploitation, and human rights violations. Similarly, organizations that do not integrate environmental sustainability issues run the risk of contributing to damaging delicate ecosystems, impacting climate change, or depleting resources. These risks can result in physical damage to operations, regulatory scrutiny, and reputational harm.

Shift 3: From Development to Interrelated Sustainability

The need for integrating frameworks for sustainability reflects the evolution of our understanding of sustainable development. Sustainability offers a more integrated approach to developing sustainability across sectors and beyond the focus on socio-economic development of Global South nations. The SDGs have been purposely designed to be integral to key social, economic, and environmental crucial objectives for humanity and apply to all nations. Unlike the Millennium Development Goals (MDGs) from 2000 to 2015 which applied to developing countries, the SDGs, from 2015 to 2030, are universal and apply to all countries with strong focus on means of implementation (financial resources and partnership mechanisms), along with capacity building and technology, as well as data measurement of progress and impact. Rio+20, the United Nations Conference on Sustainable Development held in Rio de Janeiro, Brazil, in 2012, played an important role in integrating sustainability into the 8 MDGs and the development of the 2030 Agenda for Sustainable Development with the 17 SDGs. The resulting SDGs represent a more integrated and holistic approach to sustainable development and strive for a more sustainable society calling all nations to recognize the interdependence of economic, social, and environmental sustainability. Here are the definitions of sustainable development and sustainability:

1. **Sustainable development**: Sustainable development is a concept that was introduced by the World Commission on Environment and Development in the Brundtland Report (1987), which defined it as "development that meets the needs of the present without compromising the ability of future generations to meet their own needs." This definition highlights the idea that development should be focused on meeting the needs of people in the present, while also ensuring that natural resources and the environment are protected for future generations.

2. **Sustainability**: Sustainability is a broader concept that refers to the ability of an ecosystem, society, or individual to persist over time. Sustainability is often used to refer to the three interrelated pillars of economic, social, and environmental sustainability, which must be balanced and integrated for a system to be truly sustainable.

In other words, sustainable development is a subset of the broader concept of sustainability and focuses on meeting the needs of the present without compromising the ability of future generations to meet their own needs. Sustainability, on the other hand, is a broader interrelated concept because it encompasses multiple dimensions that are interdependent and interrelated. It is a concept that encompasses economic, social, and environmental factors and the ability of systems to persist over time. The field of sustainable development has played a crucial role in shaping our understanding and practice of sustainability by promoting a more integrated and balanced approach to development that considers economic, social, and environmental objectives together. It has also highlighted the need for integrating policies and good governance in promoting well-being and prosperity beyond health and profit.

Shift 4: From Profit to Prosperity and Well-Being

The more recent interpretation of the 3Ps economic model has replaced "profit" with "prosperity" and draws the attention away from profit for a few shareholders and legitimizes the economic activity for a larger and shared benefit for all stakeholders (Mayer, 2018). In order to achieve sustainability, it is essential to move beyond a narrowly-focused profit-driven approach and focus instead on creating shared prosperity for all. This means not only looking at economic growth, but also considering the social, environmental, and cultural impacts of our actions. It also means taking into account the needs of future generations and ensuring that our actions today do not undermine the ability of future generations to meet their own needs. Profit and prosperity are related concepts, but they have distinct differences:

1. **Profit**: Profit refers to the financial gain or surplus that a business or organization generates after accounting for all its expenses. Profit is the key measure of success for many businesses and is used to

determine the value of the company, pay dividends to shareholders, and invest in future growth.

2. **Prosperity**: Prosperity refers to a state of being successful and thriving, especially in terms of economic growth and development. Prosperity is a more holistic concept that goes beyond financial measures and considers factors such as quality of life, well-being, and access to resources.
3. **Focus**: Profit is focused on financial gain, while prosperity takes a more comprehensive approach and considers a wider range of factors that contribute to success and well-being.
4. **Time horizon**: Profit is often measured in the short term, while prosperity is focused on the long-term health and well-being of individuals, communities, and the planet.
5. **Stakeholders**: Profit primarily focuses on the interests of shareholders, while prosperity takes into account the interests and well-being of a wider range of stakeholders, including employees, customers, communities, and the environment.

Profit is a financial measure of success, while prosperity is a more comprehensive concept that takes into account a wider range of factors that contribute to success and well-being. Prosperity and well-being are better terms than profit in sustainability because they are more comprehensive and holistic measures of human welfare and progress, and they better reflect the multidimensional nature of sustainable development. Well-being refers to the state of being healthy, happy, and prosperous, while prosperity refers to the ability to thrive and flourish in a sustainable manner. In recent years, sustainable development scholars and practitioners have been shifting their concerns from economic growth to well-being economics which center around the notion of prosperity (Saunders, 2018). The various definitions of well-being reflect the multidimensional nature of sustainable development, and they recognize the need to balance economic, social, and environmental objectives to achieve long-term sustainability. Integrating sustainability demands us to move away from a strict focus on short-term profits and towards a more holistic approach which takes into account the well-being of people, the planet, and future generations. This means investing in renewable energy sources, developing sustainable technologies, and creating policies and initiatives that are equitable and just. By doing so, we can create a more prosperous, equitable, and sustainable future.

Shift 5: From Needs to Multiple Capitals

Sustainability is about more than just meeting basic needs as expressed in the Gro Brundtland's definition of sustainable development. Meeting the needs of the present without compromising the ability of future generations to meet their own needs is an important starting point for understanding sustainability, but it can also be problematic for several reasons. Here are a few examples:

1. **Subjectivity**: Needs are subjective and can vary greatly depending on factors such as culture, geography, and individual preferences. This means that determining what constitutes a "basic need" can be difficult, and there is often disagreement about what should be included. For example, some people might consider access to high-speed internet a basic need, while others might not.
2. **Unsustainable consumption**: The focus on meeting basic needs can sometimes be used to justify unsustainable consumption patterns. For example, some argue that it is necessary to consume natural resources in order to meet basic human needs like food and shelter, without considering the impacts of such consumption on the environment and future generations.
3. **Insufficient attention to long-term sustainability**: The emphasis on needs can sometimes lead to a focus on short-term solutions rather than long-term sustainability. For example, if the focus is only on meeting the basic needs of people today, without considering the long-term sustainability of the resources used to meet those needs, it may not be possible to meet the needs of future generations.
4. **Overlooked social and environmental needs**: The focus on needs can sometimes overlook social and environmental needs that are not considered basic needs. For example, the need for access to clean air, water, and a healthy environment may not be considered basic needs, but they are essential for sustainable development.

Other frameworks, such as the multiple capitals framework, can help to better understand and achieve sustainability by considering a wider range of resources and factors that contribute to well-being and prosperity. Considering multiple capitals can give value to multiple assets in our collective existence and can create a more equitable and sustainable future (Sfeir-Younis & Tavanti, 2020). For example, by investing in renewable energy sources, we can create jobs and support economic growth while also reducing our dependence on non-renewable resources. Similarly, by investing in social capital, we can help ensure that our communities are safe and supportive, while also creating a more equitable and just society. By considering multiple capitals, we can create a more sustainable and prosperous future for all. Here are some of the diverse capitals that can play an important role in the integration and recognition of true values and contributing factors:

1. **Natural capital**: Natural capital refers to the natural resources and ecosystems that provide the raw materials, energy, and services that are necessary for economic and social activities. This includes things like clean air and water, biodiversity, and healthy ecosystems. Natural capital is important because it provides the foundation for sustainable economic and social development, and it supports human well-being. For example, sustainable management of natural resources can help to ensure that they are available for future generations.
2. **Human capital**: Human capital refers to the knowledge, skills, and abilities that individuals possess and can apply to economic and social activities. This includes things like education, training, and experience. Human capital is important because it is a critical input to sustainable economic development, and it helps to foster social and environmental sustainability. For example, a highly educated workforce is more likely to be able to adapt to new technologies and approaches that promote sustainability.
3. **Social capital**: Social capital refers to the networks, relationships, and norms of behavior that facilitate cooperation and coordination among individuals and groups. This includes things like trust, reciprocity, and social norms. Social capital is important because it helps to foster collaboration and collective action, which is critical for promoting sustainable development. For example, social capital can help mobilize communities to take collective action on issues like climate change or social inequality.
4. **Financial capital**: Financial capital refers to the monetary resources that are used to fund economic activities. This includes assets such as cash, investments, and other financial instruments. Financial capital

is important because it provides the funding necessary for sustainable economic development, such as investment in renewable energy infrastructure, sustainable agriculture, and other green technologies.

5. **Physical capital**: Physical capital refers to the physical infrastructure that is used to support economic and social activities. This includes things like buildings, roads, and other forms of infrastructure. Physical capital is important because it provides the material foundation for economic and social activities, and it is necessary for sustainable development. For example, investing in sustainable infrastructure can help to reduce environmental impacts and increase the resilience of communities to climate change.
6. **Institutional capital**: Institutional capital refers to the formal systems, rules, and structures that govern economic, social, and environmental activities. This includes institutions such as governments, regulatory bodies, and financial institutions. Institutional capital is important because it provides the legal and regulatory framework that enables sustainable economic development, protects natural resources, and supports social equity. For example, regulations that limit pollution and protect public health are an important form of institutional capital that can help promote environmental sustainability.
7. **Cultural capital**: Cultural capital refers to the non-material aspects of culture that contribute to social sustainability. This includes things like shared values, beliefs, and customs that promote social cohesion, diversity, and inclusion. Cultural capital is important because it supports social stability and helps build resilient communities. For example, promoting cultural diversity and respecting different perspectives can help build a more inclusive society, which can in turn promote social sustainability.
8. **Spiritual capital**: Spiritual capital refers to the values, beliefs, and worldviews that guide individual and collective behavior. This includes aspects such as ethical and moral values, faith-based traditions, and spiritual practices. Spiritual capital is important because it can help provide a sense of purpose and meaning, promote social and environmental responsibility, and foster a deeper sense of connection with others and the natural world. For example, organizations that prioritize social and environmental responsibility as part of their mission and values can help build spiritual capital by aligning their actions with a deeper sense of purpose.

By considering the interrelationships between these different capitals, the multiple capitals framework provides a more comprehensive and integrated approach to sustainability, recognizing that economic, social, and environmental factors are not the only elements that contribute to sustainable development. The multiple capital model of sustainability highlights the importance of considering the interplay of these various forms of capital in promoting sustainable development. In addition, the institutional, cultural, and spiritual capitals are important dimensions of the multiple capital model of sustainability because they provide complementary and intersecting perspectives on how to promote sustainable economic, social, and environmental development. By taking a holistic approach that considers financial, human, social, natural, and physical capital, organizations and societies can build a more sustainable future that supports human well-being, economic prosperity, and environmental stewardship.

Shift 6: From Shareholders to Multi-stakeholders Inclusion

Clearly, a business leader has several responsibilities towards shareholders, including maximizing shareholder value, ensuring financial reporting accuracy, communicating effectively with shareholders, fostering shareholder trust, protecting shareholder rights, and balancing the interests of different stakeholders. A sustainability business leader is called to go beyond fiduciary responsibilities towards the company and its shareholders. Today's business leaders and sustainability companies need to be concerned with stakeholders because stakeholders are a crucial aspect of any business or organization. Stakeholder inclusion in sustainability refers to the process of engaging and involving stakeholders in the decision-making and implementation processes of sustainable development. Multi-stakeholder inclusion refers to the process of engaging and involving multiple stakeholders from different sectors and perspectives in the decision-making and implementation processes of sustainable development. It recognizes that sustainable development challenges are complex and interconnected, and that they require a diverse range of actors to work together to find solutions. Stakeholders are individuals or groups who have an interest or concern in the activities and outcomes of a business, and can include employees, customers, suppliers, shareholders, government, and the broader community. Including stakeholder values into sustainable leadership and managerial practices implies entering into an ecosystem of socially and globally responsible organizations, institutions, and champions. It implies that sustainable business leaders move from a focus solely on creating shareholder value to becoming globally responsible for stakeholder value for several reasons:

1. **Changing Expectations**: There has been a shift in societal expectations, with stakeholders, including customers, employees, investors, and communities, increasingly looking for businesses to be responsible corporate citizens and to address societal and environmental challenges.
2. **Long-term Sustainability**: Addressing stakeholder values, including social and environmental impacts, is key to ensuring the long-term sustainability of a business. A narrow focus on shareholder value can lead to short-term thinking and decision-making with possible negative impacts on other stakeholders and the environment.
3. **Increased Reputation and Brand Value**: By being responsible corporate citizens and addressing stakeholder values, businesses can improve their reputation and brand value, attract and retain customers and employees, and potentially increase financial performance.
4. **Improved Financial Performance**: By considering stakeholder values, companies can better identify and manage sustainability risks and opportunities, and potentially improve financial performance. ESG data, which includes environmental, social, and governance factors, is increasingly being used by investors and stakeholders to assess a company's sustainability performance and potential financial risks.
5. **Addressing Global Challenges**: Finally, businesses have a significant impact on society and the environment, and a responsibility to help address global challenges such as climate change, poverty, and inequality. Addressing stakeholder values is essential for businesses to fulfill this responsibility and contribute to a more sustainable and equitable world.

Overall, engaging with stakeholders is an essential part of doing business in a sustainable and responsible way. By considering the needs and interests of all stakeholders, companies can build trust, reduce risk, improve decision-making, increase innovation, and meet societal expectations.

Shift 7: From One Sector to Multi-sector and Multi-disciplinary Approaches

Today, sustainability has become synonymous with multi-disciplinary research and multi-sector collaborations. Adopting multi-disciplinary and multi-sector perspectives in sustainability leadership is important for several reasons:

1. **Holistic Approach**: Sustainability challenges are complex and often cross multiple sectors and disciplines, such as the environment, economy, and social issues. By adopting a multi-disciplinary and multi-sector perspective, sustainability leaders can better understand the interconnections and interdependencies of these challenges and develop more effective solutions.
2. **Broader Expertise**: Bringing together experts from multiple disciplines and sectors can help to identify new and innovative solutions to sustainability challenges. For example, a team with expertise in environmental science, business, and policy can develop more comprehensive and effective solutions than one with expertise in just one field.
3. **Collaboration and Partnership Building**: Sustainability leaders who adopt a multi-disciplinary and multi-sector approach are more likely to engage in collaboration and partnership building, which is essential for addressing complex sustainability challenges. By working together, different organizations and stakeholders can share resources, knowledge, and expertise and develop more comprehensive and impactful solutions.
4. **Improved Decision-Making**: Adopting a multi-disciplinary and multi-sector perspective can help to ensure that sustainability decisions are based on the best available evidence and are informed by a range of perspectives. This can lead to more informed and effective decision-making, and ultimately, better outcomes for the economy, environment, and society.

5. **Increased Innovation**: A multi-disciplinary and multi-sector approach helps foster innovation as it brings together diverse perspectives and encourages the development of new ideas and creative solutions.

Overall, adopting a multi-disciplinary and multi-sector perspective in sustainability leadership is essential for addressing complex sustainability challenges and to finding more effective, innovative, and comprehensive solutions. This requires a shift in mindsets. Developing an integrated and multi-disciplinary mindset is vital for managerial practices, organizational strategies, and systemic operations. A multi-sector and multi-disciplinary mindset for sustainability refers to an approach that involves the collaboration and integration of knowledge and skills from different sectors and disciplines to achieve sustainable outcomes. It recognizes that sustainability challenges are complex and interconnected, and that addressing them requires the involvement of multiple sectors (such as government, business, and civil society) and disciplines (such as environmental science, social sciences, economics, and engineering). Such a mindset is essential to identify and address the interrelated environmental, social, and economic dimensions of sustainability challenges. It can also promote innovation and creativity by bringing together diverse perspectives and expertise. It can provide sustainability leaders with the predisposition for collaborations and partnerships between government, business, and civil society organizations to develop policies and initiatives that promote sustainable development. It is an essential mindset shift for creating sustainable solutions that address the complex and interconnected challenges facing our world today.

Shift 8: From Status Quo to Innovation Opportunities

We live in a new time for leaders and managers in organizations. One that cannot accept managing the status quo and instead welcomes opportunities for integrating innovations. Current and future sustainability innovations are about developing new sustainability integrated organizations, companies, and enterprises whose mission and performances combine integrated "bottom lines" through innovative approaches and impactful solutions.

Sustainability requires moving away from managing the status quo and implementing innovative solutions because:

1. **Status quo is unsustainable**: The current practices and systems are often unsustainable, as they are based on the depletion of natural resources and the emission of harmful pollutants. Moving away from the status quo and towards innovative solutions is necessary to address these challenges and ensure a more sustainable future.
2. **Limitations of current solutions**: The current solutions to sustainability challenges are often limited and ineffective, as they only address part of the problem. Moving towards innovative solutions that take a more holistic approach is necessary to find solutions that are more effective and durable.
3. **The need for transformational change**: Sustainability challenges are complex and often require transformational change, rather than incremental improvements. Moving towards innovative solutions is necessary to drive this change and ensure that it is meaningful and impactful.
4. **The opportunities for positive impact**: Implementing innovative solutions can not only help to address sustainability challenges but also create opportunities for positive impact. For example, investing in renewable energy can not only reduce greenhouse gas emissions but also create jobs and boost the local economy.
5. **The need to stay ahead of the curve**: Sustainability challenges are constantly evolving, and new challenges are emerging. Moving towards innovative solutions is necessary to stay ahead of the curve and ensure that the solutions remain relevant and effective over time.

Sustainability is an innovation opportunity for businesses to renew their approaches and become agents of positive impact in society. This change requires moving away from managing the status quo and implementing innovative solutions in order to address complex sustainability challenges, drive transformational change, create positive impact, and stay ahead of the curve.

These mindset shifts for sustainability are not mutually exclusive and need to be considered in the overall challenge of embracing sustainability changes in our leadership perspective and organizational management practices. Sustainability requires mindset shifts at multiple levels, including individual, organizational, and societal levels. This is because sustainability is not just a technical problem that can be solved through technology or policy alone, but it is also a social and cultural challenge that requires changes in the way we think, behave, and make decisions.

At the individual level, achieving sustainability requires a shift in mindset from a consumption-oriented lifestyle to a more sustainable one that values conservation, efficiency, and social and environmental responsibility. At the organizational level, achieving sustainability requires a shift in mindset from a short-term profit-oriented approach to a long-term sustainable business model that takes into account the social and environmental impacts of their activities.

At the societal level, achieving sustainability requires a shift in mindset from a growth-oriented economic model to a more sustainable and equitable one that promotes well-being and environmental protection. Society must recognize the need for systemic changes in the way we produce and consume goods and services, and adopt policies and practices that promote sustainable development, such as investing in renewable energy, promoting sustainable agriculture, and reducing social and economic inequalities.

In other words, achieving sustainability requires mindset shifts at multiple levels because the systemic solutions offered by sustainability require changes in the way we think, behave, and make decisions.

Key Takeaways

1. The Anthropocene, characterized by unprecedented environmental challenges, has created an urgent need for sustainable practices across all sectors of society.
2. Sustainability and resilience are essential for ensuring a prosperous future for both humanity and the planet, and the Sustainable Development Goals (SDGs) provide a framework for achieving these goals.
3. A sustainability mindset shift is necessary to address the complex challenges of the Anthropocene, including whole systems thinking, integrated bottom lines, interrelated sustainability, prosperity and well-being, multiple capitals, multi-stakeholder inclusion, multi-sector and multi-disciplinary collaboration, and innovation opportunities.

4. Embracing sustainability can create value for businesses by reducing costs, increasing efficiency, building brand reputation, and increasing customer loyalty.
5. The future of value lies in sustainability, as businesses and consumers increasingly recognize the importance of creating a more sustainable future for the planet.

References

Brundtland, G. H. (1987). *Our common future*. WCED.

Friedman, T. L. (2008). *Hot, flat, and crowded: Why we need a green revolution—And how it can renew America* (1st ed.). Farrar, Straus and Giroux.

Gates, B. (2022). *How to prevent the next pandemic*. Knopf.

Hawken, P. (2007). *Blessed unrest: How the largest movement in the world came into being, and why no one saw it coming*. Viking.

Head, B. W. (2022). Wicked problems in public policy. *Springer Nature*. https://doi.org/10.1007/978-3-030-94580-0

Hull, R. B., Mortimer, M., & Robertson, D. P. (2020). *Leadership for Sustainability: Strategies for Tackling Wicked Problems*. United States: Island Press.

Maathai, W. (2006). *Unbowed: A memoir* (1st ed.). Alfred A. Knopf.

Mayer, C. P. (2018). *Prosperity: Better business makes the greater good*. Oxford University Press.

Meadows, D. H. (1972). *The limits to growth: A report for the club of Rome's project on the predicament of mankind*. Universe Books.

Nunes, R. (2022). *Healthcare as a universal human right : Sustainability in global health*. Routledge.

Rawson, M. (2021). *The nature of tomorrow: A history of the environmental future*. Yale University Press.

Rifkin, J. (2011). *The third industrial revolution: How lateral power is transforming energy, the economy, and the world*. Palgrave Macmillan.

Rifkin, J. (2022). *The age of resilience: Reimagining existence on a rewilding earth*. Swift Press.

Sachs, J. (2015). *The age of sustainable development*. Columbia University Press.

Saunders, C., et al. (2018). *Wellbeing economics: The capabilities approach to prosperity*. Springer International Publishing.

Sfeir-Younis, A., & Tavanti, M. (2020). *Conscious sustainability leadership: A new paradigm for next generation leaders*. Planet Healing Press.

Thunberg, G. (2023). *The climate book: The facts and the solutions*. Penguin Press.

PART I

Sustainability Leadership

This part of this book sets the stage and explains the core elements of sustainability leadership. It provides practical examples of how sustainability leadership is first and foremost about the practice of values and principles. These are anchored in the leader's and organization's higher purpose, connected to sustainability mindsets, and determining ethical choices. The sustainability values and principles ground the practice of leadership beyond personal and organizational growth and for protecting the environment, promoting social justice, and creating economic prosperity for all.

Sustainability values are based on the idea that our current and future generations should be able to benefit from the natural world without damaging it or disrupting the delicate balance of nature. For leaders today, sustainability values are essential for creating a future that is both prosperous and sustainable. Sustainability values emphasize the need for wise resource management, equitable distribution of wealth, and responsible business practices. By following sustainability values, leaders can create a future that is prosperous, equitable, and environmentally conscious.

The principles of sustainability leadership involve taking a holistic approach to sustainability, involving all stakeholders, and making sure that ethical considerations are taken into account when making decisions. This includes the belief that the environment, society, and economy are interrelated and need to be managed in an integrated way. It also involves creating long-term strategies that are focused on diminishing negative impact and promoting net positive effects promoting environmental protection, social equity, and economic prosperity. Sustainability leadership also involves setting a good example for others to follow, setting long-term goals, and having a commitment to transparency and accountability. Additionally, it involves developing innovative solutions to environmental and social problems, integrating environmental and social considerations into business decisions and operations, and advocating for responsible public policies.

In this first section of the book, we want to explore the core dimensions of sustainability leadership starting from its core values and principles emerged from sustainability-related documents and initiatives (Chapter 2). We pay special attention to higher purpose through many inspiring examples of sustainability leaders and by considering purpose as a driving force for sustainability action and organizational transformation (Chapter 3). We finally consider ethics and ethos in their role for ethical decision making in organizations and sustainability leadership practice (Chapter 4). Throughout these chapters, we offer examples of leading organizations in the sustainability movements and practical implications for applying these concepts to real-world situations.

CHAPTER 2

Values and Principles for Sustainability Leadership

Abstract This chapter reviews the foundational importance of values and principles for sustainability leadership. It explores various initiatives and documents like the Earth Charter, the UNGC Principles, and the 2030 Agenda to understand the role of values in sustainability and leadership practices. It connects universal values with professional applications and personal values-based priorities for people, planet, prosperity, peace, and partnership. It looks at studies that consider how values and principles are essential for sustainability leadership, providing a framework for decision-making, promoting responsible behavior, fostering innovation, and building trust and credibility. By prioritizing ethical values and principles, sustainability leaders can help to create a more sustainable future for their organization and for society as a whole.

Keyword Sustainability values · Sustainability principles · Shared values · Earth charter · 2030 Agenda

> *Making values a bedrock of your culture is far more wise and sustainable than applying them selectively or intermittently, or scrambling to put them in place in reaction to a crisis. All of this might sound like a minefield, but I firmly believe that in the future, equality will be the key to unlocking a*

M. Tavanti, *Developing Sustainability in Organizations*, Sustainable Development Goals Series,
https://doi.org/10.1007/978-3-031-36907-0_2

company's full and sustainable value. That doesn't mean it's easy to achieve. But those who fail to try will be on the wrong side of history.

—Marc R. Benioff, CEO of Salesforce, in *Trailblazer*

The Foundational Role of Values and Principles

Value and principles play a crucial role in business ethics and even more in sustainability leadership. They help to establish ethical standards that guide business conduct. They encourage responsible behavior and produce shared values as businesses and consumers increasingly recognize the importance of creating a more sustainable future for the planet (Lowitt, 2011). Sustainability creates value through competitive differentiation by providing businesses with a unique selling proposition, reducing costs and increasing efficiency, and building brand reputation and customer loyalty. As such, businesses that embrace sustainability will be well positioned to thrive in the future of value. Sustainability values promote social responsibility through ethical principles such as community engagement and social justice. They help to build trust with their stakeholders. The following are some additional ways that values and principles are important in sustainability leadership:

1. **Setting the tone for ethical behavior**: Sustainability leaders must model ethical behavior and set the tone for a culture of sustainability within the organization. Values such as integrity, transparency, and accountability can help to create a culture of ethical behavior that supports sustainability.
2. **Providing a framework for decision-making**: Values and principles can provide a framework for decision-making that considers the long-term impacts of actions on economic, social, and environmental sustainability. This can help to prioritize sustainability in decision-making and ensure that decisions are consistent with the organization's mission and values.
3. **Encouraging responsible behavior**: Values and principles can encourage responsible behavior that is consistent with sustainability goals. Leaders can use values such as responsibility, respect, and stewardship to encourage employees to act in ways that protect the environment, promote social well-being, and create economic value that is sustainable.

4. **Promoting innovation**: Sustainability leadership requires creativity and innovation to develop new solutions that balance economic, social, and environmental considerations. Values such as collaboration, creativity, and innovation can help to promote new ideas and solutions that support sustainability goals.
5. **Fostering trust and credibility**: Values and principles can help to foster trust and credibility with stakeholders. Sustainability leaders who prioritize values such as transparency, accountability, and stakeholder engagement can build trust with employees, customers, suppliers, and the wider community, which can support long-term success (Fig. 2.1).

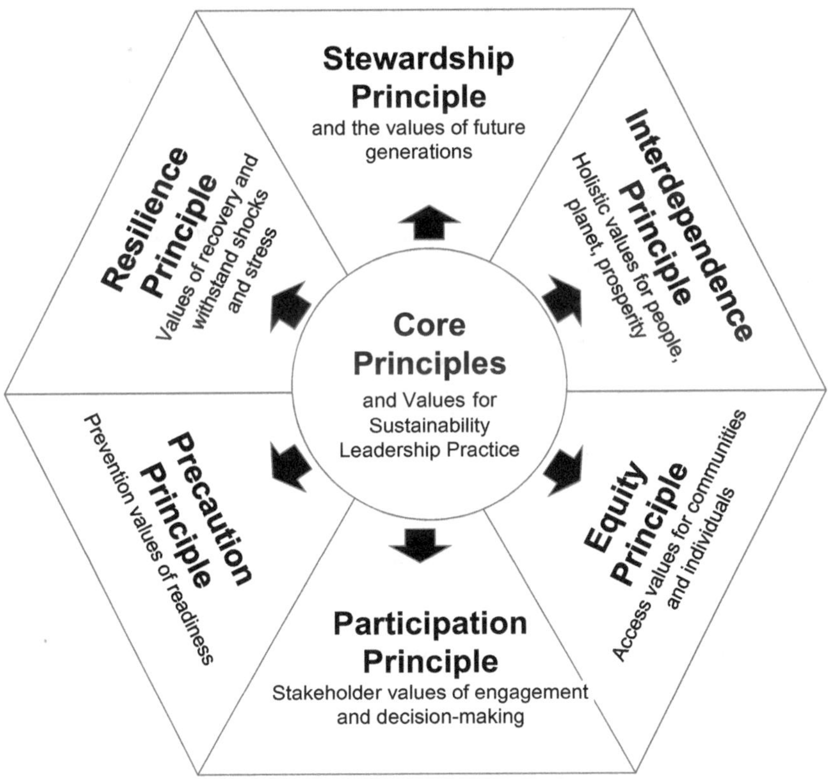

Fig. 2.1 Core principles and values in sustainability practices

Sustainability values and principles are critical for developing mindsets and impactful practices (Rimanoczy, 2021). Sustainability itself is a value that emerges from a set of principles that emphasize the importance of balancing economic, social, and environmental considerations in order to meet the needs of the present generation without compromising the ability of future generations to meet their own needs. In general, sustainability includes core values and principles such as:

1. **Stewardship**: The principle of stewardship emphasizes the responsibility that individuals and organizations manage resources in a way that ensures their sustainability for future generations.
2. **Interdependence**: The principle of interdependence emphasizes the interconnectedness of social, economic, and environmental systems, and the need to take a holistic approach to sustainability.
3. **Equity**: The principle of equity emphasizes the importance of ensuring that all individuals and communities have access to the resources and opportunities necessary to achieve a sustainable and prosperous life.
4. **Participation**: The principle of participation emphasizes the importance of involving all stakeholders, including individuals, communities, and organizations, in decision-making processes related to sustainability.
5. **Precaution**: The principle of precaution emphasizes the need to take action to prevent harm to the environment and human health, even in the absence of full scientific certainty.
6. **Resilience**: The principle of resilience emphasizes the importance of building resilience into social, economic, and environmental systems in order to withstand and recover from shocks and stresses.

The role of these core values and principles is to provide a framework for action that ensures the sustainability of our natural resources and social systems. By adopting a sustainability perspective, individuals and organizations can make decisions that balance economic, social, and environmental considerations and contribute to a more sustainable and prosperous future for all.

Values and principles are often used interchangeably, but they actually have correlated but different roles. Values refer to the beliefs and attitudes that guide an individual's actions and decisions. They are the fundamental beliefs that underpin a person's behavior, and they often reflect their personal and cultural backgrounds. They are at the core identity of a leader and an organization. They are difficult to change, and they can shape a person's worldview and approach to sustainability leadership. For example, someone who values community and social equity might prioritize these values in their sustainability initiatives, while someone who values economic growth might prioritize initiatives that promote economic development. Principles, on the other hand, are a set of fundamental rules or guidelines that guide the behavior of individuals, organizations, and institutions. They are the fundamental guidelines that shape an organization's behavior and decision-making. They are the rules or standards that are considered to be universally applicable and serve as the foundation for ethical conduct in a company. In sustainability leadership, principles can include things like the precautionary principle, the principle of intergenerational equity, and the principle of the polluter pays. These principles help guide leaders in making decisions and taking action in a way that is consistent with sustainability principles.

Values and principles are interconnected in business ethics because an organization's values influence the principles it adopts, and the principles it adopts reflect its values. For example, if an organization values integrity, it will likely adopt a principle of honesty and transparency in its dealings with customers, suppliers, and other stakeholders. If an organization values social responsibility, it may adopt a principle of sustainability and work to minimize its impact on the environment. In business ethics, values and principles are related because an organization's values shape the principles it adopts, and the principles it adopts reflect its values. Both principles and values are essential for establishing ethical conduct in a company. In sustainability leadership, values are the underlying beliefs that guide a person's behavior, while principles are the specific rules and guidelines that help leaders make decisions and take action in a sustainable way. Both are important for sustainability leadership, as they help guide leaders in making decisions that are consistent with their values and that promote a more sustainable future.

Several studies have attempted to identify the values that characterize sustainability leaders. While there is some variation in the specific values that are identified, there are some commonalities that emerge. A study conducted by Bansal and Roth (2000) identifies four core values that are associated with sustainable business leaders: environmental stewardship, social responsibility, employee empowerment, and customer satisfaction.

Environmental stewardship refers to the commitment to protecting the natural environment, while social responsibility refers to the commitment to broader social and economic issues. Employee empowerment refers to the belief in the value of employees and the importance of treating them fairly and respectfully, while customer satisfaction refers to the focus on meeting the needs and expectations of customers in a sustainable way. Henriksson and Grunewald (2020) in their edited volume *Sustainability Leadership: A Swedish Approach to Transforming Your Company, Your Industry and the World* highlight a set of core values that are associated with sustainability leadership. These values include: responsibility, long-term thinking, collaboration, innovation, transparency, human rights, diversity, and inclusiveness. These values reflect a holistic and systemic approach to sustainability leadership, emphasizing the importance of collaboration, innovation, and long-term thinking, as well as a strong commitment to responsibility and transparency. The authors argue that these values are essential for companies and organizations that wish to succeed in the long term and to contribute to a more sustainable economy. These findings are consistent with the values that are commonly associated with sustainability leadership.

Other studies have identified additional values that are associated with sustainability leadership, such as ethical behavior, transparency, and adaptability. The values identified in these studies suggest that sustainability leaders are characterized by a deep commitment to environmental and social issues, a willingness to collaborate and innovate, and a strong sense of responsibility and stewardship. The values associated with sustainability leadership are:

1. **Integrity**: Sustainability leaders are committed to ethical and transparent behavior and to being accountable for their actions and decisions.
2. **Responsiveness**: Sustainability leaders are responsive to the needs and concerns of stakeholders and are committed to engaging in active and open communication.
3. **Innovation**: Sustainability leaders are committed to exploring new and innovative solutions to sustainability challenges and to continuously improving their performance.
4. **Collaboration**: Sustainability leaders recognize that sustainability challenges are complex and often require collaboration across sectors

and disciplines, and are committed to working with others to find solutions.

5. **Long-term thinking**: Sustainability leaders understand the importance of considering the long-term implications of their actions and decisions, and are committed to creating sustainable systems and practices that will benefit future generations.
6. **Inclusivity**: Sustainability leaders understand that sustainability is not only about the environment, but also about the well-being of people and communities, and that it is important to consider the needs and perspectives of all stakeholders, especially the most marginalized.
7. **Adaptability**: Sustainability leaders understand that the sustainability challenges are complex, ever-evolving and are committed to continuously learning and adapting their approach.
8. **Systems thinking**: Sustainability leaders understand the interconnectedness of environmental, social, and economic systems and are committed to taking a holistic and systems-based approach to sustainability.

Sustainability as Value Creation

Sustainable value creation (SVC) is the practice of generating long-term economic, environmental, and social benefits for all stakeholders, including shareholders, employees, customers, communities, and the environment. It involves generating long-term value for stakeholders, including shareholders, employees, customers, suppliers, and the wider community, while minimizing negative environmental impacts and promoting social well-being. SVC creates long-term value across both the risks and opportunities associated with economic, environmental, and social developments. There are several studies of well-known scholars who have argued in favor of creating sustainability values and their shared benefits for the organization and society at large.

Michael Porter, a leading management scholar, has written extensively on the topic of sustainable value creation. In their Harvard Business Review article *Creating Shared Value*, Michael Porter and Mark Kramer (2011) argued that companies can move beyond traditional corporate social responsibility (CSR) and gain competitive advantage by creating shared value (CSV). According to Porter and Kramer, CSV involves creating economic value in a way that also creates value for society and addresses societal challenges. Companies that embrace CSV create a virtuous cycle of mutually reinforcing economic and social benefits, rather than just seeking to mitigate social and environmental harms or simply engaging in philanthropy. Porter and Kramer argue that there are three key ways that companies can create shared value:

1. **Reconceiving products and markets**: Companies can create shared value by innovating products and services that address societal needs and challenges. For example, Nestle created shared value by developing a nutritious, affordable product called "Milo" that helps address malnutrition in developing countries.
2. **Redefining productivity in the value chain:** Companies can create shared value by improving the efficiency and sustainability of their operations and supply chains. For example, Walmart created shared value by implementing a sustainable seafood sourcing program that not only reduced its environmental impact but also provided economic benefits to fishermen and improved food security for local communities.
3. **Enabling local cluster development**: Companies can create shared value by investing in the social and economic development of the communities in which they operate. For example, Intel created shared value by investing in education and infrastructure development in Costa Rica, which helped create a more skilled workforce and a more robust local economy.

Overall, Porter and Kramer argue that companies who embrace CSV can create a competitive advantage by improving their reputation, reducing risks, accessing new markets, improving efficiency, and attracting and retaining talent. By creating shared value, companies can contribute to the economic, social, and environmental well-being of society while also creating long-term value for their shareholders. In relation to sustainability, the CSV model relates to three dimensions of sustainable value creation, which are:

1. **Economic Dimension**: According to Porter, sustainable value creation begins with creating economic value. This involves generating profits and creating economic growth while also addressing

social and environmental challenges. Companies can achieve economic sustainability by pursuing efficiency in their operations, innovating new products and services, and creating shared value for their stakeholders.

2. **Social Dimension**: The social dimension of sustainable value creation involves addressing social challenges such as poverty, inequality, and social exclusion. Companies can achieve social sustainability by investing in their employees, creating safe and healthy workplaces, supporting local communities, and engaging in philanthropic activities.
3. **Environmental Dimension**: The environmental dimension of sustainable value creation involves minimizing negative impacts on the natural environment and promoting sustainable practices. Companies can achieve environmental sustainability by reducing their carbon footprint, conserving natural resources, and promoting sustainable production and consumption practices.

Other scholars have similarly argued on the benefits of value creation in sustainability. John Elkington (2001), for example, has been a pioneer in framing sustainability values. In his book, *The Chrysalis Economy: How Citizen CEOs and Corporations Can Fuse Values and Value Creation,* he presents a vision for a more sustainable and equitable future, based on seven key arguments. First, Elkington argues that the current economic model is unsustainable, with growing inequalities, environmental degradation, and social unrest. He proposes a new economic model based on sustainable value creation. Second, Elkington sees sustainability innovation as a key driver of economic growth and transformation, with the potential to create new markets and business opportunities. Third, Elkington emphasizes the need for systems thinking to address complex sustainability challenges and the need to consider the interconnectedness of social, environmental, and economic systems. Fourth, Elkington argues that businesses have a critical role to play in sustainable development, and that they must shift from a focus on short-term profits to a longer-term view that incorporates social and environmental impacts. Fifth, Elkington argues that traditional measures of economic growth, such as GDP, are inadequate to capture the true value of sustainable development. He proposes new metrics that incorporate social, environmental, and economic factors. Sixth, Elkington emphasizes the need for collaboration and partnership among stakeholders, including businesses, governments, NGOs, and communities, to achieve sustainable development goals. Seventh, Elkington sees the potential for a new social contract that values sustainability, equity, and well-being, which can then help build more resilient and inclusive societies. Elkington also introduces the seven levels of sustainable value creation:

1. **Financial Value**: This level refers to creating economic value through sustainable business practices that generate revenue and profits.
2. **Social Value**: This level involves creating positive social impacts through sustainable business practices that benefit communities, employees, and other stakeholders.
3. **Environmental Value**: This level focuses on reducing the negative impacts of business activities on the environment, such as reducing waste and greenhouse gas emissions.
4. **Material Value**: This level involves creating value by conserving natural resources and minimizing the use of non-renewable resources.
5. **Intellectual Value**: This level involves creating value through innovation, research, and development of new products and technologies.
6. **Cultural Value**: This level involves creating value by preserving and promoting cultural heritage and diversity.
7. **Spiritual Value**: This level involves creating value by promoting values such as compassion, empathy, and mindfulness, which can help build more sustainable and equitable societies.

Chris Laszlo and Nadya Zhexembayeva (2011) in their book, *Embedded Sustainability: The Next Big Competitive Advantage*, make a convincing argument that companies can better leverage global challenges by integrating all these seven levels of sustainability value creation which include:

1. **Individual level**: Supporting the personal growth and development of employees and stakeholders.
2. **Functional level**: Optimizing business processes and systems to minimize waste and environmental impact.
3. **Product level**: Creating sustainable products that meet customer needs and promote sustainability.

4. **Customer level**: Engaging with customers to create sustainable value and build brand loyalty.
5. **Societal level**: Contributing to the well-being of society and addressing social and environmental issues.
6. **Global level**: Addressing global sustainability challenges through collaborations and partnerships.
7. **Planetary level**: Creating solutions that address the long-term sustainability of the planet.

They argue that by embedding sustainability into a company's operations at each of these seven levels, companies can achieve competitive advantage by mitigating risks, achieving higher operational efficiency, differentiating products, entering or creating new markets, protecting and enhancing brand identity, reshaping market rules, and regulatory contexts. The book emphasizes the importance of radical innovation, which involves creating new business models, products, and services that are based on sustainable principles and practices. In other words, embedding sustainability into a company's core business strategy and operations can create a competitive advantage by addressing sustainability challenges, mitigating risks, and creating opportunities for innovation and growth. The seven levels of value creation provide a framework for companies to achieve this goal.

Stuart Hart, an internationally known scholar on the implications of the environment and poverty for business strategy, developed a *Sustainable Value Framework* for linking societal challenges of global sustainability to the creation of shareholder value by the firm (Hart & Milstein, 2003). The framework identifies opportunities for businesses to create value by addressing environmental and social challenges. His framework reflects four core dimensions of sustainability strategy linked to corporate performance and value creation:

1. **Pollution Prevention**: Minimizing waste and emissions from current facilities and operations);
2. **Product Stewardship**: Engaging stakeholders and managing the full life cycle of today's products;
3. **Clean Technology**: Developing and deploying "next-generation" clean technologies;
4. **Base of the Pyramid**: Co-creating new businesses to serve the unmet needs of the poor and underserved.

He also makes a call for a sustainable value proposition, which is the way a company creates value by addressing sustainability challenges. The sustainable value proposition can take many forms, including eco-efficiency, eco-effectiveness, and social innovation. By creating a sustainable value proposition, companies can differentiate themselves from their competitors, build brand value, and create new markets. By integrating these elements, the Sustainable Value Framework provides a comprehensive approach for businesses to create value while also addressing sustainability challenges. The framework recognizes that economic, social, and environmental sustainability is all interdependent, and that businesses can create value by addressing all three spheres of sustainability throughout the value chain. The sustainable value proposition provides a way for businesses to differentiate themselves and create new markets by addressing sustainability challenges. Ultimately, the Sustainable Value Framework provides a roadmap for businesses to create both shareholder and societal values.

Mariana Mazzucato's book *The Value of Everything* (2018) explores the role of value creation in modern economies and argues that current measures of economic value do not fully capture the contribution of public goods, social value, and environmental sustainability. From this perspective, there are several sustainable value implications that emerge from her arguments, including:

1. **The need to measure and reward social value creation**: Mazzucato argues that traditional economic measures, such as GDP, do not fully capture the value created by public goods and social investments. To address this, she suggests that we need new measures of value that take into account the contribution of social value, such as investments in education, healthcare, and social welfare.
2. **The importance of public-private partnerships**: Mazzucato argues that public investments in research and development have been crucial to driving technological innovation and economic growth. This highlights the importance of public-private partnerships in driving sustainable innovation that benefits both the economy and society.
3. **The need for responsible innovation**: Mazzucato argues that innovation should be directed towards solving societal challenges and creating sustainable value, rather than solely focusing on commercial

gain. This requires a shift in business practices towards responsible innovation that prioritizes social and environmental sustainability.

4. **The role of the state in promoting sustainable value creation**: Mazzucato argues that the state has a critical role to play in promoting sustainable value creation through investments in research and development, social welfare, and infrastructure. This highlights the importance of public policies that promote sustainability, such as subsidies for renewable energy and regulations that incentivize sustainable practices.

Overall, Mazzucato's arguments emphasize the need to broaden our understanding of value creation to include social and environmental sustainability. This requires a shift in the way we measure and reward economic activity, as well as a more collaborative approach to innovation that focuses on solving societal challenges and creating sustainable value.

In the following sections, we want to explore in more detail the contributions that some international initiatives have given to the understanding and practices of sustainability leadership. These contributions have enriched our understanding of a principled approach to sustainability leadership. As illustrated and summarized in Fig. 2.1, they represent a values-based perspective for the practice of sustainability leadership for people, planet, prosperity, peace, partnership, and personal-professional values and principles. We consider initiatives and fundamental documents that have emerged along the history and evolution of our understanding of sustainability leadership in its core values. These are correlated principles for sustainability leadership and include the principles of the 2030 Agenda behind the SDGs, the Earth Charter principles, the Global Compact's principles and its connected responsible management education principles, the business human rights principles, and the diversity and inclusion principles (Fig. 2.2).

The 2030 Agenda Principles

The United Nations (2015) document *Transforming our world: the 2030 Agenda for Sustainable Development* is a plan of action adopted by the UN in 2015 that outlines 17 SDGs with their 169 targets and 232 indicators to guide global efforts towards sustainable development by 2030. The SDGs are viewed as a set of interconnected goals designed to end

Fig. 2.2 Correlated principles for sustainability leadership

poverty, protect the planet, and ensure prosperity for all. The principles of the 2030 Agenda for Sustainable Development include:

1. **Universality**: The 2030 Agenda is a universal agenda, applying to all countries, regardless of their level of development.
2. **Integration**: The agenda is integrated and indivisible, meaning that all of the goals and targets are interrelated and must be pursued in an integrated manner.
3. **Leave no one behind**: The agenda is focused on reaching the most vulnerable and marginalized populations, to ensure that no one is left behind in the pursuit of sustainable development.

4. **Partnership**: The agenda emphasizes the need for partnerships and cooperation between governments, civil society, the private sector, and other stakeholders, to achieve the sustainable development goals.
5. **Human rights**: The agenda is grounded in human rights, including the right to development, and emphasizes the need for gender equality, empowerment of women and girls, and the protection of human rights for all.
6. **Sustainability**: The agenda emphasizes the need for sustainable development, which means meeting the needs of the present generation without compromising the ability of future generations to meet their own needs.

The principles of the 2030 Agenda emphasize the need for a collaborative and integrated approach to sustainable development, focused on leaving no one behind and ensuring a sustainable future for all. The document also groups the sustainability agenda inherent to SDG leadership implications for the 5Ps pillars of People, Planet, Prosperity, Peace, and Partnership. The 5Ps are a framework used to guide sustainable development and promote a more sustainable future for all. The 5Ps have important implications for sustainability leadership, as they provide a framework for guiding organizations and leaders towards a more sustainable future. The principles and goals behind each of the 5Ps pillars are as follows:

1. **People**: This pillar focuses on the well-being of people, both now and in the future. It aims to ensure that all people have access to basic needs such as food, clean water, healthcare, education, and social services. The goal is to promote human development and human rights, reduce inequality and discrimination, and ensure that everyone can participate in and benefit from economic and social development. Sustainability leadership requires a focus on the well-being of people, both within and outside of the organization. Leaders must prioritize the needs and concerns of stakeholders, including employees, customers, suppliers, and the wider community and work to create a culture of inclusion, diversity, and equity.
2. **Planet**: This pillar focuses on protecting the natural environment and preserving natural resources for future generations. The goal

is to promote sustainable use of natural resources, reduce pollution and waste, combat climate change, and protect biodiversity and ecosystems. Sustainability leadership requires a commitment to protecting the natural environment and preserving natural resources. Leaders must be proactive in promoting environmentally sustainable practices and reducing their organization's carbon footprint and other negative environmental impacts.

3. **Prosperity**: This pillar focuses on promoting economic growth and development that is inclusive, sustainable, and benefits everyone. The goal is to promote job creation, innovation, and entrepreneurship, while ensuring that economic growth is environmentally sustainable, socially inclusive, and promotes social justice. Sustainability leadership requires a focus on creating economic value that is socially and environmentally sustainable. Leaders must prioritize long-term value creation, consider the impacts of their business on society and the environment, and work to create economic growth that is inclusive and benefits all stakeholders.
4. **Peace**: This pillar focuses on promoting peaceful and inclusive societies, where everyone has access to justice and the rule of law. The goal is to promote human security, reduce conflict and violence, and ensure that people can live in safety and security. Sustainability leadership requires a commitment to promoting peace, stability, and security in the wider society. Leaders must promote human security, reduce conflict and violence, and ensure that their organization is committed to human rights, social justice, and the rule of law.
5. **Partnership**: This pillar focuses on promoting partnerships between different stakeholders, including governments, civil society, the private sector, and international organizations. The goal is to promote collaboration and cooperation, share knowledge and resources, and build a global community committed to sustainable development. Sustainability leadership requires a commitment to building partnerships and collaborations, both within and outside of the organization. Leaders must work to build relationships with stakeholders, engage in dialogue and cooperation, and share knowledge and resources to advance sustainable development.

The 5Ps pillars provide a framework for a comprehensive and integrated approach to sustainable development, taking into account the interrelatedness of different aspects of human development and the environment.

The goal is to create a sustainable future for all, where people can live in harmony with the planet and with each other. The 5Ps have significant implications for sustainability leadership as it requires adopting an integrated approach to consider sustainability practices, objectives, and measurable contributions mapped on social, environmental, and economic sustainability, as well as peace and partnership performances.

The United Nations Global Compact's *Blueprint for Business Leadership: A Principles-Based Approach* (2017) provides a framework for businesses to align their strategies and operations with the SDGs. It emphasizes the critical role of business leadership in achieving the SDGs and outlines several key principles of SDG leadership. Some of the key points from the Blueprint on SDG leadership include leadership commitment to integrate sustainable development into their core business strategies. It also recommends businesses to take an integrated approach to sustainable development, considering social, environmental, and economic factors in their decision-making processes. It also makes a case for cross-sector collaboration, transparency, and accountability through SDG reporting and encourages SDG leaders to advance innovation and technology and respect human rights, including labor rights and social and environmental justice. The principles of SDG leadership outlined in the Blueprint align with the broader ethical principles of responsible business conduct and sustainable development and outline three principles-based steps as integral to promotion and practices of SDG leadership:

Step 1: Prioritize Principle: Prioritizing, involves identifying the SDGs that are most relevant to the business's operations and stakeholders, and determining which goals the business can have the most impact on. This can involve assessing the business's value chain, engaging with stakeholders, and considering the social and environmental challenges faced by the business and its industry.

Step 2: Act Principle: Acting, involves implementing strategies and initiatives to address the SDGs identified in the prioritization process. This can involve changes to business practices, such as reducing greenhouse gas emissions or promoting sustainable supply chain practices, as well as collaboration with stakeholders to drive progress towards the SDGs.

Step 3: Learn Principle: Learning, involves monitoring and evaluating the impact of the business's actions on the SDGs, and using this information to improve and refine strategies going forward. This can involve measuring and reporting on progress towards the SDGs, engaging with stakeholders for feedback, and learning from best practices and innovations.

Overall, the three-step process of prioritizing, acting, and learning provides a principles-based framework for businesses to continually improve their leadership on the SDGs and respond to changes in the business environment and social and environmental challenges. By repeating this process, businesses can stay responsive and adaptive, and help drive progress towards the achievement of the SDGs.

The Earth Charter Principles

The idea of the Earth Charter originated in 1987 by members of the Club of Rome, when the United Nations World Commission on Environment and Development called for a new charter to guide the transition to sustainable development. In 1972, the Club of Rome published the book *The Limits to Growth* (Meadows et al., 1972) which explored the consequences of exponential growth on a finite planet and helped to popularize the idea that economic growth must be balanced with environmental and social sustainability, and it continues to be a reference point for discussions on sustainable development. The 27 principles of the Earth Charter were created in response to the 1987, *Our Common Future* from the World Commission on Environment and Development (aka, Brundtland Commission), with the "new charter" with "new principles" and "new norms" as discussed in 1992 Earth Summit in Rio de Janeiro.

The Earth Charter principles cover a wide range of areas, including respect and care for the community of life, ecological integrity, social and economic justice, and nonviolence and peace. These fundamental ethical principles have been elaborated to give a comprehensive framework for building a just, sustainable, and peaceful global society in the twenty-first century. These are the 27 principles of the Earth Charter:

I. **Respect and care for the community of life**

1. Respect Earth and life in all its diversity.
2. Care for the community of life with understanding, compassion, and love.

3. Build democratic societies that are just, participatory, sustainable, and peaceful.

II. **Ecological integrity**

4. Secure Earth's bounty and beauty for present and future generations.
5. Protect and restore the integrity of Earth's ecological systems.

III. **Social and economic justice**

6. Prevent harm as the best method of environmental protection and, when knowledge is limited, apply a precautionary approach.
7. Eradicate poverty as an ethical, social, and environmental imperative.
8. Ensure that economic activities and institutions at all levels promote human development in an equitable and sustainable manner.
9. Affirm gender equality and equity as prerequisites to sustainable development and ensure universal access to education, healthcare, and economic opportunity.

IV. **Democracy, nonviolence, and peace**

10. Uphold the right of all, without discrimination, to a natural and social environment supportive of human dignity, bodily health, and spiritual well-being, with special attention to the rights of Indigenous peoples and minorities.
11. Strengthen democratic institutions at all levels and provide transparency and accountability in governance, inclusive participation in decision-making, and access to justice.
12. Integrate into formal education and lifelong learning the knowledge, values, and skills needed for a sustainable way of life.
13. Treat all living beings with respect and consideration.
14. Promote a culture of tolerance, nonviolence, and peace.

V. **Partnerships**

15. Strengthen the role of international cooperation in achieving sustainable development and address the inequities in global systems of trade and finance.

16. Enhance the participation of civil society in decision-making and governance.
17. Encourage and support the development of sustainable communities at the local level.
18. Recognize and support the critical role and value of Indigenous cultures and traditional knowledge.

VI. **Responsible consumption and production**

19. Adopt patterns of production, consumption, and reproduction that safeguard Earth's regenerative capacities, human rights, and community well-being.
20. Advance the study of ecological sustainability and promote the open exchange and wide application of the knowledge acquired.

VII. **Human rights**

21. Secure the universal right to water and food.
22. Protect and restore the health of the planet's ecosystems.
23. Ensure universal access to healthcare that fosters reproductive health and responsible reproduction.
24. Secure the rights of all to an environment that meets human needs for dignity, livelihood, and well-being.

VIII. **Cultural diversity**

25. Support international and national cultural diversity and ensure that the cultural heritage of minorities and Indigenous peoples is respected and maintained.
26. Promote the use of information and communications technologies that serve the common good and are accessible to all.
27. Use science and technology to enhance ecological sustainability and support a culture of peace.

The principles of the Earth Charter have significant implications for sustainability leadership. Leaders who prioritize the principles of the Earth Charter can create a vision for a just, sustainable, and peaceful world and take action to achieve this vision. By incorporating the principles of the Earth Charter into their leadership practices, leaders can help to foster a culture of respect, care, and compassion for the community of life, which includes all living beings and ecosystems. The Earth Charter's principles can help sustainability leaders to articulate their promotion of the integrity of ecological systems, recognizing the critical role they play in sustaining life on Earth. The principles can also address social and economic inequities, including poverty, and work towards ensuring that economic activities and institutions promote humans. These principles serve as a powerful framework for creating a sustainable and ethical business model. They encourage organizations to build a culture of respect and care for all living things, minimize their environmental impact, and promote equity and social justice in all their endeavors. Additionally, they emphasize the importance of nonviolence and peace, both internally and externally. Finally, the Earth Charter Principles provide a strong ethical foundation for business leadership as they work to create a better world.

The Global Compact Principles

The United Nations Global Compact (UNGC) is a voluntary initiative which aims to encourage businesses and organizations to adopt sustainable and socially responsible policies and practices (Conaway & Laasch, 2015). These principles were developed through a global consultation process involving businesses, labor organizations, civil society, and other stakeholders. The initiative is based on ten principles that cover four key areas: human rights, labor, environment, and anti-corruption:

Key Area 1: Human Rights

Principle 1: Businesses should support and respect the protection of internationally proclaimed human rights.
Principle 2: Businesses should make sure that they are not complicit in human rights abuses.

Key Area 2: Labor

Principle 3: Businesses should uphold the freedom of association and the effective recognition of the right to collective bargaining.
Principle 4: Businesses should eliminate all forms of forced and compulsory labor.
Principle 5: Businesses should effectively abolish child labor.

Principle 6: Businesses should eliminate discrimination in respect of employment and occupation.

Key Area 3: Environment

Principle 7: Businesses should support a precautionary approach to environmental challenges.
Principle 8: Businesses should undertake initiatives to promote greater environmental responsibility.
Principle 9: Businesses should encourage the development and diffusion of environmentally friendly technologies.

Key Area 4: Anti-corruption

Principle 10: Businesses should work against corruption in all its forms, including extortion and bribery.

The ten principles of the UNGC were officially launched by the UN Secretary-General in 2000, after a year-long consultation process that involved thousands of stakeholders from around the world. The principles were designed to provide a framework for businesses and organizations to adopt sustainable and socially responsible policies and practices, and to encourage dialogue and collaboration between businesses, civil society, and other stakeholders. Since its launch, the UNGC has become one of the world's largest corporate sustainability initiatives, with over 14,000 signatories from over 160 countries along with more than 3,000 non-business participants representing civil society organizations and academia among others. For business leadership, the UNGC principles serve as a guide for creating sustainable, ethical, and responsible business practices. They help to ensure that companies are creating value for all stakeholders, while also protecting the environment and contributing to a more prosperous and equitable world.

Connected to the Global Compact principles are the responsible management education principles. In 2007, the UNGC worked with academic institutions and higher education associations for the development of the Principles of Responsible Management Education (PRME) with over 800 business schools in 98 countries (Morsing, 2021). The PRME initiative seeks to promote sustainability and responsibility in management education and it is based on six principles, which outline the role of business schools in promoting responsible management education. The principles are as follows:

1. **Purpose**: Business schools should develop a clear sense of purpose that is consistent with sustainable development and social responsibility.
2. **Values**: Business schools should promote values of global social responsibility and ethical behavior.
3. **Method**: Business schools should use a learning and teaching approach that encourages critical thinking and creativity, and that incorporates sustainability and social responsibility issues.
4. **Research**: Business schools should engage in research that advances our understanding of sustainable development and social responsibility.
5. **Partnership**: Business schools should seek to establish partnerships with businesses, governments, civil society, and other stakeholders in order to create a more sustainable and equitable world.
6. **Dialogue**: Business schools should engage in dialogue with their stakeholders, including their students, faculty, staff, and the wider community, in order to promote sustainable development and social responsibility.

For business schools, these principles provide a framework for promoting responsible management education and ensuring that their graduates are prepared to lead organizations in a sustainable and socially responsible manner. Business schools that commit to the PRME principles are expected to integrate sustainability and social responsibility issues into their curriculum, research, and outreach activities. This can involve revising course materials, creating new programs, and promoting research and dialogue that addresses sustainability and social responsibility issues. By committing to the PRME principles, business schools can play a crucial role in preparing future business leaders to create a more sustainable and equitable world. They can also enhance their reputation and build stronger relationships with stakeholders who value sustainability and social responsibility. For academics and MBA programs, the PRME is a commitment that gives a framework for integrating sustainability, social responsibility, and ethical education into management and leadership education. Through the engagement in the PRME chapters, the Sharing Information on Progress (SIP), and the conferences and seminars, academic leaders can learn from each other's best practices for integrating sustainability into higher education. This principle-based forum for academic business leaders promotes the integration of responsible management education. The mindsets, best teaching and learning practices, and the administration leadership commitments demonstrate that principles matter in the education of future business leaders who can then navigate complex global challenges, including climate change, inequality, and poverty.

Business Human Rights Principles

The *Guiding Principles on Business and Human Rights* (UNGPs) were developed by the United Nations in 2011 to provide a framework for businesses to respect human rights in their operations (OHCHR, 2011). The UNGPs are based on three pillars and correlated principles:

1. **Protect**: The states' duty is to protect human rights. States have a duty to protect human rights from abuse by third parties, including businesses. This means that states should establish laws, policies, and regulations to prevent human rights abuses by businesses and to ensure that victims of such abuses have access to effective remedies.
2. **Respect**: The corporate responsibility is to respect human rights. Businesses have a responsibility to respect human rights in their operations and to avoid infringing on the human rights of others. This means that businesses should conduct due diligence to identify and address human rights risks in their operations and should put in place policies, procedures, and mechanisms to prevent and mitigate human rights abuses.
3. **Remedy**: The need for effective remedies for victims of human rights abuses. Victims of human rights abuses should have access to effective remedies, including judicial and non-judicial remedies. Businesses have a responsibility to provide or contribute to effective remedies for harms that they have caused, or to which they have contributed.

The UNGPs also provide guidance on how businesses can implement these principles in practice, including through the development of human rights policies, due diligence processes, and grievance mechanisms. The UNGPs emphasize the importance of engaging with stakeholders, including affected communities, workers, and civil society organizations, and of ensuring transparency and accountability in business operations.

The UNGPs were developed by John Ruggie, who served as the United Nations Secretary-General's Special Representative for Business and Human Rights from 2005 to 2011. They were developed through an extensive and inclusive consultation process that involved a wide range of stakeholders, including businesses, civil society organizations, governments, and academics. Ruggie's work was based on the recognition that while businesses have the potential to contribute to human rights, they can also negatively impact human rights through their operations, and that there was a need for a framework to guide businesses in respecting human rights.

The UNGPs were unanimously endorsed by the United Nations Human Rights Council (UNHCR) in 2011, and they have since been widely recognized as the authoritative framework for business and human rights. The UNGPs have been integrated into a variety of initiatives and frameworks, including the United Nations Global Compact, the Organization for Economic Co-operation and Development (OECD) Guidelines for Multinational Enterprises, and the SDGs.

The UNGPs have several implications for sustainability leadership, including:

1. **Corporate Responsibility**: The UNGPs emphasize the responsibility of businesses to respect human rights, including the right to a safe and healthy work environment, the right to freedom of association and collective bargaining, and the right to non-discrimination. Sustainability leaders must integrate these principles into their business operations and supply chain management.
2. **Due Diligence**: The UNGPs call for companies to conduct human rights due diligence, which involves identifying, assessing, and mitigating potential human rights risks in their operations and supply chains. Sustainability leaders must ensure that their organizations are conducting robust due diligence to prevent and mitigate human rights abuses.
3. **Stakeholder Engagement**: The UNGPs call for businesses to engage with a wide range of stakeholders, including affected communities, workers, and civil society organizations. Sustainability leaders must ensure that their organizations are engaging with stakeholders in a meaningful and transparent manner, and incorporating stakeholder feedback into their decision-making processes.

4. **Remedy**: The UNGPs call for companies to provide effective remedies for victims of human rights abuses. Sustainability leaders must ensure that their organizations have effective grievance mechanisms in place to provide remedy to those who have been harmed by their operations.

Overall, the UNGPs provide a framework for businesses to respect human rights in their operations and supply chains, and sustainability leaders must integrate these principles into their business practices to ensure that they are contributing to a sustainable future. For business leaders, the UNGPs provide an authoritative global standard for preventing and addressing the risk of adverse human rights impacts linked to their business activity. Through the UNGPs, business leaders can ensure that their business operations are compliant with human rights laws and regulations, and that they are promoting human rights throughout their business operations.

The Inclusion IDEA Principles

The principles for Inclusion, Diversity, Equity, and Accessibility (IDEA) focus on creating a work environment that is inclusive, equitable, and accessible to all employees, regardless of their background. These perspectives and values are increasingly becoming essential elements in responsible leadership practices (Marques & Dhiman, 2022). They have important implications for sustainability leadership, as sustainable leaders must strive to build a diverse and inclusive workplace that reflects the values of sustainability and social responsibility. Here are some of the key principles for IDEA and their implications for sustainability leadership:

1. **Inclusion**: Inclusion means creating a work environment where all employees feel valued, respected, and supported. Sustainable leaders should work to foster an inclusive culture by promoting open communication, creating a safe and welcoming work environment, and providing opportunities for employees to share their perspectives and ideas.
2. **Diversity**: Diversity means valuing and embracing differences in ethnicity, race, gender, age, religion, sexual orientation, and other characteristics. Sustainable leaders should work to build a diverse workforce that reflects the communities in which their organization

operates, and that encourages diversity of thought, experience, and perspective.

3. **Equity**: Equity means ensuring that all employees have access to the same opportunities and resources, regardless of their background. Sustainable leaders should work to create an equitable workplace by promoting fair and equitable hiring, promotion, and pay practices and by providing equal opportunities for growth and development.
4. **Accessibility**: Accessibility means ensuring that the work environment is accessible to all employees, including those with disabilities. Sustainable leaders should work to provide an accessible workplace by making physical accommodations as needed, providing assistive technology, and ensuring that employees with disabilities are fully included in all aspects of the workplace.

The book *Corporate Social Responsibility and Diversity Management: Theoretical Approaches and Best Practices* by Seierstad and Hansen (2018) gives a series of principles for diversity and inclusion for companies who can enhance their social responsibility and sustainability performance. They show how companies can create a more diverse, inclusive, and socially responsible workplace, which in turn can lead to improved employee satisfaction, innovation, and financial performance. These principles have important implications for sustainability leadership. Here are some of the ways that these principles can inform sustainable leadership:

1. **Building a diverse and inclusive workforce**: Sustainable leaders should work to build a diverse and inclusive workforce that reflects the communities where their organization operates. This means ensuring that recruitment and retention practices are inclusive and equitable, and that employees from diverse backgrounds are provided with equal opportunities for growth and development.
2. **Promoting a culture of respect and inclusivity**: Sustainable leaders should work to create a culture of respect and inclusivity where all employees feel valued, respected, and supported. This includes fostering open communication and dialogue across differences, providing cultural competency training, and creating a safe and welcoming work environment for all.
3. **Embracing supplier diversity**: Sustainable leaders should embrace supplier diversity and seek out partnerships with diverse suppliers,

including those owned by women, people of color, and members of other underrepresented groups. This can help to build a more equitable and sustainable supply chain and can also help to promote economic development in underrepresented communities.

4. **Incorporating diversity and inclusion into decision-making**: Sustainable leaders should incorporate diversity and inclusion considerations into their decision-making processes. This means seeking out diverse perspectives, actively engaging with underrepresented stakeholders, and considering the potential social and environmental impacts of their decisions on different groups.

Overall, the principles of IDEA can inform sustainable leadership by helping leaders to build a more inclusive, equitable, and accessible workplace which reflects the values of sustainability and social responsibility. By prioritizing IDEA, sustainable leaders can create a more sustainable and responsible business culture that benefits both the organization and the broader community. The principles of diversity and inclusion can inform sustainable leadership by helping leaders to build more inclusive and equitable organizations that promote social and environmental sustainability. Companies and their leaders know that, as we will see in detail in Part 2: Sustainability Management, DEI reporting is often an integral or parallel effort along sustainability reporting. Sustainability leaders are necessarily inclusive leaders.

Therefore, sustainability leaders should welcome into their companies expert training for all employees, including managers and executives, for increased awareness and understanding of different cultures, perspectives, and experiences. This training should focus on building empathy, cultural competence, and effective communication across differences. They know that diversity is a strength to be valued in their supply chain. This means seeking out and partnering with diverse suppliers, including those owned by women, people of color, and members of other underrepresented groups. These principles can help companies create a more diverse, inclusive, and socially responsible workplace, which in turn can lead to improved employee satisfaction, innovation, and financial performance. By prioritizing diversity and inclusion, sustainable leaders can create a more sustainable and responsible business culture that benefits both the organization and the broader community. Diversity and inclusion in the workplace is key for companies who strive to become more globally relevant, interculturally competent, and internationally recognized.

Personal-Professional Values and Principles

Sustainability leaders know the importance of embedding values and principles into their leadership and organizations. The moral compass, as we explore in Chapter 5, is pivoted around personal and professional values and principles. Values and principles play a critical role in developing sustainability leadership, as they provide a framework for ethical decision-making and behavior that is necessary to achieve sustainability goals. Some of the core personal/professional values and principles for sustainability leadership include responsibility, innovation, respect, and collaboration. Others, like the CEC European Managers (2018), in their *Sustainable Leadership Guidelines,* enlist personal sustainability values as skills along the other necessary competencies for social (for SDG 1–5, 10), economic (for SDG 6–9, 11), environmental (for SDG 12–15), and procedural (for SDG 16–17). They describe how sustainability leaders exhibit mindfulness, continuous learning, adaptability and flexibility, sense of responsibility and ethics, and thinking in multiple perspectives (for the inner dimension) along team building, formulating vision, building network and trust, facilitating, and understanding social settings (for the social dimension). Identifying and developing these skills are crucial in their work of promoting sustainable development and responsible business practices. Four core values are highlighted here to show how these skills and competencies are linked to principled-based sustainability leadership practices:

1. **Responsibility**: The value of responsibility is central to sustainability leadership, as it emphasizes the importance of taking action to address sustainability issues and to minimize negative impacts on society and the environment. Leaders who prioritize responsibility are committed to ensuring that their organizations are acting in a way that is accountable and transparent, and that minimizes harm to the environment and society. Examples of responsible leadership include companies that implement sustainable production methods, reduce waste, and invest in renewable energy.
2. **Innovation**: The principle of innovation is also important in sustainability leadership, as it encourages leaders to think creatively about how to achieve sustainability goals. Innovative leaders are willing to take risks, experiment with new technologies, and challenge established ways of doing things. Examples of innovative sustainability

leadership include companies that use cutting-edge technology to reduce emissions, develop new products that promote sustainability, or engage in sustainable business practices.

3. **Respect**: The principle of respect emphasizes the importance of treating others with dignity and fairness, which is crucial to developing sustainable business practices. Leaders who prioritize respect are committed to promoting social justice, protecting human rights, and creating a culture of inclusivity and diversity. Examples of respectful sustainability leadership include companies that implement fair labor practices, promote gender equality, and invest in education and job training programs.
4. **Collaboration**: The principle of collaboration is also essential in sustainability leadership, as it emphasizes the importance of working together with stakeholders to achieve shared goals. Collaborative leaders are committed to building partnerships with governments, NGOs, and other organizations to create sustainable solutions that benefit everyone. Examples of collaborative sustainability leadership include companies that engage with local communities, work with suppliers to promote sustainable sourcing, and support sustainability initiatives through philanthropy and partnerships.

Overall, values and principles play a critical role in developing sustainability leadership, as they provide a framework for ethical decision-making and behavior that is necessary to achieve sustainability goals. By prioritizing responsibility, innovation, respect, and collaboration, sustainability leaders can create a culture of sustainable business practices that benefit both the environment and society. A great example of a sustainability leader who has successfully embedded values and principles into his career, service, and legacy is Mark Moody-Stuart.

Sir Mark Moody-Stuart KCMG is a British businessman and sustainability leader who has held senior leadership positions at several major corporations, including Shell, Anglo American, and HSBC. He is known for his work in promoting responsible and sustainable business practices, and has written extensively on topics such as climate change, sustainability, and corporate responsibility. Moody-Stuart has been recognized for his promotion of responsible and sustainable business practices in the companies that he led as well as influencing other leaders and companies. He served as the chairman of Anglo American from 2002 to 2009, during which time he focused on promoting sustainable development in the mining industry. He also served as the chairman of the Global Reporting Initiative (GRI), a nonprofit organization that promotes sustainability reporting, from 2007 to 2011. Moody-Stuart's work in promoting sustainability and responsible business practices has earned him numerous accolades and recognition. He was named a Commander of the British Empire in 2000 for his services to the oil and gas industry, and has received several other awards and honorary degrees for his work in sustainability and corporate responsibility. Moody-Stuart is considered an example of a sustainability leader due to his extensive experience and expertise in promoting responsible and sustainable business practices, and his commitment to addressing the environmental and social challenges facing the world today.

Mark Moody-Stuart's book (2017) entitled *Responsible Leadership: Lessons from the Front Line of Sustainability and Ethics* argues that embedding values and principles is critical to creating a culture of responsible and sustainable leadership within organizations. Here are some of the main arguments he makes:

1. **Values and principles guide behavior**: According to Moody-Stuart, values and principles provide a framework for ethical decision-making and behavior. By embedding these values and principles within an organization, leaders can guide their behavior and decision-making towards responsible and sustainable outcomes.
2. **Values and principles create a shared vision**: Embedding values and principles can help create a shared vision of what responsible and sustainable leadership looks like within an organization. This shared vision can help align employees and stakeholders around a common goal and encourage them to work together towards that goal.
3. **Values and principles build trust**: Moody-Stuart argues that embedding values and principles within an organization can help build trust between the organization and its stakeholders. By demonstrating a commitment to responsible and sustainable behavior, organizations can build long-term relationships with customers, investors, and other stakeholders.
4. **Values and principles drive innovation**: Moody-Stuart suggests that embedding values and principles can also drive innovation within organizations. By setting ambitious goals and pushing employees to think creatively about how to achieve those goals,

organizations can find new and innovative ways to operate in a responsible and sustainable manner.

5. **Values and principles create resilience**: Finally, Moody-Stuart argues that embedding values and principles can help organizations weather crises and setbacks. By having a clear set of values and principles to guide their decision-making, organizations can respond quickly and effectively to unexpected challenges, without sacrificing their commitment to responsible and sustainable behavior.

Moody-Stuart's leadership example and insightful biography emphasize the importance of embedding values and principles within organizations as a way to promote responsible and sustainable leadership. By creating a culture that prioritizes these values and principles, organizations can build trust, drive innovation, and create a more resilient and sustainable future.

The Limits of Principles

Principles play an essential role in guiding sustainable leadership practices, but they are not enough. They don't necessarily offer specific guidance on how to navigate the complex situations that businesses may face in the course of their operations. Principles may not account for trade-offs as sustainable leadership practices often require balancing competing considerations, such as economic, social, and environmental goals. Also, principles may not provide a clear framework for making these trade-offs. In other words, while having principles is a critical starting point for ethical business practice, it is not enough on its own. Sustainable leadership and ethical business practice requires a thoughtful, nuanced approach to decision-making that takes into account the specific context of each situation and balances competing considerations. Sustainable leaders must use principles as a starting point but must also rely on critical thinking, creativity, and empathy to navigate the complex challenges of leading a sustainable business. Here are a few reasons why solely having principles alone is not enough for sustainability leadership and ethical business practice:

1. **Principles are open to interpretation**: Principles can be interpreted differently by different people, and what one person considers to be ethical may not be perceived the same way by someone else.

2. **Principles don't cover every situation**: Principles may not be detailed enough to cover every situation that a business may encounter. For example, a principle such as "do no harm" is important, but it may not provide specific guidance on how to address a complex ethical dilemma.
3. **Principles may not be specific enough**: While principles provide a general framework for ethical behavior, they may not offer specific guidance for the complex challenges that sustainable leaders face. For example, while the principle of "minimizing waste" is essential, it may not provide specific guidance on how to reduce waste in a particular supply chain.
4. **Principles can be overridden by other factors**: While principles are important, they may not be the only consideration in a decision. Businesses must balance ethical considerations with other factors such as financial considerations, legal requirements, and stakeholder interests.
5. **Principles may be ignored**: Unfortunately, some businesses may prioritize profits over ethical principles and may make decisions that are unethical in order to achieve their financial goals.
6. **Principles may not account for evolving challenges**: Sustainable leadership practices must adapt to changing circumstances, such as emerging technologies or new regulatory frameworks. Principles may not be sufficiently dynamic to accommodate these changes.
7. **Principles may not account for diverse stakeholder perspectives**: Sustainable leadership requires considering the needs and interests of multiple stakeholders, including employees, customers, investors, and the broader community. However, principles may not account for the diversity of perspectives and interests that exist among stakeholders.
8. **Principles may not account for unintended consequences**: Sustainable leadership practices must consider the potential unintended consequences of their actions. However, principles may not provide adequate guidance for anticipating and mitigating these consequences.

Values, like principles, are also a good starting point and a term of reference in decision-making processes, but alone are insufficient. They too can be interpreted differently by different people. While values such as integrity, respect, and accountability are essential to sustainable leadership, they may not offer clear guidance on how to address specific sustainability challenges. Values, like principles, may inspire and motivate, but they may not translate into tangible action without a clear plan and strategy.

Sustainable leadership requires setting concrete goals and creating a roadmap for achieving them. Values, like principles, must also align with broader business goals and objectives. Sustainable leaders must balance sustainability considerations with other business priorities, such as profitability and growth. In addition, values, especially in reference to inner qualities of leaders, may not address systemic issues such as inequality, social justice, and environmental degradation. While values such as fairness and social responsibility are essential, they may not offer clear guidance on how to address complex systemic challenges. Values may be the deeper elements of culture, but they may not reflect diverse perspectives.

Sustainable leadership requires engaging with diverse perspectives and stakeholders. Values, however, may reflect the perspectives of a particular group or culture, and may not account for the diversity of views and experiences that exist in the broader community.

In conclusion, values and principles are essential foundations for sustainable leadership, but they are not sufficient on their own to ensure good performance and ethical practices. Sustainable leaders must use values as a starting point and principles as references but must also rely on concrete action, strategic planning, and engagement with diverse perspectives to achieve sustainability goals. They must also engage in discernments for their ethical decision-making processes.

Key Takeaways

1. Values and principles play a foundational role in sustainability leadership and practices, as they guide decision-making, actions, and behaviors towards a sustainable future.
2. Sustainability is not only about mitigating negative impacts but also about creating value for all stakeholders, including the environment, society, and the economy.
3. Core principles and values in sustainability practices include intergenerational equity, ecological integrity, social justice, and economic viability.

4. The 2030 Agenda, Earth Charter, Global Compact, Business and Human Rights, and Inclusion IDEA principles provide frameworks for sustainability leadership and practices, emphasizing the importance of human rights, corporate responsibility, and stakeholder engagement.
5. Personal and professional values and principles are also important for sustainability leadership, as they influence individual behaviors, attitudes, and perspectives towards sustainability.
6. However, the limits of principles must also be acknowledged, as they can be interpreted and implemented differently by different individuals and organizations, and may not always lead to the intended outcomes.

References

Bansal, P., & Roth, K. (2000). Why companies go green: A model of ecological responsiveness. *Academy of Management Journal, 43*(4), 717–736.

Benioff, M. R. (2019). *Trailblazer : The power of business as the greatest platform for change*. Currency.

Conaway, R. N., & Laasch, O. (2015). *Principles of responsible management: Global sustainability, responsibility, and ethics*. Cengage Learning.

CEC European Managers. (2018). *Sustainable leadership guidelines*. https://www.cec-managers.org/wp-content/uploads/2018/11/CEC-Sustainable-Leadership-Guidelines.pdf

Elkington, J. (2001). *The Chrysalis economy: How citizen CEOs and corporations can fuse values and value creation*. Wiley.

Hart, S. L., & Milstein, M. B. (2003). Creating sustainable value. *Academy of Management Perspectives, 17*(2), 56–67.

Henriksson, H., & Grunewald, E. W. (2020). *Sustainability leadership: A Swedish approach to transforming your company, your industry and the world*. Springer International Publishing.

Laszlo, C., & Zhexembayeva, N. (2011). *Embedded sustainability: The next big competitive advantage*. Stanford Business Books.

Lowitt, E. (2011). *The future of value: How sustainability creates value through competitive differentiation*. Wiley.

Marques, J., & Dhiman, S. (2022). *Leading with diversity, equity and inclusion: Approaches, practices and cases for integral leadership strategy*. Springer International Publishing.

Mazzucato, M. (2018). *The value of everything: Making and taking in the global economy*. Penguin Books Limited.

Meadows, D. et.al. (1972). *The limits to growth: A report for the club of Rome's project on the predicament of mankind*. Universe Books.

Moody-Stuart, M. (2017). *Responsible leadership: Lessons from the front line of sustainability and ethics*. Taylor & Francis.

Morsing, M. (Ed.). (2021). *Responsible management education: The PRME global movement*. Taylor & Francis.

OHCHR. (2011). *Guiding principles on business and human rights: Implementing the United Nations "protect, respect and remedy" Framework*. UN.

Porter, M. E., & Kramer, M. R. (2011). Creating shared value: How to reinvent capitalism—and unleash a wave of innovation and growth. *Harvard Business Review, 89*, 1–2. https://hbr.org/2011/01/the-big-idea-creating-shared-value. Accessed 14 March 2023.

Rimanoczy, I. (2021). *The sustainability mindset principles a guide to develop a mindset for a better world*. Routledge.

Seierstad, C., & Hansen, K. (2018). *Corporate social responsibility and diversity management: Theoretical approaches and best practices*. Springer International Publishing.

UN Global Compact. (2017). *Blueprint for business leadership on the SDGs*. Retrieved March 10, 2023, from Unglobalcompact.org website: https://unglobalcompact.org/library/5461

United Nations. (2011). *Guiding principles on business and human rights: Implementing the United Nations "Protect, Respect and Remedy" framework*. Switzerland.

United Nations. (2015). *Transforming our world: The 2030 agenda for sustainable development*. United States. https://sdgs.un.org/2030agenda. Accessed 14 March 2023.

CHAPTER 3

Higher Purpose in Sustainability Leaders

Abstract This chapter explores the concept of higher purpose in sustainability leadership through examples of leaders and organizations driving long-lasting business transformation and sustainable prosperity. It highlights the importance of values in purpose-driven organizations and how they can help to align stakeholders towards a common goal. The bulk of the chapter features nine case studies of sustainability leaders with a higher purpose, including Wangari Maathai, Elinor Ostrom, Mohammad Younis, Vandana Shiva, Paul Hawken, Christiana Figueres, Gro Harlem Brundtland, Greta Thunberg, Autumn Peltier, Xiye Bastida, Paul Polman, and Ray Anderson. These cases demonstrate how these leaders integrated sustainability into their businesses and made a positive impact on society and the planet. Finally, the chapter identifies common elements of higher purpose in sustainability companies and provides guidance on how to assess the impact of higher purpose on sustainability leadership.

Keywords Higher purpose · Purpose-driven organizations · Sustainable business transformation · Inspiring cases · Positive impact

M. Tavanti, *Developing Sustainability in Organizations*, Sustainable Development Goals Series,
https://doi.org/10.1007/978-3-031-36907-0_3

The best time to plant a tree was 20 years ago. The second best time is now.
—Chinese proverb

Higher Purpose as a Central Paradigm

There are many inspiring examples of sustainability leaders with a higher purpose in life. Paul Polman, former CEO of Unilever, as we will show in the cases of this chapter, is one of them. His vision to make Unilever a leader in sustainable business practices, while also working towards achieving the SDGs, has earned him numerous accolades and recognition, including being named one of the "World's 100 Most Influential People" by TIME magazine and the recipient of the Oslo Business for Peace Award. Polman's example demonstrates the importance of having a higher purpose in sustainability leadership, as it provides a sense of direction, motivation, and fulfillment, while also driving positive change for society and the planet.

Higher purpose is the central paradigm for sustainability leaders. But what is it? While purpose and higher purpose are related concepts, there is a difference between them in their relevance to sustainability.

1. **Purpose**: Purpose is a sense of direction or meaning that gives individuals and organizations a clear sense of what they are trying to achieve. Purpose can be defined in different ways, and it can relate to a variety of goals, both personal and professional. In the context of leadership, purpose can help leaders align their actions with their values and create a sense of meaning and motivation for themselves and their followers.
2. **Higher purpose**: on the other hand, refers to a purpose that goes beyond individual self-interest and is connected to a broader societal or environmental goal. Higher purpose is often associated with sustainability, as it involves a commitment to creating positive social and environmental outcomes in addition to achieving financial success. Higher purpose can inspire and align people around a common goal that goes beyond individual self-interest and creates a sense of meaning and significance.

In the context of sustainability leadership, higher purpose is particularly important because it can help leaders navigate complex sustainability challenges and build the trust and collaboration necessary for creating positive change. Higher purpose can create a sense of shared purpose that drives positive action and can help leaders overcome resistance to change and create new opportunities for innovation and growth.

Indeed, purpose and higher purpose are related concepts, but higher purpose is particularly relevant to sustainability leadership because it involves a commitment to creating positive social and environmental outcomes in addition to achieving financial success. Higher purpose can inspire and align people around a common goal that goes beyond individual self-interest and can help sustainability leaders navigate complex sustainability challenges and build the trust and collaboration necessary for creating positive change.

Higher purpose is connected to the notion of leading with the benefit of all humanity. In the book *Leading Sustainably: The Path to Sustainable Business and How the SDGs Changed Everything* by Testa Bridges and Donald Eubank (2021), the phrase "Pro bono humani generis" (for the good of all humanity) is used to emphasize the importance of sustainability and the need for businesses to act in a way that benefits all of humanity, not just their own interests. They suggest that leaders and businesses have a responsibility to consider the impact of their actions on society as a whole and to work towards sustainability in order to create a better future for everyone. They argue that by adopting sustainable practices and focusing on long-term goals rather than short-term profits, leaders and businesses can contribute to the well-being of society and the planet as a whole.

A leader with a strong, higher, and shared sense of purpose is able to create a culture of sustainability in society and within the organization, where employees feel motivated and engaged to work towards a common goal of sustainability. Ultimately, the role of purpose in sustainability leaders is to provide a clear and compelling direction for the organization's sustainability efforts and to inspire and engage employees, customers, and other stakeholders in the pursuit of sustainability goals. A higher purpose for sustainability leaders goes beyond themselves, their career aspirations, and their organization's mission. It aims at having a net positive impact in solving urgent social, environmental, and economic problems affecting both current and future populations. It offers a review of the purposes that inspired selected current and past sustainability leaders. Higher purpose sustainability leaders commit to address social, environmental, and economic issues to create a better world.

There are several emerging studies on the role of purpose in value leadership. Indeed, purpose and higher purpose, in particular, matter considerably in making a difference and instilling net positive impact in companies, societies, and the world. Here is an examination of critical aspects of purpose and higher purpose in their relevance to sustainability leadership.

Why Purpose Matters in Sustainability Leadership

On Purpose Leadership: Master the Art of Leading Yourself to Inspire and Impact Others by Dominick Quartuccio (2021) is a book that offers guidance on how to become a more effective and authentic leader. The book presents several key arguments on why purpose matters for today's practices of sustainability leadership.

1. **Leading oneself is the foundation for leading others**: Quartuccio argues that becoming an effective leader starts with mastering the art of leading oneself. He emphasizes the importance of self-awareness, self-regulation, and self-care, which are essential for developing the inner strength and resilience necessary for effective leadership. This argument is particularly relevant for sustainability leaders, who often face complex and challenging situations that require a high degree of personal resilience and adaptability.
2. **Purpose is the key to inspiring and impacting others**: The book emphasizes the importance of purpose as the key driver of effective leadership. Quartuccio argues that when leaders are clear about their purpose, they are better able to inspire and impact others, and create a sense of shared purpose that can drive positive change. For sustainability leaders, having a clear sense of purpose is crucial to creating a sense of urgency around the need to address environmental and social challenges.
3. **Authenticity is the foundation of trust and influence**: Quartuccio argues that authentic leadership is based on the alignment between one's values, beliefs, and actions. He emphasizes the importance of building trust with others through transparency and vulnerability,

and the power of vulnerability to inspire and connect with others. This argument is particularly relevant for sustainability leaders, who often need to build trust with diverse stakeholders and communicate complex and often controversial issues.

4. **Collaboration and collective impact are key to creating systemic change**: Quartuccio argues that effective leadership requires the ability to collaborate with others and create collective impact. He emphasizes the importance of building partnerships and alliances, and the need to create a shared vision and common goals that can drive systemic change. This argument is particularly relevant for sustainability leaders, who often need to work with diverse stakeholders and create multi-stakeholder partnerships to address complex sustainability challenges.

In summary, *On Purpose Leadership* offers a comprehensive framework for becoming a more effective and authentic leader. The book's emphasis on self-leadership, purpose, authenticity, collaboration, and collective impact is particularly relevant for today's sustainability leaders, who need to navigate complex and rapidly changing sustainability challenges and build the trust and collaboration necessary for creating positive change.

Start with Why in Sustainability Leadership

The arguments made by Simon Sinek in his book *Start with Why* (2011) are decidedly relevant to the idea of higher purpose in sustainability leadership because they emphasize the importance of having a clear and compelling purpose for organizations. Sinek argues that successful organizations are those that are driven by a sense of purpose or "why," which he defines as the reason an organization exists beyond just making a profit. In the context of sustainability leadership, having a clear purpose can help organizations to align their activities and decision-making with their values and goals, and to make choices that are in line with the long-term health and sustainability of the organization and its stakeholders. Sinek's arguments are clearly relevant to purpose in sustainability leadership in the following ways:

1. **Fostering a sense of meaning and purpose**: By focusing on the "why" behind their actions, organizations can create a sense of meaning and purpose for their employees, customers, and other stakeholders. This can help to build stronger relationships and foster a sense of shared responsibility for sustainability outcomes.
2. **Driving innovation and creativity**: When organizations are guided by a clear sense of purpose, they are more likely to be innovative and creative in their approach to sustainability challenges. This can help to create new and more sustainable solutions that have a positive impact on the environment, society, and the economy.
3. **Building a resilient organization**: By having a strong sense of purpose, organizations are better able to withstand challenges and obstacles, and to bounce back from setbacks in a sustainable manner. This can help organizations to be more resilient in the face of environmental and social changes, and to maintain their commitment to sustainability over the long term.

Overall, Sinek's arguments can help organizations to create a strong sense of purpose and direction that is aligned with the principles of sustainability leadership.

Purpose for Long-Lasting Business Transformation

John Elkington and Jochen Zeitz, in their book *The Breakthrough Challenge* (2014), argue that companies need to have a higher purpose beyond just profit and shareholder value, and that this higher purpose should be connected to sustainability and social impact. They suggest that companies can create "net positive" outcomes by aligning their purpose with the sustainability challenges facing the world. Here are some of the key arguments made in the book that are relevant to sustainability leadership:

1. **The need for a higher purpose**: Elkington and Zeitz argue that companies need to have a higher purpose beyond just profit and shareholder value. They suggest that a higher purpose can inspire and align people around a common goal that goes beyond individual self-interest and creates a sense of meaning and significance. This argument is particularly relevant to sustainability leaders, who need

to navigate complex sustainability challenges and build the trust and collaboration necessary for creating positive change.

2. **The importance of sustainability and social impact**: The authors emphasize the importance of sustainability and social impact as a core part of a company's higher purpose. They suggest that companies can create "net positive" outcomes by aligning their purpose with the sustainability challenges facing the world and by pursuing strategies that create both financial and social/environmental value. This argument is relevant to sustainability leaders, who need to ensure that their organizations are not only financially successful but also socially and environmentally responsible.
3. **The value of cross-sector partnerships**: Elkington and Zeitz argue that cross-sector partnerships are critical for addressing sustainability challenges. They suggest that companies can create breakthrough solutions by collaborating with governments, NGOs, and other stakeholders and by leveraging the resources and expertise of multiple sectors. This argument is relevant to sustainability leaders, who often need to work with diverse stakeholders and create multi-stakeholder partnerships to address complex sustainability challenges.
4. **The need for innovation and systems thinking**: The authors emphasize the importance of innovation and systems thinking in addressing sustainability challenges. They suggest that companies need to adopt a long-term perspective and focus on creating sustainable solutions that are integrated with the natural and social systems in which they operate. This argument is relevant to sustainability leaders, who need to think creatively and systematically about how to create sustainable and resilient organizations that can thrive over the long term.

In summary, Elkington and Zeitz's arguments are relevant to sustainability leadership because they highlight the importance of a higher purpose, sustainability and social impact, cross-sector partnerships, and innovation and systems thinking in creating sustainable and resilient organizations. These arguments can help sustainability leaders navigate complex sustainability challenges and build the trust and collaboration necessary for creating positive change.

Higher Purpose for Sustainable Prosperity

In their book, *The Economics of Higher Purpose*, Robert Quinn et al. (2019) argue that companies that operate with a higher purpose, beyond just maximizing profits, can achieve superior financial performance in the long run. The authors contend that a higher purpose can provide a unifying focus that aligns the interests of all stakeholders, including customers, employees, shareholders, and society at large.

The book emphasizes the importance of leadership in creating and maintaining a higher purpose, and outlines several key characteristics of purpose-driven leaders, including a commitment to creating value for all stakeholders, a focus on long-term outcomes, and a willingness to challenge the status quo.

The authors also argue that a higher purpose can drive innovation, foster employee engagement and motivation, and enhance a company's reputation and brand. This, in turn, can lead to increased customer loyalty, improved financial performance, and a competitive advantage in the marketplace.

In terms of sustainability leadership, the book suggests that a higher purpose can be a powerful tool for creating a sustainable business model. By focusing on the long-term interests of all stakeholders, companies can avoid short-term thinking that may be detrimental to the environment, society, or future generations. Moreover, purpose-driven companies may be more likely to adopt environmentally and socially responsible practices, as these align with their higher purpose and values.

Overall, *The Economics of Higher Purpose* argues that purpose-driven companies can achieve both financial success and positive social and environmental impact, and that leadership plays a critical role in creating and maintaining a higher purpose. This has important implications for sustainability leadership, as it suggests that companies that prioritize sustainability and social responsibility may be more likely to achieve long-term financial success, while also benefiting society and the planet.

Values Matter in Purpose Driven Organizations

Richard Barrett, in his book *The Values-Driven Organization* (2013), argues that organizations that are driven by a higher purpose and a strong set of values are more sustainable and resilient over the long term. He suggests that a higher purpose can help organizations navigate complex challenges and build trust with stakeholders. In his long career as an influential developer of values in organizations, he makes a case for strategically prioritizing values-driven organizational cultures that create positive social and environmental impact. Here are some of the key arguments made in the book that are relevant to higher purpose in sustainability leadership:

1. **The importance of values**: Barrett argues that values are the key to creating a strong organizational culture that is aligned with a higher purpose. Values serve as a guide for decision-making and behavior, and they can help organizations build trust, foster collaboration, and create a sense of meaning and purpose. This argument is relevant to sustainability leadership because values such as social and environmental responsibility can be used to guide sustainable decision-making and behavior.
2. **The role of leadership**: Barrett suggests that leaders play a critical role in creating a values-driven culture and a higher purpose. Leaders need to model the values they want to see in their organization, and they need to create a sense of purpose and meaning that inspires and motivates their followers. This argument is relevant to sustainability leadership because leaders need to create a sense of purpose and meaning that goes beyond individual self-interest and is connected to a broader societal or environmental goal.
3. **The benefits of a values-driven culture**: Barrett argues that organizations that have a values-driven culture are more successful in the long run. They are more resilient, more innovative, and more adaptable to change. A values-driven culture can also create positive social and environmental impact, as organizations are more likely to take responsibility for their impact and seek to create positive change. This argument is relevant to sustainability leadership because organizations that are committed to sustainability and social impact are more likely to create positive change and thrive over the long term.
4. **The need for a higher purpose**: Barrett suggests that organizations need to have a higher purpose that goes beyond just making a profit. A higher purpose can inspire and align people around a common goal that goes beyond individual self-interest and creates a sense of meaning and significance. This argument is particularly relevant to sustainability leadership, where a higher purpose can create a sense of shared purpose that drives positive action and can help

leaders overcome resistance to change and create new opportunities for innovation and growth.

Barrett Seven Levels Model of values, which resembles Maslow's hierarchy of needs, has been used for developing sustainability leadership competencies in numerous national and international organizations. His model is relevant to higher purposes in sustainability leadership because it emphasizes the importance of values, leadership, a values-driven culture, and a higher purpose in creating sustainable and resilient organizations that can create positive social and environmental impact. Similarly, Fig. 3.1 illustrates how Maslow's hierarchy of needs links to sustainability responsibilities at different levels and how purpose drives sustainability actions at different levels of needs and priorities. These values-driven approaches to sustainability leadership with its responsibilities can create a sense of shared purpose that drives positive action and can help leaders overcome resistance to change and create new opportunities for innovation and growth.

Higher Purpose Cases in Sustainability Leaders

Here are a few examples of sustainability leaders and how their higher purpose has shaped their leadership. These leaders and many others like them have been able to overcome adversity and achieve their goals because of their strong sense of purpose and their commitment to creating a more sustainable and just world.

Case 3.1 Wangari Maathai and the Green Belt Movement

Wangari Maathai was a Kenyan environmental and political activist who is widely regarded as a sustainability leader. She was the founder of the Green Belt Movement, an organization that has planted over 50 million trees in Kenya, and she was the first African woman to win the Nobel Peace Prize in 2004.

Maathai's higher purpose was to improve the lives of Kenyan people by addressing the root causes of poverty, environmental degradation, and political oppression. She believed that environmental conservation and sustainable development were inextricably linked, and that by addressing these issues, she could improve the social, economic, and political conditions in her country. Her focus on environmental issues was not only

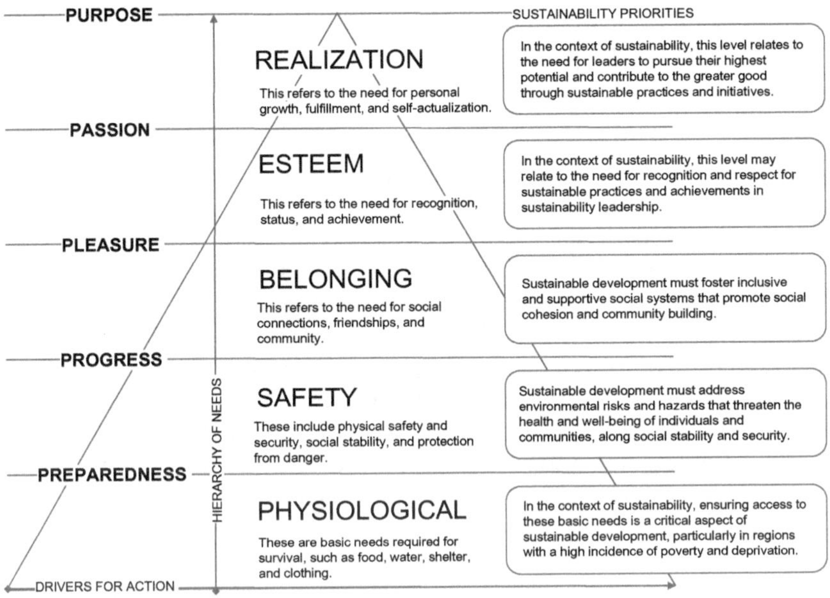

Fig. 3.1 Purpose as driving force in sustainability actions

about planting trees and preserving wildlife, but also about empowering people and communities to take charge of their own development.

Maathai's work had a significant impact on sustainability and environmental conservation in Kenya and beyond. By founding the Green Belt Movement, she was able to bring attention to the importance of reforestation and ecological restoration, and her work inspired many people to take action on these issues. She was also a strong advocate for women's rights, and she recognized the importance of empowering women to become leaders in their communities.

In summary, Wangari Maathai is an example of a sustainability leader because of her focus on environmental conservation, sustainable development, and social justice. Her higher purpose was to improve the lives of people in Kenya by addressing the root causes of poverty, environmental degradation, and political oppression. Through her work with the Green Belt Movement and her advocacy for women's rights, Maathai inspired many people to take action on sustainability issues and created a lasting legacy for environmental conservation and social justice.

Explore more in the book Maathai (2006) *Unbowed* and the website http://www.greenbeltmovement.org/.

Case 3.2 Elinor Ostrom and Governing the Commons

Elinor Ostrom was an American political economist and Nobel Prize laureate who is widely regarded as a sustainability leader for her groundbreaking work on common-pool resources and collective action. Her research has had a significant impact on the field of environmental governance and sustainability. She became the first woman to win the Nobel Prize in Economics for her refutation of the "tragedy of the commons" (Hardin, 1968) through "governing the commons."

Ostrom's higher purpose was to better understand the complex social and ecological systems that govern common-pool resources, such as forests, fisheries, and water systems. She was interested in understanding how communities could collectively manage these resources without depleting them or causing environmental harm. Her work challenged the conventional wisdom that common-pool resources were best managed through government regulation or privatization, and instead showed that local communities could develop effective governance systems based on collective action and shared norms.

Ostrom's research focused on identifying the key factors that enable communities to successfully manage common-pool resources, such as clear and enforceable rules, monitoring and enforcement mechanisms, and mechanisms for dispute resolution. She also emphasized the importance of local knowledge and community participation in designing and implementing effective governance systems.

Ostrom's work has had a significant impact on sustainability and environmental governance, and has influenced policy and practice around the world. Her research has shown that local communities can be effective stewards of natural resources, and that decentralized governance systems can be more effective than top-down regulation or privatization. Her work has also highlighted the importance of social and ecological complexity in understanding sustainability issues, and the need for interdisciplinary approaches to address these challenges.

In summary, Elinor Ostrom is an example of a sustainability leader because of her groundbreaking research on common-pool resources and collective action. Her higher purpose was to better understand the social and ecological systems that govern these resources and to identify effective governance mechanisms based on collective action and shared norms. Her work has had a significant impact on sustainability and environmental governance, and has influenced policy and practice around the world.

Explore more in the book Ostrom (1990) *Governing the Commons* and the website https://ostromworkshop.indiana.edu/.

Case 3.3 Mohammad Younis and the Grameen Bank

Muhammad Yunus is a Bangladeshi economist and social entrepreneur who founded the Grameen Bank and pioneered the concept of microfinance. His higher purpose was to provide financial services to poor people who were excluded from traditional banking systems, and to help lift them out of poverty. His leadership in the Grameen Bank to expand the microfinance solutions benefitted impoverished communities around the world through innovative, engaging, and inclusive financial solutions. Despite facing skepticism and resistance from traditional banking institutions and government officials, Yunus persevered and was able to build a successful microfinance institution that has lifted millions of people out of poverty. Muhammad Yunus is an inspiring example of a sustainability leader in the field of microfinance and its significant impact on poverty reduction, women empowerment, and sustainable economic development in many parts of the world.

Yunus recognized that access to credit was a key barrier for poor people to start businesses or improve their lives, and he developed the concept of microcredit to address this issue. He founded the Grameen Bank in Bangladesh in 1983, which provided small loans to poor people, particularly women, without requiring collateral or other traditional requirements for loans. This approach helped to empower poor people to start businesses and improve their economic situation, and it has been replicated in many parts of the world.

Yunus's values of social justice and empowerment helped him to overcome adversity in the early days of the Grameen Bank. He faced skepticism and resistance from traditional banking institutions and government officials, who did not believe that poor people were creditworthy or that microcredit could be a sustainable model for banking. However, Yunus persisted in his vision, and his commitment to social justice and empowerment helped to inspire others to support his work.

Yunus's values also helped him to expand the scope of his work beyond microfinance. He recognized that poverty was not just an economic issue, but was also linked to broader social and environmental challenges. He founded the Grameen Foundation, which focuses on promoting sustainable development, and has worked on a range of issues such as healthcare, education, and environmental sustainability.

In summary, Muhammad Yunus is an example of a sustainability leader because of his pioneering work in microfinance and his commitment to social justice and empowerment. His higher purpose was to provide financial services to poor people and to help lift them out of poverty. Yunus's values helped him to overcome adversity and to inspire others to support his work, and they also, in turn, helped him to expand the scope of his work beyond microfinance to address broader social and environmental challenges.

Explore more in the book Muhammad Yunus (2003) *Banker to the Poor* and the website https://www.muhammadyunus.org/.

Case 3.4 Vandana Shiva and the Green Movement

Vandana Shiva is an Indian environmental activist and author who is a leading voice in the movement for sustainable agriculture and food systems. Her higher purpose is to promote ecological and social justice and to challenge the corporate control of the food system. Despite facing opposition from agribusiness companies and government officials, Shiva has been able to build a successful grassroots movement that has helped to promote organic farming, preserve traditional seed varieties, and promote sustainable agriculture. She is an inspiring sustainability leader for her work on environmental sustainability and social justice, particularly in the context of small farmers rights, sustainable agriculture, environmental activism, food sovereignty advocacy, and ecofeminism. She is often referred to as "Gandhi of grain" for her activism associated with the anti-GMO movement, intellectual property rights, and biodiversity. Her higher purpose is to promote sustainable and equitable practices in agriculture and to protect the rights of small farmers and Indigenous communities.

Shiva's work has focused on promoting traditional and organic farming practices that are sustainable and environmentally friendly, while also empowering small farmers and communities to have control over their own food systems. She has been a vocal critic of industrial agriculture, genetically modified organisms (GMOs), and the use of pesticides and other harmful chemicals in farming.

Shiva's values of social justice, environmental sustainability, and empowerment have helped her to overcome adversity in her work. She has faced criticism and opposition from powerful corporations and governments who are invested in the industrial agriculture system, but her commitment to her higher purpose has helped her to persist in her efforts. Beside her controversial stands on GMOs, her example of sustainability advocate has inspired many women ecologists and food sovereignty advocates.

Shiva has also been an advocate for the rights of small farmers and Indigenous communities, who often face discrimination and marginalization in the agricultural sector. She has worked to promote their participation in decision-making processes related to agriculture and food systems and to protect their land and resources from exploitation by large corporations.

Overall, Vandana Shiva's higher purpose of promoting sustainable and equitable agriculture has helped her to overcome adversity in her work, and her values of social justice and empowerment have inspired others to join her in her efforts. Her work is an important example of sustainability leadership, and her ideas and actions have had a significant impact on the global conversation around agriculture and food systems.

Explore more in the book Shiva (2005) *Earth Democracy* and the website http://www.navdanya.org/.

Case 3.5 Paul Hawken and the Natural Capital Institute

Paul Hawken is an American environmentalist and entrepreneur who has been a leader in the movement for sustainable business and clean energy. Paul Hawken is considered an influential sustainability leader because of his extensive work and contribution to the environmental movement. He is an environmentalist, entrepreneur, author, and activist who has dedicated his life to advocating for sustainability and climate change. Hawken is the author of several books, including *Natural Capitalism: Creating the Next Industrial Revolution* (1999) where he writes about the idea of natural capital and direct accounting for ecosystem services. Together with *The Ecology of Commerce: A Declaration of Sustainability* (1993), he has been among the first authors and leaders to point the way towards a sustainable global economy. In these and other of his publications, he has presented his ideas on sustainability, social justice, and climate change, which have influenced environmentalists, policymakers, and business leaders around the world.

His higher purpose is to promote a regenerative economy that works in harmony with nature and to address climate change and other environmental challenges. Hawken's higher purpose is rooted in his deep conviction that the Earth and all its inhabitants deserve a healthy and vibrant environment to thrive. His love for nature and his desire to create a sustainable world for future generations have driven him to work tirelessly towards his goal. This higher purpose has helped him to overcome difficulties and challenges along the way and has motivated his leadership.

Despite facing opposition from fossil fuel companies and government officials, Hawken has been able to build successful businesses and organizations that are promoting clean energy and sustainable business practices. One example of how his higher purpose has helped him to overcome difficulty is when he created the Natural Capital Institute in the early 2000s. The institute sought to find solutions to environmental and social challenges by using market-based approaches. Hawken's passion for his mission and his higher purpose helped him persevere to keep the institute afloat and eventually turn it into a successful organization that has made a significant impact on the environmental movement.

In conclusion, Paul Hawken is considered a sustainability leader because of his extensive work and contribution to the environmental movement. His higher purpose, which is rooted in his love for nature and his desire to create a sustainable world, helped him to overcome challenges and has motivated his leadership. His work continues to inspire individuals and organizations worldwide to take action on climate change and sustainability.

Explore more in the book Hawken (2007) *Blessed Unrest* and its official website https://www.paulhawken.com/.

Case 3.6 Christiana Figueres and the Paris Agreement

Christiana Figueres is a Costa Rican diplomat who led the United Nations Framework Convention on Climate Change. She played an instrumental role in negotiating the historic 2015 Paris Agreement on climate change. Her higher purpose has been to promote sustainable development and to protect the planet from the devastating impacts of climate change

(Figueres & Rivett-Carnac, 2020). Figueres' values of collaboration, inclusivity, and determination have helped her in her leadership role. She recognized early on in her career that the issue of climate change was not just an environmental problem, but also a political and economic one that required collaboration and partnership among diverse stakeholders. She has worked to engage a wide range of actors, including governments, civil society organizations, businesses, and individuals, in efforts to address climate change.

Figueres has also been a strong advocate for inclusivity in the global climate negotiations. She recognized that the voices and needs of marginalized communities and developing countries were often overlooked in these discussions, and she worked to ensure that their perspectives and interests were represented in the negotiations. Her commitment to inclusivity helped to build trust and cooperation among diverse stakeholders and to foster a sense of shared responsibility for addressing climate change.

Finally, Figueres' determination and optimism have been critical in her leadership role. She has faced many challenges and setbacks in her efforts to address climate change, but her belief in the possibility of a better future and her unwavering commitment to her higher purpose have helped her to persist in her efforts. Her leadership and advocacy have been instrumental in securing the Paris Agreement and in galvanizing global action on climate change.

In summary, Christiana Figueres is a sustainability leader due to her leadership and advocacy in the global efforts to address climate change. Her higher purpose has been to promote sustainable development and to protect the planet from the devastating impacts of climate change. Her values of collaboration, inclusivity, and determination have helped her to overcome adversity and to inspire others to join her in her efforts to create a more sustainable and equitable future.

Explore more in the book Figueres and Rivett-Carnac (2020) *The Future We Choose* and on the website https://christianafigueres.com/.

Case 3.7 Gro Harlem Brundtland and Our Common Future

Gro Harlem Brundtland is a well-known sustainability leader for her significant contributions to the definition of sustainable development. She is a Norwegian politician and diplomat who has held several prominent positions in government and international organizations. In her leadership capacity on the World Commission on Environment and Development, she was able to reconcile diverse (conflicting) priorities and concerns into the shared values and common concerns for current and future generations.

One of Brundtland's most notable accomplishments is the publication of the Brundtland Report in 1987, also known as *Our Common Future* (1987) which coined the term "sustainable development." She defined sustainable development as "Development that meets the needs of the present without compromising the ability of future generations to meet their own needs." Through her leadership, the reports presented a new vision for global development that integrates economic, social, and environmental considerations. This report is widely recognized as a landmark document that has influenced global policy on sustainability.

Brundtland's higher purpose has been to create a better future for all people, and this has helped her to overcome difficult negotiations. For example, during her tenure as the Director-General of the World Health Organization (WHO), she faced significant opposition from member countries who did not agree with her approach to global health issues. However, her commitment to improving global health outcomes and her vision of creating a healthier world for all people helped her to overcome these challenges and reach agreements that benefited all parties.

Similarly, as the Prime Minister of Norway, Brundtland played a key role in negotiations that led to the adoption of the United Nations Framework Convention on Climate Change (UNFCCC) in 1992. Her higher purpose of creating a more sustainable and equitable world drove her to be a strong advocate for climate action, and her leadership helped to secure an agreement that set the stage for international cooperation on climate change.

In conclusion, Gro Harlem Brundtland is a sustainability leader because of her significant contributions to sustainable development and environmental protection. Her higher purpose of creating a better future for all people has helped her to overcome difficult negotiations and reach agreements that benefit all parties. Her work has inspired people around the world to take action on sustainability and work towards a more equitable and sustainable future.

Explore more in the book Brundtland (2011) *Daughter of the Vikings* and on the website https://www.groharlembrundtland.com/.

Case 3.8 Greta Thunberg, Autumn Peltier, and Xiye Bastida

Greta Thunberg, Autumn Peltier, and Xiye Bastida are recognized young leaders who have become prominent voices in the sustainability movement worldwide. They share a common goal of advocating for environmental protection and climate action. Here's a brief introduction of each leader:

Greta Thunberg is a Swedish activist who first gained international attention for her solo "school strike for climate" sign in front of the Swedish Parliament in 2018. Since then, she has become a prominent voice for climate action, inspiring millions of young people around the world to join the "Fridays for Future" movement. She has addressed world leaders at the United Nations Climate Action Summit and other high-level events, calling for immediate action to address the climate crisis. Thunberg's leadership style is characterized by her direct and uncompromising approach, which has earned her both praise and criticism. Thunberg is motivated by a sense of urgency and a deep concern for the future of the planet. Her higher purpose is to raise awareness about the urgent need for climate action and to pressure governments and corporations to take immediate and bold action to address the climate crisis (Thunberg, 2022). Thunberg's values are centered around honesty, transparency, and a willingness to speak truth to power. She emphasizes the need for action to be based on scientific evidence and emphasizes the importance of accountability for those in power.

Autumn Peltier is an Indigenous Canadian water protector and activist who has been advocating for clean water since she was eight years old. She has addressed the United Nations and Canadian Parliament, advocating for clean water rights and protection of water sources. Peltier's leadership style is rooted in her cultural and spiritual values, and she emphasizes the need for environmental protection and sustainability to be grounded in Indigenous knowledge and practices. Peltier is motivated by a deep love and respect for the natural world and her Indigenous culture. Her higher purpose is to protect the water and the land and to ensure that future generations have access to clean water and a healthy environment. Peltier's values are grounded in Indigenous knowledge and practices, and she emphasizes the importance of intergenerational responsibility and the need to protect the sacred relationship between Indigenous people and the natural world.

Xiye Bastida is a Mexican climate activist who grew up in a town that was severely impacted by hurricanes and floods. She is a co-founder of the Fridays for Future movement in New York City and has been a vocal advocate for climate justice and the need for systemic change to address the climate crisis. Bastida's leadership style is characterized by her focus on inclusivity and collaboration, working to build a diverse coalition of people and groups to address the climate crisis. Bastida is motivated by a sense of justice and a desire to create a more equitable world. Her higher purpose is to fight for climate justice and to ensure that the most vulnerable communities are not disproportionately impacted by the climate crisis. Bastida's values are centered around inclusivity, collaboration, and the importance of building a diverse coalition to address the climate crisis. She emphasizes the need for systemic change and the need to address the root causes of the climate crisis.

In conclusion, Greta Thunberg, Autumn Peltier, and Xiye Bastida are all young leaders who have become prominent voices in the sustainability movement. While they share a common goal of advocating for environmental protection and climate action, their approaches and styles are unique. Their specific values and higher purposes may differ, but they clearly reflect strong alignment and passion for a better future for the current and future generation. They are all motivated by a deep sense of purpose and a desire to create a more sustainable and equitable world. They are all inspiring examples of how young people can make a significant impact on the world and work towards a more sustainable and equitable future.

Explore more in the books Thunberg (2019) *No One Is Too Small to Make a Difference* and Ayana and Wilkinson (2020) *All We Can Save: Truth, Courage, and Solutions for the Climate Crisis* and on their official websites https://www.gretathunberg.org/, and http://www.autumn.peltier.ca/ and https://www.xiyebastida.com/.

Case 3.9 Paul Polman and Ray Anderson

Paul Polman and Ray Anderson are both well-known sustainability leaders who have made significant contributions to the business world. While their approaches to sustainability may differ, their higher purpose has inspired other business leaders to prioritize sustainability and social responsibility.

Ray Anderson was the founder of Interface, a modular carpet manufacturer that became a sustainability leader under his leadership. Anderson believed that businesses had a responsibility to address environmental and social issues and worked to create a company culture that reflected these values. He developed a vision for Interface to become a "restorative enterprise," which meant that the company would not only reduce its negative impact on the environment but would also work to create positive social and environmental outcomes. Anderson's higher purpose was to create a more sustainable and equitable world, and his leadership inspired other business leaders to prioritize sustainability in their own companies.

Paul Polman was the CEO of Unilever, a multinational consumer goods company. Under his leadership, Unilever became a leader in sustainable business practices, with a focus on reducing the company's environmental footprint and promoting social responsibility. Polman believed that businesses had a responsibility to contribute to a more sustainable and equitable world, and he worked to integrate sustainability into every aspect of Unilever's operations. His higher purpose was to create a more sustainable future for all, and he used his platform as a business leader to advocate for global action on climate change and other sustainability issues. Polman's leadership and advocacy inspired other business leaders to prioritize sustainability and to view it as a key component of long-term business success.

In conclusion, while Ray Anderson and Paul Polman may have different approaches to sustainability, they share a higher purpose of creating a more sustainable and equitable world. Their leadership and vision have inspired other business leaders to prioritize sustainability and to view it as an essential component of long-term business success. Both leaders have demonstrated that it is possible to run a profitable business while also making a positive impact on the environment and society, and their legacies continue to inspire and motivate others to work towards a more sustainable future.

Explore more in the books Anderson (2009) *Confessions of a Radical Industrialist;* Csikszentmihalyi (2004) *Good Business;* Kumar (2019) *The Business of Changing the World*; and Polman and Winston (2019) *Net Positive.* Check also on the official websites https://www.paulpolman.com/ and http://www.interface.com/.

The Common Elements of Higher Purpose in Sustainability Companies

From the analysis of the literature and the examples of leaders considered here, it emerges that the concept of higher purpose in sustainability leadership is multidimensional, and there are several ways in which leaders can define and articulate their higher purpose. Here are a few examples of the dimensions of higher purpose in sustainability leadership:

1. **Social and environmental impact**: Sustainability leaders often see their higher purpose as making a positive impact on society and the environment. For example, B Lab, the nonprofit corporation that has developed the B Corp certification, has a mission to use business as a force for good, and it has developed a global movement of certified B Corps that are committed to creating a more sustainable and equitable world.
2. **Stakeholder orientation**: Higher purpose in sustainability leadership is often focused on creating value for all stakeholders, not just shareholders. For example, Unilever's higher purpose is to "make sustainable living commonplace," which involves creating products and services that meet the needs of consumers while also minimizing negative environmental and social impacts. Unilever engages with a wide range of stakeholders, from customers and suppliers to NGOs and governments, to ensure that its sustainability efforts are aligned with stakeholder needs and expectations.
3. **Values and culture**: Higher purpose can also be expressed through a company's values and culture. For example, Patagonia has made sustainability a core part of its values and culture. The company's mission is to "build the best product, cause no unnecessary harm, use business to inspire and implement solutions to the environmental crisis." Patagonia has taken a number of innovative steps to reduce its environmental impact, such as using recycled and organic materials in its products, reducing energy and water use, and supporting grassroots environmental organizations.
4. **Innovation and disruption**: Sustainability leaders often see their higher purpose as driving innovation and disrupting traditional business models. Consider the plant-based meat substitute company Beyond Meat. Their mission is to create plant-based meat products

that taste and feel like real meat while having a lower environmental impact. Beyond Meat has gained popularity in recent years as more consumers seek alternatives to traditional meat products due to concerns about the environmental impact of meat production and animal welfare.

5. **Long-term orientation**: Sustainability leaders often have a long-term orientation. They focus on creating sustainable solutions that will benefit future generations. Natura & Co is a Brazilian cosmetics company with long-term sustainability plans as part of its core business strategy. It has set ambitious sustainability goals, including becoming carbon neutral by 2030, using 100% renewable energy by 2023, and achieving zero deforestation in its supply chain. Natura & Co also has a strong commitment to social responsibility, such as empowering women entrepreneurs and supporting local communities in the Amazon.

Overall, the dimensions of higher purpose in sustainability leadership are diverse and multifaceted, but they all share a common focus on creating positive social and environmental impact, value for all stakeholders, and a long-term orientation.

Assessing Higher Purpose Impact for Sustainability Leadership

Assessing and analyzing higher purposes in sustainability companies and leaders can be a complex task that requires a multifaceted approach. We will consider this more specifically in Part 4: Sustainability Impact. This is a field that is rapidly growing to reflect more coherent measurements, parameters, and metrics. In general, the higher purpose impact of a company in its sustainability leadership includes some of the following key considerations and strategies:

1. **Evaluate the company's mission and values**: One way to assess higher purpose in sustainability companies is to look at their mission and values statements. Companies that have a clear commitment to sustainability and social responsibility are more likely to have a higher purpose that aligns with these values.

2. **Examine sustainability reports**: Sustainability reports can provide valuable insights into a company's sustainability strategy and performance. These reports can help to identify key sustainability issues, goals, and initiatives, as well as progress towards sustainability targets.
3. **Analyze stakeholder engagement**: Companies that engage with a wide range of stakeholders, including customers, employees, suppliers, and communities, are more likely to have a higher purpose that is aligned with stakeholder needs and expectations. Stakeholder engagement can be assessed through surveys, focus groups, and other feedback mechanisms.
4. **Look at leadership and management practices**: The values and priorities of sustainability leaders and managers can have a significant impact on a company's higher purpose and sustainability performance. Analyzing leadership and management practices can help to identify areas of strength and areas for improvement.
5. **Assess the impact of sustainability initiatives**: Companies that are truly committed to higher purpose in sustainability will have a track record of implementing sustainable initiatives and measuring the impact of these initiatives. Assessing the impact of sustainability initiatives can be done through environmental and social impact assessments, as well as financial metrics.
6. **Compare against industry benchmarks and standards**: Comparing a company's sustainability performance against industry benchmarks and standards can provide useful context and help to identify areas for improvement.

Overall, assessing and analyzing higher purpose in sustainability companies and leaders require a holistic approach that considers a wide range of factors, including mission and values, sustainability reports, stakeholder engagement, leadership and management practices, impact of sustainability initiatives, and industry benchmarks and standards. By using a multifaceted approach, it is possible to gain a more comprehensive understanding of a company's higher purpose in sustainability and its sustainability performance.

At a more personal and professional level, sustainability leaders too could be assessed in the impact of higher purpose in their performance. Personal leadership characteristics and value assessments for sustainability higher purpose can vary depending on the individual and the context.

However, here are some examples of key characteristics and values that are commonly associated with sustainability leadership:

1. **Vision and strategic thinking**: Sustainability leaders must be able to envision a better future and develop a long-term strategy to achieve it. They must be able to think creatively and strategically to address complex sustainability challenges and identify new opportunities.
2. **Commitment to sustainability values**: Sustainability leaders must have a deep commitment to sustainability values, such as environmental protection, social responsibility, and economic viability. They must be able to articulate and communicate these values to others and integrate them into their personal and professional decision-making.
3. **Collaboration and stakeholder engagement**: Sustainability leaders must be able to work collaboratively with a wide range of stakeholders, including customers, employees, suppliers, and communities. They must be able to listen to diverse perspectives and build consensus around sustainability goals.
4. **Resilience and adaptability**: Sustainability leaders must be able to adapt to changing circumstances and overcome obstacles. They must be able to navigate complex and uncertain environments and maintain a positive outlook in the face of challenges.
5. **Integrity and ethical leadership**: Sustainability leaders must be committed to ethical leadership practices, including transparency, accountability, and fairness. They must be able to maintain high standards of integrity in their personal and professional conduct.
6. **Learning and continuous improvement**: Sustainability leaders must be committed to learning and continuous improvement. They must be willing to take risks, learn from mistakes, and adapt their approach based on feedback and new information.
7. **Personal sustainability**: Sustainability leaders must be committed to personal sustainability, including physical, emotional, and spiritual well-being. They must be able to balance their personal and professional responsibilities and maintain a healthy work-life balance.

In conclusion, to assess personal leadership characteristics and value assessments for sustainability higher purpose, individuals can engage in self-reflection and self-assessment activities, such as identifying personal values, strengths and weaknesses, and setting personal sustainability goals. They can also seek feedback from others, participate in leadership development programs, and engage in ongoing learning and development activities to enhance their leadership skills and competencies. Values-centered leadership development programs can also be very helpful to assess the alignment of purpose with practice and improve sustainability performances at the personal, professional, and corporate level. As these types of development are a long-term commitment, it is imperative that consultations, retreats, strategic processes, and other actions are inserted into an ongoing long-term orientation for continuous education and discernment.

Key Takeaways

1. Having a higher purpose in sustainability leadership can inspire, motivate, and provide direction for individuals and organizations working towards a sustainable future.
2. The "Start with Why" approach to leadership can be applied to sustainability and can help align stakeholders towards a common goal.
3. Values play a crucial role in purpose-driven organizations and can help drive long-lasting business transformation and sustainable prosperity.
4. The featured inspiring case studies of sustainability leaders have integrated sustainability into their businesses and made a positive impact on society and the planet.
5. There are common elements to be considered as guidance on how to assess the impact of higher purpose on sustainability leadership.

References

Anderson, R. (2009). *Confessions of a radical industrialist: profits*. St. Martin's Press.

Ayana, E. J., & Wilkinson, K. K. (2020). *All we can save: Truth, courage, and solutions for the climate crisis*. Penguin Books.

Barrett, R. (2013). *The values-driven organization: Unleashing human potential for performance and profit*. Taylor & Francis.

Bridges, T., & Eubank, D. (2021). *Leading sustainably: The path to sustainable business and how the SDGs Changed everything*. Taylor & Francis.

Brundtland, G. H. (2011). *Daughter of the vikings: Growing up in Norway*. University of Minnesota Press.

Csikszentmihalyi, M. (2004). *Good business: Leadership, flow, and the making of meaning*. Penguin Books.

Elkington, J., & Zeitz, J. (2014). *The breakthrough challenge: 10 ways to connect today's profits with tomorrow's bottom line*. Wiley.

Figueres, C., & Rivett-Carnac, T. (2020). *The future we choose: surviving the climate crisis*. Knopf Doubleday Publishing Group.

Hardin, G. (1968). The tragedy of the commons. *Science*, 162(3859), 1243–1248. https://science.sciencemag.org/content/162/3859/1243.full

Hawken, P. (1993). *The ecology of commerce: A declaration of sustainability*. HarperCollins.

Hawken, P. (2007). *Blessed unrest: How the largest movement in the world came into being, and why no one saw it coming*. Penguin Books.

Hawken, P. et al. (1999). *Natural capitalism: Creating the next industrial revolution*. Little, Brown and Company.

Kumar, R. (2019). *The business of changing the world: how billionaires, Tech Disrupters, and social entrepreneurs are transforming the global aid industry*. Harvard Business Review Press.

Maathai, W. (2006). *Unbowed: A memoir* (1st ed.). Knopf.

Ostrom, E. (1990). *Governing the commons: The evolution of institutions for collective action*. Cambridge University Press.

Polman, P., & Winston, A. (2019). *Net positive: How courageous companies thrive by giving more than they take*. Harvard Business Review Press.

Quartuccio, D. (2021). *On purpose leadership: Master the art of leading yourself to inspire and impact others*. Lifestyle Entrepreneurs Press.

Quinn, R. E., et al. (2019). *The economics of higher purpose: eight counterintuitive steps for creating a purpose-driven organization*. Berrett-Koehler Publishers.

Shiva, V. (2005). *Earth democracy: Justice, sustainability, and peace*. Springer.

Sinek, S. (2011). *Start with why: How great leaders inspire everyone to take action*. Penguin Books Limited.

Thunberg, G. (2019). *No one is too small to make a difference*. Penguin Books.

Thunberg, G. (2022). *The climate book*. Penguin Books, Limited.

Yunus, M. (2003). *Banker to the poor: Micro-lending and the battle against world poverty*. Public Affairs.

CHAPTER 4

Mindsets for Sustainability Leadership

Abstract Why do leadership mindsets matter for addressing today's sustainability challenges? This chapter reviews how mindsets influence sustainability leadership through different competencies. We review scholarly works which have examined mindset characteristics in sustainability leaders and highlight the most important areas to be considered in the development of leadership for individuals and organizations. We propose a model of an integrated sustainability leadership mindset with merged characteristics from influential studies.

Keywords Leadership mindsets · Sustainability mindset · Leadership consciousness · Spiritual values

> *The Sustainability Mindset breaks away from traditional management disciplinary silos by integrating management ethics, entrepreneurship, environmental studies, systems thinking, self-awareness and spirituality within the dimensional contexts of being (values), thinking (knowledge) and doing (competency). [...] Developing a sustainability mindset means moving from a worldview that is fragmented to one that is systemic, recognizing patterns of interdependence, and acting accordingly.*
>
> — Isabel Rimanoczy, Convener of the PRME Working Group on the Sustainability Mindset.

M. Tavanti, *Developing Sustainability in Organizations*, Sustainable Development Goals Series,
https://doi.org/10.1007/978-3-031-36907-0_4

Challenges Requiring New Leadership Mindsets

Today's sustainability challenges require new mindsets and skill sets to adequately respond and make a net positive impact. Sustainability is a complex and multifaceted issue that presents a number of significant challenges impacting the leader's mindset. For instance, sustainability requires finding a balance between economic growth, social equity, and environmental protection, which can make it difficult to achieve. Sustainability requires addressing global issues such as climate change, biodiversity loss, and resource depletion, which have far-reaching impacts and require coordinated international action. In addition, sustainability often requires significant changes in the way we live and do business, which can be difficult to implement and meet resistance from those who benefit from the status quo. Other significant challenges connected to sustainability are the persisting and growing inequities. Sustainability leadership must be properly equipped to address this challenge and adopt mindsets for inclusiveness and equality. One must take into account the needs and perspectives of marginalized communities, which can be challenging in practice. Sustainability reflects systemic challenges that, to be solved, would need to overcome political impasse, which can be very difficult challenging to achieve, particularly in the face of competing interests and conflicting priorities. All of these challenges require renewed mindsets, principles, competencies, and skill sets.

In this context, the word "mindsets" refers to the attitudes, beliefs, and values that shape a leader's approach to sustainability. A sustainability mindset means that a leader recognizes the importance of environmental, social, and economic sustainability and is committed to integrating sustainable practices into the organization's operations (Henriksson & Grunewald, 2020). The relationship between skill sets and mindsets in sustainability is that while skill sets are necessary for effective sustainability management, they must be supported by a sustainability mindset. A manager with a strong sustainability skill set, but lacking a sustainability mindset, may view sustainability as an added cost or burden rather than an opportunity to create value for the organization and society. On the other hand, a leader with a strong sustainability mindset but lacking the necessary skill sets may have difficulty turning their vision into action. Therefore, to be effective in promoting sustainability, leaders need to have both the skill sets and mindsets necessary to drive change. By combining strong sustainability skill sets with a sustainability mindset, leaders can foster a culture of sustainability within their organization, encourage innovation, and drive positive environmental, social, and economic outcomes.

Paradigms Affecting Mindsets

Addressing these challenges will require sustained effort and collaboration across sectors. It will need innovative solutions and approaches to creating a more sustainable future. It will require a leadership approach that reflects new paradigms and new mindsets. Here are a few ways that sustainability challenges can affect a leader's mindset:

1. **Increased awareness**: As sustainability challenges become more pressing and visible, leaders are becoming more aware of the importance of environmental, social, and economic sustainability. This increased awareness can lead to a shift in mindset, as leaders begin to recognize the need for sustainable business practices and start to consider the impact of their decisions on the environment and society.
2. **Emphasis on long-term thinking**: Sustainability challenges often require long-term solutions, which can encourage leaders to adopt a more strategic and forward-looking mindset. Instead of focusing on short-term gains, leaders who are committed to sustainability are more likely to prioritize investments and initiatives that deliver long-term value for the organization and society.
3. **Collaborative approach**: Addressing sustainability challenges often requires collaboration with stakeholders both within and outside the organization. This collaborative approach can encourage leaders to adopt a more open and inclusive mindset, as they seek out diverse perspectives and work together to develop sustainable solutions.
4. **Innovation and creativity**: Sustainability challenges require innovative solutions, which can encourage leaders to adopt a more creative and flexible mindset. By embracing new ideas and taking calculated risks, leaders can drive sustainable innovation and create new opportunities for growth and development.

Overall, sustainability challenges can be a catalyst for the development of a leader's mindset, as they encourage leaders to adopt a more strategic, collaborative, and innovative approach to decision-making. By embracing sustainability and making it a core part of their leadership philosophy, leaders can drive positive change, promote sustainable growth, and create value for their organization and society as a whole.

Principles for Leadership Mindsets

Isabel Rimanoczy has contributed to the understanding of sustainability mindset in her scholarship and leadership as convener of the PRME working group on sustainability mindset. Her book *Sustainability Mindset Principles* (Rimanoczy, 2020), advances a model that includes interconnected principles. Sustainability mindset reflects principles associated with four main areas identified as essential characteristics for sustainability leadership: ecological worldview, systems perspectives, emotional intelligence, and spiritual intelligence. Rimanoczy suggests 12 sustainability mindset principles as a set of guidelines for business leaders to help them shift their thinking and behaviors towards a more sustainable and responsible approach to business.

The principles expressing the ecological worldview are:

1. **Eco-literacy**: This principle emphasizes the importance of understanding the principles of ecology, such as the interconnectedness of living systems and the importance of biodiversity, in order to promote sustainability.
2. **My Contribution**: This principle emphasizes that every individual has a role to play in promoting sustainability, and encourages people to take responsibility for their own impact on the environment.

The principles expressing systems perspectives are:

1. **Long-term thinking**: This principle encourages a long-term perspective, recognizing that sustainability challenges require solutions that are sustainable over the long term.
2. **Flow in cycles**: This principle emphasizes the importance of designing systems that work in cycles, mimicking natural systems, in order to minimize waste and promote sustainability.

3. **Both-and**: This principle emphasizes the importance of embracing both/and thinking, recognizing that there are often multiple solutions to sustainability challenges, and that these solutions can be complementary rather than competing.
4. **Interconnectedness**: This principle emphasizes that social, economic, and environmental systems are interconnected, and that sustainability requires an integrated approach that considers all of these systems.

The principles expressing emotional intelligence are:

1. **Creative innovation**: This principle emphasizes the importance of creative thinking and innovation in promoting sustainability.
2. **Reflection**: This principle emphasizes the importance of reflection and learning, recognizing that sustainability is an ongoing process that requires ongoing evaluation and adjustment.
3. **Self-awareness**: This principle emphasizes the importance of self-awareness, recognizing that individual actions and decisions can have a significant impact on sustainability.

The principles expressing spiritual intelligence are:

1. **Purpose**: This principle emphasizes the importance of having a clear purpose or mission that guides sustainability initiatives and decision-making.
2. **Mindfulness**: This principle emphasizes the importance of mindfulness, or being present in the moment and fully engaged with one's surroundings, as a means of promoting sustainability.
3. **Oneness with nature**: This principle emphasizes the importance of recognizing our interconnectedness with the natural world and treating it with respect and reverence in order to promote sustainability.

By following these principles, business leaders can help to create more sustainable, responsible, and resilient organizations that contribute to a better future for all. They can promote transformative leadership practices that reflect principles for the common good and our shared global responsibility (Ritz & Rimanoczy, 2021). These principles reflect what other studies of sustainability leadership have highlighted as essential elements. Clarke Murphy (2022), for example, in his book *Sustainable Leadership* argues that sustainable leadership is essential for organizations to survive and thrive in the long term. He defines sustainable leadership as the ability to create and maintain a healthy and productive work environment, while also ensuring that the organization is responsible and responsive to the needs of its stakeholders. He argues that we need a new leadership paradigm that is more adaptive, responsive, and inclusive. Like Rimanoczy, Murphy highlights the critical role that empathy and emotional intelligence play in sustainable leadership. He argues that leaders who are able to understand and respond to the needs and emotions of their employees, customers, and other stakeholders are more likely to create a sustainable and successful organization. He also makes a case that sustainable leadership requires a holistic approach which takes into account not just financial performance but also social and environmental impact. He suggests that leaders must consider the long-term consequences of their decisions and actions, and strive to balance the interests of multiple stakeholders.

Competencies for Sustainability Mindsets

The report *Leadership for the Decade of Action* by Russell Reynolds Associates and the UNGC (2020), identifies several leadership competencies required to address the sustainability challenges faced by organizations and society. The report highlights the importance of leadership in addressing sustainability challenges, as the world faces a last "decade of action" to achieve the SDGs by 2030. It recognizes the central role that sustainability mindsets have in the transformation of business as commercial activity integrated with the wider societal and environmental context in which it operates. For business leaders, these sustainability mindsets shape their priorities and decision-making processes targeting success and impact in the long term. They welcome innovation and manage across commercial, societal, and environmental outcomes and align all aspects of running their organization with these core values and beliefs. The report outlines a model for sustainability leadership mindsets resulting from interconnected ecosystems for the greater good of the whole and reflecting specific leadership characteristics along four key competencies: (1) Multi-level Systemic Thinking, (2) Purpose-Driven Long-term Activation, (3) Stakeholder Inclusion and Engagement, and (4) Disruptive and Adaptive Innovation. These competencies include specific abilities and values-based capacities associated with these competencies (Fig. 4.1).

1. **Multi-level Systemic Thinking**: The ability to see the big picture and understand the interconnections between different parts of the system, including the impact of business on the environment and society. This includes the ability to recognize interdependencies in complex systems, such as the social, economic, and environmental

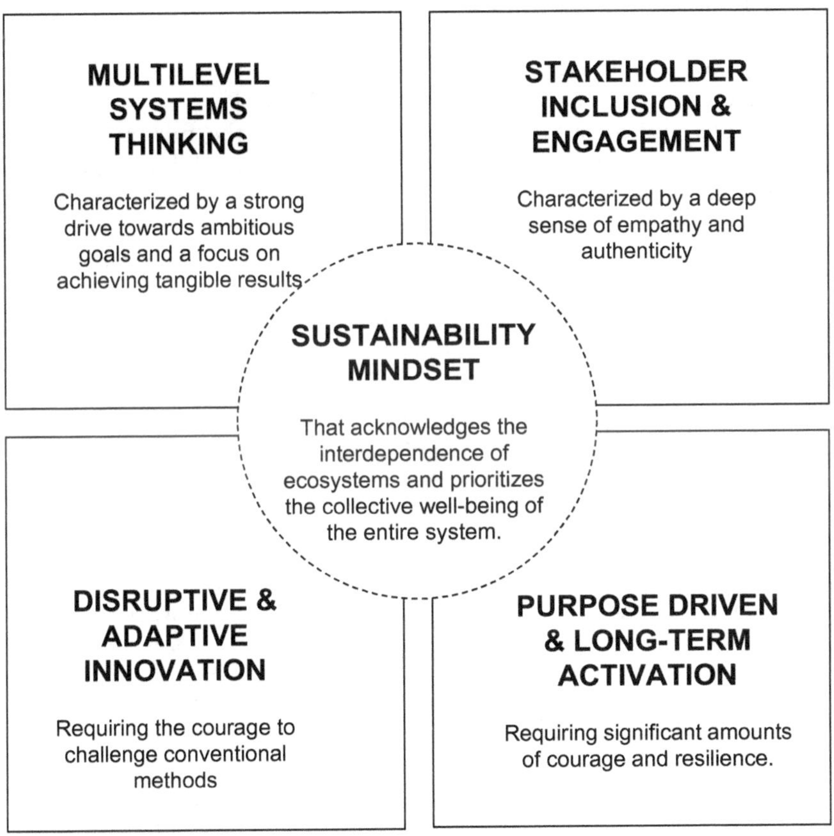

Fig. 4.1 Competencies for sustainability mindsets

systems, and to take a holistic approach in addressing sustainability challenges. Sustainability leaders with these competencies have a result-oriented focus using cross-sector and multi-sector collaborations.

2. **Purpose-Driven Long-term Activation**: The ability to align personal and organizational values with a strong sense of purpose, and to lead with a long-term vision that takes into account the impact of business on the environment and society. This includes the ability to articulate a clear and inspiring purpose and set of values, and to lead with integrity, transparency, and accountability in order to drive sustainable and responsible business practices. The purpose and audacious goals of sustainability leaders do not simply have an orientation towards the long term. They drive concerted actions and attract strategic investment for the pursuit of them. Sustainability leaders with these competencies exhibit a great deal of courage and resilience to stay the course in the face of setbacks. They may become unpopular with some short-term-oriented stakeholders when they make decisions that have a long-term benefit to the higher purpose.
3. **Stakeholder Inclusion and Engagement**: The ability to engage with a wide range of stakeholders, including employees, customers, suppliers, investors, and communities, to understand their needs and perspectives and to build mutually beneficial relationships. This includes the ability to recognize and prioritize the interests of multiple stakeholders in relation to their socio-economic contexts, cultural communities and ecosystems to align business decisions and actions with their needs. Sustainability leaders do not manage stakeholders; they include them, empower them, and enable them to fully participate and thrive. They welcome divergent thinkers and diversity or perspectives as they employ a wide range of points of view in order to drive decision-making with all those stakeholders in mind and where possible, actively involve those stakeholders in actioning the decisions and sharing the benefits. Sustainability leaders with these competencies exhibit a great deal of empathy, authenticity, flexibility, active listening, fairness, and cultural competency.
4. **Disruptive and Adaptive Innovation**: The ability to be agile and flexible, and to respond to changes in the external environment and to anticipate and prepare for future challenges. This includes the ability to adapt to changing circumstances, to continuously improve

operations, products, and services, and to develop new and innovative solutions to sustainability challenges. Sustainability leaders with these competencies exhibit high-level capacity and courage to challenge traditional approaches and seek new solutions to enduring challenges.

The implications of this model for sustainability leadership mindsets are significant. By focusing on these key competencies, organizations can develop leaders who are equipped to address the complex sustainability challenges faced by society and the business world. By aligning personal and organizational values with a strong sense of purpose and engaging with stakeholders, sustainability leaders can drive positive change and create a more sustainable and equitable future. The ability to think systemically and to be adaptive is also critical, as the world faces an uncertain future and the need for leaders who can anticipate and respond to change. Overall, the report by Russell Reynolds Associates and the UNGC highlights the importance of leadership in driving sustainable change and provides a framework for developing leaders who are equipped to address the challenges of the decade of action. These competencies represent mindset shifts and concrete capabilities intended to help organizations and individuals develop a more comprehensive and integrated approach to sustainability, and to make a meaningful contribution to the SDGs.

Paradigms for Sustainable Leadership Mindsets

Dr. Alfredo Sfeir Younis, known for promoting sustainable development through his role as the first environmental economist at the World Bank, has a similar but deeper approach to consider the new paradigms for sustainability leadership. He considers consciousness as the paradigm for recognizing our interdependence and constructed a model of multiple capitals that include cultural, spiritual, and human rights as assets for sustainable development. In the book I co-authored with him, *Conscious Sustainability Leadership* (2021), we propose holistic dimensions that integrate intellectual and physical dimensions with emotional and spiritual dimensions. Specifically, we propose the following six paradigms for conscious sustainability leadership:

1. **Consciousness**: The first paradigm is the recognition that leadership begins with self-awareness and a deep understanding of one's own values and beliefs.
2. **Interconnectedness**: The second paradigm is the understanding that all things are interconnected and that sustainable leadership requires a holistic view of the world.
3. **Purpose**: The third paradigm is the belief that leadership must be guided by a clear and meaningful purpose that goes beyond personal gain.
4. **Ethics**: The fourth paradigm is the importance of ethical behavior in leadership and the need for leaders to act with integrity and in the best interests of all stakeholders.
5. **Systems thinking**: The fifth paradigm is the understanding that leadership must consider the larger systems and impacts of their actions and decisions.
6. **Collaboration**: The sixth paradigm is the belief that effective leadership requires collaboration and the ability to work effectively with others towards a common goal.

These paradigms provide a framework for leaders to develop a more conscious and sustainable approach to leadership and decision-making. The paradigm recalls some of the values indicated in the conscious leadership notion, an approach in business that emphasizes the importance of social and environmental considerations alongside financial performance. It recognizes that businesses have a broader responsibility to create value for all stakeholders, including employees, customers, suppliers, communities, and the environment, rather than solely focusing on maximizing profits for shareholders. Conscious leadership is connected to the notion of conscious capitalism that is built on the following values: (1) Purpose: Businesses should have a higher purpose beyond just making money, such as creating a positive impact on society or the environment; (2) Stakeholder orientation: Businesses should consider the needs and interests of all stakeholders and strive to create value for all of them; (3) Ethical Leadership: Business leaders should prioritize ethical and moral decision-making, act with integrity, and foster a culture of trust and collaboration; (4) Conscious culture: Businesses should foster a culture that values and promotes social and environmental responsibility, innovation, and continuous learning. Conscious leadership has been embraced by a growing number of companies, entrepreneurs, and investors as a way to create more sustainable, inclusive, and purpose-driven businesses that benefit all stakeholders. The ontologically different paradigms represented by consciousness in sustainability leadership mindsets have been described as "Quantum Leadership" (Tsao & Laszlo, 2019). Through these perspectives, sustainability leaders can view reality in four ontologically different paradigms: mechanistic, organic, mindful, and integral. Each paradigm offers a unique perspective on the nature of reality, and each provides a different approach to sustainability leadership. Understanding these paradigms can help leaders develop a more nuanced understanding of sustainability and guide them in creating effective strategies for promoting sustainable practices in their organizations.

Integral Models for Sustainability Mindsets

E. F. Schumacher, a British economist, philosopher, and author who is best known for his work on sustainability and human-scale development offers us inspiring insights for an integrated model of sustainability leadership. He is considered a pioneer of the sustainability movement and a key figure in the development of ecological economics. In his most famous book *Small Is Beautiful: Economics as if People Mattered*, Schumacher (1973) argues that the pursuit of economic growth at all costs is unsustainable and that we need to prioritize human well-being and environmental sustainability. He emphasizes the importance of small-scale, decentralized, and community-led approaches to development, and advocates for a "Buddhist economics" that prioritizes human dignity, ecological sustainability, and spiritual fulfillment over materialism and consumerism. Schumacher's contribution to sustainability leadership lies in his pioneering ideas about sustainable development and his advocacy for a more holistic and human-centered approach to economics. He recognized the importance of ecological sustainability long before it became a mainstream concern, and his work has influenced generations of sustainability leaders and thinkers.

In his book *A Guide for the Perplexed*, Schumacher (1977) presented his concept of four fields of knowledge that are necessary for a complete understanding of the world. These fields are: (1) Nature, which includes the study of the physical world, including natural sciences such as physics, chemistry, biology, and ecology; (2) Society, which includes the study of human behavior and social institutions, including social sciences such as economics, political science, sociology, and psychology; (3) Spiritual, which includes the study of religion, philosophy, and spirituality. It encompasses questions about the nature of reality, the purpose of life, and the human experience; and (4) Personal, which includes the study of the individual and personal development, including psychology, self-reflection, and meditation. Understanding the self is important for personal growth and fulfilling one's potential. According to Schumacher, these four fields of knowledge are interconnected and interdependent. To solve complex (wicked) problems, it is necessary to integrate knowledge from all four fields and develop a holistic understanding of the world.

Other authors have expanded on these fields and created similar models for integrated leadership and conscious leadership. Ken Wilber's integral leadership theory offers a similar holistic and comprehensive approach to leadership to address the complex challenges of sustainability. In his book *Integral Leadership: The Next Half-Step*, Wilber (2014) applies his integral framework to the domain of leadership and offers a comprehensive model for understanding leadership in a more holistic and integrated way. The book explores the different dimensions of leadership, including the individual, collective, interior, and exterior dimensions, and how these dimensions can be integrated into a more comprehensive and effective approach to leadership. Wilber also discusses the developmental stages of individuals and collectives and the relationship between different levels of consciousness and effective leadership. Similarly, Schumacher's four fields of knowledge encompass the physical, social, spiritual, and personal dimensions of knowledge, while Wilber's integral theory includes a broader range of dimensions, including the individual, collective, interior, and exterior dimensions of experience. Wilber's integral theory includes a focus on the relationship between different levels of consciousness and the types of problems that can be solved at each level. Wilber argues that leadership needs to operate at multiple levels of consciousness to effectively address complex sustainability challenges. Both Schumacher's four fields of knowledge and Wilber's integral theory provide important frameworks for understanding the complex challenges of sustainability and the need for more comprehensive and integrated approaches to leadership.

Schumacher's four fields of knowledge and Wilber's integral theory also share some similarities with the four directions of the indigenous medicine wheel, which is a sacred symbol and teaching tool used in many indigenous cultures. The indigenous medicine wheel is a circular symbol divided into four quadrants, or directions, commonly associated with the physical, emotional, mental, and spiritual aspects of human experience. All three models highlight the importance of a more holistic and integrated approach to understanding human experience and the complex sustainability challenges we face in the world.

The Need for New Integral Models

We need new integrated models for sustainability leadership to address the complexity, challenges, need for collaboration, and integration of diverse forms of knowledge for our short-term and long-term goals. Reflecting on the contributions from other disciplines. We consider four major priority areas: higher-purpose as mission, well-being as happiness, prosperity as the conditions for thriving, and consciousness as awareness of our interconnectedness. These four areas of higher purpose, collective well-being, shared prosperity, and consciousness are also important for the business and leadership world, particularly with regard to sustainability goals, outcomes, and impact. Figure 2.2 is a revised model for integrated sustainability leadership mindsets. It comprises the UNGC mindset study of sustainability leaders and Schumacher's four fields of knowledge with Wilber's integral theory and the Indigenous people's medicine wheel. At the center is the Fibonacci sequence and the golden ratio which remind us of the recurring pattern of nature. The spiral builds upon itself to continue to grow and evolve. When incorporated into designing and developing sustainability leadership programs, it offers a symbolic representation of sustainable solutions that work in harmony with nature (Fig. 4.2).

1. **Purpose**: A purpose-driven sustainability mindset involves having a clear understanding of the organization's mission and goals, and aligning actions with that purpose. Leaders with a purpose-driven mindset are motivated by a desire to make a positive impact on society and the environment, and they are committed to driving sustainable change. The purpose encompasses political capacity and spiritual and systemic intelligence. It is connected to the attitude of openness and unconditional service (Seva, in Sanskrit).
2. **Well-being**: A sustainability mindset that emphasizes well-being involves prioritizing the physical, emotional, and mental health of individuals within the organization and the broader community. Leaders with a well-being-focused mindset recognize the importance of sustainable practices in supporting human health and

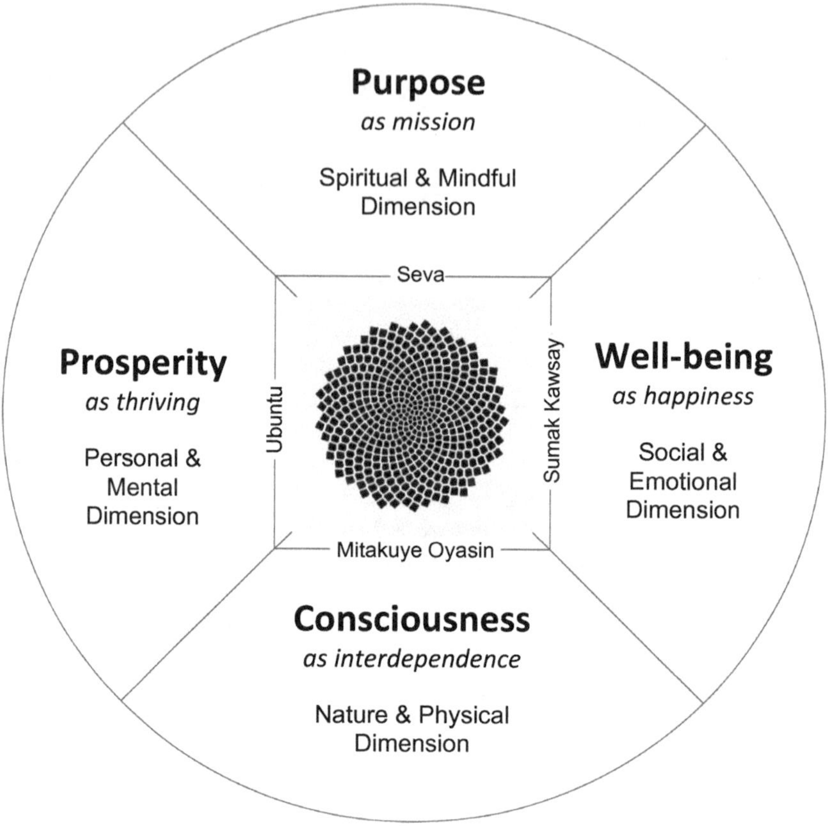

Fig. 4.2 Dimensions of sustainability leadership mindsets

well-being, and they strive to create environments that promote health and happiness. The well-being dimension encompasses inter-relational capacity and social and cultural intelligence. It is connected to the attitude of solidarity, flexibility, and compassion and expressed in the idea of "good life" (Sumak Kawsay, in Quechua).

3. **Consciousness**: A consciousness-focused sustainability mindset involves cultivating a deep awareness of the interconnectedness of all things and recognizing the impact of individual actions on the broader system. Leaders with a consciousness-focused mindset

are mindful of the consequences of their decisions and actions, and they strive to make choices that are aligned with their values and the values of their organization. The consciousness dimension encompasses empathy capacity and environmental intelligence. It is connected to the attitude of protection and respect and the realization of our interdependence (Mitakuye Oyasin, in Lakota).

4. **Prosperity**: A sustainability mindset that prioritizes prosperity involves recognizing that sustainable practices can lead to economic growth and long-term success. Leaders with a prosperity-focused mindset seek to create economic value while also promoting social and environmental sustainability. They recognize that sustainable practices can lead to increased innovation, improved customer loyalty, and enhanced brand reputation, all of which contribute to long-term prosperity. The prosperity dimension encompasses strategic capacity and business intelligence. It is connected to the values of flourishing and thriving in the community (Ubuntu, in Zulu).

This integrated model of sustainability leadership mindsets suggests that when purpose, well-being, consciousness, and prosperity are integrated and prioritized, they can result in more effective and impactful leadership performance. Leaders with a purpose-driven mindset are motivated by making a positive impact on society and the environment, while those with a well-being-focused mindset prioritize the health and happiness of individuals within the organization and the broader community. Consciousness-focused leaders are mindful of their actions' impact on the system and strive to make choices aligned with their values, and prosperity-focused leaders recognize that sustainable practices can lead to economic growth and long-term success.

Applications of this model to sustainability leadership include developing a clear sense of purpose and aligning actions with it, prioritizing the health and well-being of individuals within and outside the organization, cultivating awareness of interconnectedness and consequences of decisions and actions, and recognizing the potential for sustainable practices to lead to economic growth and long-term success. By incorporating these mindsets into their leadership approach, sustainability leaders can drive positive change and create a better future for all.

Key Takeaways

1. Sustainability challenges require new mindsets and skill sets to adequately respond and make a net positive impact. Leaders need to adopt principles, competencies, and skill sets to address complex and multifaceted sustainability challenges such as balancing economic growth, social equity, and environmental protection, addressing global issues like climate change, biodiversity loss, and resource depletion, and overcoming political impasse, among others.
2. Sustainability mindsets involve attitudes, beliefs, and values that shape a leader's approach to sustainability, and they are essential for driving positive environmental, social, and economic outcomes. Leaders need to have both the skill sets and mindsets necessary to drive change and foster a culture of sustainability within their organization.
3. Integral models for sustainability mindsets provide a useful framework for understanding the different dimensions of sustainability leadership mindsets, including purpose, well-being, consciousness, and prosperity. These dimensions encompass competencies such as political capacity, environmental intelligence, strategic capacity, and business intelligence, among others.
4. Leadership consciousness and spiritual values play an important role in sustainability mindsets, as they involve cultivating a deep awareness of the interconnectedness of all things, recognizing the impact of individual actions on the broader system, and being motivated by a desire to make a positive impact on society and the environment.

References

Henriksson, H., & Grunewald, E. W. (2020). *Sustainability leadership: A swedish approach to transforming your company, your industry and the world*. Springer International Publishing.

Murphy, C. (2022). *Sustainable leadership: Lessons of vision, courage, and grit from the CEOs who dared to build a better world*. Wiley.

Rimanoczy, I. (2020). *The sustainability mindset principles: A guide to developing a mindset for a better world*. Taylor & Francis.

Ritz, A. A., & Rimanoczy, I. eds. (2021) *Sustainability mindset and transformative leadership: a multidisciplinary perspective*. Springer Nature.

Russell Reynolds Associates & United Nations Global Compact (2020). *Leadership for the decade of action*. https://unglobalcompact.org/library/5745
Schumacher, E. F. (1973). *Small is beautiful: economics as if people mattered*. Harper & Row.
Schumacher, E. F. (1977). *A Guide for the perplexed*. HarperCollins Publishers.
Sfeir-Younis, A., & Tavanti, M. (2020). *Conscious sustainability leadership: A new paradigm for next generation leaders*. Planet Healing Press.
Tsao, F., & Laszlo, C. (2019) *Quantum leadership: New consciousness in business*. Tantor Media, Inc.
Wilber, K. (2014). *Integral leadership: The next half-step*. Integral Publishers.

CHAPTER 5

Ethos of Sustainability Leadership

Abstract This chapter discusses the importance of developing an ethos of sustainability leadership. The chapter begins by exploring the concept of sustainability ethics and the role of ethical decision-making in promoting sustainability. A framework for ethical decision-making is presented, which includes the precautionary principle, intergenerational equity principle, and stakeholder engagement principle. The chapter then focuses on developing an ethos for a sustainability culture, emphasizing the need to move beyond greenwashing and unsustainable ethics. Overall, the chapter highlights the critical role that ethos and ethics play in promoting sustainability leadership and fostering a sustainable future.

Keywords Ethics · Ethos · Decision-making · Precautionary principle · Intergenerational equity · Greenwashing

The Ultimate Measure of a Man is not Where He Stands in Moments of Comfort and Convenience, but Where He Stands at Times of Challenge and Controversy.

- Martin Luther King Jr.

M. Tavanti, *Developing Sustainability in Organizations*, Sustainable Development Goals Series,
https://doi.org/10.1007/978-3-031-36907-0_5

Promoting a Sustainability Ethics and Ethos

Considering ethics and ethos in sustainability leadership is crucial because it helps ensure that decisions and actions taken in pursuit of sustainability are not only effective but also responsible and just. Sustainability leadership involves making decisions that balance environmental, social, and economic factors to meet the needs of the present without compromising the ability of future generations to meet their own needs. This requires a deep commitment to ethical principles and a strong sense of ethos, or values and beliefs that guide behavior and decision-making. Dion et al. (2022) goes further and suggests that ethical leadership requires a deep sense of personal, organizational, and global responsibility demonstrated by the equilibrium between personal ethics (characterized by humility and altruism) and universal ethos (primarily characterized by social justice).

Ethics are important because they provide a framework for evaluating the morality of actions and decisions. In the context of sustainability leadership, ethical principles can help guide decision-making by ensuring that actions taken are fair, just, and sustainable. The precautionary principle, for example and as we will examine later, suggests that in situations where the potential for harm is great, it is better to err on the side of caution, which can help prevent unintended consequences of sustainability initiatives. Ethos, on the other hand, is important because it helps establish a culture of sustainability within organizations and communities. An ethos of sustainability promotes shared values and beliefs that guide behavior and decision-making towards sustainability goals. This can lead to more effective and sustained efforts towards sustainability, as well as greater accountability and transparency in decision-making.

Ethics and ethos are related concepts, but they have slightly different meanings.

Ethics for Responsible Business

1. **Ethics for Responsible Business**: Ethics refers to a set of principles and values that guide behavior and decision-making. It is concerned with questions of right and wrong, and it provides a framework for evaluating actions and making moral judgments. In the context of business, ethics often involves considerations of fairness, responsibility, and accountability to stakeholders, as well as the broader social and environmental impacts of business activities.

2. **Ethos for Organizational Cultures**: Ethos, on the other hand, refers to the characteristic spirit or culture of a community or organization. It is the set of beliefs, values, and practices that shape the identity and behavior of a group of people. In the context of business, ethos refers to the culture and values of an organization, including its commitment to sustainability, ethical behavior, and responsible environmental stewardship.

Sustainability leadership requires the incorporation of both ethics and ethos. A leader who prioritizes ethics ensures that business activities are conducted in a responsible and transparent manner, while a leader who prioritizes ethos creates a culture of sustainability that encourages innovation and responsible environmental stewardship throughout the organization. Ethics for sustainability involves applying ethical principles to the pursuit of sustainable development and balancing the pursuit of profit with consideration for the broader social and environmental impacts of business activities. A sustainability ethos is a set of values and practices that prioritize sustainability and responsible environmental stewardship, providing a framework for decision-making that takes into account the long-term health and well-being of the environment and society. Building a sustainability ethos can lead to better business outcomes, improve stakeholder relationships, and enhance a company's reputation and credibility by promoting responsible and ethical behavior.

Overall, the development of both sustainability ethics and sustainability ethos is important for leadership because it provides a framework for decision-making that takes into account the long-term health and well-being of the environment and society, and helps create a culture of sustainability that can enhance a company's innovation, reputation, and long-term profitability. For business ethics, sustainability ethics promotes responsible, transparent, and accountable business practices that take into account the broader social and environmental impacts of business activities. By adopting a framework of ethics for sustainability, businesses can build trust and credibility with their stakeholders, enhance their innovation and creativity, and contribute to the long-term well-being of the environment and society.

Ethical Decision-Making for Sustainability

Ethical decision-making for sustainability involves making decisions that are guided by ethical principles and values, and that prioritize the long-term health and well-being of the environment and society. It involves considering the impacts of decisions on a wide range of stakeholders, including future generations, and taking a proactive approach to risk management and sustainability. Thiele et al. (2011) emphasize the importance of ethical decision-making in achieving sustainability. They argue that sustainability is not just about technological solutions, but it also involves ethical considerations, such as justice, equity, and responsibility. The authors provide a framework for ethical decision-making that considers the environmental, social, and economic impacts of actions and promotes a long-term perspective that considers the needs of future generations. They also suggest that sustainability requires a shift in values and mindset, where individuals and organizations prioritize the well-being of the natural world and the broader community over short-term economic gain. The book provides case studies and practical tools to help individuals and organizations implement ethical decision-making practices and move towards a more sustainable future. In order to make ethical decisions for sustainability, it is important to consider a range of factors, such as:

1. **Environmental impact**: Consider the potential environmental impacts of decisions, and take steps to minimize harm to the environment.
2. **Social impact**: Consider the potential social impacts of decisions, including impacts on workers, local communities, and other stakeholders.
3. **Economic impact**: Consider the economic impacts of decisions, and seek to balance economic considerations with environmental and social considerations.
4. **Stakeholder engagement**: Engage with a wide range of stakeholders in decision-making processes, and consider their perspectives and concerns.
5. **Transparency**: Be transparent about decision-making processes, and provide clear and accurate information to stakeholders about the potential impacts of decisions.

6. **Continuous improvement**: Continuously monitor and evaluate the impacts of decisions, and make changes as needed to improve sustainability performance over time.

Ultimately, ethical decision-making for sustainability involves taking a holistic and proactive approach to decision-making, and recognizing the interdependence of economic, social, and environmental factors. By prioritizing sustainability and considering the impacts of decisions on a wide range of stakeholders, leaders can help to promote a more sustainable and equitable approach to business.

Frameworks for Ethical Decision-Making

There are various frameworks for ethical decision-making. For example, Meinhold (2021) discusses the TBL, stakeholder theory, and ethical leadership as ethical decision-making frameworks that can promote sustainability in business. Similarly, Rendtorff (2019) argues that ethical decision-making for sustainability should be grounded in a holistic and interdisciplinary approach and proposes that we should consider the long-term consequences and impacts of actions on the environment, society, and economy. The following are some commonly suggested steps that can be useful to promote sustainability in organizations and society:

1. **Identify the ethical issues**: The first step is to identify the ethical issues at hand. This involves understanding the potential social, economic, and environmental impacts of a decision or action.
2. **Gather information and assess the impact**: The next step is to gather information and assess the potential impact of the decision or action on the environment and society. This may involve conducting a sustainability impact assessment, using sustainability indicators, or consulting with stakeholders.
3. **Evaluate the options**: After assessing the potential impacts, evaluate the options available and consider the potential consequences of each. This may involve weighing the potential benefits and costs of each option and identifying any trade-offs that may be required.

4. **Apply ethical principles and values**: Use ethical principles and values to evaluate the options and determine the best course of action. This may involve considering the principles of environmental justice, fairness, and the precautionary principle.
5. **Implement and monitor the decision**: Once a decision has been made, it is important to implement it and monitor its impact. This may involve setting performance indicators and reporting on progress, as well as engaging stakeholders and seeking feedback on the outcomes of the decision.
6. **Continually review and improve**: Finally, it is important to continually review and improve the decision-making process, seeking to identify areas for improvement and taking steps to incorporate lessons learned into future decision-making processes. This may involve developing a sustainability management plan or seeking external verification of sustainability performance.

By following these steps, leaders can make ethical decisions for sustainability that are informed by a range of perspectives and that balance economic, social, and environmental considerations. This can help to promote a more sustainable and equitable approach to business, and contribute to long-term sustainability and resilience.

The Precautionary Principle for Sustainability Decisions

Some key principles are very important for ethical decision-making for sustainability. One of them includes the precautionary principle, which requires businesses to take action to prevent harm to the environment and society even when there is uncertainty about the exact nature and scope of the harm. More precisely, the precautionary principle is a guiding principle in decision-making that emphasizes caution, especially in situations where scientific knowledge is incomplete or there is a risk of harm to human health or the environment. The principle states that when an activity or product poses a potential threat to human health or the environment, in the absence of scientific consensus, the burden of proof falls on those who support the activity or product. In other words, if there is a reasonable suspicion that an activity or product may cause harm, precautionary measures should be taken, even if it is not yet possible to establish a direct causal relationship between the activity or product and the harm. The precautionary principle is often invoked in debates around environmental policy, public health, and technology regulation (Peel, 2005).

There are many examples of leaders and organizations that have used the precautionary principle in their decision-making process. Here are a few examples:

1. **European Union**: The EU has incorporated the precautionary principle into its decision-making process for a range of environmental and public health issues, including regulation of genetically modified organisms and chemicals. The EU's REACH (Registration, Evaluation, Authorization, and Restriction of Chemicals) regulation is a key example of the precautionary principle in action, as it requires companies to demonstrate the safety of chemicals before they are allowed on the market.
2. **Greenpeace**: The environmental organization Greenpeace has been a strong advocate for the precautionary principle, using it to push for the phase-out of hazardous chemicals, the regulation of genetically modified organisms, and the protection of the Arctic from oil drilling.
3. **California Air Resources Board (CARB)**: CARB is a regulatory agency that oversees air quality in California. The agency has used the precautionary principle to develop a range of regulations, including standards for vehicle emissions and limits on toxic air pollutants.
4. **Seventh Generation**: The household products company Seventh Generation has incorporated the precautionary principle into its product development process, using it to guide decisions about product ingredients and packaging.
5. **Organic Consumers Association**: The Organic Consumers Association, a consumer advocacy group, has advocated for the precautionary principle in the regulation of genetically modified organisms, arguing that more research is needed to understand the potential risks to human health and the environment.

These examples demonstrate how the precautionary principle can be applied in a range of contexts, from government regulation to product development to advocacy. By prioritizing caution and proactive risk management, leaders and organizations can help to reduce the likelihood of environmental harm, and promote a more sustainable approach to business that balances economic, social, and environmental considerations.

The Intergenerational Equity Principle for Sustainability Decisions

Another impact principle is the intergenerational equity principle which emphasizes that present generations have a responsibility to consider the needs and interests of future generations in their decision-making processes. This means that decisions and policies should be made with consideration of the long-term effects on the environment, economy, and society, and that natural resources should be managed sustainably to ensure their availability for future generations. This principle is recognized as an important component of environmental ethics and sustainability, and is often invoked in debates around environmental policy, natural resource management, and sustainable development. Some examples of leaders and organizations that have used the intergenerational equity principle in their decision-making process include:

1. **Norway's Government Pension Fund Global**: This fund, which is one of the largest sovereign wealth funds in the world, has a mandate to invest in a way that ensures long-term returns for future generations of Norwegians. As part of this mandate, the fund has divested from companies that are deemed to be harmful to the environment and society, and has invested in renewable energy and other sustainable industries.
2. **The Natural Resources Defense Council (NRDC)**: The NRDC is an environmental advocacy organization that works to protect the environment for present and future generations. The organization uses the intergenerational equity principle in its advocacy efforts, pushing for policies and practices that will protect the environment and public health for generations to come.
3. **The World Future Council**: The World Future Council is an international organization that works to promote the interests of future generations in policy and decision-making. The organization has worked to promote policies such as renewable energy, sustainable

agriculture, and environmental conservation, in order to ensure a sustainable future for all.

4. **The 7th Generation Interfaith Coalition for Responsible Investment**: This coalition of religious institutions uses the intergenerational equity principle in its investment decisions, seeking to invest in companies that are environmentally and socially responsible, and that will create long-term value for future generations.
5. **Bhutan**: The country of Bhutan is known for its commitment to intergenerational equity, which is enshrined in its constitution. Bhutan has prioritized the protection of its natural environment, and its policies are guided by the principle of "Gross National Happiness" (GNH) which seeks to balance economic development with environmental protection and social well-being.
6. **New Zealand**: In 2018, New Zealand became one of the first countries in the world to pass a law that requires the government to consider the impact of its policies on future generations. The law requires the government to produce a "well-being budget" each year, which considers the long-term impact of spending decisions on the environment, social equity, and intergenerational equity.
7. **Seventh Generation**: Seventh Generation is a US-based cleaning products company that is committed to environmental sustainability and intergenerational equity. The company's name is based on the idea that its products should be made in a way that ensures a sustainable future for the next seven generations. Seventh Generation uses plant-based ingredients and recycled packaging, and has a strong commitment to transparency and corporate social responsibility.
8. **The Future Fit Foundation**: The Future Fit Foundation is a nonprofit organization that has developed a set of standards for business sustainability, which includes a focus on intergenerational equity. The standards require companies to consider the long-term impact of their decisions on the environment and future generations, and to take a proactive approach to risk management and sustainability.

Other examples would obviously include the SDGs as the goals are based on the intergenerational equity principle, and seek to ensure that current development efforts do not compromise the ability of future generations to meet their own needs. By using the intergenerational equity principle in their decision-making, these leaders and organizations are working to ensure a more sustainable and equitable future for all. These country level decisions are helping to ensure that future generations have the same opportunities to enjoy a healthy environment and sustainable economy as current generations of their citizens do.

The Stakeholder Engagement Principle for Sustainability Decisions

Another important principle in ethical decision-making for sustainability is the principle of stakeholder engagement, which emphasizes the importance of involving stakeholders in the decision-making process and being accountable to them for business activities. According to this principle, organizations should engage with and consider the interests and perspectives of all relevant stakeholders in their decision-making processes. Manetti and Bellucci (2018) argue that stakeholder engagement is an ongoing process that should result in quality organizational sustainability reporting. Here are some examples of how some well-known sustainability companies and perhaps less well-known organizations have used this principle in their decision-making process:

1. **World Wildlife Fund (WWF)**: The WWF is an international conservation organization that works to protect endangered species and their habitats. The organization has a stakeholder engagement strategy that includes working with governments, businesses, and communities to develop conservation plans that meet the needs of all stakeholders.
2. **Environmental Protection Agency (EPA)**: The EPA is a US government agency that works to protect human health and the environment. The agency has a stakeholder engagement strategy that includes consulting with a wide range of stakeholders, including industry, environmental groups, and community organizations, to develop regulations and policies that balance economic, social, and environmental considerations.
3. **The Rockefeller Foundation**: The Rockefeller Foundation is a philanthropic organization that supports a wide range of initiatives to promote social and economic progress. The foundation has a

stakeholder engagement strategy that includes working with partners in government, civil society, and the private sector to develop innovative solutions to global challenges.

4. **United Nations (UN)**: The UN is an international and global organization that brings together governments, civil society, and other stakeholders to promote sustainable development and peace. The UN has a stakeholder engagement strategy that includes consulting with member states, civil society organizations, and the private sector to develop policies and programs that address the world's most pressing challenges.
5. **The Natural Step**: The Natural Step is a global nonprofit organization that helps businesses and communities to become more sustainable. The organization has developed a sustainability framework called The Natural Step Framework, which includes stakeholder engagement as a key principle. The Natural Step works with businesses and communities to help them engage with all stakeholders and create a more sustainable future.
6. **The Forest Stewardship Council (FSC)**: The FSC is an international organization that promotes responsible forest management. The FSC engages with a range of stakeholders, including forest owners, Indigenous peoples, NGOs, and companies, to develop its forest management standards and certification program.
7. **Patagonia**: Patagonia, an outdoor apparel company, has a strong commitment to sustainability and engages with a wide range of stakeholders in its decision-making process. The company seeks input from employees, customers, suppliers, and environmental groups, and has been known to make major business decisions based on the feedback it receives.
8. **The Body Shop**: The Body Shop, a cosmetics and skincare company, has a long history of stakeholder engagement. The company has a dedicated stakeholder engagement team, and seeks input from a wide range of stakeholders, including customers, employees, suppliers, and NGOs. The Body Shop has used stakeholder feedback to develop new products, change sourcing practices, and develop more sustainable packaging.
9. **Unilever**: Unilever, a global consumer goods company, has a strong commitment to sustainability and stakeholder engagement. The company has established a Sustainable Living Plan, which sets ambitious goals for reducing its environmental impact and

improving social conditions. Unilever engages with a wide range of stakeholders, including customers, suppliers, employees, and NGOs, and has used stakeholder feedback to inform its sustainability strategy.

10. **Interface**: Interface, a carpet and flooring company, has a strong commitment to sustainability and stakeholder engagement. The company has established a comprehensive stakeholder engagement program, which includes regular meetings with suppliers, customers, and environmental groups. Interface has used stakeholder feedback to develop new products, reduce waste, and improve its environmental performance.

By engaging with stakeholders and considering their interests and perspectives, these leaders and organizations are able to make more informed and sustainable decisions that benefit both the organization and the wider community.

Developing an Ethos for a Sustainability Culture

The quote "Culture eats strategy for breakfast" is often attributed to management consultant and author Peter Drucker. The quote suggests that an organization's culture is a more powerful force in determining its success than any strategy that it may devise. In the context of ethical leadership, this quote highlights the importance of creating a culture of ethical behavior within an organization. No matter how well-crafted an ethical strategy may be, it is unlikely to be effective if it is not supported by the culture of the organization. Combe (2022) suggests that an effective development of a sustainability culture requires leadership that is fully committed to the ethos of sustainability.

Ethical leadership involves not only developing and communicating ethical standards and policies, but also creating a culture in which ethical behavior is expected, supported, and rewarded. This means modeling ethical behavior at all levels of the organization, fostering a sense of personal responsibility for ethical conduct, and promoting open communication about ethical issues. An organization with a strong ethical culture is one in which employees are more likely to make ethical decisions even in the absence of explicit rules or guidance. They will be more likely to speak up when they see unethical behavior, and more likely to report incidents of misconduct. This can help to prevent ethical violations before they occur, and can help to mitigate the damage if they do occur. Developing an ethical sustainability culture in an organization means placing at the core of operations, decisions, and stakeholder relations those values, beliefs, practices, and behaviors that prioritize the well-being of the environment, society, and the economy. This value prioritization is done in a way that is consistent with ethical principles. Such a culture reflects a company's commitment to sustainability and responsible business practices.

In an ethical sustainability culture, companies make conscious efforts to minimize their negative impact on the environment and society while contributing to sustainable development. This involves adopting sustainable business practices, such as reducing greenhouse gas emissions, minimizing waste and pollution, conserving natural resources, promoting social justice, and investing in renewable energy. A strong ethical sustainability culture also involves engaging with stakeholders and promoting transparency, accountability, and ethical behavior throughout the organization. This means involving stakeholders in the decision-making process, actively seeking feedback, and regularly reporting on the company's sustainability performance. Building an ethical culture is also an important component of sustainability leadership, as both concepts are closely linked. An ethical culture is one in which employees and stakeholders are encouraged to act with integrity and in the best interests of the organization and society as a whole. A sustainable organization, on the other hand, is one that is able to meet the needs of the present without compromising the ability of future generations to meet their own needs.

Paradigms for Sustainable Ethical Leadership

Paradigms are conceptual frameworks that shape our values, beliefs, and principles that guide our actions and choices. They influence how we perceive ethical issues, evaluate moral perspectives, and make decisions about right and wrong. Paradigms also shape how we interpret and apply ethical theories and influence the way we approach moral dilemmas. Our paradigms affect how we perceive sustainability issues and the ethical implications of our decisions, influencing the way we prioritize values, weigh trade-offs, and consider the interests of different stakeholders. For instance, a paradigm that emphasizes short-term gains and immediate economic benefits may prioritize profits over environmental sustainability or social justice. On the other hand, a paradigm that emphasizes intergenerational equity and responsibility for future generations may prioritize the conservation of natural resources, the protection of biodiversity, and the reduction of greenhouse gas emissions. Someone who holds a utilitarian paradigm may prioritize the greater good or the outcomes that produce the most happiness for the greatest number of people, while someone who holds a deontological paradigm may prioritize following moral rules or principles regardless of the consequences. Therefore, it is essential to understand our own paradigms and the paradigms of others to engage in constructive dialogue and reach ethical solutions that are just and equitable.

The following interconnected paradigms can be helpful framework for organizational and professional discernment for sustainable ethical decision-making:

1. **Conscious Interdependence (Responsibility)**: Conscious interdependence is a higher-purpose value that promotes the common good, social-global responsibility, and shared social progress. This paradigm centers the sustainability leader into a journey of self-realization beyond ego and eco leadership into seva leadership as interdependence with purpose to make the world a better place. It emphasizes the importance of leaders taking a holistic, systems-level approach to decision-making, and recognizing the impact of their decisions on all stakeholders and the natural world. Leaders who practice conscious interdependence are mindful of their role as stewards of the environment, and seek to balance the needs of different stakeholders in a way that ensures long-term sustainability.
2. **Stakeholder Inclusiveness (Diversity)**: Stakeholder inclusiveness is a paradigm for sustainable ethical leadership that emphasizes the importance of engaging with and considering the perspectives and interests of all stakeholders who are affected by an organization's actions. It involves seeking out and listening to a wide range of stakeholders, considering the long-term and indirect impacts of decisions, and balancing the needs of different stakeholders while respecting the natural world. By incorporating stakeholder inclusiveness into their approach, leaders can build trust and legitimacy, promote transparency and equity, and create a more just and sustainable society.

3. **Systemic Justice (Rights)**: The Systemic Justice paradigm emphasizes the importance of addressing the root causes of social and environmental problems, and creating more just and equitable systems for long-term sustainability. This involves focusing on systemic solutions, addressing power imbalances, and considering the long-term impacts of decisions. Sustainability leaders who incorporate the Systemic Justice paradigm into their approach can help create a more just and sustainable world, where social and environmental problems are addressed at their roots.
4. **Global Citizenship (Rights-Responsibilities)**: The Global Citizenship paradigm is a framework for sustainable ethical leadership that emphasizes the responsibilities of individuals and organizations to contribute to a more just, equitable, and sustainable world. It recognizes the interconnectedness of global challenges and promotes a sense of shared responsibility and solidarity across borders and cultures. The paradigm involves a mindset and set of values that prioritize the common good, respect for diversity, and active engagement in addressing global challenges. It can help sustainable ethical decision-making by providing a broader perspective that considers the social and environmental impacts of decisions on a global scale. The Global Citizenship paradigm can inspire us to adopt sustainable and ethical practices in our personal and professional lives and contribute to a more sustainable, just, and peaceful world.
5. **Collective Well-being (Solidarity-Subsidiarity)**: The collective well-being paradigm is a framework for sustainable ethical leadership that emphasizes the interdependence of individuals, communities, and ecosystems. It promotes the well-being of all members of society and recognizes that individual well-being is interconnected with the well-being of others and the natural world. This paradigm can help with sustainable ethical decision-making by providing a broader perspective that considers the social and environmental impacts of decisions on all members of society, especially the most vulnerable and marginalized. It also promotes collaboration, participation, and empowerment, recognizing the importance of listening to diverse perspectives and experiences, promoting social equity and justice, and fostering a culture of solidarity and empathy. By embracing this paradigm, we can create a more sustainable and ethical society

that prioritizes the well-being of all members and recognizes the interconnectedness of social, economic, and environmental systems.

6. **Eco-stewardship (Respect-Interdependence)**: The eco-stewardship paradigm emphasizes the responsibility of individuals and organizations to care for the natural world and promote ecological sustainability. Sustainable leaders who embrace this paradigm prioritize the long-term health and well-being of the environment, develop strategies to reduce waste, promote resource efficiency and renewable energy, and educate stakeholders about the ecological impacts of their actions. By adopting a more proactive and values-based approach to sustainability, leaders can create a more sustainable and resilient organization that contributes to a more just and sustainable society.

Beyond Greenwashing and Unsustainable Ethics

The blindside of sustainability leadership is greenwashing. Vollero (2021) has analyzed numerous corporate cases of deceptive marketing and corporate communication practices that overemphasize a company's sustainability practices and offers some lessons in how to avoid greenwashing traps. Miller (2018) makes a cultural critical analysis of greenwashing. He argues that culture has become complicit in our environmental crisis through its promotion of image-friendly environmental credentials and engagement with big industry polluters. Greenwashing is a marketing tactic used by companies to mislead consumers into believing that their products, services, or operations are environmentally friendly or sustainable when they are not. This can harm both consumers and the environment by promoting false environmentally responsible choices and undermining genuine sustainability efforts. To avoid greenwashing, consumers should look for third-party certifications and companies should provide clear, verifiable information to support environmental claims. Greenwashing can also undermine the values of transparency, integrity, and responsibility that are essential for sustainability ethics and damage the credibility and trust necessary for sustainable leadership. Specifically, greenwashing can have the following negative consequences:

1. **Undermining Values and Principles**: Greenwashing can undermine the values of transparency and integrity that are central to sustainability ethics. When companies make false or misleading environmental claims, they are not being transparent about their environmental practices or their impact on the environment. This can erode trust and confidence in their commitment to sustainability, and it can create a sense of cynicism or distrust among consumers and stakeholders.
2. **Damaging Credibility and Trust**: Greenwashing can damage the credibility and trust that are essential for sustainable leadership. When companies make false or misleading environmental claims, they are not demonstrating the responsible leadership that is necessary to address the environmental challenges facing our planet. This can undermine the credibility of their sustainability initiatives and make it more difficult to engage and inspire others to take meaningful action.
3. **Promoting a Culture of Complacency**: Greenwashing can perpetuate a culture of complacency and inaction, leading people to believe that sustainability is not a serious issue or that it is being adequately addressed when it is not. This can have serious consequences for the environment and for future generations, as it can delay or prevent the adoption of sustainable practices and policies that are necessary for a more just and sustainable society.

To address the implications of greenwashing for sustainability ethics and leadership, it is essential that companies and leaders adopt a culture of transparency, honesty, and responsibility. This means providing clear, verifiable information about their environmental practices and impact, avoiding vague or misleading environmental claims, and adopting independent, third-party certifications and labels that provide clear and transparent information about a product's environmental impact. It also means demonstrating responsible leadership by taking meaningful action to address the environmental challenges facing our planet and inspiring others to do the same.

Like greenwashing, other terms have been used to describe the unethical practices towards sustainability. These include:

1. **Blue-washing**: "Blue-washing" is a term sometimes used to describe the practice of companies or organizations that claim to be environmentally responsible or sustainable, but do not address the impact of their activities on the world's oceans or water resources. Alternatively, blue-washing has been used to signify the superficial affiliation of organizations with the United Nations. "Referring to the color of the United Nations flag, bluewashing came to mean that some participating companies were using the Global Compact to improve the public perception of their values, social programs, and governance practices without introducing any real changes or reforms" (McClimon, 2022).
2. **SDG-washing**: "SDG-washing" is a term used to describe the practice of companies or organizations that claim to support or contribute to the SDGs, without actually taking meaningful action to address the global challenges that the SDGs aim to address. Some critics say businesses use the goals to highlight positive contributions without referencing the areas where they're making a negative impact. In other cases, businesses reflect another trend towards SDG-washing, with companies "cherry-picking" the SDGs that they feel comfortable with (Heras Saizarbitoria et al., 2022).
3. **Brown-washing**: Trying to appear as being supportive of Black, Brown, Indigenous, and People of Color (BIPoC) without implementing real or substantial empowerment initiatives or inclusive initiatives into their own business. Alternatively, the term "brownwashing" is sometimes used to describe the practice of companies or organizations that attempt to present themselves as environmentally responsible or sustainable, but whose core business or operations have a significant negative impact on the environment. "When consumers see brown they think green, say companies that sell products like paper towels, napkins and diapers. Brown is the New White" (Nassauer, 2012)

Unsustainable and unethical leadership practices go beyond greenwashing and its variation. It can unfortunately result in ethical violations and often criminal transgressions. These are actions or behaviors that are considered ethically wrong or morally unacceptable, and at the same time have negative impacts on the environment, society, or economy, making them unsustainable in the long term. Some unsustainable and unethical practices may include:

1. **Exploitation of natural resources**: Practices that exploit natural resources beyond their limits, without regard for future generations, can be considered unethical and unsustainable. This includes activities such as overfishing, deforestation, and mining that cause irreversible damage to the environment.
2. **Labor abuses**: Practices that involve exploitation or mistreatment of workers, such as child labor, unsafe working conditions, and discrimination, are unethical and unsustainable because they can lead to social unrest, conflict, and decreased productivity.
3. **Unfair business practices**: Practices such as bribery, corruption, and fraud are considered unethical and unsustainable because they undermine the rule of law, damage the reputation of the business or organization, and lead to economic inefficiencies and inequality.
4. **Environmental pollution**: Practices that cause environmental pollution, such as air and water pollution, and the release of greenhouse gasses that contribute to climate change, are considered unethical and unsustainable because they have negative impacts on human health, biodiversity, and the planet as a whole.
5. **Waste and resource consumption**: Practices that involve excessive waste and resource consumption, such as the use of disposable products, single-use plastics, and non-renewable energy sources, are considered unethical and unsustainable because they contribute to environmental degradation and depletion of resources.

To promote sustainable ethical practices, individuals, businesses, and organizations should be aware of the potential negative impacts of their actions on the environment, society, and economy, and take steps to reduce or mitigate those impacts. This includes adopting sustainable practices and technologies, promoting transparency and accountability, and engaging with stakeholders to understand and address their concerns.

There have been many business leaders throughout history who have promoted unsustainable and unethical ethical practices. Here are some notable examples:

1. **Andrew Carnegie**: While Carnegie is remembered for his philanthropic activities, his steel company was known for its poor treatment of workers, including low wages and long hours. The

company also used controversial practices such as lockouts and strikebreaking to suppress labor organizing.

2. **John D. Rockefeller**: Rockefeller built his fortune through the oil industry, but his company, Standard Oil, was notorious for its aggressive business practices, including monopolistic behavior, price-fixing, and bribery.
3. **Enron**: In the early 2000s, Enron was one of the largest energy companies in the world, but it collapsed in a financial scandal that exposed widespread fraud, corruption, and unethical business practices. It is insightful and a case that I often use in my business ethics classes, that Eron's Value Statements were well-written and inspiring but clearly disjointed from their practices.
4. **Volkswagen**: In 2015, it was revealed that Volkswagen had installed software in its diesel cars that allowed them to cheat on emissions tests, leading to a massive scandal and a loss of public trust.
5. **Wells Fargo**: In 2016, it was revealed that Wells Fargo had engaged in fraudulent practices, including opening millions of unauthorized bank accounts, to meet aggressive sales targets and boost profits.
6. **H&M**: The company has been a target of criticism for its fast fashion practices, despite the company's efforts to promote sustainability and ethical practices. It has been criticized for its greenwashing practices using vague labeling language like "close the loop" and "a conscious choice," and calling their products "sustainable." While the company has implemented some sustainable initiatives, such as using organic cotton and recycled materials, it still operates within the fast fashion business model, which encourages overconsumption and creates environmental and social impacts.
7. **Jack Welch**: The former CEO of General Electric (GE), has been criticized for promoting unsustainable business practices during his tenure. Some of the criticisms include his financial engineering (focus on short-term financial gains came at the expense of long-term sustainability and innovation), environmental impact (expansion of fossil fuel-based energy and the production of plastics), workforce reduction (strategy of continuous downsizing and restructuring), and lack of transparency (ambiguous financial reporting). While Welch is credited with transforming GE into a highly profitable company, his legacy is also seen as a cautionary tale about the dangers of pursuing financial engineering at the expense of long-term sustainability and social responsibility.

8. **Jair Bolsonaro:** The 38th president of Brazil has been criticized by many as an example of an unsustainable leader for his environmental and social policies. His environmental policies supported agribusiness and opposed measures to protect the Amazon rainforest. His government has been accused of dismantling environmental protections and regulations, leading to increased deforestation, illegal mining, and land grabbing in the Amazon region. Bolsonaro has been known for his denial of climate change and his dismissal of scientific evidence about the environmental impacts of human activities. He has been accused of undermining efforts to address climate change and of contributing to the global climate crisis. In the areas of human rights and social justice, his administration has been accused of undermining the rights of Indigenous people, women, and the LGBTQ + community, as well as of promoting violence and police brutality. His handling of the COVID-19 pandemic in Brazil, particularly for his opposition to measures such as social distancing and mask mandates have contributed to the high number of infections and deaths in the country. His policies and actions have had negative impacts on the environment, social justice, and public health, making him an example of an unsustainable leader.

In summary, these examples show how business leaders who prioritize short-term profits over ethical and sustainable practices can harm their companies, their employees, and the wider community. To promote sustainable and ethical business practices, leaders should prioritize transparency, accountability, and stakeholder engagement, and should recognize that long-term success requires a commitment to social and environmental responsibility. We can avoid unsustainable and unethical leadership practices through several concrete steps and commitments:

1. **Set clear sustainability goals:** Organizations and leaders should set clear and measurable sustainability goals, such as reducing carbon emissions, improving working conditions, or increasing diversity and inclusion. These goals should be aligned with the organization's values and mission.
2. **Adopt a sustainability-focused culture:** Organizations should create a culture that prioritizes sustainability and ethical values.

This can be done by involving employees in sustainability initiatives, recognizing and rewarding sustainable practices, and providing sustainability training and education.

3. **Foster transparency and accountability:** Organizations should promote transparency and accountability in their sustainability practices by reporting on their sustainability performance, engaging stakeholders in sustainability decision-making, and being open to feedback and criticism.
4. **Implement sustainable managerial practices:** As we will explore in more detail in Part 2, organizations should implement sustainable management practices in the operations, processes, sectors, and stakeholder relations. These practices should include reducing waste and energy consumption, using renewable resources, and promoting sustainable supply chains.
5. **Prioritize stakeholder engagement:** Leaders should prioritize stakeholder engagement, such as engaging with employees, customers, suppliers, and local communities, to understand their needs and perspectives and develop solutions that are socially and environmentally responsible. This includes establishing a truly inclusive and participatory culture in the organization.
6. **Foster ethical decision-making:** Leaders should foster ethical decision-making by promoting a culture of integrity, providing ethics training, and ensuring that ethical considerations are part of all decision-making processes including strategic planning, risk management, and performance evaluation.
7. **Holding leaders accountable:** Organizations should hold leaders accountable for ethical and sustainable practices by establishing clear performance metrics, monitoring and reporting on sustainability performance, and rewarding leaders who achieve sustainability goals.
8. **Encouraging innovation and collaboration:** As we will explore in more detail in Part 3, leaders should encourage innovation and collaboration to find new and creative ways to promote sustainability and ethical practices. This can be achieved by creating cross-functional teams, engaging external partners, and exploring new technologies and approaches.

By adopting these steps, organizations and leaders can avoid unsustainable and unethical leadership practices, promote sustainability and ethical values, and create a more responsible and sustainable future. Sustainability leaders have the responsibility to go beyond traditional CSR efforts and instead seek to create a net positive impact on society and the environment. This means aiming to leave the world in a better place than they found it, rather than simply minimizing their negative impacts. To achieve this, leaders need welcoming systems approaches to seek root causes, collaborating with multiple and diverse stakeholders, and becoming more competent in managing, innovating, and creating impactful sustainability solutions.

Key Takeaways

1. Sustainability leadership requires both ethics and ethos, with a focus on promoting responsible and transparent business activities that take into account the broader social and environmental impacts.
2. Ethical decision-making for sustainability involves considering the Precautionary Principle, the Intergenerational Equity Principle, and the Stakeholder Engagement Principle, which emphasize the need to prioritize long-term impacts and involve all relevant stakeholders in decision-making.
3. Developing a sustainability ethos involves promoting a set of values and practices that prioritize sustainability and responsible environmental stewardship, and creating a culture that encourages innovation and responsible behavior throughout the organization.
4. It is important to go beyond greenwashing and unsustainable ethics, and to prioritize genuine sustainability efforts that are backed by responsible decision-making and a strong sustainability ethos.

References

Dion, M., et al. (2022). *Humanizing business: What humanities can say to business*. Springer International Publishing.

Combe, C. (2022). *Introduction to global sustainable management*. SAGE Publications.

Manetti, G., & Bellucci, M. (2018). *Stakeholder engagement and sustainability reporting*. Taylor & Francis.

Meinhold, R. (2021). *Business ethics and sustainability*. Taylor & Francis.

McClimon, T. J. (2022, November 8). Bluewashing joins greenwashing as the new corporate whitewashing. *Forbes*. https://www.forbes.com/sites/timothyjmcclimon/2022/10/03/bluewashing-joins-greenwashing-as-the-new-corporate-whitewashing/?sh=5b141629660c

Miller, T. (2018). *Greenwashing culture*. Routledge.

Nassauer, S. (2012, January 24). Trying on shades of brown to scream green. Retrieved February 18, 2023, from *WSJ website*. https://www.wsj.com/articles/SB10001424052970203718504577180852718515394

Peel, J. (2005). *The precautionary principle in practice: Environmental decision-making and scientific uncertainty*. Federation Press.

Rendtorff, J. D. (2019). *Philosophy of management and sustainability: Rethinking business ethics and social responsibility in sustainable development*. Emerald Publishing Limited.

Heras Saizarbitoria, I., et al. (2022). Organizations' engagement with sustainable development goals: From cherry picking to SDG washing? *Corporate Social Responsibility and Environmental Management, 29*(2), 316–328.

Thiele, L. P., et al. (2011). *Working toward sustainability: Ethical decision-making in a technological world*. Wiley.

Vollero, A. (2021). *Greenwashing: Foundations and emerging research on corporate sustainability and deceptive communication*. Routledge.

PART II

Sustainability Management

This part of the book focuses on sustainability management, exploring various approaches and effective practices for managing sustainability across different sectors. Sustainability management plays a crucial role in achieving sustainability goals, and it is closely linked to sustainability leadership. This part of the book is designed to provide readers with a comprehensive understanding of the different tools, frameworks, and strategies used in sustainability management, as well as the challenges and opportunities associated with them. We explore the various practical aspects of sustainability practices at the organizational level and across sectors, specifically aspects of sustainability management through the lens of organizational effectiveness and stakeholders' well-being and we concentrate on the economic, environmental, social, and governance (E-ESG) model for understanding sustainability management organizational practices. We review core values-driven practices for sustainability management in organizations including the triple bottom line, life cycle assessment, and circular economy among others. The selected cases aim at giving a better and more concrete understanding of how these concepts apply in specific fields and contexts and along the examples of leading organizations and insightful initiatives. We explore the field of sustainability management across economic and industry sectors and review the emergence and value contribution that sustainability management makes to the 2030 Sustainability Agenda and some of its specific goals and targets.

We first introduce readers to different approaches to managing sustainability, including the Triple Bottom Line (TBL), Life Cycle Assessment, Circular Economy, Sustainable Risk Management, and Corporate Social Responsibility (Chapter 6). Then, we examine the importance and implications of an integrated model for ESG Framework for Sustainability Management, which integrates the economic, environmental, social, and governance (EESG) factors of sustainable development into an integrated approach (Chapter 7). We then explore sustainability management practices and applications across different sectors, including business, government, social, academic, healthcare, and technology. We also examine case studies from each sector to provide readers with a deeper understanding of the challenges and opportunities associated with sustainability management (Chapter 8). We also delve into sustainable management effective practices, including sustainable stakeholder management, supply chain management, social marketing, human resource management, financial sustainability management, sustainability strategy, negotiation, reporting, and alternative organizational structures (Chapter 9). We finally explore the future of sustainability management, discussing the main trends and challenges that are likely to shape the field in the years to come. We also highlight the importance of monitoring future sustainability management trends and the potential limits and downsides of sustainability management (Chapter 10).

CHAPTER 6

Approaches to Managing Sustainability

Abstract This chapter focuses on sustainability management and explores various approaches to managing sustainability. It reviews five key approaches to sustainability management, including the Triple Bottom Line (TBL), Life Cycle Assessment (LCA), Circular Economy (CE), Sustainable Risk Management (SRM), and Corporate Social Responsibility (CSR). Each approach is discussed in detail, highlighting its benefits and limitations. The sixth approach, ESG management, is reviewed in more detail in the subsequent chapter. The TBL approach emphasizes the importance of considering social, environmental, and economic impacts of business operations. LCA is a tool for analyzing the environmental impact of a product or service throughout its life cycle. CE is an economic system that aims to minimize waste and maximize the use of resources by keeping them in the economy for as long as possible. SRM involves identifying and managing potential risks associated with sustainability issues. Finally, CSR focuses on the responsibility of businesses to contribute to society and the environment. Overall, this chapter provides a comprehensive overview of different approaches to sustainability management, highlighting their potential to help organizations become more sustainable and responsible.

Keywords Sustainability management · Triple Bottom Line · Life Cycle Assessment · Circular Economy · Corporate Social Responsibility

M. Tavanti, *Developing Sustainability in Organizations*, Sustainable Development Goals Series, https://doi.org/10.1007/978-3-031-36907-0_6

"It's not purpose ahead of profits. It's purpose that drives better profits." "By putting itself to the service of others; by putting purpose above profit; and by holding up shared responsibility and prosperity as the kitemarks of success, business can and will be the catalyst for the transformative progress that the world so desperately needs."

—Paul Polman, Former CEO of Unilever

Developing and Shaping Sustainability Management

Warren Bennis, one of the pioneers of contemporary leadership studies, was fond of saying, "The manager does things right; the leader does the right thing." In relation to sustainability, this signifies the importance of connecting sustainability leadership for good mindsets with sustainability management for good skill sets. Sustainability management is therefore essential for optimizing existing processes and resources to achieve specific goals, whereas sustainability leadership is focused on setting the strategic direction of the organization and ensuring that it aligns with broader societal and environmental goals. Sustainability requires a long-term perspective and a commitment to balancing economic, social, and environmental considerations. Effective leaders are those who are able to articulate a compelling vision of a sustainable future and inspire their teams to work towards that goal. They need to be able to balance short-term demands with long-term objectives, and make difficult decisions that may require sacrificing short-term profits for long-term sustainability. Managers, on the other hand, are responsible for implementing the strategies and plans set by leaders, and ensuring that they are carried out in an efficient and effective manner. They need to be able to measure and monitor progress towards sustainability goals, and make adjustments as needed to ensure that they are being achieved in a responsible and cost-effective manner (Hahn, 2022). In short, both leadership and management are essential for achieving sustainability, but they play different roles in the process. Effective sustainability requires a strong partnership between leaders and managers, who are able to work together to create a vision of a sustainable future and implement the strategies needed to achieve it.

Sustainability management is rooted in responsible management, a field that has been advanced by numerous scholars and leaders in the field of sustainability and corporate social responsibility. We are grateful to them and their contribution to the practices and principles of sustainability management. Among the many we need to recognize in particular Klaus Schwab (2017), author of the book *The Fourth Industrial Revolution* and founder of the World Economic Forum, has been a leading voice in promoting the concept of stakeholder capitalism, which emphasizes the importance of balancing the interests of all stakeholders, including employees, customers, suppliers, and the environment. Michael Porter (2011) is well-known for developing the concept of *Creating Shared Value*, which emphasizes the interdependence between business and society and the importance of creating value for both. His contribution has been very important for making a case of sustainable values integration for competitive advantages. John Elkington (1999), also well-known for his book *Cannibals with Forks*, that introduced the TBL approach for responsible management. Professor Jeffrey Sachs (2015, 2020) at Columbia University has been a leading advocate for the SDGs and has worked extensively on issues related to sustainable development and poverty reduction. Paul Polman (2021), through his leadership at Unilever, has been a vocal advocate for responsible management and sustainable business practices, and has been recognized for his leadership in promoting the SDGs. Mary Robinson (2018), former President of Ireland and UN Special Envoy on Climate Change, has been instrumental for the promotion of human and indigenous rights in responsible business and has voiced the notion of climate justice in relation to gender and the SDGs. Peter Senge (1990), the author of the best-selling book *The Fifth Discipline* (1990), has been a leading voice in promoting the concept of "learning organizations," which emphasizes the importance of continuous learning and adaptation in the context of complex, rapidly changing environments. These scholars, leaders, and authors, among many others, have made important contributions to shape our understanding of CSR and its implications for sustainability management practices. They have set the foundation for framing and understanding how businesses can contribute to the achievement of the SDGs.

The Triple Bottom Line Approach

There are many approaches to sustainability management. One of the most well-known approaches, along the ESG management model reviewed in Chapter 7, is The Triple Bottom Line (TBL or 3BL). This is an approach for organizational management that takes into account three bottom lines: social, environmental, and financial. It involves balancing the economic, social, and environmental aspects of an organization's activities and can be used in various ways, including project evaluation (Ding & Runeson, 2020). It emphasizes the need for organizations to create value not only for shareholders but also for society and the environment. The triple bottom line approach recognizes that sustainability is not only about reducing negative impacts but also about creating positive impacts. Adopting a TBL approach can bring many advantages to organizations, including:

1. **Holistic view of performance**: The TBL approach encourages organizations to take a more holistic view of their performance, considering not just financial performance, but also social and environmental impact. This can help organizations to make more informed and responsible decisions, and to build a more sustainable and resilient business.
2. **Improved stakeholder relationships**: By considering the needs and interests of all stakeholders, including employees, customers, communities, and the environment, organizations can build stronger and more positive relationships with these groups. This can lead to increased trust, loyalty, and support from stakeholders, and can help to improve the organization's reputation.
3. **Risk management**: Adopting a TBL approach can help organizations to manage risk more effectively. By considering the social and environmental impact of their operations, organizations can identify and address potential risks before they become significant issues. This can help to reduce liability, avoid costly lawsuits, and protect the organization's reputation.
4. **Cost savings**: Adopting a TBL approach can help organizations to identify opportunities for cost savings. By reducing waste, improving energy efficiency, and using resources more efficiently, organizations can reduce their operating costs and improve their financial performance.
5. **Innovation**: Adopting a TBL approach can also foster innovation, as organizations are encouraged to develop new products and services that meet social and environmental needs in addition to financial ones. This can lead to the development of new markets, the creation of new revenue streams, and increased competitiveness.

Overall, the TBL approach can bring many advantages to organizations, including improved performance, better stakeholder relationships, risk management, cost savings, and innovation. By taking a more holistic view of organizational performance, organizations can build a more sustainable and resilient business, and contribute to a more sustainable and equitable world.

There are many organizations that have successfully integrated the TBL into their management practices. Beside the well-known leading example of Patagonia, Unilever, Interface, and Danone, here are a few more examples to highlight their successful TBL management integrations:

1. **Greyston Bakery**: Greyston Bakery is a social enterprise that has integrated a TBL approach into its management practices. The company provides employment opportunities and job training for people facing barriers to employment, including homelessness and incarceration. Greyston also sources its ingredients from local, sustainable suppliers and has implemented a range of environmental initiatives to reduce its impact.
2. **IKEA**: IKEA is a global home furnishing retailer that has integrated a TBL approach into its management practices. The company has set ambitious sustainability targets, including sourcing 100% renewable energy and using only sustainable materials by 2030. IKEA also works to improve the well-being of its customers and employees, and to support local communities.
3. **Grameen Bank**: Grameen Bank is a microfinance organization in Bangladesh that has integrated a TBL approach into its management practices. The bank provides small loans to low-income individuals, particularly women, to support entrepreneurship and economic development. Grameen Bank also promotes social and environmental sustainability through its lending practices.
4. **Natura & Co Natura**: Natura & Co is a Brazilian cosmetics company that has a strong commitment to sustainability and the TBL approach. The company uses natural and organic ingredients in its products and works to reduce its environmental impact. Natura & Co also has a strong commitment to social responsibility, including promoting fair labor practices and supporting local communities.
5. **Seventh Generation**: Seventh Generation is a US-based home and personal care product company that has integrated a TBL approach into its management practices. The company's products are designed

to be environmentally friendly and socially responsible. Seventh Generation also works to promote sustainable practices throughout its value chain, including sourcing sustainable materials and reducing waste.

These are just a few examples of the many organizations that have successfully integrated a TBL approach into their management practices. By considering social, environmental, and financial impact, these organizations have been able to build more sustainable and responsible businesses, and contribute to a more sustainable and equitable world.

It is important to also note studies pointing out TBL's shortcomings. For example, Savitz and Weber (2013) examine the limitations and practical implementation of TBL in CSR and consider it in comparison with the sometimes more effective role of regulation and legislation in promoting sustainable business practices. As we will see in more detail in Ch. 10, even John Elkington (1998), who coined the term in 1994, has offered some critiques of the TBL approach he helped popularize.

The Life Cycle Assessment Approach

The Life Cycle Assessment (LCA) approach involves assessing the environmental impacts of an organization's products or services throughout their entire life cycle, from raw material extraction to end-of-life disposal. LCA is sometimes called Environmental Life Cycle Assessment and it is commonly referred to as a "cradle-to-grave" analysis. The life cycle assessment approach can help organizations identify opportunities to reduce their environmental footprint and improve the sustainability of their products and services.

The LCA's key elements are: (1) identify and quantify the environmental loads involved; e.g., the energy and raw materials consumed, the emissions and wastes generated; (2) evaluate the potential environmental impacts of these loads; and (3) assess the options available for reducing these environmental impacts. Expanding on these, we identify five stages as core LCA elements:

1. **Goal and scope definition:** This is the first stage of LCA, where the purpose of the assessment is defined, and the system boundaries are established. The goal and scope definition stage includes identifying

the product or process to be assessed, determining the functional unit, and setting the system boundaries.

2. **Life cycle inventory (LCI)**: In this stage, data is collected on the inputs and outputs of each stage of the product or process life cycle. This includes raw materials extraction, production, distribution, use, and disposal.
3. **Life cycle impact assessment (LCIA)**: The data collected in the LCI stage is used to assess the potential environmental impacts associated with each stage of the life cycle. This includes impacts on climate change, air quality, water use, and other environmental factors.
4. **Interpretation**: In the interpretation stage, the results of the LCA are analyzed and communicated. This includes identifying areas of high environmental impact and opportunities for improvement, as well as communicating the findings to stakeholders.
5. **Review**: The review stage includes an independent review of the LCA process and results to ensure that the assessment is consistent with established standards and that the results are accurate and reliable.

Overall, the core elements of LCA provide a framework for evaluating the environmental impact of a product or process throughout its entire life cycle. By considering all stages of the life cycle, companies can identify areas for improvement and make more informed decisions about the environmental impact of their products or processes.

There are several advantages of using LCA in sustainability organizational management:

1. **Holistic approach**: LCA provides a comprehensive view of the environmental impact of a product or process throughout its entire life cycle. It considers all stages, from raw material extraction and production to use and disposal. This holistic approach helps companies identify areas of their operations that have the greatest environmental impact and where they can make the most significant improvements.
2. **Identifies hotspots**: LCA can identify hotspots or areas of a product's life cycle that have the most significant environmental impact. This can help companies focus their efforts on reducing the

impact of these areas, rather than spreading their efforts too thinly across the entire life cycle.

3. **Comparison of alternatives**: LCA can be used to compare the environmental impact of different products or processes, allowing companies to make more informed decisions when selecting materials or designing processes. This can help companies choose materials or processes that have a lower environmental impact.
4. **Encourages innovation**: LCA can encourage innovation by highlighting areas where new technologies or processes could be developed to reduce the environmental impact of a product or process.
5. **Stakeholder engagement**: LCA can be used to engage stakeholders, including customers, suppliers, and regulators, in discussions about the environmental impact of products or processes. This can help companies build trust and credibility with stakeholders and identify areas for collaboration and improvement.

Overall, LCA can be a valuable tool for companies looking to manage their environmental impact and promote sustainability. By providing a comprehensive view of the environmental impact of their products or processes, companies can make more informed decisions and identify areas for improvement.

Many companies, nonprofit organizations, and public agencies have used LCA in their sustainability management practices. Here are a few examples:

1. **Nestle**: Nestle used LCA to assess the environmental impact of its packaging and to identify opportunities for improvement. The company has set a goal of using 100% recyclable or reusable packaging by 2025.
2. **Patagonia**: Patagonia used LCA to assess the environmental impact of its clothing products and to identify areas for improvement. The company has implemented several initiatives to reduce its environmental impact, including using recycled materials and reducing water usage in production.
3. **Toyota**: Toyota used LCA to assess the environmental impact of its Prius hybrid car and to identify opportunities for improvement. The

company has implemented several initiatives to reduce its environmental impact, including using sustainable materials and reducing emissions in its production process.

4. **US Environmental Protection Agency (EPA)**: The EPA has used LCA to assess the environmental impact of various products and processes, including renewable energy sources and biofuels. The agency has also developed LCA tools and resources to help businesses and organizations evaluate their environmental impact.
5. **World Business Council for Sustainable Development (WBCSD)**: The WBCSD has developed a set of LCA guidelines and tools to help companies and organizations evaluate their environmental impact and identify areas for improvement.
6. **Nike**: Nike has used LCA to evaluate the environmental impact of its products and identify areas for improvement. The company has used LCA to assess the environmental impact of its footwear, apparel, and equipment, and has used the results to make changes to its products and manufacturing processes.
7. **Procter & Gamble**: Procter & Gamble has used LCA to assess the environmental impact of its products, including Pampers diapers and Tide laundry detergent. The company has used LCA to identify areas where it can reduce its environmental impact and has set goals to improve the sustainability of its products and operations.
8. **Environmental Defense Fund**: The Environmental Defense Fund has used LCA to assess the environmental impact of products and to develop guidelines for sustainable product design. The organization has used LCA to evaluate products such as paper bags, plastic bags, and disposable plates, and has used the results to develop recommendations for reducing the environmental impact of these products.

Overall, LCA is a widely used tool in sustainability management, and many companies, nonprofit organizations, and public agencies have successfully used LCA to identify areas for improvement and to reduce their environmental impact. By providing a comprehensive view of the environmental impact of a product or process, LCA can help organizations identify areas for improvement and make more informed decisions about sustainability.

The Circular Economy Approach

Circular Economy (CE) is an approach involving designing products and processes that minimize waste and pollution and maximize the reuse and recycling of materials. Charter (2017), Lacy and Rutqvist (2019), and Beckers et al. (2021) are some of the influential studies on the values of the circular economy in sustainability management. The circular economy approach emphasizes the need for organizations to shift from a linear "take-make-dispose" model to a more circular model that prioritizes resource efficiency and closed-loop systems. The four main concepts of the circular economy are:

1. **Designing out waste and pollution**: In a circular economy, products and processes are designed to minimize waste and pollution throughout their life cycle, from production to disposal. This involves designing products with the end in mind, so that materials can be easily recovered and reused or recycled.
2. **Keeping products and materials in use**: The circular economy aims to maximize the use of existing products and materials, rather than continually extracting and consuming new resources. This involves strategies like reuse, refurbishment, and recycling to keep products and materials in use for as long as possible.
3. **Regenerating natural systems**: In a circular economy, natural systems are valued and conserved, and efforts are made to restore and regenerate them. This involves practices like regenerative agriculture, reforestation, and habitat restoration to support healthy ecosystems and the services they provide.
4. **Fostering collaboration and innovation**: The circular economy requires collaboration among stakeholders across the value chain, including producers, consumers, and policymakers. It also requires innovation to develop new technologies, business models, and policy frameworks that can support a circular economy.

Adopting a circular economy approach can bring many advantages to organizations, including:

1. **Reduced environmental impact**: By designing products for longevity and reuse, and by prioritizing the use of recycled and

renewable materials, organizations can significantly reduce their environmental impact and carbon footprint.
2. **Increased efficiency**: Adopting circular practices can help organizations to streamline their operations, reduce waste, and use resources more efficiently. This can lead to cost savings and increased profitability.
3. **Improved resilience**: A circular economy approach can help organizations to become more resilient in the face of supply chain disruptions, resource scarcity, and other challenges. By relying less on finite resources and by building a more self-sustaining system, organizations can reduce their vulnerability to external shocks.
4. **New business opportunities**: The circular economy offers a range of new business opportunities, including the development of new products and services that are designed for circularity, the creation of new value chains based on resource sharing and collaboration, and the exploration of new business models that prioritize sustainability.
5. **Enhanced brand reputation**: Adopting circular practices can enhance an organization's brand reputation and increase customer loyalty. Consumers are increasingly concerned about sustainability and environmental impact, and are more likely to support businesses that prioritize these issues.

Overall, the adoption of a circular economy approach can bring significant benefits to organizations, including environmental, economic, and social benefits, and can help to drive a more sustainable and resilient future.

There are several organizations that have successfully integrated circular economy principles into their management. Here are some examples:

1. **Philips**: The Dutch multinational company has adopted a circular business model that involves leasing lighting solutions and other products to customers rather than selling them outright. Philips then takes back the used products and recycles the materials to create new products.
2. **Patagonia**: The outdoor clothing company has adopted a circular economy approach by encouraging customers to repair and reuse their clothing, rather than throwing it away. The company also

uses recycled materials to make new products and has launched a program to collect and recycle used clothing.

3. **Interface**: The carpet tile manufacturer has implemented a closed-loop system in which old carpets are collected and used to create new carpets. The company has also developed a range of environmentally friendly products, including carpets made from recycled fishing nets.
4. **MUD Jeans**: The sustainable denim company offers a leasing program that allows customers to rent a pair of jeans for a fixed period of time. At the end of the lease, the jeans are returned to the company, which then recycles the materials to make new jeans.
5. **Lego**: The toy manufacturer has set a target to make all its products from sustainable materials by 2030. It has also developed a program to collect and recycle used Lego bricks, which are then used to make new products.
6. **Renault**: This is a global car manufacturer that has been a leader in the circular economy in the automotive sector. The company has developed a range of circular initiatives, including a remanufacturing program that allows components to be reused, a battery recycling program, and a car-sharing service that promotes resource sharing. Renault has also set a goal to become carbon–neutral by 2050.
7. **Ellen MacArthur Foundation**: The Ellen MacArthur Foundation is a nonprofit organization that is dedicated to promoting the circular economy. The foundation works with businesses, governments, and academics to develop circular economy strategies and initiatives, and has been instrumental in driving the circular economy agenda forward.

These organizations are just a few examples of the many businesses that have successfully integrated circular economy principles into their management and operations. The circular economy is a growing movement, and more and more organizations are recognizing the benefits of this approach to sustainability.

The Sustainable Risk Management Approach

Sustainable Risk Management (SRM) is an approach involving identifying, assessing, and managing sustainability risks that could impact an organization's ability to achieve its sustainability goals. This includes risks related to climate change, resource depletion, regulatory compliance, social and environmental impacts, and reputation. SRM involves integrating sustainability risks into an organization's overall risk management framework and developing strategies to mitigate or manage those risks. SRM is a growing field that reflects how risks have shifted from traditional economic and financial risks to those posed by environmental and social factors. In addition, the management of organizations today considers external factors such as climate change, migration flows, stakeholders, partnerships, etc. Therefore, organizations would need to mitigate risks that are often social, global, cross-sector, and cross-generational. Sustainability offers a framework of analysis and action that goes beyond environmental concerns into diversity issues, governance aspects, and international/global supply chain. The sustainability management approach is an integrated approach to risk management that is necessary and promising. While apparently more basic than an approach for integrating sustainability, the risk management approach can also be very helpful for organizations who need to implement a practical sustainability strategy. SRM is an approach to managing sustainability risks that could impact an organization's ability to achieve its sustainability goals. It involves integrating sustainability risks into an organization's overall risk management framework and developing strategies to mitigate or manage those risks. Some of the core aspects of SRM include:

1. **Identifying sustainability risks**: This involves identifying and assessing the sustainability risks that are most relevant to the organization. This could include risks related to climate change, resource depletion, social and environmental impacts, regulatory compliance, and reputation.
2. **Assessing the potential impact of sustainability risks**: This involves assessing the potential impact of sustainability risks on the organization, including financial, reputational, and operational impacts.
3. **Developing risk management strategies**: This involves developing risk management strategies to mitigate or manage sustainability risks. This could include strategies such as diversifying supply chains, reducing resource consumption, implementing environmental management systems, and engaging stakeholders in sustainability initiatives.

4. **Implementing risk management strategies**: This involves implementing the risk management strategies that have been developed, and monitoring and evaluating their effectiveness.
5. **Reviewing and updating risk management strategies**: This involves regularly reviewing and updating risk management strategies to ensure that they remain relevant and effective in addressing the sustainability risks facing the organization.

Some examples of sustainable risk management strategies could include:

- Developing a climate change adaptation plan to mitigate the impacts of climate change on the organization's operations and supply chain.
- Conducting a life cycle assessment of the organization's products to identify opportunities for reducing their environmental footprint.
- Developing a stakeholder engagement strategy to ensure that the organization is addressing the social and environmental concerns of its stakeholders.
- Implementing an environmental management system (such as ISO 14,001) to systematically manage the organization's environmental impacts.
- Conducting due diligence on suppliers to ensure that they are meeting the organization's sustainability standards and minimizing the risks associated with their operations.

While SRM is a useful approach to managing sustainability risks, there are some limits to its effectiveness. Here are a few examples:

1. **Difficulty in predicting future risks**: SRM is based on the assumption that organizations can identify and manage sustainability risks effectively. However, it can be challenging to predict future sustainability risks, especially those that are related to emerging technologies or regulatory changes. This means that SRM may not always be effective in preventing or mitigating risks that were not anticipated.
2. **Lack of data**: SRM relies on accurate and reliable data to identify and assess sustainability risks. However, in some cases, data on sustainability risks may be limited or difficult to obtain, especially for smaller organizations or those operating in developing countries.

This can make it challenging to develop effective risk management strategies.

3. **Cost**: Implementing SRM strategies can be costly, especially for smaller organizations or those operating in sectors with thin profit margins. This can limit the ability of these organizations to invest in sustainability risk management.
4. **Limited scope**: SRM typically focuses on the sustainability risks that are most relevant to an organization's operations and supply chain. However, sustainability risks can be complex and interconnected, and it can be challenging to address them comprehensively.
5. **Over Reliance on risk management**: Finally, while SRM is an important approach to managing sustainability risks, it should not be relied on exclusively. Organizations should also take a proactive approach to sustainability by setting clear sustainability targets and embedding sustainability into their core business practices.

In summary, while SRM is an important approach to managing sustainability risks, it has its limits, and organizations should be aware of these limitations when developing their risk management strategies.

The Corporate Social Responsibility Approach

Corporate social responsibility (CSR) can be considered as an approach to sustainability management, as it involves integrating social, environmental, and economic concerns into business operations (Gutterman, 2020). This approach involves taking responsibility for the social and environmental impacts of an organization's activities. It includes engaging with stakeholders, supporting social and environmental causes, and implementing sustainable business practices. However, some argue that CSR, at its basic levels, is not adequate on its own for ensuring sustainability.

The levels of CSR are often described as a three-tiered model which includes the following:

1. **First Level - Compliance**: The first level of CSR involves compliance with legal and regulatory requirements. Companies at this level focus on meeting the minimum legal and ethical standards that are required by law, such as adhering to workplace health and safety regulations or complying with environmental regulations.

2. **Second Level - Philanthropy**: The second level of CSR involves philanthropic activities, such as charitable giving or volunteer work. Companies at this level may donate money or resources to social or environmental causes, or may encourage employees to volunteer in their local communities.
3. **Third Level - Strategic**: The third level of CSR is the most comprehensive, and involves integrating sustainability principles into the core business strategy. Companies at this level seek to create long-term value by addressing social and environmental issues in a way that is aligned with their overall business strategy. This may involve developing products or services that are more sustainable, adopting environmentally friendly practices in their operations, or creating partnerships with stakeholders to address social or environmental challenges.

It's important to note that these levels are not necessarily hierarchical, and companies can engage in multiple levels of CSR at the same time. However, by moving beyond basic legal compliance and engaging in strategic CSR, companies can create more meaningful and lasting impact on the environment and society.

Chris Laszlo, a sustainability expert and a professor at Case Western Reserve University, has written extensively on the integration of CSR and sustainability in companies. One of his key arguments is that companies should move beyond a traditional CSR approach and instead aim to create what he calls a "sustainable enterprise." Laszlo (2014) argues that a sustainable enterprise should move past philanthropic CSR activities and instead seek to integrate social and environmental considerations into the core business strategy. This involves developing new products and services that are designed to be more sustainable, adopting environmentally friendly practices in operations, and engaging with stakeholders to address social and environmental challenges. According to Laszlo (2003 and 2008), a sustainable enterprise is not only good for society and the environment, but it can also lead to greater financial performance and competitiveness. By adopting a more comprehensive approach to CSR and sustainability, companies can differentiate themselves from their competitors, reduce risks, and tap into new market opportunities. Overall, Laszlo's argument is that companies should move beyond a narrow view of CSR and instead aim to create more sustainable, long-term value by integrating sustainability principles into their core business strategy.

Through the integration of sustainability values, companies can become agents for change and enterprises for human flourishing.

CSR typically involves voluntary actions by companies to address social and environmental issues, such as reducing greenhouse gas emissions, implementing ethical labor practices, and donating to charitable causes. While these actions are positive and can make a difference, they may not be sufficient to address the systemic challenges that contribute to unsustainability. Critics argue that CSR can be used as a way for companies to appear socially and environmentally responsible while continuing to pursue profit at the expense of the planet and society. In some cases, companies may engage in greenwashing, or making misleading claims about their environmental practices to improve their public image.

Therefore, while CSR can be a useful approach for sustainability management, it may not be sufficient on its own. Many experts argue that a more comprehensive approach is needed, such as integrating sustainability principles into the core business strategy, adopting a circular economy approach, and using life cycle assessment to evaluate the environmental impact of products and processes. CSR can be a good framework for expressing a company's organizational commitment to sustainability. By adopting CSR policies and practices, companies can demonstrate their commitment to sustainability and show that they are taking steps to operate in a more responsible and ethical manner. However, it is important to note that CSR should not be the only approach that companies use to address sustainability issues. In order to truly integrate sustainability into their operations, companies should also consider adopting more comprehensive approaches such as the TBL, the SDG, or the SRM. These approaches go beyond CSR by considering the economic, social, and environmental impacts of business operations, and can help companies to develop more holistic sustainability strategies.

The Sustainable Development Goals Approach

Sustainable Development Goals (SDG), is an approach involving setting specific sustainability goals and objectives, and managing the organization towards achieving them. The organizational goals can be aligned and mapped with the SDGs. The approach uses SDG mapping tools that help organizations to identify and align their actions in a way that they can be associated and measured with 17 SDGs and its 169 targets. Management through sustainability goals involves tracking and reporting progress towards the goals but also engaging in a process for systematically and strategically integrating sustainability across all operations of the organization. Overall, the SDGs provide a useful framework for companies to manage their sustainability performance. Here are some steps that a company can take to use the SDGs for this purpose:

1. **Identify relevant SDGs**: Companies should identify the SDGs that are most relevant to their business operations, products and services, and stakeholders. They should also consider the SDGs that relate to their industry, geographic location, and impact areas.
2. **Set goals and targets**: Once the relevant SDGs have been identified, companies should set specific goals and targets that align with the SDGs. These goals should be measurable, time-bound, and relevant to the company's sustainability performance.
3. **Develop a sustainability strategy**: Companies should develop a sustainability strategy that incorporates the SDGs and outlines how they will achieve their goals and targets. The strategy should address all aspects of the company's operations, including supply chain management, product design, production processes, and customer engagement.
4. **Monitor and report progress**: Companies should regularly monitor their progress towards achieving their sustainability goals and targets. This can be done by tracking key performance indicators (KPIs) and reporting on them in sustainability reports. The reports should be transparent and accessible to stakeholders, including customers, investors, and employees.
5. **Engage stakeholders**: Companies should engage with stakeholders, including customers, suppliers, employees, and local communities, to ensure that their sustainability efforts are aligned with their needs and expectations. This can be done through regular communication, stakeholder consultations, and partnerships.

There are several tools available to map a company's performance towards the SDGs. Here are some examples described in general. Chapter 17 will analyze these tools in the context of impact measurements:

1. **SDG Compass**: The SDG Compass is a guide that provides practical guidance and tools for companies to align their strategies with

the SDGs. The tool includes a self-assessment questionnaire, which helps companies to assess their current performance and identify areas for improvement. The tool has useful and practical steps for organizations to map their own goals and performances with the SDGs (GRI, UNGC, WBCSD 2016).

2. **Global Reporting Initiative (GRI)**: The GRI provides a sustainability reporting framework that includes indicators for tracking progress towards the SDGs. The GRI Standards cover a wide range of sustainability topics and can be used to report on a company's performance in relation to the SDGs.
3. **The SDG Action Manager**: This is an online tool developed by the UNGC and B Lab to help businesses take action towards achieving the SDGs. The SDG Action Manager provides companies with a step-by-step guide to assess their sustainability performance, set goals, and track progress towards the SDGs.
4. **Sustainable Development Goals Knowledge Platform**: The Sustainable Development Goals Knowledge Platform provides a range of tools and resources to support companies in mapping their performance towards the SDGs. The platform includes a set of indicators and targets for each SDG, which can be used to track progress.
5. **Business Call to Action (BCtA)**: The BCtA is a platform that supports companies in developing business models that contribute to the SDGs. The platform provides a range of tools and resources, including a monitoring and evaluation framework that helps companies to track their progress towards the SDGs.
6. **Impact Management Project (IMP)**: The IMP is a forum that brings together investors, companies, and other stakeholders to develop a common approach to impact measurement and management. The IMP provides a set of standardized metrics for tracking progress towards the SDGs.

These tools can help companies to map their sustainability performance towards the SDGs and demonstrate their commitment to sustainable development. It is important to note that no single tool or framework can fully capture a company's performance towards the SDGs, and companies may need to use multiple tools and approaches to map their performance comprehensively. By using the SDGs as a framework for managing their sustainability performance, companies can demonstrate their commitment to sustainable development and contribute to a more sustainable future.

Many companies, nonprofit organizations, academic institutions, and government agencies have mapped their performance along the SDGs. Here are a few examples:

1. **Danone**: Danone is a global food and beverage company that has integrated the SDGs into its corporate strategy. The company has mapped its performance along the SDGs and reports on its progress annually. Danone has set a goal to become a B Corp, which is a certification for companies that meet high social and environmental standards.
2. **Unilever**: Unilever is a global consumer goods company that has integrated the SDGs into its sustainability strategy. The company has mapped its performance along the SDGs and has set targets to achieve a positive social and environmental impact across its value chain.
3. **The World Wildlife Fund (WWF)**: The WWF is a nonprofit organization that works to conserve nature and reduce the most pressing threats to the diversity of life on Earth. The organization has mapped its performance along the SDGs and has aligned its conservation efforts with the SDGs. The WWF also works with companies and governments to promote sustainable practices that contribute to the SDGs.
4. **Higher Education Institutions**: Arizona State University, USA, University of Waterloo, Canada, University of Bologna, Italy, University of Manchester, UK, University of Cape Town, South Africa, are few examples of universities who have made a commitment to the SDGs. They have integrated the SDGs into their sustainability strategy, set targets for each relevant SDG, and report on their sustainability performance in research, teaching, service, operations, and administration.
5. **The City of Buenos Aires**: The City of Buenos Aires, Argentina, has mapped its performance along the SDGs and has developed a strategic plan to align its policies and programs with the SDGs. The city has set targets for each of the SDGs and has developed a monitoring and evaluation framework to track progress.
6. **The Government of Colombia**: The Government of Colombia has integrated the SDGs into its national development plan and set

targets for each SDG. The government also reports on its progress in its Voluntary National Review.

7. **The United Nations Development Programme (UNDP)**: The UNDP is a United Nations agency that works to reduce poverty, promote sustainable development, and empower communities. The organization has mapped its performance along the SDGs and works with governments, civil society organizations, and the private sector to achieve the SDGs.

These are just a few examples of organizations across different sectors that have mapped their performance along the SDGs. Many other organizations are also working towards the SDGs and have integrated them into their sustainability strategies. Organizations are also contributing to the achievements of specific goals through their SDG commitments and demonstrated performances. Here are some examples of companies, nonprofits, and international organizations contributing to each of 17 Sustainable Development Goals:

1. **SDG 1—No Poverty**: The World Food Programme (WFP) provides food assistance to people affected by conflicts and disasters, contributing to the eradication of poverty.
2. **SDG 2—Zero Hunger**: Nestle, a food and beverage company, has committed to achieving zero net greenhouse gas emissions by 2050 and promoting sustainable agriculture, contributing to the goal of zero hunger.
3. **SDG 3—Good Health and Well-being**: Johnson & Johnson, a healthcare company, has developed a range of products and services that improve access to healthcare and support the prevention and treatment of diseases.
4. **SDG 4—Quality Education**: LEGO, a toy company, has developed a range of educational products that promote creativity, innovation, and problem-solving skills, contributing to the goal of quality education.
5. **SDG 5—Gender Equality**: Unilever, a consumer goods company, has set targets to achieve gender balance across all levels of its workforce and eliminate stereotypes in advertising, contributing to the goal of gender equality.

6. **SDG 6—Clean Water and Sanitation**: PepsiCo, a food and beverage company, has set targets to improve water efficiency across its operations and promote access to safe drinking water in the communities where it operates.
7. **SDG 7—Affordable and Clean Energy**: Tesla, an electric vehicle and renewable energy company, has developed innovative products that promote the transition to a low-carbon economy and support the goal of affordable and clean energy.
8. **SDG 8—Decent Work and Economic Growth**: Patagonia, an outdoor apparel company, has committed to promoting fair labor practices and environmental sustainability throughout its supply chain, contributing to the goal of decent work and economic growth.
9. **SDG 9—Industry, Innovation, and Infrastructure**: Google, a technology company, has developed a range of innovative products and services that support sustainable development and promote the goal of industry, innovation, and infrastructure.
10. **SDG 10—Reduced Inequalities**: The Body Shop, a cosmetics company, has developed a range of products that promote fair trade, gender equality, and social justice, contributing to the goal of reduced inequalities.
11. **SDG 11—Sustainable Cities and Communities**: Cisco, a technology company, has developed a range of smart city solutions that promote sustainable urban development and support the goal of sustainable cities and communities.
12. **SDG 12—Responsible Consumption and Production**: IKEA, a furniture and home goods company, has set targets to reduce its carbon footprint and promote circular economy principles in its operations and supply chain, contributing to the goal of responsible consumption and production.
13. **SDG 13—Climate Action**: Apple, a technology company, has committed to achieving carbon neutrality across its operations and supply chain by 2030 and developing innovative products that support the transition to a low-carbon economy.
14. **SDG 14—Life Below Water**: The Ocean Cleanup, a nonprofit organization, has developed a range of technologies and strategies to remove plastic waste from the oceans, contributing to the goal of life below water.

15. **SDG 15—Life On Land**: Conservation International is a nonprofit organization that works to protect biodiversity and promote sustainable land use practices around the world. The organization works with local communities, governments, and businesses to develop sustainable land use practices and protect threatened ecosystems.
16. **SDG 16—Peace, Justice, and Strong Institutions**: The International Committee of the Red Cross (ICRC) provides humanitarian assistance to people affected by conflicts and disasters and promotes respect for international humanitarian law, contributing to the goal of peace, justice, and strong institutions.
17. **SDG 17—Partnerships for the Goals**: The United Nations Global Compact, a voluntary initiative for companies to align their strategies with the SDGs, promotes collaboration and partnerships among businesses, civil society, and governments to achieve the global goals.

Small companies and organizations may face several challenges when it comes to using the SDGs to map their sustainability management and performance. Here are a few reasons why:

1. **Lack of Resources**: Small companies and organizations often have limited resources and may lack the capacity to devote time and money to sustainability initiatives. Mapping sustainability performance against the SDGs may require additional resources such as staff, tools, and data that small organizations may not have.
2. **Lack of Awareness**: Some small companies and organizations may not be aware of the SDGs and their relevance to their operations. Without a clear understanding of the SDGs and their potential impact, small organizations may not see the value in mapping their sustainability performance against them.
3. **Lack of Expertise**: Mapping sustainability performance against the SDGs requires expertise in sustainability reporting and data analysis. Small organizations may not have the in-house expertise needed to undertake such an analysis, and may not have the resources to hire external consultants.
4. **Limited Data Availability**: Small organizations may have limited data on their sustainability performance, which makes it difficult to

map their performance against the SDGs. Without access to reliable data, small organizations may struggle to understand their impact on sustainability issues and identify areas for improvement.

5. **Limited Stakeholder Engagement**: Engaging stakeholders such as customers, employees, and suppliers is essential for effective sustainability management. Small organizations may have limited resources to engage stakeholders and may struggle to build the necessary partnerships to achieve the SDGs.

While these challenges can be daunting, small companies and organizations can still take steps to use the SDGs to map their sustainability management and performance. For example, they can start by prioritizing a few SDGs that are most relevant to their business and focusing on improving their performance in those areas. They can also leverage existing sustainability reporting frameworks and tools to help them collect and analyze data on their sustainability performance. In addition, as technology rapidly advances, more tools will be available to make the SDG mapping more easily accessed and integrated. In any case, small and medium enterprises (SME) and small organizations with limited resources and capacity can engage with stakeholders and partners to build the necessary collaborations to make their contribution to the SDGs' count.

In this chapter, we reviewed some of the main approaches for integrating sustainability management into organizations. We included examples of companies, organizations, and government agencies who have successfully integrated these approaches and used the tools associated with them. These approaches are not mutually exclusive, and organizations can adopt multiple approaches depending on their goals, sector, and stakeholders. The key is to embed sustainability into an organization's core business practices and to take a long-term perspective that balances economic, social, and environmental considerations.

Key Takeaways

1. Sustainability management has several approaches that include Triple Bottom Line (TBL), Life Cycle Assessment (LCA), Circular Economy (CE), Sustainable Risk Management (SRM), Corporate Social Responsibility (CSR), and Sustainable Development Goals (SDG) approaches.

2. The TBL approach emphasizes the importance of considering social, environmental, and economic impacts of business operations, while LCA is a tool for analyzing the environmental impact of a product or service throughout its life cycle.
3. CE is an economic system that aims to minimize waste and maximize the use of resources by keeping them in the economy for as long as possible, while SRM involves identifying and managing potential risks associated with sustainability issues.
4. CSR focuses on the responsibility of businesses to contribute to society and the environment while the SDG approach focuses on identifying organizational goals and mapping them along the common goals.
5. These approaches are not mutually exclusive, and organizations can adopt multiple approaches depending on their goals, sector, and stakeholders.

References

Beckers, S., Borch, K., & van Dun, J. (2021). *Circular business: Collaborate and circulate*. Routledge.

Charter, M. (2017). *Designing for the circular economy*. Routledge.

Ding, G. K. C., & Runeson, G. (2020). A 'triple bottom line' approach to advanced project evaluation. Cambridge Scholars Publishing.

Elkington, J. (1998). Towards the sustainable corporation: Win-win-win business strategies for sustainable development. *California Management Review, 40*(2), 90–100. https://www.proquest.com/docview/216128357 [Accessed 14 Mar. 2023].

Elkington, J. (1999). *Cannibals with forks: The triple bottom line of 21st Century business*. New Society Publishers.

GRI, UNGC, WBCSD. (2016). *SDG compass: The guide for business action on the SDGs TM*. Retrieved March 14, 2023, from https://sdgcompass.org/aligning-your-business-with-the-sdgs/

Hahn, R. (2022). *Sustainability management: Global perspectives on concepts, instruments, and stakeholders*. Rüdiger Hahn.

Lacy, P., & Rutqvist, J. (2019). *The circular economy handbook: Realizing the circular advantage*. Palgrave Macmillan.

Laszlo, C. (2003). *The Sustainable Company*. Island Press.

Laszlo, C. (2008). *Sustainable Value: How the World's Leading Companies are Doing Well by Doing Good*. Stanford Business Books.

Laszlo, C., & Sorum Brown, J. (2014). *Flourishing Enterprise: The New Spirit of Business*. Stanford Business Books.

Polman, P., & Winston, A. (2021). *Net positive: How courageous companies thrive by giving more than they take*. Harvard Business Review Press.

Porter, M. E., & Kramer, M. R. (2011). Creating shared value. How to reinvent capitalism—and unleash a wave of innovation and growth. *Harvard Business Review*, *89*, 1–2. https://hbr.org/2011/01/the-big-idea-creating-shared-value [Accessed 14 Mar. 2023].

Robinson, M. (2018). *Climate justice: A man-made problem with a feminist solution*. Bloomsbury Publishing.

Sachs, J. (2015). *The age of sustainable development*. Columbia University Press.

Sachs, J. (2020). *The ages of globalization: Geography, technology, and institutions*. Columbia University Press.

Savitz, A., & Weber, K. (2013). *The triple bottom line: Does it all add up*. Wiley.

Schwab, K. (2017). *The fourth industrial revolution*. Crown Business.

Senge, P. M. (1990). *The fifth discipline: The art and practice of the learning organization*. Doubleday.

CHAPTER 7

EESG Organizational Sustainability Management

Abstract This chapter reviews and expands on the ESG framework, a frequently used approach for sustainability management. It provides case studies for crucial and emerging organizational practices for sustainability-related factors. It makes a case for an approach that integrates economic and financial performances to environmental, social, and governance (EESG). It explains how the ESG and EESG strategic frameworks are crucial for a more integrated and balanced assessment of the organizational objectives and activities in relation to sustainability. Many commitments to social and environmental performance such as carbon footprint are integrated with participatory and inclusive governance practices such as workplace culture and commitment to diversity and inclusion. Although not standardized, the ESG framework, becomes increasingly important for socially responsible investors who want to invest in companies that have a high ESG rating or score.

Keywords ESG Framework · Economic Factor · Carbon Credits · Community-Driven Development · Good Governance

M. Tavanti, *Developing Sustainability in Organizations*, Sustainable Development Goals Series,
https://doi.org/10.1007/978-3-031-36907-0_7

Business is a vital partner in achieving the Sustainable Development Goals. Companies can contribute through their core activities, and we ask companies everywhere to assess their impact, set ambitious goals and communicate transparently about the results.

—Ban Ki-moon, Former United Nations Secretary-General

About the ESG Framework for Sustainability Management

ESG (Environmental, Social, and Governance) is an approach to sustainability management. ESG refers to a set of criteria that investors use to evaluate a company's performance on environmental, social, and governance issues. However, in recent years, the ESG approach has also been adopted by companies themselves as a way to manage their sustainability impacts. For instance, McKinsey (2023) is one of the many organizations that build capacity for better integrating ESG management for creating sustainable, inclusive growth and increasing financial, societal, and environmental impact while ensuring long-term competitiveness. This is achieved by benchmarking, strategy development, initiative design, program execution, investor and external communications, and reporting. They use data-driven and proprietary solutions to support clients throughout their ESG journey and combine expertise in what drives value and impact within sectors with social expertise across ESG dimensions such as sustainability, net-zero, culture and talent, diversity, equity, and inclusion, economic development, public health, education, and future of work. The focus is on creating value and impact while managing risks and opportunities, setting measurable goals, and building capabilities that broaden impact.

Specifically, ESG factors are used to evaluate a company's performance in the areas of environmental sustainability, social responsibility, and corporate governance and for identifying the following objectives:

1. **Identifying Risks and Opportunities:** ESG factors can help organizations identify the risks and opportunities associated with environmental, social, and governance issues. By assessing their performance in these areas, companies can identify potential risks that could impact their operations, and identify opportunities for improvement and growth.

2. **Improving Corporate Governance:** ESG factors can help organizations improve their corporate governance by promoting transparency, accountability, and ethical behavior. This can help companies build trust with stakeholders and reduce the risk of negative impacts on the environment and society.
3. **Reducing Environmental Impact:** ESG factors can help organizations reduce their environmental impact by identifying areas where they can improve their energy efficiency, reduce waste and emissions, and adopt more sustainable business practices.
4. **Enhancing Social Responsibility**: ESG factors can help organizations enhance their social responsibility by promoting fair labor practices, respecting human rights, and contributing to the development of local communities.
5. **Attracting Investment:** ESG factors are increasingly important to investors who are looking for companies that are committed to sustainable business practices. By focusing on ESG factors, organizations can improve their reputation and attract investment from socially responsible investors.

The use of ESG factors in organizational sustainability management can help companies achieve their sustainability goals, reduce risk, and enhance their reputation as responsible corporate citizens. They can also be very useful to organizations that want to identify and manage risks and opportunities related to environmental, social, and governance issues. In other words, ESG can be seen as a more comprehensive approach to sustainability management, as it recognizes that sustainability issues go beyond just environmental concerns. By taking a broader view of sustainability, companies can identify areas where they can make a positive impact and develop strategies to address potential risks.

It's worth noting that there is some debate about the effectiveness of ESG as an approach to sustainability management. Proponents of ESG argue that it can be a useful tool for promoting sustainability and responsible business practices. On the other hand, some critics argue that the ESG approach can be superficial and fail to address deeper structural issues within companies and the broader economic system. Here are some of the known limits of using ESG factors in organizational sustainability management.

1. **Lack of Standardization**: There is no standardized way of measuring ESG factors, which means that companies may use different methods to evaluate their performance in these areas. This can make it difficult to compare companies and assess their ESG performance.
2. **Data Availability**: There may be a lack of reliable and consistent data on ESG factors, which can make it difficult for companies to accurately evaluate their performance and make informed decisions.
3. **Subjectivity**: ESG factors are often based on subjective criteria, which means that different stakeholders may have different opinions on what constitutes good or bad performance in these areas. This can make it challenging for companies to develop an ESG strategy that satisfies all their stakeholders.
4. **Time Horizon**: ESG factors may focus on long-term sustainability issues, such as climate change or social justice, which can be difficult to address in the short term. This can make it challenging for companies to balance short-term and long-term objectives.
5. **Limited Scope**: ESG factors may not cover all relevant sustainability issues, such as supply chain management or product design. This can limit the effectiveness of ESG strategies in addressing broader sustainability challenges.

While ESG factors can be a useful tool for organizational sustainability management, it is important to recognize their limitations and use them in conjunction with other tools and strategies to effectively address sustainability challenges. More evidently, the lack of integration of economic and financial measures is one of the major limitations of traditional ESG (only environmental, social, and governance factors) frameworks. ESG frameworks traditionally focus on non-financial measures of sustainability, such as environmental and social impact, but often fail to incorporate and effectively integrate financial performance and economic factors into their assessments. This can limit the effectiveness of ESG strategies in creating sustainable value for companies and investors.

The EESG Framework as an Integrated Approach

To address this limitation, a new framework called EESG (Economic with Environmental, Social, and Governance) has emerged. EESG takes a more integrated approach to sustainability by incorporating economic and financial factors into the assessment of environmental, social, and governance risks and opportunities. By doing so, EESG aims to provide a more comprehensive assessment of a company's sustainability performance, and to create more sustainable value for companies and investors. According to Bellucci and Bini (2019), the traditional sequential approach to sustainability reporting using ESG as an additive approach that separates environmental, social, and economic issues can be overcome with an integrated approach. This new approach will enable companies to effectively communicate their commitment to sustainability and demonstrate how environmental, social, and governance issues truly have a role and impact on their operations (Fig. 7.1).

EESG typically stands for Economic with Environmental, Social, and Governance factors. These factors are used to assess the sustainability and ethical impact of a company or an investment. They provide a framework for evaluating how well a company is managing its responsibilities in each of these areas.

1. **Economic (E):** This factor evaluates the financial performance and stability of a company, including its revenue, profitability, and long-term growth prospects. It also considers how the company creates value for its stakeholders, such as customers, employees, suppliers, and investors. Companies with strong economic performance are more likely to attract investors and maintain a competitive edge in the market.
2. **Environmental (E):** This factor considers the impact a company has on the natural environment, such as its carbon footprint, waste management, energy efficiency, and overall ecological impact. Companies with strong environmental practices are more likely to be sustainable and successful in the long term.
3. **Social (S):** This factor assesses the company's impact on society, including its relationships with employees, customers, suppliers, and local communities. It considers issues such as diversity and inclusion, employee health and safety, customer satisfaction, and community engagement. Companies with strong social practices are more likely to build trust, loyalty, and goodwill with stakeholders, which can contribute to long-term success.
4. **Governance (G):** This factor examines the company's leadership, board structure, and management practices, focusing on transparency, accountability, and ethical behavior. Good governance

Fig. 7.1 Economic with Environmental, Social, and Governance factors

practices help to minimize risks and ensure that a company is run with the best interests of its stakeholders in mind.

EESG factors have gained significant attention from investors, regulators, and other stakeholders in recent years, as they recognize the importance of these factors in determining the long-term success and sustainability of companies. By evaluating EESG performance, investors can make more informed decisions and potentially mitigate risks associated with companies that do not effectively manage their EESG responsibilities.

Overall, the EESG framework is a better and more comprehensive model for integrating financial and economic factors with non-financial environmental, social, and governance factors. By doing so, it provides a better understanding of the economic impact of sustainability on a company's long-term financial performance. This can help companies to identify new business opportunities, reduce costs, and mitigate risks associated with sustainability challenges. In other words, while traditional ESG frameworks have limitations related to the lack of integration of economic and financial measures, the emerging EESG framework takes a more integrated approach to sustainability management, and seeks to create more sustainable value for companies and investors by considering the economic, environmental, social, and governance aspects of a company's performance.

The concept of EESG is relatively new. The slow adoption of integrated reporting (IR) explains its novelty but also its future directions for more comprehensive and better integrated sustainability reporting (Bellucci & Bini, 2019). Academic studies are still limited and some of them use the term to indicate "ethics" instead of "economic" factor for the added E (Razaee, 2021). In addition, many companies are still in the process of integrating this approach into their sustainability management strategies. However, there are some companies that have already started to use the EESG approach to manage sustainability. Here are a few examples:

1. **Siemens:** Siemens is a global technology company that has integrated EESG factors into its sustainability strategy. The company's sustainability program is called "Vision 2020+," and it includes targets for both financial performance and sustainability performance. Siemens has set targets for reducing greenhouse gas emissions, increasing renewable energy capacity, and promoting sustainable business practices.
2. **Danone:** Danone is a food and beverage company that has integrated EESG factors into its sustainability strategy. The company's sustainability program is called "One Planet. One Health" and it includes targets for both financial performance and sustainability performance. Danone has set targets for reducing greenhouse gas emissions, increasing the use of renewable energy, and promoting sustainable agriculture.
3. **Royal DSM:** Royal DSM is a global science-based company that has integrated EESG factors into its sustainability strategy. The

company's sustainability program is called "Brighter Living Solutions," and it includes targets for both financial performance and sustainability performance. DSM has set targets for reducing greenhouse gas emissions, increasing the use of renewable energy, and promoting sustainable products and solutions.

4. **Ørsted**: Ørsted is a Danish renewable energy company that has integrated EESG factors into its sustainability strategy. The company's sustainability program is called "Green Energy for All," and it includes targets for both financial performance and sustainability performance. Ørsted has set targets for reducing greenhouse gas emissions, increasing renewable energy capacity, and promoting sustainable business practices.
5. **Allianz:** Allianz is a global insurance and financial services company that has integrated EESG factors into its sustainability strategy. The company's sustainability program is called "Allianz Purpose," and it includes targets for both financial performance and sustainability performance. Allianz has set targets for reducing greenhouse gas emissions, promoting diversity and inclusion, and investing in sustainable infrastructure.
6. **Enel**: Enel is an Italian multinational energy company that has integrated EESG factors into their sustainability management strategy. They have set ambitious sustainability goals, including becoming carbon-neutral by 2050 and promoting sustainable energy solutions. They have also developed an EESG performance dashboard that allows them to monitor and report on their sustainability performance.
7. **BlackRock:** BlackRock is the world's largest asset management firm, and they have integrated EESG factors into their investment strategy. They use EESG analysis to identify risks and opportunities related to sustainability issues and to inform their investment decisions. They have also developed a sustainability reporting framework that integrates EESG factors into their financial reporting.
8. **Nestle:** Nestle is a global food and beverage company that has integrated EESG factors into their sustainability management strategy. They have set ambitious sustainability goals, including reducing their environmental impact, promoting sustainable agriculture, and improving access to clean water. They have also developed an EESG performance framework that allows them to monitor and report on their sustainability performance.

9. **BBVA**: BBVA is a global financial services company that has integrated EESG factors into their sustainability management strategy. They have set ambitious sustainability goals, including reducing their carbon footprint, promoting financial inclusion, and improving access to sustainable finance. They have also developed an EESG risk management framework that integrates sustainability considerations into their decision-making processes.
10. **Toyota:** Toyota, a Japanese multinational automotive manufacturer, has integrated EESG factors into their sustainability strategy. They have set ambitious sustainability goals, such as achieving zero carbon emissions from their operations by 2050 and promoting sustainable mobility solutions. They also consider the economic impact of their sustainability initiatives, such as the potential for increased profitability through the development of sustainable products and services.

These are just a few examples of companies that have used EESG factors for managing sustainability. As EESG gains more popularity, it is likely that more companies will integrate this framework into their sustainability management strategies. In the near future, we can expect to see more companies integrating economic, environmental, social, and governance factors into their sustainability reporting and strategies for integrating sustainability in all aspects of the organization (Sikka & Luo, 2017).

As we will review in more detail in Part IV where we examine sustainability impact, there are several tools and methods that can be used to integrate the EESG framework in the evaluation of a company's sustainability performance. These include:

1. **Integrated reporting:** Integrated reporting is a framework that aims to provide a holistic view of a company's performance by integrating financial and non-financial information. It involves reporting on the company's financial performance alongside its sustainability performance, including its EESG performance.
2. **Sustainability accounting**: Sustainability accounting involves measuring and reporting on the social and environmental impacts of a company's activities, as well as the economic impacts of sustainability initiatives. This can help to identify the economic benefits

of sustainability initiatives, such as cost savings or new business opportunities.

3. **Life cycle assessment:** Life cycle assessment (LCA), as we introduced it earlier, is a method for evaluating the environmental impact of a product or service over its entire life cycle, from production to disposal. LCA can be used to identify the environmental impact of a company's activities and to evaluate the economic and social implications of different sustainability strategies.
4. **Social return on investment:** Social return on investment (SROI) is a framework for measuring the social and environmental impact of a company's activities. It involves identifying and valuing the social and environmental benefits of a company's activities and comparing them to the costs.
5. **Environmental, social, and governance (ESG) ratings**: ESG ratings are a tool for evaluating a company's sustainability performance based on its environmental, social, and governance practices. ESG ratings can be used to identify areas for improvement and to benchmark a company's performance against its peers.

These tools and methods can be used individually or in combination to integrate the EESG framework in the evaluation of a company's sustainability performance. By using these tools, companies can gain a more comprehensive understanding of their sustainability performance and identify opportunities for improvement. Overall, EESG reporting, parallel to other kinds of sustainability reporting, and integrated reporting is to provide stakeholders with a more comprehensive view of a company's performance and impact beyond traditional financial reporting. The important value added with these more recent approaches is the more balanced and integrated reporting of the overall financial and non-financial reports of the organization. By providing greater transparency and accountability, these forms of reporting can help companies build trust and credibility with their stakeholders, and ultimately support more sustainable and responsible business practices.

E-Economic Factor for Sustainable Development

Economic and financial factors play a critical role in sustainability management as it is the engine that drives many human activities, including production, consumption, and investment (Bose et al., 2019). Economic factors often explain the success and failures of implementing sustainability in numerous contexts and cases (Brinkmann & Garren, 2018). Sustainable economic development aims to promote economic growth while minimizing negative impacts on the environment and society. It is about creating an economic system that can be sustained over the long term without degrading the natural and social resources on which it depends. In a way, the economic dimension of sustainability goes to the core of what we mean by sustainable development. The very notion of sustainable development encompasses sustainability and the idea of achieving economic, social, and environmental goals simultaneously. It is an approach to development that seeks to balance economic growth, social progress, and environmental protection in a way that benefits present and future generations. Sustainable development recognizes that economic growth is necessary for the well-being of people, but it should be achieved in a way that is environmentally and socially sustainable. This means that economic development should not be pursued at the expense of the environment or the well-being of people, and that the benefits of economic growth should be shared equitably.

That is why economic sustainable development uses the term "prosperity" instead of "profit" because it reflects a broader and more holistic view of economic progress (Mayer, 2018). While profit is an important component of economic activity, it is a narrow measure that only considers financial gain. Prosperity, on the other hand, encompasses a wider range of factors that contribute to overall well-being and quality of life. Prosperity takes into account not only economic factors like income and employment, but also social and environmental factors such as health, education, equality, and ecological sustainability. By considering these factors, prosperity promotes a more balanced and sustainable approach to economic development that benefits all members of society. Moreover, sustainable economic development emphasizes the long-term well-being of society, rather than short-term gains for a few individuals or corporations. Prosperity aligns better with this goal since it focuses on creating shared value for all stakeholders, rather than just maximizing profits for a few. Prosperity reflects a more holistic and long-term view of economic progress that includes social, environmental, and economic factors.

In other words, sustainable economic development is an approach to economic growth that aims to balance economic progress with environmental protection and social well-being. There are important relations to be taken into consideration for economic sustainability in relation to social economy and circular economy. To use the analogy of a pie, economic systems whose only concern is economic growth ask the question: *How can we grow the pie?* Social economy solutions, whose main concern is the economic effect on society in terms of equity and social development, ask the questions: *Who accesses the pie? How is the pie distributed?* Circular economies that are concerned with environmental aspects and how the needs of future generations will be met, ask the question: *How long will the pie last?* Sustainable economic development asks all these questions together. It is an approach to economic growth that aims to balance economic progress with environmental protection and social well-being. Therefore, there are several key aspects of sustainable economic development that affect efficiency, energy, production, but also social equity and green innovation:

1. **Resource Efficiency**: Sustainable economic development promotes the efficient use of resources, including energy, water, and raw materials. This can be achieved by adopting technologies and practices that reduce waste, improve energy efficiency, and minimize environmental impacts. Economic solutions may include measures such as building retrofits, which improve the energy performance of buildings, and the use of efficient appliances and lighting.
2. **Renewable Energy**: Sustainable economic development encourages the use of renewable energy sources such as wind, solar, hydro, and geothermal power. This reduces reliance on fossil fuels and helps to mitigate the negative impacts of climate change.
3. **Sustainable Agriculture:** Sustainable economic development promotes environmentally sustainable farming practices that protect soil, water, and biodiversity. This includes practices such as organic farming, agroforestry, and the use of integrated pest management. It may also include techniques such as regenerative agriculture, which focuses on building healthy soil and improving ecosystem health.
4. **Social Equity:** Sustainable economic development aims to improve social equity by creating opportunities for all members of society to benefit from economic growth. This includes promoting access to education, healthcare, and basic services, as well as creating job opportunities and supporting small businesses.
5. **Green Innovation:** Sustainable economic development encourages the development of innovative technologies and practices

that promote sustainability. This includes developing new eco-friendly products and services, as well as improving existing products and processes to reduce environmental impacts. This may include sustainable transportation solutions for low-carbon modes of transportation (public transit, biking, and walking) including the use of electric and hybrid vehicles, and the development of sustainable fuels.

6. **Circular Economy:** Sustainable economic development aims to promote a circular economy, which involves reducing waste and reusing and recycling resources. This can be achieved by designing products to be more durable, repairable, and recyclable, as well as encouraging the development of recycling and reuse infrastructure.

Overall, sustainable economic development is about promoting economic growth while protecting the environment and improving social well-being. It involves a shift towards more sustainable practices and technologies that can support long-term prosperity and sustainability. In addition, sustainable economic development can also create new business opportunities and jobs, particularly in sectors such as renewable energy, green technology, and sustainable agriculture. These economic solutions also include social enterprises. As we will explore in detail in Part III, social entrepreneurship involves the creation of businesses that have a social or environmental mission, as well as a financial goal. It can include the creation of products and services that address social and environmental challenges, such as clean water, affordable housing, and renewable energy. These industries not only provide economic benefits but also contribute to reducing environmental degradation and improving social well-being.

Economic Aspects of the SDGs

All of the 17 SDGs include economic, environmental, and social aspects of sustainability. Here are some examples of the economic aspects of sustainability exemplified in each of the goals:

1. **No Poverty**: This goal focuses on reducing poverty, which is often caused by economic inequalities. Economic aspects of sustainability are exemplified by promoting inclusive economic growth and creating decent work opportunities.

2. **Zero Hunger**: This goal focuses on ensuring food security and promoting sustainable agriculture. Economic aspects of sustainability are exemplified by supporting small farmers, promoting rural development, and investing in sustainable agriculture.
3. **Good Health and Well-being**: This goal focuses on improving health outcomes and well-being. Economic aspects of sustainability are exemplified by promoting access to affordable and quality healthcare services and supporting research and development of new health technologies.
4. **Quality Education**: This goal focuses on ensuring inclusive and quality education for all. Economic aspects of sustainability are exemplified by investing in education infrastructure, promoting access to educational resources, and supporting vocational training programs.
5. **Gender Equality:** This goal focuses on promoting gender equality and empowering women and girls. Economic aspects of sustainability are exemplified by promoting equal access to economic opportunities and reducing gender pay gaps.
6. **Clean Water and Sanitation:** This goal focuses on ensuring access to clean water and sanitation. Economic aspects of sustainability are exemplified by promoting sustainable water management practices and investing in water infrastructure.
7. **Affordable and Clean Energy**: This goal focuses on promoting access to affordable and clean energy. Economic aspects of sustainability are exemplified by investing in renewable energy sources and promoting energy efficiency.
8. **Decent Work and Economic Growth:** This goal focuses on promoting sustained, inclusive, and sustainable economic growth, full and productive employment, and decent work for all. Economic aspects of sustainability are exemplified by promoting job creation, supporting small and medium-sized enterprises, and investing in skills development.
9. **Industry, Innovation, and Infrastructure**: This goal focuses on promoting sustainable industrialization and innovation, and improving infrastructure. Economic aspects of sustainability are exemplified by promoting the development of sustainable technologies and infrastructure, and supporting the growth of sustainable industries.

10. **Reduced Inequalities**: This goal focuses on reducing inequalities within and among countries. Economic aspects of sustainability are exemplified by promoting inclusive economic growth, reducing income inequality, and promoting social protection programs.
11. **Sustainable Cities and Communities**: This goal focuses on promoting sustainable and resilient cities and communities. Economic aspects of sustainability are exemplified by promoting sustainable urban development, improving urban infrastructure, and promoting affordable housing.
12. **Responsible Consumption and Production:** This goal focuses on promoting sustainable patterns of consumption and production. Economic aspects of sustainability are exemplified by promoting sustainable production practices, reducing waste and pollution, and promoting the use of eco-friendly products.
13. **Climate Action:** This goal focuses on combating climate change and its impacts. Economic aspects of sustainability are exemplified by promoting the development of low-carbon technologies, reducing greenhouse gas emissions, and supporting the growth of the green economy.
14. **Life Below Water**: This goal focuses on conserving and sustainably using the oceans, seas, and marine resources. Economic aspects of sustainability are exemplified by promoting sustainable fishing practices, reducing marine pollution, and promoting the growth of the blue economy.
15. **Life on Land:** This goal focuses on protecting, restoring, and promoting sustainable use of terrestrial ecosystems, sustainably managing forests, combating desertification, halting and reversing land degradation, and halting biodiversity loss. Economic aspects of sustainability are exemplified by promoting sustainable land use practices, investing in sustainable forestry, and supporting the growth of sustainable tourism.
16. **Peace, Justice, and Strong Institutions:** This goal focuses on promoting peaceful and inclusive societies and strengthening institutions. Economic aspects of sustainability are included in the investments for the targets aiming at reducing corruption and promoting the rule of law and human rights.
17. **Partnerships for the Goals:** This SDG aims to strengthen global partnerships for sustainable development. Economic aspects are evident in the targets for increasing international cooperation and

promoting multi-stakeholder partnerships for sustainable development.

Overall, the economy plays a vital role in achieving the SDGs and for prompting sustainability management in organizations. The blueprint of the SDGs with its targets integrates those economic development with human development, social well-being, and environmental health. Promoting sustainable economic development is essential to achieving long-term sustainability goals.

Economic Mechanisms for Sustainability

Other key economic aspects of sustainability management include the responsibility to promote sustainable finance through responsible impact investing through sustainable supply chains and specific carbon exchange mechanisms. It involves growth of sustainability investing, impact investing, and other financial mechanisms promoting and scaling sustainable solutions. There are various financial, trade, and economic mechanisms and solutions that can promote sustainability. Here are some examples:

1. **Carbon pricing:** Carbon pricing is a mechanism that puts a price on carbon emissions to incentivize businesses and individuals to reduce their carbon footprint. It can include measures such as a carbon tax or a cap-and-trade system. Examples of countries that have implemented a carbon tax include Sweden, Norway, and Switzerland. Examples of countries that have implemented a cap-and-trade system include the European Union and China. At the company level, Microsoft has implemented an internal carbon fee that charges each business unit within the company for its carbon emissions. The proceeds from the fee are used to fund renewable energy and energy efficiency projects.
2. **Sustainable investment:** Sustainable investment, also known as socially responsible investing, involves investing in companies and projects that prioritize environmental, social, and governance (ESG) criteria. It may include investments in renewable energy, sustainable agriculture, and other sectors which promote sustainability. Examples of sustainable investing include renewable energy, sustainable

agriculture, clean technology, social impact, corporate governance, environmental conservation, and community development. These investments aim to promote sustainable practices, generate positive social and environmental impacts, and provide financial returns for investors.

3. **Green bonds:** Green bonds are financial instruments that raise funds for environmentally friendly projects, such as renewable energy and energy efficiency. An example is when Apple Inc. in 2016 issued a $1.5 billion green bond to fund renewable energy projects, such as solar and wind power generation, in its supply chain. Another example is Iberdrola S.A., a Spanish energy company that in 2019 issued a €1.5 billion green bond to fund renewable wind and solar power energy projects in Europe.
4. **Sustainable public procurement:** Sustainable public procurement involves using public procurement policies and procedures to promote sustainability. It measures such as requiring suppliers to meet sustainability criteria, such as using sustainable materials and reducing carbon emissions. One example of socially responsible procurement is when governments use sustainable public procurement to promote social sustainability by encouraging the purchase of goods and services from companies that demonstrate good labor practices and provide safe working conditions for their employees. The European Union (EU), for example, has adopted a comprehensive framework for sustainable public procurement that includes guidelines and criteria for environmental, social, and economic factors in procurement processes. The EU has also set ambitious targets for the use of sustainable procurement in its member states. The United States has established the Sustainable Acquisition Program to promote sustainable public procurement in federal agencies. The program includes guidelines and training for federal procurement officers to help them incorporate sustainability considerations into their procurement processes.
5. **Sustainable trade agreements:** Sustainable trade agreements include measures to promote sustainability in international trade, such as requirements for sustainable production practices and protection of environmental and labor standards. Examples include the Africa Continental Free Trade Area (AfCFTA), a trade agreement between 54 African countries which is designed to promote sustainable development, create jobs, and reduce poverty. Another

example is The Comprehensive and Progressive Agreement for Trans-Pacific Partnership (CPTPP), a trade agreement between 11 countries in the Asia–Pacific region that has provisions for protecting the environment, promoting labor rights, and encouraging sustainable development.

6. **Payment for ecosystem services (PES):** Payment for ecosystem services involves paying landowners and communities to provide ecosystem services, such as carbon sequestration and biodiversity conservation. Examples of PES programs include: Water Funds (where individuals and organizations contribute to the conservation and restoration of watersheds); Conservation Easements (legal agreements in which landowners agree to limit the use of their land in exchange for payments); Carbon Offset Programs (where individuals and organizations offset their carbon emissions by paying for projects that reduce greenhouse gas emissions or sequester carbon); Biodiversity Conservation Payments (where individuals and organizations pay for the conservation and restoration of ecosystems and biodiversity); and Soil Carbon Sequestration (where individuals and organizations pay for activities that increase the amount of carbon stored in soils). See the REDD+ Case.
7. **Eco-labeling:** Eco-labeling involves the use of labels to identify products that meet environmental and social sustainability criteria, such as using sustainable materials and reducing carbon emissions. Examples of eco-labeling include: ENERGY STAR managed by the U.S. Environmental Protection Agency that certifies products such as appliances, electronics, and lighting; the Forest Stewardship Council (FSC) for paper, wood, and furniture; Fairtrade Certification program that ensures that products (such as coffee, tea, and chocolate) are produced and traded under fair and sustainable conditions; Green Seal, a certification program for cleaning products, paints, and office supplies; and LEED (Leadership in Energy and Environmental Design) a certification program managed by the U.S. Green Building Council that promotes sustainable building design and construction. These are just a few examples of eco-labeling programs. By providing consumers with information about the environmental impact of products and services, eco-labeling programs can help to promote sustainable consumption and support the growth of a green economy.

In summary, financial, trade, and economic mechanisms and solutions that promote sustainability include carbon pricing, sustainable investment, green bonds, sustainable public procurement, sustainable trade agreements, eco-labeling, sustainable development goals, and payment for ecosystem services. These programs aim to incentivize sustainable practices, promote sustainable investment, and provide economic incentives for sustainability efforts.

Case 7.1 REDD+ and Carbon Credits

REDD+ stands for "Reducing Emissions from Deforestation and Forest Degradation" and is a global program aimed at reducing greenhouse gas emissions by protecting and restoring forests. REDD+ program is an example of Payment for Ecosystem Services (PES) because it provides financial incentives for the conservation and sustainable management of forests, which are critical ecosystems that provide a range of services such as carbon sequestration, biodiversity conservation, and water regulation. The program works by providing financial incentives to developing countries that take action to reduce deforestation and forest degradation. REDD+ is related to sustainable economic development because it creates economic incentives for countries to protect their forests, which can provide significant economic benefits. These benefits include:

1. **Carbon credits:** REDD+ provides financial incentives to developing countries that reduce their carbon emissions by protecting their forests. These countries earn carbon credits that can be sold on carbon markets, creating a new source of revenue.
2. **Biodiversity conservation**: Forests are home to a diverse range of plant and animal species, many of which are not found anywhere else on Earth. Protecting these species and their habitats creates economic opportunities in fields such as ecotourism and bioprospecting.
3. **Sustainable forestry:** REDD+ can incentivize sustainable forestry practices that promote long-term economic benefits, such as selective logging and forest restoration.
4. **Community development**: REDD+ can also support local communities by providing new sources of income, such as through payments for ecosystem services, and promoting sustainable livelihoods that do not rely on forest destruction.

In other words, REDD+ is a program that promotes forest protection and restoration as a way to reduce greenhouse gas emissions, and it creates economic incentives for countries to take action. This program can promote sustainable economic development by providing new sources of revenue, promoting sustainable forestry practices, conserving biodiversity, and supporting local communities. While REDD+ has the potential to contribute to sustainable economic development and climate change mitigation, it has also faced several critiques. Some of the main critiques are:

1. **Permanence:** One concern is that forest protection and restoration measures may not be permanent and may be subject to reversal in the future. This could lead to carbon emissions being released back into the atmosphere and undermining the effectiveness of the program.
2. **Additionality:** Another concern is that the financial incentives provided by REDD+ may not be sufficient to change the behavior of those responsible for deforestation and forest degradation. This could result in REDD+ payments being made for actions that would have happened anyway, leading to no real net reduction in emissions.
3. **Leakage:** REDD+ may also lead to leakage, which occurs when deforestation or forest degradation activities simply shift to other areas not covered by the program, leading to no real net reduction in emissions.
4. **Social and environmental impacts:** There are also concerns about the social and environmental impacts of REDD+, including potential land grabbing, displacement of local communities, and impacts on biodiversity.

To address these critiques, a number of remedies have been put in place. These include:

1. **Monitoring and verification**: REDD+ programs typically require monitoring and verification to ensure that emissions reductions are real and permanent. This can be done through satellite monitoring, field inspections, and other methods.

2. **Additionality safeguards:** REDD+ programs often include additionality safeguards to ensure that payments are only made for actions that would not have happened without the program.
3. **Leakage safeguards**: REDD+ programs may also include leakage safeguards to prevent deforestation and forest degradation activities from simply shifting to other areas outside the program.
4. **Social and environmental safeguards**: REDD+ programs often include social and environmental safeguards to ensure that the program does not have negative impacts on local communities or biodiversity.

In summary, while REDD+ has faced criticism related to permanence, additionality, leakage, and social and environmental impacts, these concerns have been addressed through monitoring and verification, additionality safeguards, leakage safeguards, and social and environmental safeguards. By implementing these safeguards, REDD+ can contribute to sustainable economic development and climate change mitigation while also protecting local communities and biodiversity.

Explore more on the REDD+ initiative at https://redd.unfccc.int/.

E-Environmental Factors for Sustainable Development

Biologists, public policymakers, economists, and others have written about the need to review business practices and their impact on the environment. Groundbreaking books such as *Silent Spring* (Carson, 1962), *Our Common Future* (WCED, 1987), and *Natural Capitalism* (Hawken et al., 1999), are a few of the seminal works that have moved public opinion about environmental factors in business practices and sustainable development. Contemporary books to read include *The Sixth Extinction: An Unnatural History* (Kolbert, 2014), *This Changes Everything: Capitalism vs. The Climate* (Klein, 2014), and *The Uninhabitable Earth: Life After Warming* (Wallace-Wells, 2019). This heightened awareness of business practices and their impact on the environment has influenced the ESG framework. In particular, it has changed the business practices in the extractive industries and other businesses that significantly affect the environment and local communities (Spitz et al., 2022). The focus is on how to better integrate environmental factors in the mining industries in relation to environmental sustainable development standards. The environmental factor in the ESG criteria is particularly focused on how a company addresses environmental concerns and manages its ecological footprint from climate change to biodiversity conservation and habitat protection, and from green products to green supply chain.

The key principles of environmental sustainable development include:

1. **Environmental conservation**: This involves protecting and preserving natural resources and ecosystems such as forests, oceans, rivers, and wildlife, to maintain their ecological balance and biodiversity.
2. **Resource efficiency**: This involves using natural resources in a way that minimizes waste and pollution, and promotes the efficient use of resources to reduce environmental impact.
3. **Pollution prevention:** This involves reducing or eliminating pollution from all sources, including industry, agriculture, transportation, and households.
4. **Climate change mitigation and adaptation:** This involves reducing greenhouse gas emissions and adapting to the impacts of climate change to avoid its worst effects on the environment and society.
5. **Community participation and engagement**: This includes involving local communities, stakeholders, and Indigenous peoples in decision-making processes, ensuring that their needs and priorities are considered in environmental policy and planning.

Therefore, environmental sustainable development is about balancing economic development with environmental protection and promoting the long-term health and well-being of both people and the planet. In the context of ESG ratings and the newest EESG model, the E for "environment" refers to the environmental impact of a company's operations, products, and services. It includes factors such as resource use, pollution, waste generation, climate change, and biodiversity. Some examples of environmental factors that are evaluated in ESG ratings include the following companies that have used the ESG model for reducing their environmental impact and have modeled these sustainable practices:

1. **Carbon emissions reduction and capture**: This includes the amount of greenhouse gasses (such as carbon dioxide) that a company emits as a result of its operations and activities that contributes to climate change. Companies can set targets to reduce their greenhouse gas emissions and adopt energy-efficient technologies and processes to achieve those targets. This may include using renewable energy, improving building insulation, and optimizing transportation and logistics. Microsoft, for example, has set a goal of being carbon-negative by 2030, and has already taken significant steps to reduce its carbon emissions. The company has committed to being carbon–neutral by 2022, and has developed a plan to remove all the carbon it has ever emitted by 2050. In addition, there are some interesting technologies and companies invested in carbon capture (pre- and post-combustion or with oxy-fuel combustion or direct air capture). Some of these companies include Carbon Clean Solutions (India), Carbon Engineering (Canada), Climeworks (Switzerland), ExxonMobil (USA), and Shell (Holland).
2. **Water usage conservation**: This includes the amount of water that a company uses in its operations, as well as the quality of the water that is discharged as waste. Companies can adopt practices to reduce their consumption of natural resources such as water, energy, and raw materials. For example, they can implement water conservation programs, recycle materials, and adopt circular economy models that reduce waste and promote resource efficiency. Levi Strauss & Co, for example, has set a goal of reducing its water usage by 50% by 2025. The company has already reduced its water usage by 26% since 2015, and is using innovative technologies to improve water efficiency in its manufacturing processes. Another example is Colgate-Palmolive. The company has set a goal of reducing its water usage by 35% by 2025 and it has already reduced its water usage by 30% since 2010. It is now using innovative technologies to improve water efficiency in its operations.
3. **Waste generation and design**: This includes the amount and type of waste that a company produces, as well as its waste management practices. This is connected to the company's sustainable supply chain management. They can ensure that their suppliers follow environmentally sustainable practices by setting sustainability standards and regularly monitoring and auditing their suppliers. It is also linked to the company's ability to design products that are more

environmentally sustainable and that have a reduced environmental footprint throughout their life cycle. This includes using sustainable materials, reducing waste and pollution, and promoting reuse and recycling. Adidas, for example, has set a goal of using only recycled polyester in all of its products by 2024. The company has already reduced the amount of waste it generates in its manufacturing processes, and is working to use more sustainable materials in its products. Toyota is another example. The company has set a goal of achieving zero waste to landfill in all of its operations. Toyota has already reduced its waste generation by 66% since 2010, and is using innovative technologies to improve waste reduction in its manufacturing processes.

4. **Energy efficiency and renewables**: This includes the efficiency of a company's energy use, such as how much energy is consumed per unit of output. Connected to efficiency is the increase in use of renewable energy. Companies are increasingly investing in renewable energy sources, such as wind and solar power, to reduce their carbon footprint and decrease reliance on fossil fuels. Google and Amazon have some interesting examples. Google has committed to being carbon-free by 2030, and to operate on 24/7 carbon-free energy by 2030. To achieve this, the company is investing in renewable energy and energy efficiency measures, such as using machine learning to optimize data center cooling systems and using renewable energy to power its operations. Amazon has set a goal to achieve net-zero carbon emissions by 2040. To achieve this, the company is investing in renewable energy and energy efficiency measures, such as using electric delivery vehicles, and investing in energy-efficient data centers and buildings.
5. **Biodiversity impact:** This includes the impact of a company's activities on natural habitats, ecosystems, and endangered species. Companies can protect and promote biodiversity by adopting sustainable land management practices, conserving natural habitats, and reducing their impact on wildlife. The Nature Conservancy for example, has protected biodiversity and restored critical ecosystems around the world. The organization has protected more than 119 million acres of land and more than 5,000 miles of rivers worldwide, and has helped to establish more than 100 marine protected areas. Danone is another example. It has made a commitment to biodiversity conservation and is partnering with organizations such as the

World Wildlife Fund to promote sustainable agriculture and protect biodiversity.

Overall, environmental factors are an important part of ESG ratings, as they provide a measure of a company's impact on the natural environment and its ability to manage and mitigate environmental risks. By considering environmental factors in their investment decisions, investors can help promote sustainable business practices and support companies that are working to reduce their environmental impact.

The Environmental Factors of Climate Change and Mitigation

Climate change is driven by a complex set of economic factors, and mitigating its impacts also involves a range of economic considerations. Here are some of the main economic factors driving climate change and its mitigation:

1. **Fossil fuels:** The burning of fossil fuels such as coal, oil, and natural gas is the primary source of greenhouse gas emissions, which are the main driver of climate change. Fossil fuels are economically attractive because they are abundant, cheap, and convenient, but transitioning away from them will require significant investment in renewable energy sources and infrastructure.
2. **Land use and agriculture:** Land use changes such as deforestation and conversion of grasslands for agriculture are also significant contributors to climate change. Mitigating these impacts will require a shift towards more sustainable land use practices and reducing food waste.
3. **Industrial processes**: Certain industrial processes, such as cement production and steelmaking, are also significant sources of greenhouse gas emissions. Reducing these emissions will require the development and deployment of more sustainable production methods.
4. **Economic growth and consumption:** Economic growth and increasing consumption patterns are driving many of the above factors, as well as increasing demand for energy and other resources.

Mitigating climate change will require a shift towards more sustainable consumption patterns, as well as investment in low-carbon economic development.

5. **Investment and policy**: Finally, addressing climate change will require significant investment in new technologies and infrastructure, as well as policy interventions such as carbon pricing and regulations to encourage more sustainable practices.

These are just a few of the economic factors driving climate change and its mitigation. Addressing these challenges will require a multifaceted approach that addresses both the root causes of climate change and the economic and political barriers to mitigating its impacts. Managing climate change implies managing risks at four levels: (1) Mitigation as efforts to reduce greenhouse gas emissions; (2) Adaptation as an increase capacity of society to cope with changes in climate; (3) Geoengineering as to find solutions for carbon capture and manipulate earth systems to counteract the impact of greenhouse gasses; and (4) Knowledge through measurements and understanding of climate systems. Climate change is such a daunting task that it requires more than the ESG commitments of the business sector. International agreements also play an important role in addressing climate change by setting targets for greenhouse gas emissions reduction, coordinating efforts among countries, and providing a framework for global cooperation on climate issues. Here are some examples of major international agreements related to climate change:

1. **United Nations Framework Convention on Climate Change (UNFCCC):** This treaty was signed by nearly all countries in the world at the 1992 Rio Earth Summit. It provides a framework for international cooperation to address climate change. The most significant outcome of the UNFCCC has been the adoption of the Paris Agreement.
2. **Paris Agreement:** Adopted in 2015 under the UNFCCC, the Paris Agreement aims to limit global temperature increase to well below 2 degrees Celsius above pre-industrial levels, and pursue efforts to limit the increase to 1.5 degrees Celsius. The agreement includes targets for greenhouse gas emissions reductions, and provides a framework for countries to regularly assess and report on their progress.

3. **Kyoto Protocol:** Adopted in 1997, the Kyoto Protocol was the first international agreement to set binding targets for greenhouse gas emission reductions. The protocol required developed countries to reduce their emissions by an average of 5% below 1990 levels by the end of 2012. While the Kyoto Protocol has largely been superseded by the Paris Agreement, it remains an important precedent for international cooperation on climate issues.
4. **Montreal Protocol:** While not specifically focused on climate change, the 1987 Montreal Protocol is an important international agreement related to the environment. The protocol aims to protect the ozone layer by phasing out the use of ozone-depleting substances, which are also potent greenhouse gasses. The success of the Montreal Protocol in reducing these substances has also had a positive impact on climate change.

These are just a few examples of major international agreements related to climate change. While these agreements are not sufficient on their own to address the complex challenges of climate change, they provide an important framework for global cooperation and progress on this critical issue.

Case 7.2 SDG 15 and Biodiversity

SDG 15 (Life on Land) specifically focuses on biodiversity in its goal to protect, restore, and promote the sustainable use of terrestrial and inland freshwater ecosystems, sustainably manage forests, combat desertification, halt and reverse land degradation, and halt biodiversity loss. The targets under SDG 15 that specifically relate to biodiversity include:

15.1 By 2020, ensure the conservation, restoration, and sustainable use of terrestrial and inland freshwater ecosystems and their services, in particular forests, wetlands, mountains and drylands, in line with obligations under international agreements.
15.2 By 2020, promote the implementation of sustainable management of all types of forests, halt deforestation, restore degraded forests, and increase afforestation and reforestation.
15.5 Take urgent and significant action to reduce the degradation of natural habitats, halt the loss of biodiversity, and protect and prevent the extinction of threatened species.

15.9 By 2020, integrate ecosystem and biodiversity values into national and local planning, development processes, poverty reduction strategies, and accounts.

These targets aim to ensure the protection and conservation of biodiversity, and to promote the sustainable use of natural resources in a way that benefits both current and future generations. The foundation of these biodiversity SDG 15 targets is the Convention on Biological Diversity (CBD), an international treaty adopted at the United Nations Conference on Environment and Development (UNCED) in Rio de Janeiro in 1992. The CBD is one of the most important international agreements related to biodiversity, and has been ratified by 196 countries. The goal of the CBD is to conserve biodiversity, promote its sustainable use, and ensure the fair and equitable sharing of the benefits arising from the use of genetic resources. The convention recognizes that biodiversity is a global asset of tremendous value to present and future generations, and that it is essential for sustainable development. The CBD has three main objectives:

1. **Conservation of biological diversity**: To conserve biological diversity, including ecosystems, species, and genetic resources.
2. **Sustainable use of biological diversity**: To use biological diversity in a sustainable way, ensuring that it is available for future generations.
3. **Fair and equitable sharing of the benefits arising from the use of genetic resources:** To ensure that the benefits from the use of genetic resources are shared fairly and equitably.

The CBD has several key provisions, including the development of national biodiversity strategies and action plans, the establishment of protected areas, and the promotion of sustainable use and access to genetic resources. The convention also includes provisions for the transfer of technology and financial resources to developing countries to support their efforts to conserve biodiversity. Overall, the CBD plays a critical role in global efforts to conserve biodiversity, and provides a framework for international cooperation on this important issue.

Companies can contribute to these biodiversity targets and commitments in several ways. Here are a few examples:

1. **Sustainable land use:** Companies can adopt sustainable land use practices that support the conservation of natural habitats and promote the restoration of degraded land. This can include measures such as reforestation, habitat restoration, and the use of sustainable agriculture practices that minimize negative impacts on biodiversity.
2. **Sustainable forestry:** Companies that rely on forestry resources can adopt sustainable forestry practices that help to protect and restore forests. This can include measures such as reducing deforestation, planting new trees, and promoting the use of certified sustainable forest products.
3. **Reduction of negative impacts:** Companies can work to reduce their negative impacts on biodiversity, such as reducing pollution and waste, and minimizing the impact of their operations on natural habitats.
4. **Collaboration with stakeholders:** Companies can collaborate with stakeholders, including governments, NGOs, and local communities, to support the protection and conservation of biodiversity. This can involve supporting community-based conservation initiatives, partnering with NGOs on conservation projects, and engaging in multi-stakeholder initiatives to promote sustainable land use and biodiversity.
5. **Disclosure and Reporting:** Companies can disclose their impacts on biodiversity and report on their efforts to support the conservation of biodiversity. This can include reporting on metrics such as land use, carbon emissions, and the use of sustainable forestry products, and using tools such as the Global Reporting Initiative to communicate their sustainability performance.

Overall, companies have an important role to play in supporting biodiversity as expressed in the CBD and SDG 15, and can make a significant contribution through their operations, partnerships, and reporting. Commendable is the example of Unilever who has committed to sourcing 100% of its agricultural raw materials sustainably, including a commitment to zero net deforestation by 2023. The company has also worked to protect and restore forests and wetlands in its supply chain, and has partnered with NGOs and other stakeholders to support biodiversity conservation. Danone has also integrated biodiversity conservation into its climate strategy. The company has worked to promote regenerative agriculture practices that support soil health and biodiversity, and has partnered with

NGOs and other stakeholders to support landscape-scale conservation efforts. Nestle has made a commitment to source 100% of its key commodities from sustainable sources by 2020, and has worked to promote sustainable agriculture practices that support biodiversity conservation. The company has also developed a biodiversity strategy that includes the restoration of degraded ecosystems and the protection of biodiversity hotspots.

Also commendable is the initiative that some companies have made to reduce the biodiversity devastation of palm oil plantations. The Roundtable on Sustainable Palm Oil (RSPO) is a certification system and voluntary initiative aimed at promoting sustainable palm oil production. It was established in 2004 by a group of palm oil producers, traders, and NGOs, and is recognized as one of the most important initiatives in the palm oil industry. The RSPO aims to promote the production and use of sustainable palm oil, and to support social and environmental sustainability in the industry. The RSPO has developed a set of principles and criteria for sustainable palm oil production, and certification is granted to companies that meet these standards.

The principles and criteria of the RSPO cover a range of issues, including the protection of natural resources, the rights of workers and local communities, and the use of best management practices in palm oil production. The RSPO also includes requirements for the transparency of the supply chain, so that the end users of palm oil can be sure that it is produced in a sustainable and responsible way. In 2021, RSPO registered more than 4,000 members worldwide, including producers, traders, processors, and retailers. While it has faced criticism from some environmental groups for not doing enough to address deforestation and other environmental issues, it remains an important initiative for promoting more responsible practices in the palm oil industry.

Explore more on SDG 15 at https://www.globalgoals.org/goals/15-life-on-land/.

S-Social Factor for Sustainable Development

The social factor of EESG management is important because it addresses the impact of a company's operations on people, communities, and society as a whole. The organizational impact on employees, customers, and communities are increasingly being used by investors and stakeholders to evaluate a company's long-term sustainability and impact on society. It considers issues such as labor standards, human rights, community engagement, diversity and inclusion, and product safety. A company that manages its social impacts effectively is more likely to attract and retain talented employees, maintain positive relationships with its customers, for employees and suppliers, prevent exploitation and discrimination, and promote gender and racial equity. These are some of the core topics relevant to the society factor in ESG:

1. **Human rights:** Addressing human rights violations in the company's operations and supply chain, such as forced labor, child labor, and human trafficking. Many companies have made efforts to address human rights violations in their operations and supply chains. For example, Adidas has worked with independent auditors to assess its suppliers' compliance with human rights standards. Nestle, Apple, and Unilever have worked with NGOs and other stakeholders to address issues related to child labor, forced labor, and human trafficking in its supply chain. Patagonia has implemented a traceability program to ensure that its products are not made with forced labor or other human rights abuses.
2. **Community engagement:** Engaging with local communities and stakeholders to understand and address their concerns, and ensuring that the company's operations do not harm their health, safety, or well-being. Many companies engage with communities as part of their corporate social responsibility initiatives, which can help to build trust, create positive social impact, and promote sustainability. For example, Ben & Jerry's has a social mission that includes a commitment to supporting local communities. The company has implemented a community action program that provides grants and other resources to grassroots organizations working on issues such as social and economic justice, environmental sustainability, and food security. Starbucks has a community service program that includes

initiatives to support economic development, environmental sustainability, and social justice in communities where it operates. The company has also implemented a coffee sourcing program that includes partnerships with local farmers and initiatives to support sustainable agriculture practices.

3. **Product safety:** Ensuring the safety and quality of the company's products and services, and preventing harm to customers and the environment. Many companies prioritize product safety and take measures to prevent harm to customers and the environment. For example, Johnson & Johnson has learned from its past failures and has implemented numerous measures to prevent harm to customers such as rigorous testing, screening processes, and prompt recalls. Procter & Gamble, in addition to their product safety program, has also implemented a product stewardship program that includes initiatives to reduce the environmental impact of its products and promote sustainability.
4. **Diversity and inclusion:** Promoting diversity and inclusion in the company's workforce, leadership, and decision-making, and preventing discrimination based on gender, race, ethnicity, age, or other factors. EESG companies can contribute to greater diversity and inclusion in the workplace, which can create more opportunities for underrepresented groups and help to reduce inequality. For example, Microsoft has a diversity and inclusion program that aims to increase the representation of underrepresented groups in its workforce and create a more inclusive culture.
5. **Access to healthcare and education**: Addressing issues related to healthcare and education access and equity, and supporting initiatives that promote social welfare and well-being. Numerous companies prioritize access to healthcare and education as part of their corporate social responsibility initiatives. For example, Novartis has implemented a program called "Novartis Access" which provides affordable medicines to low-income communities in developing countries. The company has also implemented a program to improve healthcare infrastructure and provide healthcare services to underserved communities. Cisco has implemented a program called "Cisco Networking Academy" which provides IT education and training to underserved communities around the world. The program is designed to help people acquire the skills needed to succeed in the digital economy.

Companies and organizations across sectors can significantly contribute to finding solutions to these challenges. The commitment for ESG reporting and the SDGs they represent help companies prioritize and partner with others in order to make a more positive impact. That is why we need effective social management. Companies that address these challenges are more likely to build trust, maintain a positive reputation, and create long-term value for their stakeholders. Many organizations across private, public, and social sectors, are actively involved and positively contribute to the main social challenges of sustainable development. They work to promote social sustainable development by prioritizing human rights, diversity inclusion, gender equality, children's rights, decent work, and human security. Here are some examples of such organizations:

1. **UNICEF**: UNICEF works to promote children's rights and improve the lives of children around the world through programs focused on education, healthcare, and protection from violence and exploitation.
2. **Amnesty International:** Amnesty International is a global organization that works to promote human rights by advocating for the release of political prisoners, ending torture, and fighting against discrimination and violence.
3. **International Labor Organization (ILO)**: The ILO is a specialized agency of the United Nations that promotes decent work and social justice around the world. The organization works to promote labor rights, improve working conditions, and eradicate child labor and forced labor.
4. **Global Fund for Women**: The Global Fund for Women is a nonprofit organization that works to promote gender equality and women's rights by providing funding and support to women-led organizations around the world.
5. **Human Rights Watch**: Human Rights Watch is an international organization that promotes human rights by conducting research, advocating for policy change, and exposing human rights abuses.
6. **United Nations Development Programme (UNDP)**: The UNDP works to promote sustainable development and reduce poverty by supporting countries in the areas of governance, economic development, and environmental sustainability.

These are just a few examples of organizations that work to promote social sustainable development by prioritizing human rights, diversity inclusion, gender equality, children's rights, decent work, and human security. Many other organizations and companies are also working to promote sustainable social development in various ways. Overall, EESG companies take a holistic approach to social issues, recognizing that they are interconnected with other aspects of sustainability, such as environmental impact and good governance.

Company approaches to address social issues can include setting specific goals and targets related to social issues, such as improving diversity and inclusion in the workplace or reducing the environmental impact of their operations. They can also engage with a wide range of stakeholders, including employees, customers, suppliers, and local communities, to understand their perspectives on social issues and to identify opportunities to address them. They can conduct surveys, host town hall meetings, or establish advisory committees. They can implement policies and practices to address social issues, such as human rights, diversity and inclusion, and decent work. These may include codes of conduct, training programs, and initiatives to promote workplace safety and employee well-being.

They can also engage in reporting and transparency about their performance on social issues, and may report on their progress through sustainability reports or other forms of public disclosure. This allows stakeholders to evaluate their performance and hold them accountable for their commitments. They can collaborate with other organizations, such as NGOs, governments, and other businesses, to address social issues. This may involve joining industry coalitions or partnering with NGOs to support specific initiatives. By addressing social issues in a comprehensive and strategic way, EESG companies can help create a more just and sustainable future for all.

Case 7.3 BRAC and Community-Driven Development

Building Resources Across Communities (BRAC) is a development organization based in Bangladesh that has contributed significantly to sustainable development in its home country and around the world. It was founded in 1972 by Sir Fazle Hasan Abed, with the goal of addressing poverty and social injustice in Bangladesh. BRAC is the largest nongovernmental organization (NGO) in the world in terms of both staff and program reach. There are several reasons why BRAC has been able to achieve such a high level of scale and impact:

1. **Comprehensive approach to development:** BRAC's approach to sustainable development is multifaceted, with programs that focus on a wide range of issues, including education, healthcare, microfinance, agriculture, and more. By taking a comprehensive approach to development, BRAC is able to address the root causes of poverty and inequality, and create long-term, sustainable change.
2. **Community-led development**: BRAC's programs are designed and implemented in partnership with local communities, and are tailored to the specific needs and contexts of each community. This approach ensures that programs are culturally appropriate, responsive to local needs, and have a high level of community ownership.
3. **Innovation and learning:** BRAC is known for its innovative approach to problem-solving, and its willingness to experiment with new ideas and approaches. The organization has a strong focus on learning and continuous improvement, and regularly evaluates its programs to ensure that they are having the desired impact.
4. **Partnerships and collaborations**: BRAC works in partnership with a wide range of organizations, including governments, NGOs, and the private sector. These partnerships enable BRAC to leverage the expertise and resources of others, and to create more effective and sustainable programs.
5. **Focus on sustainability**: BRAC's programs are designed to create long-term, sustainable change, rather than providing short-term assistance. This focus on sustainability has helped the organization to achieve lasting impact and to scale its programs to reach millions of people.

Overall, BRAC's success can be attributed to its comprehensive approach to development, its community-led approach, its focus on innovation and learning, its partnerships and collaborations, and its commitment to sustainability. These factors have enabled BRAC to become a model for development organizations around the world, and to make a significant contribution to sustainable development. BRAC has had a significant impact on sustainable development in Bangladesh and 10 other countries, including Afghanistan, Myanmar, and Uganda. In addition to its work in sustainable development, BRAC has also played a key role in disaster relief efforts, providing assistance to communities affected by natural disasters and other emergencies. Overall, BRAC's focus on community-led development, its innovative approach to problem-solving, and its commitment to sustainability have made it a model for development organizations around the world, and have helped to improve the lives of millions of people in Bangladesh and beyond.

Some of the activities that BRAC engages in and had significant social impact include:

1. **Education:** BRAC operates schools in many countries, including Bangladesh, Afghanistan, Liberia, and Uganda. The organization also provides educational materials and teacher training to improve the quality of education in these schools. In terms of impact BRAC operates over 50,000 schools in Bangladesh, providing education to over 12 million children. The organization's schools have helped to improve literacy rates and increase access to education in some of the most impoverished areas of the country.
2. **Healthcare**: BRAC provides healthcare services in many countries, including maternal and child healthcare, nutrition services, and community health programs. The organization also trains community health workers to provide basic healthcare services in rural and remote areas. In terms of impact, BRAC's healthcare programs have helped to reduce infant and maternal mortality rates in Bangladesh and other countries where it operates. The organization's community health programs have also helped to increase access to healthcare services in remote and rural areas.
3. **Microfinance**: BRAC operates microfinance programs in many countries, providing small loans to entrepreneurs and small business owners to help them start or expand their businesses. In terms of impact, BRAC's microfinance programs have provided loans to over 8 million people, helping them to start or expand their businesses and improve their incomes. Through their microfinance programs, BRAC has provided access to credit, training, and support. BRAC has helped to empower women, reduce poverty, promote financial inclusion, and drive economic growth.
4. **Agriculture:** BRAC works with farmers in many countries to improve agricultural productivity, increase income, and improve food security. The organization provides training, seeds, and other

inputs to help farmers improve their yields and income. In terms of impact, BRAC's agricultural programs have helped to improve the livelihoods of over 2 million farmers in Bangladesh and other countries. The organization's work in this area has also helped to improve food security and reduce poverty.

5. **Disaster relief:** BRAC provides assistance to communities affected by natural disasters and other emergencies. This includes providing food, shelter, and other essential services to those affected. In terms of impact, the organization has a well-established disaster management program, which aims to provide immediate assistance to communities affected by natural disasters, as well as longer-term support for recovery and reconstruction. By providing immediate relief, supporting long-term rehabilitation and reconstruction, and promoting disaster preparedness, BRAC has helped to improve the resilience of communities and reduce the impact of natural disasters.

BRAC is often cited as a model for sustainability management for several reasons. The key factors that contribute to BRAC's success in sustainable development include its holistic approach to development, its community-driven approach, its focus on multiple issues, its scalability, its innovation, and its commitment to impact evaluation. These factors have helped to make BRAC a model for sustainability management, and have inspired many other organizations to adopt similar approaches to development.

Explore more at http://www.brac.net/.

G-Governance Factor for Sustainable Development

In EESG management, governance refers to the processes and structures that a company puts in place to manage its operations and ensure that it operates in a responsible, sustainable manner. Governance includes a wide range of factors, including board composition, executive compensation, risk management, and transparency. Governance is critical in sustainability management because it provides the framework for decision-making and accountability that is necessary to ensure that sustainability goals are achieved over the long term. Good governance helps to ensure that sustainability is integrated into business strategy and operations, and that it is treated as a priority by senior management and the board of directors.

Here is a list of 10 major reasons why governance and good governance is important in sustainability management:

1. **Establishing priorities and setting goals:** Governance provides a framework for setting priorities and establishing goals related to sustainability. This may involve developing sustainability policies and strategies, and identifying specific targets and metrics that can be used to measure progress.
2. **Coordination and collaboration:** Governance structures can facilitate coordination and collaboration among different stakeholders, including government agencies, businesses, civil society organizations, and local communities. This can help ensure that different actors work together to achieve sustainability goals, and can help avoid conflicts and duplication of efforts.
3. **Decision-making:** Governance structures can provide a framework for decision-making on sustainability issues. This can help ensure that decisions are based on the best available information, and that they take into account the interests of all stakeholders.
4. **Policy and regulatory frameworks:** Governance structures can create policy and regulatory frameworks that support sustainable development. For example, governments can create laws and regulations that encourage businesses to adopt sustainable practices, or provide incentives for renewable energy development.
5. **Setting and enforcing standards**: Governance provides a framework for setting and enforcing standards for sustainable practices. This includes policies and regulations that promote sustainable development, as well as incentives and support programs for businesses and individuals that adopt sustainable practices.
6. **Transparency and accountability**: Governance structures can ensure that sustainability policies and actions are transparent, and that there is accountability for the outcomes. Effective governance helps to ensure that sustainability goals are being met and that progress is being made towards those goals. This may involve establishing reporting requirements and ensuring that sustainability performance is regularly monitored and reported to stakeholders. This can help build trust among stakeholders, and can provide a basis for monitoring and evaluation of sustainability initiatives.

7. **Participation and empowerment**: Governance structures can encourage participation and empowerment of different stakeholders in decision-making and implementation of sustainable practices. This can help ensure that the benefits of sustainability are shared fairly among different groups, and can help build support for sustainability initiatives.
8. **Managing risk**: Good governance is also critical for managing risks related to sustainability. This may include identifying and mitigating risks related to climate change, natural resource depletion, and social and environmental impacts.
9. **Encouraging innovation**: Governance can also help to encourage innovation and creativity in sustainability management, by providing incentives and support for employees to develop new solutions and technologies.
10. **Building trust and credibility**: Finally, effective governance can help to build trust and credibility with stakeholders, including investors, customers, and employees. By demonstrating a commitment to sustainability and transparency, companies can enhance their reputation and improve their long-term sustainability.

In other words, governance is an essential component of sustainability management, and can help to ensure that sustainability is treated as a core business issue, rather than as an add-on or afterthought. Companies that prioritize good governance and sustainability management can achieve a range of benefits, including improved financial performance, enhanced reputation, and increased stakeholder engagement. Governance is also critical in sustainable development, as it helps to ensure that economic, social, and environmental considerations are integrated into decision-making and that progress towards sustainable development goals is monitored and evaluated over time.

Good governance can help to align the interests of different stakeholders, including businesses, governments, and civil society, towards common goals related to sustainable development. This can help to reduce conflicts and encourage collaboration in pursuit of sustainable development. Good governance can help to ensure that decisions related to sustainable development are based on a broad range of considerations, including economic, social, and environmental factors. This can help to ensure that decisions are more effective and sustainable over the long term.

Good governance can provide a framework for accountability and transparency in sustainable development, ensuring that progress towards sustainable development goals is monitored and reported on to stakeholders. This can help to build trust and engagement among stakeholders and ensure that commitments related to sustainable development are met. The value of good governance in sustainable development management is to create a framework for decision-making that takes into account economic, social, and environmental considerations, and that ensures progress is made towards sustainable development goals over the long term. By prioritizing good governance and sustainable development, businesses, governments, and civil society can achieve a range of benefits, including improved quality of life for people, protection of the planet's resources, and enhanced economic prosperity.

Companies that engage in EESG management face a range of governance issues that can impact their long-term sustainability and success. Some of the main governance issues for ESG companies include:

1. **Board composition and diversity:** The composition of the board of directors is an important governance issue for EESG companies, particularly with respect to diversity. Having a diverse board can help ensure that the company is able to consider a wide range of perspectives and make better decisions. Additionally, having board members with relevant expertise can help the company better manage EESG issues. There are several EESG companies that are considered leaders in board composition and diversity, and that have implemented policies and practices to promote diversity, equity, and inclusion (DEI) in their boardrooms. For example, Unilever has a board of directors that is 50% women and includes members from a range of different nationalities and backgrounds. The company has also established a DEI committee and is working to increase representation of underrepresented groups in its leadership and management ranks. Another example is Goldman Sachs that has made a commitment to diversity and inclusion at all levels of the organization, including the board of directors. The company has set targets for diverse representation on the board and has implemented initiatives to recruit, retain, and promote underrepresented groups.
2. **Executive compensation:** Executive compensation is another important governance issue for ESG companies, particularly with respect to the alignment of compensation with EESG goals.

Ensuring that executive compensation is tied to ESG performance can help incentivize executives to prioritize sustainability and social responsibility. Several companies have strategically aligned the interests of executives with the long-term sustainability of the company. For example, Intel's executive compensation plan includes a portion of pay that is tied to the company's progress towards sustainability goals, including those related to renewable energy, water conservation, and waste reduction. Another example is that JPMorgan Chase has implemented an executive compensation plan that includes an ESG scorecard, which measures the company's performance on a range of ESG metrics, including climate change, human rights, and diversity and inclusion.

Also, exemplary is Royal Dutch Shell that has implemented an executive compensation plan that includes targets related to the company's progress towards reducing its carbon footprint and transitioning to a lower-carbon energy system.

3. **Risk management**: ESG companies face a range of risks related to sustainability, including reputational risk, regulatory risk, and operational risk. Effective risk management is an important governance issue for ESG companies, and may involve the development of risk management policies and the establishment of risk oversight committees. Many ESG companies have prioritized risk management to identify and mitigate potential risks and capitalized on opportunities for sustainable growth and prosperity. These ESG companies implemented robust risk management frameworks that take into account a range of ESG risks and opportunities. For example, Swiss Re, a leading insurance and reinsurance company, has made risk management a central pillar of its ESG strategy. The company has implemented a comprehensive risk management framework that takes into account a range of ESG risks, including climate change, natural catastrophes, and social unrest. Enel is another interesting example. It has made risk management a central pillar of its ESG strategy and implemented a comprehensive risk management framework that takes into account a range of ESG risks, including climate change, cyber security, and human rights.
4. **Transparency and disclosure:** ESG companies are typically held to a high standard of transparency and disclosure, particularly with respect to their ESG performance. Effective governance requires that companies be transparent about their performance on ESG

issues and that they disclose relevant information to stakeholders, including investors, customers, and employees. BlackRock, one of the world's largest asset managers, has set an example in ESG governance management by promoting transparency and disclosure in its investment practices. The company has developed a range of ESG-focused investment products and has committed to integrating ESG factors into its investment decision-making processes. BlackRock has also established an ESG oversight committee to provide oversight and guidance on its ESG strategy and performance. Coca-Cola has also set an example in ESG governance management by providing detailed disclosures on its ESG performance and commitments, including through an annual ESG report and a dedicated sustainability website. The company has also established an independent Sustainability Advisory Council to provide oversight and guidance on its ESG strategy.

5. **Stakeholder engagement**: Effective governance for ESG companies requires that they engage with a wide range of stakeholders, including investors, customers, employees, and local communities. This may involve developing stakeholder engagement policies and establishing channels for dialogue and feedback. All major standards in sustainability reporting expect companies to engage with stakeholders. For instance, B Lab, GRI, Sustainability Accounting Standards Board (SASB), and the UNGC all require companies to engage with a range of stakeholders, including employees, customers, and suppliers, in their decision-making processes and in their development and reporting of their sustainability strategies and performance.
6. **Ethics and Compliance:** Good governance requires a strong commitment to ethics and compliance, with clear policies and procedures in place to ensure that all actions are legal, ethical, and aligned with the company's values. ESG companies often prioritize this area, with a focus on transparency, accountability, and ethical decision-making. Some best practices reported by ESG companies include clear codes of conduct, regular ethics training, strong whistle-blower protection policies, third-party due diligence, and independent oversight. These practices help to ensure that ESG companies are operating ethically and in compliance with relevant laws and regulations, and can help to build trust with stakeholders.

Addressing these governance issues requires a commitment to transparency, accountability, and stakeholder engagement. ESG companies that prioritize good governance can help build trust and credibility with stakeholders and can better manage the risks and opportunities associated with sustainability and social responsibility. Good governance will surely become a more determinant factor in ESG ratings and sustainability management. Increasingly, stakeholders are demanding more precise regulatory frameworks that include a set of characteristics that contribute to effective and ethical decision-making and leadership. In addition to transparency, accountability, participation, rule of law, and responsiveness, other factors will likely be added to the good governance ESG framework. Organizational performance including topics such as: climate adaptation solutions, data privacy, security practices, supply chain resilience, social justice and equity including racial and gender equality, and circular economy practices are more likely to be integrated in future ESG or EESG ratings.

Case 7.4 SDG 16.5 and Good Governance

SDG 16.5 refers to one of the targets under SDG 16 of the United Nations. SDG 16 aims to promote peaceful and inclusive societies, provide access to justice for all, and build effective, accountable, and inclusive institutions at all levels. Good governance plays a critical role in achieving SDG 16.5, as well as other sustainable development goals. Effective governance can help ensure that institutions are accountable, transparent, and responsive to the needs and concerns of citizens.

SDG 16.5 specifically calls for the development of "effective, accountable and transparent institutions at all levels" as a means of reducing corruption and bribery. The target includes a range of measures to strengthen institutional transparency and accountability, including the development of laws, policies, and procedures that promote transparency and accountability, as well as the strengthening of institutions responsible for preventing and combating corruption. In other words, the SDG 16.5 target recognizes the importance of good governance in the fight against corruption and promotes the adoption of measures to strengthen institutional transparency and accountability.

SDG 16.5 and the UNGC Principle 10 are closely related as they both aim to promote transparency, accountability, and anti-corruption practices in businesses and institutions. UNGC Principle 10 focuses on anti-corruption and requires companies to work against corruption in all its forms, including extortion and bribery. The principle encourages companies to implement anti-corruption measures and to engage in partnerships with governments, civil society, and other stakeholders to prevent and combat corruption.

SDG 16.5, on the other hand, is a global target that calls for the development of effective, accountable, and transparent institutions at all levels to reduce corruption and bribery. In essence, both UNGC Principle 10 and SDG 16.5 emphasize the importance of promoting transparency, accountability, and anti-corruption practices in institutions and businesses. By implementing these principles, businesses and institutions can help to promote sustainable development, build trust with stakeholders, and contribute to the achievement of the SDGs.

Good governance and anti-corruption measures are essential for sustainable management because they help to promote transparency, accountability, and responsible decision-making. When institutions and businesses are transparent and accountable, it becomes easier to ensure that resources are managed sustainably, and that the impacts of decisions are carefully considered. There are several reasons why good governance and anti-corruption are important for sustainable management:

1. **Ensuring the efficient and effective use of resources**: When institutions and businesses are transparent and accountable, it is easier to ensure that resources are managed efficiently and effectively. This is particularly important in the context of natural resource management, where it is essential to ensure that resources are used sustainably and that the benefits are shared fairly.
2. **Building trust with stakeholders:** Good governance and anti-corruption measures can help to build trust with stakeholders, including investors, customers, and the public. By promoting transparency and accountability, institutions and businesses can demonstrate their commitment to responsible management and build their reputation as ethical and trustworthy actors.
3. **Promoting long-term planning and decision-making**: Good governance and anti-corruption measures can help to promote long-term planning and decision-making. By ensuring that decision-making processes are transparent and accountable, institutions and businesses can take a more strategic and forward-thinking approach to their management practices.

4. **Reducing the risk of negative social and environmental impacts:** When institutions and businesses are transparent and accountable, it is easier to ensure that their activities do not have negative social or environmental impacts. By promoting responsible decision-making, good governance and anti-corruption measures can help to prevent harm and protect communities and the environment.

Organizations like Transparency International (TI), a German-based international NGO has been at the forefront of promoting good governance and anti-corruption measures worldwide. The organization was founded in 1993 and is dedicated to fighting corruption and promoting transparency, accountability, and integrity in government and business. It contributes to good governance and anti-corruption by:

1. **Raising awareness**: TI has played a significant role in raising awareness about the negative impacts of corruption and the importance of promoting good governance. The organization has conducted extensive research and advocacy to highlight the impact of corruption on economic growth, social development, and democracy.
2. **Promoting transparency and accountability**: TI has worked to promote transparency and accountability in government and business by developing tools and standards for measuring corruption, such as the Corruption Perceptions Index and the Bribe Payers Index. These tools provide important benchmarks for measuring progress in anti-corruption efforts and promote greater transparency in government and business.
3. **Advocacy and campaigning**: TI has conducted extensive advocacy and campaigning to promote anti-corruption measures and good governance. The organization has worked with governments, civil society, and the private sector to promote reforms, such as stronger laws, greater transparency, and more effective anti-corruption measures.

Building partnerships and networks: TI has built partnerships and networks with other organizations and stakeholders to promote anti-corruption and good governance measures. The organization works with governments, international organizations, and civil society to develop effective strategies and promote best practices in anti-corruption.

Overall, Transparency International has made a significant contribution to promoting good governance and anti-corruption measures worldwide. The organization's work has helped to raise awareness, promote transparency and accountability, advocate for reforms, and build partnerships and networks to combat corruption and promote good governance.

There have been several initiatives that have significantly contributed to SDG 16.5 for promoting good governance and anti-corruption for sustainable development. Here are a few examples:

1. **United Nations Convention Against Corruption (UNCAC)**: UNCAC is a legally binding international agreement that provides a comprehensive framework for preventing, detecting, and punishing corruption. It has been ratified by over 180 countries and serves as a powerful tool for promoting good governance and anti-corruption efforts worldwide.
2. **Open Government Partnership (OGP)**: The OGP is a multilateral initiative that aims to promote transparency, accountability, and citizen participation in government. It brings together governments and civil society organizations to work together to develop and implement open government reforms, including anti-corruption measures.
3. **Extractive Industries Transparency Initiative (EITI)**: The EITI is a global standard that promotes transparency and accountability in the management of natural resources. It requires companies and governments in the extractive industries to disclose information about payments made and received, which helps to prevent corruption and promote sustainable management of natural resources.
4. **Global Initiative for Fiscal Transparency (GIFT)**: GIFT is a global network that promotes fiscal transparency and accountability. It brings together governments, civil society, and international organizations to promote best practices in fiscal transparency and improve the quality and availability of fiscal information.
5. **Business Integrity Initiative (BII):** The Business Integrity Initiative is a multi-stakeholder initiative launched by the World Economic Forum that aims to promote business integrity and combat corruption. The initiative brings together companies, governments, civil society, and international organizations to develop and promote best practices in business integrity and to work together to address corruption risks.

These initiatives have significantly contributed to promoting good governance and anti-corruption for sustainable development. By providing frameworks, tools, and platforms for promoting transparency, accountability, and responsible decision-making, they have helped to build momentum for anti-corruption efforts and promote sustainable management.

In summary, SDG 16.5 is a target for promoting good governance and anti-corruption measures which are essential for sustainable management because they promote transparency, accountability, responsible decision-making, and the efficient use of resources. By implementing these measures, institutions and businesses can help to build trust with stakeholders, promote long-term planning, and reduce the risk of negative social and environmental impacts. SDG 16.5 targets can reduce poverty and increase social justice. By working towards this target, countries, social sector organizations, and private sector companies can help to build more stable and resilient societies, where citizens can have greater trust in their governments and institutions.

Explore more on SDG 16 at https://sdgs.un.org/goals/goal16 and the UNCG Principles 10 Resources on Anti-Corruption https://unglobalcompact.org/what-is-gc/our-work/governance/anti-corruption.

Key Takeaways

1. The ESG framework is a commonly used approach for sustainability management that integrates economic, environmental, social, and governance factors.
2. An integrated approach, known as EESG, is needed for a balanced assessment of organizational objectives and activities in relation to sustainability.
3. The economic factor of the EESG framework involves mechanisms for sustainability, such as sustainable finance and green investments, and aligning economic aspects with the Sustainable Development Goals.
4. The environmental factor of the EESG framework involves addressing climate change and biodiversity conservation through practices like REDD+ and sustainable land use.
5. The social factor of the EESG framework involves community-driven development and initiatives that promote diversity and inclusion, such as the case study of BRAC.

6. The governance factor of the EESG framework involves promoting good governance and accountability, as exemplified by the case study of SDG 16.5.

References

Bellucci, M., & Bini, L. (2019). *Integrated sustainability reporting: Linking environmental and social information to value creation processes*. Springer International Publishing.

Bose, S., Dong, G., & Simpson, A. (2019). *The financial ecosystem: The role of finance in achieving sustainability*. Springer International Publishing.

Brinkmann, R., & Garren, S. J. (2018). *The Palgrave handbook of sustainability: Case studies and practical solutions*. Springer International Publishing.

Carson, R. (1962). *Silent spring*. Houghton Mifflin.

Hawken, P., Lovins, A., & Lovins, H. (1999). *Natural capitalism: Creating the next industrial revolution*. Little, Brown and Company.

Klein, N. (2014). *This changes everything: Capitalism vs. The climate*. Simon & Schuster.

Kolbert, E. (2014). *The sixth extinction: An unnatural history*. Henry Holt and Co.

Mayer, C. P. (2018). *Prosperity: Better business makes the greater good*. Oxford University Press.

McKinsey & Company. (2023). *Environmental, social, and governance*. McKinsey & Company. https://www.mckinsey.com/business-functions/sustainability/our-insights/environmental-social-and-governance. Accessed March 13, 2023.

Rezaee, Z. (2021). *Business sustainability: Profit-with-purpose focus*. Business Expert Press.

Sikka, P., & Luo, Z. (2017). *Sustainability accounting and integrated reporting*. Taylor & Francis.

Spitz, K., Trudinger, J., & Orr, M. (2022). *Environmental social governance: Managing risk and expectations*. CRC Press.

Wallace-Wells, D. (2019). *The uninhabitable earth: Life after warming*. Tim Duggan Books.

World Commission on Environment and Development. (1987). *Our common future*. Oxford University Press.

CHAPTER 8

Sustainability Management Across Sectors

Abstract Sustainable management has common elements and specific contributions emerging across sectors. In this chapter, we review how sustainability is managed and practiced across organizations in diverse economic sectors. We review significant challenges and promising practices and initiatives specific to the business sector (companies and enterprises), the public sector (governments at local, national, and international levels), the social sector (NGOs, nonprofits, foundations, social enterprises, etc.) and within specific sectors such as academic (universities and higher education institutions in particular), the healthcare sector (hospitals and healthcare systems), and information technology sector (high-tech industries, artificial intelligence among others). We also consider specific economic sectors of extraction, manufacturing, agriculture, retail, finance, transportation, and hospitality. We consider some insightful cases that can exemplify the challenges and solutions for sustainability management across sectors.

Keywords Business sector · Government sector · Social sector · Academic sector · Healthcare sector · Information technology sector

M. Tavanti, *Developing Sustainability in Organizations*, Sustainable Development Goals Series,
https://doi.org/10.1007/978-3-031-36907-0_8

Businesses need to recognize that they can and must be a force for good. By integrating the Ten Principles of the UN Global Compact into their operations and embracing the Sustainable Development Goals, companies have the power to create meaningful change for people and the planet. Our collective future depends on responsible and sustainable business practices that ensure no one is left behind.

—Sanda Ojiambo, Assistant Secretary-General and CEO of the United Nations Global Compact

Business Sector and Sustainability Management

Economic sectors can significantly contribute to sustainable development but they can also be unsustainable and extremely harmful for the environment and its inhabitants. The economic contribution and carbon emission contribution of each sector worldwide can vary depending on the country, region, or industry. However, here is a general overview of the economic and carbon emissions contributions of each sector globally. The agriculture and forestry sector contributes around 3% to the global GDP and is responsible for around 21% of global greenhouse gas (GHG) emissions. The manufacturing sector contributes around 16% to the global GDP and is responsible for around 22% of global GHG emissions. The energy sector contributes around 10% to the global GDP and is responsible for around 72% of global GHG emissions. The construction sector contributes around 6% to the global GDP and is responsible for around 38% of global energy-related GHG emissions. The transportation sector contributes around 5% to the global GDP and is responsible for around 15% of global GHG emissions. The service sector contributes around 65% to the global GDP and is responsible for around 10% of global GHG emissions.

It is important to note that the economic contribution and carbon emission contribution of each sector can vary significantly depending on the country and region. For example, in some developing countries, the agriculture sector may contribute significantly more to the GDP than the service sector, while in developed countries, the service sector may be the largest contributor to the GDP. Additionally, the carbon emission contribution of each sector can vary depending on the energy mix and technology used in each country or region. These measurements are important for creating appropriate policy solutions and mitigating climate change and encouraging all sectors to provide net positive impactful contributions (IPCC, 2022).

Sustainability management can vary across different sectors due to a number of factors, including the nature of the industry, the supply chain, and the environmental and social impacts of the products or services being provided. Here are some examples of how sustainability management may vary across different sectors. We consider these examples in relation to businesses but acknowledge that the contribution emerges also from public sector-specific organizations as well as independent and hybrid sectors such as social enterprises, cooperatives, benefit corporations, NGOs, etc. Part III will consider these typologies of hybrid organizations in our conversation in sustainable innovation, social enterprises, and ecopreneurship. Part IV will consider in detail these sector distinctions in references to the GRI sector-specific standards.

1. **Mining Extractive Sector**: Sustainability management in the mining and extractive sector can be particularly challenging, as these industries have significant environmental and social impacts, such as habitat destruction, water pollution, and displacement of local communities. However, there are a number of approaches and strategies that mining and extractive companies can use to manage these impacts and promote sustainability. For example, before beginning operations, companies can conduct an environmental impact assessment (EIA) to identify and evaluate potential environmental impacts and risks. Companies can prioritize responsible sourcing of materials, such as through certification schemes like the Responsible Mining Index or the Conflict-Free Smelter Program. This can help ensure that the materials being extracted are done so in a way that respects human rights and environmental sustainability. Water management, energy efficiency, and stakeholder engagement can also be important approaches to ensure more sustainable and less harmful social and environmental practices. Engaging with local communities, governments, and other stakeholders can involve consultation with local communities and respecting specific protocols as the case (see later) of Free, Prior, and Informed Consent (FPIC).
2. **Agriculture Sector**: In the agriculture sector, sustainability management may focus on reducing water usage, improving soil health, and minimizing the use of pesticides and fertilizers. This may involve

implementing sustainable farming practices, such as crop rotation, intercropping, and agroforestry, and using precision agriculture technologies to optimize resource use. Sustainable agricultural practices may include conservation agriculture to improve soil health, reduce erosion, and conserve water. These practices include minimal tillage, crop rotation, and cover cropping. They also include precision agriculture that uses technology, such as GPS and sensors, to optimize crop production and reduce waste. This includes precise fertilization and irrigation management, as well as pest and disease management.

Agroforestry with the integration of trees and shrubs with crops and livestock can improve soil health, reduce erosion, and provide additional sources of income for farmers. Organic farming can lead to healthier soils, reduced chemical pollution, and improved biodiversity. Diversification is also an effective sustainable solution. It involves growing a variety of crops and/or raising multiple species of livestock on the same farm. This can help farmers reduce risks associated with weather events and market fluctuations, and also provide additional sources of income. Finally, integrated pest management (IPM) is also a more sustainable method of pest control as it relies on a combination of biological, cultural, and chemical controls. This approach can help reduce the use of harmful pesticides and preserve beneficial insects. Technology, as we highlight later, can also promote numerous sustainable agricultural outcomes.

3. **Manufacturing Sector**: In the manufacturing sector, sustainability management often focuses on reducing waste, improving energy efficiency, and minimizing the use of toxic materials. This may involve implementing sustainable production processes, using renewable energy sources, and sourcing materials from suppliers that prioritize sustainable practices. The manufacturing sector is an important contributor to economic growth and development, but it also has significant environmental and social impacts. To ensure a sustainable future for the sector some sustainable solutions that can be implemented include implementing resource efficiency measures that can significantly reduce the use of materials, energy, and water in manufacturing processes. This can be achieved through a variety of strategies, such as lean manufacturing, energy-efficient equipment, and closed-loop production systems.

Manufacturing can switch to renewable energy sources, such as solar, wind, or hydropower that can significantly reduce the sector's carbon footprint. Many companies are also investing in on-site renewable energy generation to reduce their reliance on the grid. Manufacturing can implement a circular economy approach that can help reduce waste and increase the reuse and recycling of materials. This can involve designing products for durability and easy disassembly, implementing take-back programs for end-of-life products, and using recycled materials in production. Manufacturing can also ensure sustainability across the entire supply chain.

This can involve working with suppliers to reduce their environmental and social impacts, implementing responsible sourcing policies, and supporting local suppliers. Finally, the manufacturing sector can engage employees in sustainability initiatives and can help to increase their understanding and commitment to sustainability goals. This can involve providing training and education on sustainability issues, establishing sustainability teams, and recognizing and rewarding employees for their sustainability efforts.

4. **Retail Sector**: In the retail sector, sustainability management may focus on reducing waste, improving energy efficiency, and promoting sustainable consumption. This may involve implementing sustainable store designs, using renewable energy sources, and promoting products with eco-friendly or ethical certifications. The retail sector can also make significant contributions to sustainability efforts by reducing their environmental impact by switching to more sustainable packaging options, such as biodegradable and compostable materials, or by using recycled and recyclable materials.

   Additionally, retailers can also reduce packaging waste by minimizing the size and weight of packaging. Retail stores can improve energy efficiency by implementing energy-saving measures, such as upgrading to LED lighting, installing motion sensors, and using energy-efficient HVAC systems. Retailers can also install solar panels to generate renewable energy, which can help to reduce their carbon footprint. Retailers can work with suppliers to promote sustainability throughout the supply chain. This can include requiring suppliers to meet environmental and social sustainability criteria, as well as promoting local sourcing to reduce the environmental impact of transportation.

Retailers can reduce waste by implementing measures, such as reducing food waste through food recovery programs, using reusable shopping bags, and encouraging customers to recycle. Additionally, retailers can also implement take-back programs for end-of-life products to promote the circular economy. Finally, retailers can promote responsible consumption by educating customers on the environmental and social impacts of their purchasing decisions. Retailers can also promote sustainable and ethically produced products, as well as offering repair and recycling services to encourage customers to keep products in use for longer periods of time.

5. **Hospitality Sector**: The hospitality industry can have a significant impact on the environment and communities, but it can also contribute to sustainability by adopting sustainable solutions. The hospitality sector can reduce its environmental impact, conserve resources, and contribute to sustainable development in a variety of ways.

   First, the hospitality sector can improve energy efficiency by implementing measures, such as energy-efficient lighting and appliances, using renewable energy sources, and using smart building technology to control energy use. Second, the hospitality sector can conserve water by implementing measures, such as low-flow showerheads and faucets, using reclaimed water for irrigation, and recycling wastewater. Third, the hospitality sector can promote sustainable food practices by sourcing local, organic, and seasonal produce, reducing food waste, and offering plant-based menu options. Additionally, hotels can set up rooftop or on-site gardens to grow their own produce. Fourth, the hospitality sector can promote sustainable design practices by using environmentally friendly building materials, designing buildings that are energy-efficient, and using passive design strategies such as natural ventilation and shading to reduce energy use. Fifth, the hospitality sector can reduce waste by implementing measures, such as recycling, composting, and using refillable amenity dispensers instead of disposable single-use items. And finally, the hospitality sector can engage with local communities by supporting local businesses, promoting cultural events and attractions, and providing job opportunities for local residents.

6. **Finance Sector**: In the finance sector, sustainability management may focus on integrating environmental, social, and governance

(ESG) factors into investment decisions. This may involve screening investments for ESG risks and opportunities, engaging with companies on sustainability issues, and promoting ESG investment products. The finance sector can play a critical role in driving sustainability by financing sustainable projects and encouraging sustainable business practices. Here are some sustainable solutions.

First, the fianance sector can promote socially responsible investing, impact investing, and sustainable investing. These priorities can generate positive social and environmental outcomes alongside financial returns. The finance sector can promote sustainable investment by offering green financial products, such as green bonds and sustainability-linked loans, to finance sustainable projects. Additionally, the finance sector can also integrate environmental, social, and governance (ESG) factors into their investment decisions to support sustainable businesses. Second, it can promote sustainable landing. It can offer loans to support the development of sustainable businesses, such as renewable energy and sustainable agriculture. Additionally, the finance sector can also implement sustainability criteria for loan approval to encourage sustainable business practices. Third, the finance sector can promote sustainability by using carbon accounting tools to measure and report the carbon footprint of their portfolios. This can help to identify high-carbon investments and support the transition to a low-carbon economy. Fourth, it can promote sustainability by increasing transparency and disclosure of environmental, social, and governance (ESG) risks and opportunities.

This can help investors and customers make informed decisions and encourage sustainable business practices. The finance sector can also promote sustainability through their operations (reducing energy use, promoting sustainable transportation, and reducing waste) and by educating customers and investors on sustainable investing and financing, as well as promoting sustainable business practices. Additionally, the finance sector can engage with stakeholders to promote sustainable development and contribute to sustainability initiatives. Through these solutions, the finance sector can effectively promote sustainable development and significantly contribute to the transition to a low-carbon economy.

7. **Transportation Sector**: In the transportation sector, sustainability management may focus on reducing greenhouse gas emissions,

improving fuel efficiency, and promoting sustainable mobility. This may involve developing alternative fuel vehicles, improving public transportation infrastructure, and promoting sustainable transportation behaviors. The transportation sector is a major contributor to global GHG emissions, which contribute to climate change.

To address this challenge, there are several sustainable solutions for the transportation sector including electrification, alternative fuels, active transportation, public transportation, sustainable aviation and shipping, urban planning, and vehicle efficiency. Electrifying transportation can reduce GHG emissions and improve air quality. This includes transitioning from gasoline-powered cars to electric vehicles (EVs), as well as using electric buses, trains, and other forms of public transportation. Alternative fuels, such as biofuels and hydrogen, can also help to reduce GHG emissions from the transportation sector. These fuels can be used in vehicles, as well as in aviation and shipping. Active transportation, such as walking and cycling, can help to reduce GHG emissions from transportation and improve public health.

Encouraging the use of active transportation can be achieved through improving infrastructure, such as bike lanes and pedestrian-friendly sidewalks, and implementing policies to support active transportation. Investing in public transportation, such as buses, trains, and light rail, can reduce GHG emissions and improve accessibility. This includes promoting the use of public transportation through improved service and infrastructure, as well as providing incentives for individuals to use public transportation.

The aviation and shipping industries are responsible for a significant portion of global GHG emissions. To address this, sustainable aviation fuels and low-carbon shipping technologies can be developed and implemented. Urban planning can play a critical role in promoting sustainable transportation. This includes designing cities to be more walkable and bike-friendly, as well as improving access to public transportation. Improving the efficiency of vehicles, such as through fuel-efficient engines, lightweight materials, and aerodynamics, can reduce GHG emissions and improve fuel economy. By adopting these and other sustainable solutions, the transportation sector can reduce GHG emissions and contribute to the transition to a low-carbon economy.

Businesses can and should do more than simple sustainability management practices. Current environmental and social challenges require urgent new thinking and approaches. Their efforts should be more than just minimizing negative impacts, but creating new pathways to solve our current and future problems. By adopting net positive and regenerative approaches, businesses can create value for the environment, society, and their stakeholders. Using the SDGs as a blueprint, companies can create sustainable value and effectively contribute to global challenges (Hoek, 2018). The B Corp movement and Benefit Corporations have been instrumental in promoting net-positive business solutions and encouraging companies to adopt more responsible and sustainable practices.

Case 8.1 The B Corps Movement

The terms "B Corps" and "Benefit Corporations" are often confused as being the same. They are related but not exactly the same entity.

A "Benefit Corporation" is a legal designation for a type of company that is required to consider the impact of its decisions not only on its shareholders, but also on its stakeholders, which can include employees, customers, suppliers, the environment, and the community. Benefit Corporations are required by law to pursue a general public benefit, which is defined as a material positive impact on society and the environment.

On the other hand, "B Corps" usually refers to companies that have been certified by the nonprofit organization B Lab as meeting certain standards of social and environmental performance, transparency, and accountability. B Corps are not a legal designation, but rather a certification that is awarded to companies that meet a high standard of performance across a range of areas, including governance, workers, community, environment, and customers.

While both Benefit Corporations and B Corps share a commitment to social and environmental responsibility, there are some key differences between them. Benefit Corporations are a legal structure, while B Corps are a certification. Benefit Corporations are legally required to consider the interests of stakeholders, while B Corps voluntarily adopt a high standard of social and environmental performance. In other words, Benefit Corporations are a specific legal designation for companies that are required to consider the interests of their stakeholders and pursue a general public benefit, while B Corps are companies that have voluntarily chosen to meet a high standard of social and environmental performance as defined by B Lab.

The B Corps movement is a global movement of companies that are certified as "B Corps" and many of them are also legally registered as benefit corporations, which means that they meet high standards of social and environmental performance, accountability, and transparency. B Corps are for-profit companies that are committed to using business as a force for good and creating a positive impact on society and the environment. To become a certified B Corp, companies must undergo a rigorous assessment that evaluates their impact on the environment, their workers, their customers, and their community. The assessment covers a wide range of factors, including governance, employee benefits and culture, environmental practices, supply chain management, and community engagement. Companies must earn a minimum score on the assessment and commit to making ongoing improvements in order to maintain their B Corp certification.

The B Corps movement contributes to sustainability management in several ways:

1. **Transparency**: B Corps are required to be transparent about their impact on society and the environment, which promotes accountability and encourages companies to adopt sustainable business practices.
2. **Standards**: The B Corp certification sets a high standard for social and environmental performance, which helps to promote best practices and encourages companies to adopt sustainable business practices.
3. **Collaboration**: The B Corps movement fosters collaboration between companies, which can lead to the development of new sustainable business models and innovative solutions to social and environmental challenges.
4. **Consumer awareness**: The B Corp certification provides a way for consumers to identify companies that are committed to sustainability and social responsibility, which can help to drive demand for sustainable products and services.

5. **Policy influence**: The B Corps movement also seeks to influence policy at the local, national, and international levels, to create a regulatory environment that supports sustainable business practices and promotes social and environmental justice.

The B Corps movement is a powerful tool for promoting sustainability management, by setting high standards for corporate social and environmental responsibility and encouraging companies to adopt sustainable business practices that create a positive impact on society and the environment. The movement is expanding globally with some adaptation as in the case of Italy, the first country after the US Benefit Corporation legal designation, to establish a Società Benefit (or Benefit Corporations) as a status that is awarded to companies by a certification body recognized by the Italian government. In addition, all Italian B Corp certified companies must also become Società Benefit, "formalizing in their articles of association a purpose that goes beyond mere profit and thus protecting this corporate mission in the long term" (B Lab Italy). The B Corps movement is rapidly growing, and it is having a significant impact for sustainability management (see Part IV on sustainability impact for more detail).

Government Sector and Sustainability Management

The government sector, which includes local, national governments as well as international–intergovernmental organizations such as the United Nations, has an important role to play in sustainability management. They have the power to establish regulations, laws, and policies that can encourage or enforce sustainable practices in various sectors, including the business, social, academic, healthcare, and technology sectors. Governments can also provide financial support, incentives, and technical assistance to promote sustainable development and address environmental and social issues. Governments and the public sector can promote sustainability practices by developing and implementing policies, investing in sustainable infrastructure, educating the public, leading by example, and collaborating with other sectors. This involves creating regulations and incentives, supporting green projects, raising awareness, adopting sustainable practices internally, and fostering partnerships to advance sustainable goals.

Sustainability government management is, therefore, critical for the management of public resources and promotes sustainability opportunities for the businesses, institutions, and communities under their purview. It can also be instrumental to promoting public–private partnerships (PPP) that can maximize their contributions to sustainability (Martin & Boyd, 2021). This approach involves balancing economic growth with environmental protection and social equity, and it aims to ensure that the needs of the present are met without compromising the ability of future generations to meet their own needs. Sustainability government management is important for people's well-being and the climate crisis in several ways.

First, it promotes economic prosperity. A sustainable approach to government management can promote economic prosperity by creating jobs in green industries, reducing costs through energy efficiency measures, and stimulating innovation in areas such as renewable energy. Second, it protects the environment. Sustainability government management aims to reduce the negative impact of government operations on the environment, such as reducing greenhouse gas emissions, conserving natural resources, and protecting biodiversity. Third, it supports social equity. A sustainable approach to government management can promote social equity by ensuring that everyone has access to resources and opportunities, and that no one is unfairly burdened by environmental degradation or other negative consequences of government operations. And fourth, it helps mitigate climate change as it aims to reduce greenhouse gas emissions and other harmful environmental impacts.

Governments around the world are implementing sustainable solutions in various areas such as energy, transportation, waste management, and more. Here are a few examples:

1. **Denmark's Wind Energy**: Denmark has been a pioneer in wind energy, and it now generates more than 40% of its electricity from wind power. The government has set ambitious targets to phase out fossil fuels and has implemented policies to promote the growth of the wind energy industry.
2. **Curitiba's Sustainable Urban Planning**: Curitiba, a city in Brazil, has implemented sustainable urban planning that includes a bus

rapid transit system, bike paths, and parks. This has helped to reduce traffic congestion, improve air quality, and promote active transportation.

3. **Sweden's Waste-to-Energy Plants**: Sweden has invested heavily in waste-to-energy plants that convert household and industrial waste into energy. This has helped to reduce landfill waste and greenhouse gas emissions while generating energy for homes and businesses.
4. **China's Electric Vehicle Incentives**: China has implemented policies to promote the use of electric vehicles, including incentives for both consumers and manufacturers. This has helped to reduce air pollution and greenhouse gas emissions from transportation.
5. **New York's Green Buildings**: New York City has implemented policies to promote the construction of green buildings, which are designed to be energy-efficient and environmentally friendly. This has helped to reduce energy consumption and greenhouse gas emissions from buildings.

These are just a few examples of how governments are implementing sustainable solutions. Other examples include investments in renewable energy, carbon pricing policies, sustainable agriculture practices, and more.

Local Governments Sustainability Management

Local governments have a critical role to play in promoting sustainability as they are responsible for many of the day-to-day activities that impact the environment and the well-being of their residents. Here are some examples of the role of local governments in promoting sustainability:

1. **Planning and Zoning**: Local governments can use their planning and zoning powers to promote sustainable development by requiring new buildings to meet green building standards, setting aside areas for parks and open space, and promoting mixed-use development that reduces reliance on cars. For example, in Vancouver, Canada, the city has a "Greenest City Action Plan" that includes requirements for green buildings, incentives for sustainable development, and policies to promote active transportation.

2. **Waste Management**: Local governments are responsible for managing waste and can promote sustainability by implementing recycling and composting programs, banning single-use plastics, and promoting waste reduction. For example, in San Francisco, California, the city has a goal to achieve zero waste by 2020 and has implemented policies such as mandatory composting and a ban on plastic bags.
3. **Public Transportation**: Local governments can promote sustainable transportation by investing in public transportation, promoting walking and biking, and implementing car-sharing and bike-sharing programs. For example, in Bogotá, Colombia, the city has a successful bus rapid transit system that has reduced traffic congestion and air pollution.
4. **Energy Efficiency**: Local governments can promote energy efficiency by implementing policies to reduce energy consumption in public buildings and encouraging residents and businesses to do the same. For example, in Portland, Oregon, the city has a goal to reduce energy use by 20% by 2020 and has implemented programs to promote energy efficiency in buildings.
5. **Local Food**: Local governments can promote sustainable agriculture and local food systems by supporting farmers markets, community gardens, and urban agriculture programs. For example, in Toronto, Canada, the city has implemented policies to promote local food production and distribution, and has set a goal to increase the amount of food produced within city limits.

These are just a few examples of how local governments can promote sustainability. By taking action at the local level, governments can create more sustainable and resilient communities that protect the environment, promote economic prosperity, and improve the quality of life for residents.

National and Federal Government Sustainability Management

National and federal governments also play a very important role in promoting sustainability as they have the authority to create policies, regulations, and laws that affect entire countries or regions. Here are some examples of the role of national and federal governments in promoting sustainability:

1. **Climate Policy**: National and federal governments can implement policies to reduce greenhouse gas emissions, such as carbon pricing, renewable energy targets, and energy efficiency standards. For example, in the United States, the federal government has recently proposed a series of climate policy measures aimed at reducing greenhouse gas emissions, including a national goal of achieving a net-zero economy-wide emissions target by 2050.
2. **International Cooperation**: National and federal governments can participate in international agreements and negotiations to address global sustainability challenges. For example, the Paris Agreement is a global agreement on climate change that was signed by 197 countries, including the United States, with the goal of limiting global warming to well below 2 °C above pre-industrial levels.
3. **Conservation and Biodiversity**: National and federal governments can establish protected areas and conservation programs to preserve ecosystems and biodiversity. For example, the Brazilian government has established a system of protected areas that covers more than 18% of the country's land area.
4. **Sustainable Agriculture**: National and federal governments can support sustainable agriculture practices, such as organic farming and agroforestry, to promote food security and reduce the environmental impact of agriculture. For example, the European Union has established a Common Agricultural Policy that includes measures to support sustainable agriculture practices and protect the environment.
5. **Green Infrastructure**: National and federal governments can invest in green infrastructure, such as public transportation, bike paths, and green spaces, to promote sustainable urban development and reduce greenhouse gas emissions. For example, the Chinese government has invested heavily in public transportation infrastructure, including high-speed rail and electric buses, to reduce traffic congestion and air pollution.

These are just a few examples of how national and federal governments can promote sustainability. By taking action at the national level, governments can create opportunities and set policies that can benefit the population, communities, and industries at multiple levels. They can create legal systems for a more sustainable future and help to address the complex sustainability challenges facing the world today.

International and Intergovernmental Sustainability Management

International and intergovernmental organizations play a critical role in promoting sustainability as they have the capacity to coordinate and mobilize efforts among countries and stakeholders at a global level. Here are some examples of the role of international and intergovernmental organizations in promoting sustainability:

1. **The UN and the Sustainable Development Goals**: The UN adopted the SDGs in 2015 as an international commitment for a more sustainable and equitable future for all. The UN also tracks progress towards the SDGs and reports on achievements and challenges. With its several bodies and programs that promote sustainability, such as the United Nations Environment Programme (UNEP) and the United Nations Development Programme (UNDP), the UN is probably the most important international and intergovernmental institution to promote sustainability management worldwide.
2. **Environmental Conventions**: International agreements, such as the CBC and the UNFCCC, provide a framework for countries to cooperate on issues, such as biodiversity conservation and climate change. The conventions establish commitments, guidelines, and mechanisms to help countries work together to address global environmental challenges.
3. **Technical Assistance**: International and intergovernmental organizations provide technical assistance and capacity building support to help countries develop sustainable policies and programs. For example, the World Bank provides loans and technical assistance to support sustainable development projects in developing countries.
4. **Environmental Certification and Standards**: International and intergovernmental organizations also play a role in developing and promoting environmental certification and standards, such as the FSC certification for sustainable forestry practices. These certifications and standards help to promote sustainability in industries and supply chains, and can improve consumer awareness and demand for sustainable products. Another example of standards is the role that the International Organization for Standardization (ISO) plays in a number sustainability-related standards for Environmental Management System (ISO 14001), Energy Management System (ISO

50001), Social Responsibility (ISO 26000), and Sustainable Events Management (ISO 20121).

5. **Climate Finance**: International and intergovernmental organizations provide funding and financing mechanisms to support sustainable development and climate change mitigation and adaptation efforts. For example, the Green Climate Fund (GCF) is a global fund that supports climate change projects and programs in developing countries.

These are just a few examples of how international and intergovernmental organizations promote sustainability. By working together, countries and stakeholders can collaborate to address the complex sustainability challenges facing the world today, and promote a more sustainable and equitable future for all.

Case 8.2 C40 and Urban Sustainability

C40 is a network of cities around the world committed to taking action on climate change. The network was created in 2005 and currently has more than 90 member cities, representing more than 700 million people and one-quarter of the global economy. C40's mission is to help cities take meaningful and effective action to address climate change and promote urban sustainability.

C40 was founded in 2005 by former Mayor of London Ken Livingstone and a group of mayors from around the world. From 2021, Mayor of London, Sadiq Khan, serves as C40's Chair and former Mayor of New York City Michael Bloomberg as Board President. The organization was created in response to the urgent need for action on climate change and the recognition that cities have a critical role to play in addressing this global challenge. The founding mayors recognized that cities are responsible for a significant portion of global greenhouse gas emissions and that they are also highly vulnerable to the impacts of climate change, such as sea level rise, extreme weather events, and heatwaves. They believed that by working together and sharing knowledge and best practices, cities could take meaningful and effective action on climate change and promote sustainable urban development.

C40 was named after the 40 cities that participated in the organization's first meeting in London in 2005. Since then, the organization has expanded its focus to include a wide range of sustainability issues, from transportation and energy to waste management and green infrastructure. Today, C40 is recognized as a leading global organization for urban sustainability and is playing a critical role in driving action on climate change and promoting sustainable development in cities around the world. C40 promotes urban sustainability in several ways, including:

1. **Sharing knowledge and best practices**: C40 facilitates the sharing of knowledge and best practices among member cities. This includes sharing information on sustainable urban planning, building design, public transportation, and waste management, among other topics. City mayors have the opportunity to collaborate and share knowledge with other city leaders from around the world through C40. By working together and sharing best practices, mayors can help to accelerate the implementation of sustainable solutions and promote more sustainable urban development.
2. **Setting sustainability targets and goals**: City mayors are responsible for setting sustainability targets and goals for their cities, in line with global goals, such as the Paris Agreement. By setting ambitious targets and goals, mayors can help to drive action and ensure that their cities are making progress towards a more sustainable future.
3. **Implementing Sustainable Solutions**: C40 provides technical assistance to member cities to help them implement sustainable solutions. This can include assistance with developing sustainable transportation systems, implementing renewable energy projects, and reducing greenhouse gas emissions. City mayors are responsible for implementing sustainable solutions in their cities, such as building sustainable infrastructure, reducing greenhouse gas emissions, and promoting sustainable transportation. With the technical assistance of C40, mayors can implement urban sustainability solutions. They can help to reduce the environmental impact of their cities and improve the quality of life for their citizens.
4. **Advocacy and policy development**: C40 advocates for policies at the national and international levels that support sustainable urban development. The organization also works to develop policies and regulations that support sustainable development at the local level. City mayors have a unique platform to advocate for sustainability and climate action, both at the local and international levels. By using their position to raise awareness of sustainability issues and

advocate for policy changes, mayors can help to create momentum and drive action on these critical issues.

5. **Collaboration and partnership**: C40 facilitates collaboration and partnership between member cities, as well as between cities and other stakeholders, such as businesses and civil society organizations. This collaboration can help to accelerate the implementation of sustainable solutions and promote the sharing of knowledge and best practices.

Through these activities, C40 is helping to promote urban sustainability and support cities around the world in taking action on climate change. By bringing together cities to work on common sustainability goals, C40 is helping to drive meaningful and effective action to address one of the most pressing global challenges of our time. As members of the C40 network, mayors have the opportunity to collaborate with other city leaders from around the world to develop and implement sustainable solutions.

Social Sector and Sustainability Management

The social sector, also known as the third sector or the nonprofit sector, is made up of organizations that operate for the benefit of society, rather than for profit. These organizations may include charities, foundations, NGOs, community organizations, social enterprises, and other types of nonprofit organizations (Medine & Minto-Coy, 2023). Historically, the social sector has played and continues to play a critical role in sustainable development by addressing social and environmental challenges, promoting social equity, and building community resilience (Fowler, 2013). Some of the key ways that the social sector contributes to sustainable development include:

1. **Addressing social and environmental challenges**: The social sector plays a critical role in addressing social and environmental challenges, such as poverty, inequality, climate change, and environmental degradation. Nonprofit organizations are often well-positioned to identify and respond to these challenges, working in partnership with government, business, and other stakeholders to develop and implement solutions.

2. **Building community resilience**: The social sector is often closely connected to local communities and can play a key role in building community resilience. By working with communities to develop social, economic, and environmental initiatives, nonprofits can help to create more sustainable and resilient communities.
3. **Advocating for change**: Nonprofit organizations often advocate for policy changes and promote social and environmental justice. By advocating for policies and practices that support sustainable development, nonprofits can help to create a more sustainable and equitable society.
4. **Encouraging innovation and collaboration**: Nonprofits often encourage innovation and collaboration, bringing together stakeholders from different sectors to work towards sustainable development goals. By fostering collaboration and encouraging innovation, nonprofits can help to develop and implement new approaches to sustainable development.

Overall, the social sector plays a critical role in promoting sustainable development by addressing social and environmental challenges, building community resilience, advocating for change, and encouraging innovation and collaboration.

There are many examples of nonprofits and NGOs contributing to the SDGs through their work. Here are a few examples of best practices and organizations that are making a positive impact:

1. **Water.org**: This nonprofit organization is focused on providing access to safe water and sanitation for people around the world. Their work directly contributes to SDG 6, which aims to ensure availability and sustainable management of water and sanitation for all.
2. **The Hunger Project**: This organization is focused on ending hunger and poverty through grassroots community-led initiatives. Their work contributes to SDG 1, which aims to end poverty in all its forms everywhere, and SDG 2, which aims to end hunger, achieve food security and improved nutrition, and promote sustainable agriculture.

3. **Save the Children**: This international NGO works to improve the lives of children through education, health, and protection initiatives. Their work contributes to multiple SDGs, including SDG 3 (good health and well-being), SDG 4 (quality education), and SDG 10 (reduced inequalities).
4. **The Nature Conservancy**: This organization is focused on protecting and conserving natural resources and biodiversity. Their work contributes to SDG 13 (climate action), SDG 14 (Life Below Water), and SDG 15 (Life on Land).
5. **Ashoka**: This organization supports social entrepreneurs who are working on innovative solutions to social and environmental challenges. Their work contributes to multiple SDGs, including SDG 8 (decent work and economic growth), SDG 9 (industry, innovation, and infrastructure), and SDG 12 (responsible consumption and production).
6. **Conservation International**: Conservation International is a nonprofit organization that works to protect and sustainably manage the Earth's natural resources. It has contributed to several SDGs, including SDG 14: Life Below Water, through its efforts to protect the world's oceans and marine ecosystems. The organization has implemented marine conservation programs, promoted sustainable fishing practices, and worked to reduce plastic pollution in the oceans.
7. **BRAC**: BRAC is a global development organization based in Bangladesh that has made significant contributions to several SDGs, including SDG 1: No Poverty, and SDG 5: Gender Equality. BRAC has implemented a range of programs to address poverty, empower women, and improve access to healthcare and education in communities around the world.
8. **WaterAid**: WaterAid is a nonprofit organization that works to improve access to clean water, sanitation, and hygiene in communities around the world. The organization has contributed to SDG 6: Clean Water and Sanitation, by implementing water and sanitation programs in some of the world's poorest and most marginalized communities.
9. **Oxfam**: Oxfam's "Behind the Brands" campaign focuses on pressuring the world's biggest food and beverage companies to adopt more sustainable and responsible business practices. The campaign has successfully pushed companies to address issues such

as land rights, climate change, and gender equality. It contributes to several sustainable development goals including SDG 1: No Poverty—by working to improve the lives and livelihoods of small-scale farmers and agricultural workers; SDG 2: Zero Hunger—by promoting sustainable and responsible business practices in the food and beverage sector; SDG 5: Gender Equality—by advocating for gender equality in the agricultural sector; SDG 8: Decent Work and Economic Growth—by pushing for better working conditions and labor rights for agricultural workers; and SDG 12: Responsible Consumption and Production—by encouraging companies to adopt more sustainable and responsible business practices.

10. **CARE International**: CARE International's "She Feeds the World" campaign aims to address gender inequality in the agricultural sector and promote women's empowerment. The campaign has successfully advocated for policy changes that support women's access to land, credit, and other resources. The campaign is primarily contributing to SDG 2: Zero Hunger, which aims to end hunger, achieve food security and improved nutrition, and promote sustainable agriculture. The campaign recognizes that women play a critical role in food systems, but often face discrimination and lack of access to resources and opportunities. In addition to SDG 2, the "She Feeds the World" campaign also supports several other SDGs, including SDG 1: No Poverty: By empowering women in agriculture, the campaign is helping to reduce poverty and inequality; SDG 3: Good Health and Well-being: Improved food security and nutrition can lead to better health outcomes; SDG 5: Gender Equality: The campaign focuses on empowering women in agriculture, which supports gender equality and women's empowerment; and SDG 13: Climate Action: The campaign emphasizes the importance of sustainable agriculture practices, which can help mitigate the impacts of climate change.

These are just a few examples of the many nonprofits and NGOs that are working towards the SDGs. Best practices for contributing to the SDGs include engaging in cross-sector collaborations, building strong partnerships with local communities, and focusing on long-term impact and sustainability.

Case 8.3 The SDSN and SDG Promotion

The Sustainable Development Solutions Network (SDSN) is an international non-governmental organization (NGO) that was launched by the United Nations in 2012. The SDSN operates as an independent network, but it was established under the auspices of the UN Secretary-General to support the implementation of the Sustainable Development Goals (SDGs) and the 2030 Agenda for Sustainable Development.

The SDSN is not a part of the United Nations system, but it works closely with the UN and other international organizations to promote sustainable development. The network includes members from academia, civil society, and the private sector, and it operates through a series of national and regional networks that bring together stakeholders to advance sustainable development in their respective countries or regions.

As an NGO, the SDSN is focused on advancing sustainable development through research, education, and public policy advocacy. It does not engage in direct implementation of development projects, but rather seeks to support the development of evidence-based policies and practices that can drive sustainable development outcomes.

The SDSN mobilizes knowledge and expertise from academia, civil society, and the private sector to promote sustainable development. Since 2015, the SDSN has been prompting the implementation of the SDGs to end poverty, protect the planet, and ensure prosperity for all. The SDSN aims to advance the SDGs by promoting integrated approaches to sustainable development, including through research, education, and public policy advocacy. The network brings together a diverse range of actors, including scientists, policymakers, business leaders, and civil society organizations, to collaborate on solutions to global sustainability challenges. Some of the contributions of the SDSN to sustainability include:

1. **Research and analysis**: The SDSN produces research and analysis on sustainable development issues, including reports on the implementation of the SDGs, and works to improve the quality and availability of data on sustainable development.

2. **Education and training**: The SDSN promotes education and training on sustainable development, including through the development of curricula and training programs for students, professionals, and policymakers.
3. **Advocacy and policy advice**: The SDSN provides advocacy and policy advice to governments, businesses, and civil society organizations on how to advance sustainable development, including through the development of policy briefs and recommendations.
4. **Network building**: The SDSN builds networks of experts and stakeholders to facilitate knowledge sharing, collaboration, and the development of new solutions to sustainability challenges.

Overall, the SDSN is an important actor in the global effort to advance sustainable development and achieve the SDGs. Its contributions to research, education, advocacy, and network building help to promote integrated approaches to sustainability and support the creation of a more sustainable future for all. Here are some of the SDSN significant achievements towards its mission and the SDGs:

1. **The SDG Index and Dashboard**: The SDSN developed the SDG Index and Dashboard, which is a comprehensive measure of progress on the SDGs. The index assesses countries' performance on the SDGs and helps to identify areas where additional action is needed.
2. **Mobilizing action on climate change**: The SDSN has been a leading advocate for action on climate change and has played a key role in building momentum for the Paris Agreement on climate change. The network has also supported the development of innovative financing mechanisms, such as green bonds, to mobilize investment in sustainable development.
3. **Supporting sustainable cities**: The SDSN has supported the development of sustainable cities through the launch of the SDG Cities program. This initiative provides guidance and support to city leaders and stakeholders to help them implement the SDGs in their urban contexts.

4. **Promoting sustainable agriculture**: The SDSN has promoted sustainable agriculture through the development of the SDG Agriculture and Food Index. This index measures countries' performance on the SDGs related to agriculture and food security and helps to identify areas where additional action is needed.
5. **Advancing education for sustainable development**: The SDSN has promoted education for sustainable development through the development of the SDG Academy. This online education platform provides courses and training programs on sustainable development topics, and has reached learners in more than 190 countries.

The SDSN has promoted all 17 SDGs, but some of the SDGs it has focused on include SDG 13 (Climate Action), SDG 11 (Sustainable Cities and Communities), SDG 2 (Zero Hunger), SDG 4 (Quality Education), and SDG 6 (Clean Water and Sanitation). The network's work on these SDGs has included research, advocacy, and capacity building initiatives to support progress towards achieving the goals.

Academic Sector and Sustainability Management

Academia has a critical role to play in advancing sustainable development (Öztürk, 2022). In general, the institutions and organizations of the academic-education sector have a dual responsibility towards sustainability. First, academia in general and higher education in particular have the responsibility to educate future leaders and decision-makers who can commit to a sustainable future. Second, they need to lead the way for sustainability values through institutional commitment to administer sustainability policies and practices integrated with their promotion of sustainability related teaching, research, and engagement. Third, they can contribute to the promotion of the SDGs and drive progress toward sustainable development by promoting innovative approaches to their methods of teaching and collaboration with community partners across sectors. More specifically, academia can play a critical role in promoting sustainability through the following commitments:

1. **Research**: Academic institutions are often at the forefront of research on sustainability issues and can provide valuable insights into the environmental, social, and economic dimensions of sustainable development. Academic research can help to identify the challenges and opportunities related to the SDGs, and inform policies and practices to advance sustainable development. For example, researchers at universities around the world are investigating ways to achieve SDG 2 (Zero Hunger) by developing more sustainable agricultural practices, improving access to nutritious food, and reducing food waste.
2. **Education and training**: Academic institutions can provide education and training on sustainable development, which is critical for building a skilled workforce that can advance sustainability in a range of sectors. This includes courses on sustainability issues, as well as training on sustainability practices and tools. For example, universities can work with governments, NGOs, and businesses to develop and implement sustainable development policies and practices. One example is the Global Universities Partnership on Environment and Sustainability, which brings together universities from around the world to collaborate on sustainability research, education, and engagement.
3. **Innovation**: Academic institutions can be a source of innovation in sustainable development, by developing new technologies and approaches that can help to address sustainability challenges. This includes research on renewable energy, sustainable agriculture, and sustainable urban design, among other areas. For example, researchers at the Massachusetts Institute of Technology (MIT) are developing new technologies to address SDG 7 (Affordable and Clean Energy), such as new forms of renewable energy, energy storage systems, and energy-efficient buildings.
4. **Partnerships**: Academic institutions can form partnerships with other stakeholders, including government, civil society, and the private sector, to advance sustainable development. These partnerships can leverage academic expertise to inform policy and practice, and can also provide opportunities for research and innovation. For example, universities can work with governments, NGOs, and businesses to develop and implement sustainable development policies and practices. One example is the Global Universities Partnership

on Environment and Sustainability, which brings together universities from around the world to collaborate on sustainability research, education, and engagement.

5. **Advocacy**: Academic institutions can advocate for sustainable development, by engaging in public debates and policy discussions, and by promoting the importance of sustainability in their own operations and activities. For example, universities can commit to the SDSN's SDG Accord, which commits them to embedding the SDGs into their operations and activities, and to reporting on their progress towards sustainability.
6. **Sharing**: Academic institutions have the responsibility to promote collaboration and sharing of best practices in sustainability integration and responsible educational practices. As exemplified in the latest version of the Principles for Responsible Management Education, the Sharing Information on Progress (SIP) report is not just a matter of compliance but of systemic mainstreaming of sustainability education practices.

Overall, academia can play a critical role in promoting sustainable development, by providing research, education, innovation, partnerships, and advocacy that can help to build a more sustainable future. Academic institutions can also contribute to their sustainability practices by promoting sustainable campus operations, sustainable procurement, and community engagement. Universities can adopt sustainable practices and technologies on their campuses, such as energy-efficient buildings, renewable energy sources, water conservation measures, and sustainable transportation options. This can reduce their environmental footprint and serve as a model for sustainable practices. Universities can adopt sustainable procurement practices, by purchasing products and services that have a lower environmental and social impact. This can include buying products made from sustainable materials, reducing waste, and promoting fair labor practices. Universities can engage with their local communities to promote sustainability and contribute to local sustainable development initiatives. This can include partnering with community organizations, supporting local sustainability projects, and engaging with local policymakers to advance sustainability goals.

There are several academic specific initiatives that promote sustainability in higher education and/or management education. Here is an overview of the main ones:

1. **The Principles for Responsible Management Education (PRME)**: PRME is a United Nations-backed initiative (through the UNGC) that aims to promote sustainability and responsible management education in business schools and management education institutions around the world. The initiative was launched in 2007, and it now includes over 800 signatories from over 100 countries. The PRME initiative has contributed to academic sustainability by encouraging business schools and management education institutions to integrate sustainability and responsible management education into their curriculum, research, and campus operations. Signatories to the PRME initiative commit to advancing sustainability through a range of actions, such as incorporating sustainability topics into their courses, developing research on sustainability issues, engaging with businesses and other stakeholders to promote sustainability, and promoting sustainability in their campus operations.
2. **The United Nations Academic Impact (UNAI)**: UNAI is an initiative launched by the United Nations in 2010 to align institutions of higher education, scholarship, and research with the UN's global priorities, including sustainability. UNAI is a global network of universities and other academic institutions that work to support the SDGs and promote global citizenship and social responsibility. One of the main contributions of UNAI to sustainability education has been to promote the integration of sustainability and the SDGs into academic curricula and research. UNAI works with universities and other academic institutions to develop and promote sustainability-focused courses, research, and outreach programs, and to facilitate collaboration and partnerships between academia, governments, civil society, and the private sector. In particular, UNAI has supported a range of initiatives related to sustainability education, including: *The Sustainability Literacy Test*: UNAI developed a Sustainability Literacy Test to assess students' knowledge of sustainability concepts and practices. The test is designed to help universities and other academic institutions integrate sustainability into their curricula and assess the impact of their sustainability education initiatives. *The Sustainable Development Goals (SDG) Hubs*: UNAI has developed a network of SDG Hubs, which are regional centers of excellence that promote research, education, and

outreach related to the SDGs. The SDG Hubs support collaboration and partnerships between universities, governments, and other stakeholders to advance sustainable development. *Global Citizenship Education*: UNAI supports initiatives that promote global citizenship education, which is an approach to education that emphasizes the development of knowledge, skills, and values to empower students to contribute to a more just, peaceful, and sustainable world. *Student Engagement*: UNAI promotes student engagement in sustainability education and activities, including supporting student-led initiatives and developing opportunities for student participation in sustainability-focused research and outreach programs.

3. **The Higher Education for Sustainability Initiative (HESI)**: HESI is an initiative launched by the UN Department of Economic and Social Affairs (DESA) in 2005 to promote sustainability in higher education institutions (HEIs) around the world. The goal of HESI is to support HEIs in integrating sustainability principles and practices into their teaching, research, operations, and community engagement activities. One of the main contributions of HESI to sustainable education has been to provide a platform for collaboration and knowledge sharing among HEIs that are committed to sustainability. HESI has brought together HEIs from all regions of the world to exchange experiences, best practices, and lessons learned in implementing sustainability initiatives. HESI has also supported the development of sustainability-focused programs, courses, and research at HEIs, as well as the integration of sustainability into institutional policies and operations. HESI has provided guidance and resources to HEIs to help them develop sustainability strategies, implement sustainability programs, and measure their progress in advancing sustainability. HESI has also helped to raise awareness about the importance of sustainability in higher education and has contributed to the development of a global movement for sustainability in higher education. Through its various activities and initiatives, HESI has fostered a culture of sustainability in higher education and has helped to develop a new generation of graduates who are equipped with the skills, knowledge, and values to drive sustainable development.
4. **Education for Sustainable Development (ESD)**: ESD is a global initiative led by the United Nations Educational, Scientific, and

Cultural Organization (UNESCO) to promote sustainability and sustainable development through education. ESD is an interdisciplinary approach that aims to equip students with the knowledge, skills, values, and attitudes needed to participate in building a more sustainable future. The goal of ESD is to help individuals understand the interconnectedness of social, economic, and environmental issues and to develop the competencies needed to address these challenges in a sustainable and inclusive way. ESD emphasizes the importance of education for all, regardless of age, gender, ethnicity, or socio-economic background. ESD is based on the principle of "learning by doing" and encourages students to participate in practical, real-world projects that address sustainability challenges in their communities. It also emphasizes the importance of critical thinking, problem-solving, and collaboration, and aims to develop students' awareness and understanding of the role they can play in shaping a more sustainable future. UNESCO has been working on ESD since 2002 and launched the Global Action Programme (GAP) on ESD in 2014, which is a follow-up to the United Nations Decade of Education for Sustainable Development (2005–2014). The GAP on ESD provides a framework for countries, organizations, and individuals to work together to promote sustainability through education, with a particular focus on priority areas such as climate change, biodiversity, sustainable consumption and production, and peace and global citizenship.

5. **The Association for the Advancement of Sustainability in Higher Education (AASHE)**: AASHE is a North American-based association that works to advance sustainability in higher education institutions (HEIs) globally. AASHE provides a range of resources, professional development opportunities, and networking platforms to support HEIs in their efforts to promote sustainability on campus and beyond. One of AASHE's key initiatives is the Sustainability Tracking, Assessment, & Rating System (STARS), which is a comprehensive framework for measuring and reporting on the sustainability performance of HEIs. STARS allows HEIs to assess their sustainability performance across a range of areas, including academics, operations, engagement, and planning and administration. STARS provides a transparent and standardized method for evaluating and comparing sustainability performance among HEIs, and allows HEIs to identify areas where they can improve their

sustainability performance. In addition to STARS, AASHE has developed a new initiative called the Positive Impact Rating (PIR), which is a global sustainability rating system for HEIs. PIR aims to provide a more holistic and comprehensive assessment of HEIs' sustainability performance, taking into account their positive impact on society and the environment, as well as their efforts to mitigate negative impacts. PIR assesses HEIs across three main dimensions: research and education, operations, and outreach and engagement. PIR is based on a set of 17 sustainability goals, aligned with the SDGs. AASHE's work through initiatives such as STARS and PIR has been instrumental in promoting sustainability in higher education. These initiatives provide HEIs with the tools and resources they need to assess and improve their sustainability performance, and allow them to share their progress and best practices with other institutions. AASHE's work has also helped to raise awareness about the importance of sustainability in higher education and has contributed to the development of a global movement for sustainability in higher education.

6. **The Positive Impact Rating (PIR):** The PIR is an initiative bolstered by funders like VIVA Idea, aiming to revolutionize sustainability management education. Unlike traditional rating systems, PIR fosters collaboration and inspires change, instead of inciting competition and pressure. Supported by the academic sector, the PIR contributes to sustainable education to deliver research-based insights, helping to understand and improve current sustainability practices. Institutions participate in PIR by incorporating sustainability management into their teaching, preparing the leaders of tomorrow to understand and value sustainable business practices. Educational institutions implementing sustainable practices serve as live models for students and staff, offering firsthand experiences of these practices in action. PIR promotes cross-sector collaboration by organizing conferences and workshops on sustainability and stimulate dialogue and collaboration among academic institutions. In addition, PIR aims to influence policies and industry development through research and recommendations. In a high collaborative context, PIR leverages the research and expertise of its academic institutional partners by developing and refining tools for assessing and implementing sustainable practices. The PIR, in collaboration with the academic sector and the support of funders

like VIVA Idea, is poised to alter the paradigm of business schools globally, replacing the traditional rating competition with a system focused on positive impact and sustainable practices.

Case 8.4 PRME and Sustainability Management Education

The Principles for Responsible Management Education (PRME) were created by the United Nations Global Compact (UNGC) in partnership with a group of leading business schools and academic institutions. It was launched at the 2007 UN Global Compact Leaders Summit in Geneva, Switzerland, as a way to promote responsible management education and advance the principles of corporate social responsibility (CSR) and sustainability in business schools and management education programs around the world. The following academic institutions are considered to be the founding institutions of PRME: European Foundation for Management Development (EFMD), Association of MBAs (AMBA), Association to Advance Collegiate Schools of Business (AACSB International), Aspen Institute Business and Society Program, and United Nations Global Compact Office. Since its launch, the PRME initiative has grown to include over 800 signatories, including business schools and academic institutions from over 100 countries.

By promoting sustainability and responsible management education, the PRME initiative has helped to build a new generation of business leaders who are equipped with the skills, knowledge, and values to drive sustainable business practices and contribute to a more sustainable future. The initiative has also helped to raise awareness of the importance of sustainability in business education, and has spurred a range of sustainability-related initiatives in the academic community. The PRME initiative is based on six principles:

1. **Purpose**: To develop the capabilities of students to be future generators of sustainable value for business and society at large and to work for an inclusive and sustainable global economy.
2. **Values**: To incorporate values of global social responsibility as a foundation for management education.
3. **Method**: To create educational frameworks, materials, processes, and environments that enable effective learning experiences for responsible leadership.

4. **Research**: To engage in conceptual and empirical research that advances our understanding about the role, dynamics, and impact of corporations in the creation of sustainable social, environmental, and economic value.
5. **Partnership**: To interact with managers of business corporations to extend our knowledge of their challenges in meeting social and environmental responsibilities and to explore jointly effective approaches to meeting these challenges.
6. **Dialogue**: To facilitate and support dialogue and debate among educators, business, government, consumers, media, civil society organizations, and other interested groups and stakeholders on critical issues related to global social responsibility and sustainability.
7. **Share**: The updated PRME principles (as of June 5, 2023) introduced a 7th principle based on the value of sharing successes and failures to enable collective learning and live the common values and responsible-sustainability purpose of the initiative.

PRME is an initiative that actively promotes a growing area called Responsible Management Education (RME). RME refers to the integration of sustainability and CSR principles and practices into business and management education. RME aims to prepare current and future business leaders to be more socially and environmentally responsible in their decision-making and to contribute to sustainable development. RME is closely related to the SDGs as it aims to equip students with the knowledge and skills needed to address the social, economic, and environmental challenges facing the world. The SDGs provide a framework for addressing these challenges, and RME can play a critical role in promoting sustainable business practices and advancing progress towards the SDGs.

RME can be incorporated into business and management education in a variety of ways, including through course content, experiential learning opportunities, and research. For example, courses on sustainable business practices and social entrepreneurship can help students understand the role that businesses can play in promoting sustainable development. Experiential learning opportunities, such as internships or service learning projects, can provide students with hands-on experience working on sustainability challenges. Research on sustainability topics can help to advance knowledge and understanding in the field and can inform business and policy decisions.

RME is closely related to Sustainable Management Education (SMEd). They are often used interchangeably, but there are some differences between the two. RME is focused on teaching students about responsible business practices, with a focus on corporate social responsibility and ethics. RME aims to create a new generation of business leaders who are committed to creating social and environmental value, in addition to economic value. SMEd, on the other hand, is focused on the integration of sustainability principles and practices into management education programs. SMEd aims to provide students with the knowledge and skills needed to make business decisions that take into account the social, economic, and environmental impacts of their actions. SMEd is broader than RME and encompasses a wider range of sustainability issues, including environmental sustainability, social sustainability, and economic sustainability. In practice, RME and SMEd are often used together to promote sustainability in management education.

PRME and in general RME and SMEd promote the target SDG 4.7 that states "By 2030, ensure that all learners acquire the knowledge and skills needed to promote sustainable development, including, among others, through education for sustainable development and sustainable lifestyles, human rights, gender equality, promotion of a culture of peace and non-violence, global citizenship and appreciation of cultural diversity and of culture's contribution to sustainable development." SMEd, in particular, can help to achieve SDG 4.7 by equipping learners with the knowledge and skills needed to make business decisions that take into account the social, economic, and environmental impacts of their actions. This can include teaching about sustainable business practices, responsible consumption and production, and the role of business in promoting sustainable development more broadly. By integrating sustainability and CSR principles and practices into business and management education, RME can help to create a new generation of business leaders who are committed to creating a more sustainable and equitable world.

Healthcare Sector and Sustainability Management

Global health and well-being are major challenges worldwide and the current status of global health is a mixed picture (Foster et al., 2021). On the one hand, there has been significant progress in improving health outcomes over the past few decades. For example, global life expectancy has increased by approximately 5 years since 2000, and child mortality rates have decreased by more than half since 1990. In addition, many countries have made progress in reducing the burden of communicable diseases, such as HIV/AIDS, malaria, and tuberculosis.

However, there are still significant challenges that must be addressed. Non-communicable diseases, such as heart disease, cancer, and diabetes, are now responsible for the majority of global deaths, and these diseases are on the rise in many low- and middle-income countries. In addition, many countries continue to struggle with communicable diseases, and progress in reducing maternal and child mortality has been uneven.

The COVID-19 pandemic has also had a significant impact on global health. As of February 2023, the pandemic has resulted in over 472 million confirmed cases and over 6.1 million deaths globally. The pandemic has highlighted the vulnerabilities of health systems in many countries and the importance of investing in health security and preparedness.

In summary, while progress has been made in improving health outcomes, there are still significant challenges that must be addressed, particularly in the areas of non-communicable diseases and health equity. The COVID-19 pandemic has further underscored the need for strong and resilient health systems that can respond to emerging health threats.

SDG 3 for Global Health and Well-Being

SDG 3, "Good Health and Well-being," aims to ensure healthy lives and promote well-being for all at all ages. While progress has been made in improving health outcomes in many parts of the world, there are still several challenges that must be addressed to achieve this goal. Some of the major challenges for reaching SDG 3 include:

1. **Access to healthcare**: Many people around the world do not have access to quality healthcare, including essential medicines and vaccines, leading to preventable diseases, injuries, and deaths. Ensuring universal access to health services is critical to achieving SDG 3.
2. **Communicable diseases**: Communicable diseases such as HIV/AIDS, tuberculosis, and malaria continue to be a significant health challenge, particularly in low-income countries. Addressing these diseases requires improving health systems, increasing access to

preventive measures and treatment, and tackling social and environmental determinants of health.

3. **Non-communicable diseases**: Non-communicable diseases such as diabetes, cancer, and heart disease are on the rise globally, and they now account for a significant proportion of the global burden of disease. Addressing these diseases requires a multi-sectoral approach that includes preventative measures, early detection, and access to treatment.
4. **Mental health**: Mental health is a critical component of overall health and well-being, but it is often neglected in healthcare systems. Improving access to mental health services, reducing stigma, and increasing awareness are critical for achieving SDG 3.
5. **Environmental factors**: Environmental factors such as air pollution, climate change, and unsafe drinking water can have a significant impact on health outcomes. Addressing these factors requires policies and interventions that reduce exposure to environmental hazards and promote environmental sustainability.
6. **Health workforce**: There is a significant shortage of qualified health workers in many parts of the world, particularly in rural and remote areas. Addressing this requires investing in health worker education and training, as well as policies that incentivize health workers to work in underserved areas.
7. **Health financing**: Many low-income countries struggle to finance their health systems adequately. Addressing this requires increasing investment in health and ensuring that health financing is sustainable and equitable.

These challenges are complex and interrelated, and addressing them will require a coordinated and comprehensive approach from governments, civil society, and the private sector. However, by working together, it is possible to achieve SDG 3 and ensure that everyone has access to the highest possible standard of health and well-being.

Many companies are recognizing the importance of contributing to the achievement of SDG 3 and are taking action to improve global health and well-being. Some examples of best practices in this area include:

1. **Improving access to healthcare**: Several companies are working to improve access to healthcare, particularly in low- and middle-income

countries. For example, Novartis has launched several initiatives to improve access to essential medicines, while Johnson & Johnson has established partnerships to improve maternal and child health in underserved communities.

2. **Investing in research and development**: Many companies are investing in research and development to address global health challenges. For example, Pfizer and BioNTech developed the first mRNA vaccine for COVID-19, while GSK has developed a vaccine for malaria that is currently being piloted in several African countries.
3. **Addressing non-communicable diseases**: Many companies are taking action to address non-communicable diseases, such as diabetes, cancer, and heart disease. For example, Unilever has committed to reducing the salt, sugar, and fat content of its products to help combat obesity, while Novo Nordisk is working to improve access to diabetes care in low-income countries.
4. **Promoting mental health**: Several companies are taking action to promote mental health and well-being in the workplace. For example, Unilever has established a mental health program for employees, while SAP has developed a mental health platform that provides resources and support for employees.
5. **Addressing environmental factors**: Many companies are recognizing the impact of environmental factors on global health and are taking action to address these challenges. For example, Novartis has set targets to reduce its carbon footprint and increase its use of renewable energy.
6. **Supporting health systems**: Many companies are supporting health systems in low- and middle-income countries by investing in infrastructure and training programs. For example, GSK has established a program to strengthen health systems in sub-Saharan Africa, while Johnson & Johnson has launched a program to train health workers in underserved communities.

These are just a few examples of the many ways in which companies are taking action to contribute to the achievement of SDG 3. By working together with governments, civil society, and other stakeholders, companies can help to improve global health and well-being and contribute to a more sustainable and equitable future.

Case 8.5 COVID-19 and Resilience Lessons

COVID-19 is widely believed to be a result of unsustainable development practices, particularly those related to land use, wildlife trade, and industrial agriculture. The exact origin of the virus is not yet fully understood. Here are some of the ways in which COVID-19 is linked to unsustainable development practices:

1. **Deforestation and habitat destruction**: Deforestation and habitat destruction have disrupted natural ecosystems and brought humans into closer contact with wildlife. This has increased the risk of zoonotic diseases, which are transmitted from animals to humans. Destruction of natural habitats can also lead to loss of biodiversity, which in turn can impact ecosystem services and human health.
2. **Wildlife trade**: The trade in wildlife for food, traditional medicine, and exotic pets has created opportunities for zoonotic diseases to spread from animals to humans. The wildlife trade can also lead to the exploitation and depletion of natural resources, which can further impact ecosystems and human health.
3. **Industrial agriculture**: The expansion of industrial agriculture has led to increased use of pesticides and antibiotics, which can contribute to the emergence and spread of antimicrobial resistance. Industrial agriculture can also result in the depletion of natural resources, pollution, and loss of biodiversity, all of which can have negative impacts on human health.
4. **Globalization and travel**: The globalization of trade and travel has facilitated the rapid spread of the virus around the world. The interconnectedness of the global economy and the ease of travel have made it difficult to contain the virus and have highlighted the need for global cooperation in addressing pandemics.

In summary, COVID-19 is a result of unsustainable development practices that have disrupted natural ecosystems, created opportunities for zoonotic diseases to spread from animals to humans, and contributed to the emergence and spread of antimicrobial resistance. Addressing these underlying issues will be critical to preventing future pandemics and promoting sustainable development.

The COVID-19 pandemic has also highlighted the importance of sustainability management in several ways. Some of the lessons that can be drawn from the pandemic for sustainability management include:

1. **The importance of resilience**: The pandemic has shown that businesses and societies must be resilient in the face of unexpected shocks. Companies that had built resilience into their operations prior to the pandemic were better able to adapt to the challenges posed by the crisis.
2. **The need for agility**: The pandemic has also shown the importance of agility in responding to rapidly changing circumstances. Companies that were able to quickly pivot their operations to meet changing demand were better able to weather the storm.
3. **The interdependence of global systems**: The pandemic has highlighted the interdependence of global systems, and the need for a more integrated approach to sustainability management that considers the impact of decisions on multiple stakeholders.
4. **The importance of stakeholder engagement**: The pandemic has shown that stakeholder engagement is critical to the success of sustainability initiatives. Companies that engaged with stakeholders to understand their concerns and needs were better able to respond to the challenges posed by the pandemic.
5. **The need for supply chain resilience**: The pandemic has highlighted the importance of supply chain resilience, and the need for companies to work with suppliers to ensure continuity of operations in the face of disruptions.
6. **The importance of employee well-being**: The pandemic has shown that the well-being of employees is critical to the success of sustainability initiatives. Companies that prioritize the health and safety of their employees were better able to maintain business continuity and ensure the resilience of their operations.

In conclusion, the COVID-19 pandemic has highlighted the importance of sustainability management in building resilience, promoting agility, engaging stakeholders, ensuring supply chain resilience, and prioritizing employee well-being. By incorporating these lessons into their sustainability strategies, companies can help to create a more sustainable and resilient future for all.

Technology Sector and Sustainability Management

Technology is affecting, disrupting, and impacting every sector of the economy and our society. It has the potential to also promote more sustainable practices. Technology can benefit sustainable development by improving efficiency, reducing waste, and promoting the use of renewable resources (Stuss et al., 2021). Here are some of the main areas where technology is benefiting sustainable development:

1. **Energy**: Technology is enabling the use of renewable energy sources like solar, wind, and geothermal power. Advances in renewable energy technology have made it increasingly affordable and efficient, making it possible to transition away from fossil fuels and reduce greenhouse gas emissions. One of the main challenges with renewable energy is that it is intermittent and often doesn't match demand patterns. However, energy storage technologies like batteries and pumped hydro storage can help to store excess energy and release it when needed, making renewable energy more reliable and flexible. Smart grid technology is helping to optimize the distribution of energy, reducing waste and improving efficiency. By using sensors and data analytics to monitor energy usage, smart grids can reduce the need for energy generation and improve the reliability of the grid. Technology is also enabling greater energy efficiency in buildings, transportation, and industry. This includes energy-efficient lighting, heating and cooling systems, and efficient appliances, as well as more efficient transportation technologies like electric and hybrid vehicles. Carbon capture and storage technology captures carbon dioxide emissions from power plants and other industrial sources, and stores them underground or in other locations. This can help to reduce greenhouse gas emissions and mitigate the impacts of climate change.
2. **Agriculture**: Technology is helping to improve the efficiency and sustainability of agriculture through precision farming techniques, such as using sensors and drones to optimize crop yields and reduce

inputs. This can help to reduce the use of fertilizers and pesticides, conserve water, and promote soil health. In the agricultural sector, robotics and technology can promote sustainable agriculture through precision agriculture. Robotics and sensors can help farmers optimize the use of resources such as water, fertilizers, and pesticides. By collecting data on soil conditions, weather patterns, and plant health, farmers can make data-driven decisions about how much water, fertilizer, or pesticide to apply to their crops. Autonomous vehicles like tractors and other farm equipment can improve efficiency and reduce labor costs. This can help farmers increase yields and reduce waste while also reducing the environmental impacts associated with traditional farming practices. Drones equipped with cameras and sensors can provide farmers with real-time information about crop health and potential pest and disease outbreaks. This can help farmers identify and respond to potential problems before they become widespread, reducing the need for broad-spectrum pesticides and other harmful chemicals.

Robotics and technology can also be used to automate indoor farming systems. By using hydroponics, vertical farming, and other techniques, farmers can grow crops in controlled environments without the need for pesticides or other harmful chemicals. Data analytics can also help farmers analyze large amounts of data and make data-driven decisions. By collecting data on soil conditions, weather patterns, and other factors, farmers can optimize their production and reduce waste. Overall technology can help farmers improve the efficiency and sustainability of their agricultural production. By reducing waste, increasing yields, and using fewer resources, farmers can promote sustainable agriculture and help ensure food security for future generations.

3. **Transportation**: Technology is playing an increasingly important role in driving sustainability in the transportation sector. The development of electric vehicles is helping to reduce greenhouse gas emissions from transportation. As battery technology improves, electric vehicles are becoming more affordable and can travel longer distances on a single charge. This shift towards electric vehicles is reducing the need for fossil fuels and improving air quality. Self-driving vehicles have the potential to greatly improve transportation efficiency, reducing congestion, and reducing the need for personal car ownership. This can reduce greenhouse gas emissions

and improve access to transportation in areas with limited public transportation options.

Technology is enabling smarter traffic management systems, which can reduce congestion and improve transportation efficiency. This includes real-time traffic data, adaptive traffic signals, and intelligent transportation systems that can optimize routes and reduce emissions. Technology-enabled bike-sharing and car-sharing services are helping to reduce the number of cars on the road, making transportation more sustainable. By providing access to shared vehicles, these services can reduce the need for personal car ownership and improve transportation options in urban areas. Technology is also enabling greater fuel efficiency in transportation. This includes more efficient engines, hybrid technologies, and better aerodynamics. These advances are reducing the amount of fuel needed for transportation and reducing greenhouse gas emissions.

4. **Water**: Technology is playing an increasingly important role in driving sustainability in the water and sanitation sector. A few examples, technology is enabling more efficient and effective water treatment and purification. This includes advanced filtration systems, reverse osmosis, and ultraviolet disinfection. These technologies are improving the quality of water and reducing the need for chemical treatment, making water treatment more sustainable. Technology is enabling smarter water management systems, which can reduce water waste and improve water efficiency. This includes smart irrigation systems that can optimize water usage based on weather conditions, as well as water monitoring systems that can detect leaks and reduce water loss.

   Technology is enabling more effective water reuse, helping to reduce water consumption and increase water availability. This includes advanced wastewater treatment systems that can produce high-quality water for industrial and agricultural uses, as well as systems that can capture and reuse rainwater and other sources of non-potable water. Technology is also enabling more efficient and sustainable sanitation systems. This includes waterless toilets, which can reduce water consumption and improve sanitation in areas with limited access to clean water. It also includes systems for the treatment and disposal of human waste, such as anaerobic digestion, which can produce biogas and other valuable byproducts. Technology also enables better monitoring and management of water and sanitation systems, which can improve efficiency, reduce waste, and increase sustainability. This includes sensors and data analytics that can detect leaks and identify opportunities for improvement, as well as software tools that can optimize water and sanitation systems.

5. **Health**: Technology is playing an increasingly important role in driving sustainability in the healthcare sector. For example, technology is enabling more efficient and sustainable healthcare through digital health solutions. This includes telemedicine, which can reduce the need for in-person consultations and improve access to healthcare in rural or remote areas. It also includes health apps and wearables that can help patients monitor their health and manage chronic conditions, reducing the need for in-person visits and improving overall health outcomes. In addition, technology is enabling more sustainable and efficient management of patient health records. Electronic health records (EHRs) can reduce paper waste, streamline administrative tasks, and improve patient care by making health information more accessible to healthcare providers. Moreover, technology is enabling more sustainable management of healthcare supply chains. This includes inventory management systems that can reduce waste and improve the efficiency of healthcare operations. It also includes blockchain-based supply chain tracking systems, which can improve transparency and reduce waste in pharmaceutical and medical supply chains.

   Also, technology is enabling more sustainable and efficient medical imaging and diagnostics. This includes the use of digital imaging systems that reduce the need for film and chemicals, as well as advanced diagnostic tools that can reduce the need for invasive procedures and improve accuracy in disease diagnosis. Finally, technology is also helping to improve energy efficiency in healthcare facilities. This includes the use of energy-efficient lighting and HVAC systems, as well as renewable energy solutions, such as solar panels and geothermal systems. By reducing energy consumption, healthcare facilities can reduce their environmental impact and improve their sustainability.

6. **Education Sector**: Technology is playing an increasingly important role in driving sustainability in the education sector. Online and hybrid learning is an example. Technology is enabling more efficient and sustainable education through online learning platforms.

This includes e-learning platforms, online courses, and video conferencing tools that can reduce the need for in-person teaching and improve access to education. Technology is enabling more sustainable and efficient use of educational resources. Digital textbooks and resources can reduce the need for paper and other physical materials, reducing waste and improving accessibility to educational resources. Also, technology is helping to improve energy efficiency in educational institutions. This includes the use of energy-efficient lighting, HVAC systems, and renewable energy solutions such as solar panels and geothermal systems. By reducing energy consumption, educational institutions can reduce their environmental impact and improve their sustainability.

In addition, technology is enabling smarter building management in educational institutions. This includes building automation systems that can optimize energy use and reduce waste, as well as sensors and data analytics that can detect opportunities for improvement in building operations. Finally, technology is enabling more Green curricula and sustainability education with more effective solutions in schools and universities. This includes the use of online resources and digital tools to teach students about sustainability and encourage sustainable behaviors.

Case 8.6 EdTech and Sustainable Development

EdTech, or educational technology, refers to the use of digital technology to improve and enhance teaching, learning, and educational outcomes. Disruptive digital technologies have affected all aspects of our lives, including teaching and learning (Jagannathan, 2021). The adoption of agile and cost-effective strategies in education is creating digital and blended ecosystems and solutions for SDG 4, Quality Education. By leveraging technology and adopting flexible approaches, education leaders and practitioners can drive significant progress towards achieving these goals by 2030.

EdTech encompasses a wide range of tools and resources, including software, digital media, educational apps, online courses, learning management systems, and more. EdTech is transforming the way that education is delivered and experienced, offering new opportunities for students and teachers to engage with educational content and collaborate with others. EdTech is also helping to make education more accessible and flexible, allowing learners to access educational resources from anywhere and at any time. EdTech is an increasingly important part of modern education, with applications in K-12 education, higher education, vocational training, and professional development. EdTech has the potential to revolutionize education, making it more effective, efficient, and accessible for learners of all ages and backgrounds.

EdTech offers some promising opportunities for sustainable development and the SDG 4, which aims to ensure inclusive and equitable quality education and promote lifelong learning opportunities for all. For example, EdTech is helping to increase access to education for people all over the world, particularly those who live in remote or underprivileged areas. Online courses, educational apps, and other digital resources can help learners access educational content from anywhere, at any time.

EdTech is also helping to improve the quality of education and to enhance student engagement and motivation. Digital tools and resources can help teachers customize learning experiences to meet the needs of individual learners, and can help students develop skills that are relevant to the modern world. EdTech is helping to provide teachers with new opportunities for professional development, such as online courses, webinars, and digital communities of practice. This can help teachers to stay up-to-date with new teaching methods and technologies, and to continuously improve their instructional practices.

In addition, EdTech is helping to promote digital literacy, which is becoming increasingly important in today's digital world. By teaching students how to use digital tools and resources effectively and safely, EdTech can help prepare them for the modern workforce. Finally, EdTech is contributing to research and innovation in education, helping to identify new approaches to teaching and learning that can improve educational outcomes and support the SDG 4 agenda.

Here are a few promising examples of EdTech for sustainability:

1. **Eco-Schools**: Eco-Schools is a global program that uses online tools and resources to help schools around the world become more sustainable. The program provides a framework for students and teachers to learn about sustainability and to implement sustainability initiatives in their schools and communities.

2. **Smart Energy Education**: The Smart Energy Education program is an online platform that teaches students about energy efficiency, renewable energy, and sustainable living. The program includes interactive lessons, activities, and projects to help students learn about sustainable energy practices.
3. **Virtual Field Trips**: Virtual field trips allow students to explore different parts of the world without leaving the classroom. This can help reduce the environmental impact of travel while still providing students with the opportunity to learn about different cultures and ecosystems.
4. **Sustainable Agriculture Education**: Online courses and resources are available for students and teachers to learn about sustainable agriculture practices, including organic farming, permaculture, and regenerative agriculture.
5. **Green Chemistry Education**: Online courses and resources are available to teach students about green chemistry, which focuses on developing chemical products and processes that are safer for human health and the environment.

Overall, EdTech is playing an increasingly important role in promoting sustainability education and practices. EdTech is also an important tool for achieving SDG 4, helping to improve access to education, enhance educational quality and relevance, and promote lifelong learning opportunities for all. By continuing to develop and implement innovative educational tools and resources, we can help create a more sustainable future.

Case 8.7 RAS and Autonomous Sustainability

While Robotics and Autonomous Systems (RAS) present enormous potentials for reshaping the world, changing healthcare, food production, and biodiversity management can also deliver unsustainable solutions if not properly managed (Jawad Sajid et al., 2022). RAS could simply reinforce existing inequalities and increase the accumulation of wealth by already wealthy people. RAS has the potential to contribute to the SDGs in various sectors, but there are also potential drawbacks that need to be considered. Here are some pros and cons of RAS for sustainable development:

Pros:

1. **Improved efficiency and productivity**: RAS can improve efficiency and productivity in various sectors, including agriculture, manufacturing, and logistics. This can help reduce waste and resource consumption, ultimately contributing to sustainable development goals.
2. **Reduced environmental impact**: RAS can help reduce environmental impact by improving resource efficiency and reducing waste. For example, precision agriculture can help reduce the use of fertilizers and pesticides, while autonomous vehicles can reduce emissions from transportation.
3. **Safer working conditions**: RAS can improve working conditions and reduce the risk of accidents and injuries in hazardous industries. This can contribute to the SDG of promoting safe and inclusive work environments.
4. **Improved quality of life**: RAS can improve the quality of life for people in various ways, such as by providing assistance to the elderly or disabled, or by enabling better access to healthcare services in remote areas.

Cons:

1. **Job displacement**: RAS can lead to job displacement in various industries, which can have negative social and economic impacts. This limits the achievement of SDG 9 promoting inclusive and sustainable economic growth.
2. **Cost**: RAS can be costly to develop and implement, which can be a barrier to adoption in certain sectors.
3. **Cybersecurity and privacy risks**: RAS can be vulnerable to cybersecurity threats, which can pose risks to privacy and safety. This limits the achievement of SDG 9 and 16 promoting inclusive and sustainable economic growth and secure and resilient infrastructure.
4. **Limited human control**: RAS can operate autonomously, which can limit human control and raise ethical concerns. This limits SDG 12 promoting responsible consumption and production.

Overall, the potential benefits of RAS for sustainable development are significant, but there are also potential risks that need to be addressed. It is important to carefully consider the potential impacts of RAS on different

SDGs and to ensure that the benefits are maximized and the risks are minimized.

Case 8.8 GMOs and Monsanto Controversy

GMOs, or genetically modified organisms, are living organisms whose genetic material has been altered in a way that does not occur naturally through mating or natural recombination. GMOs are often created through the use of genetic engineering techniques, which allow scientists to insert specific genes into an organism's DNA in order to give it certain desired traits or characteristics.

The controversy surrounding GMOs and their impact on sustainability arises from a number of concerns, including:

1. **Environmental impacts**: GMOs can potentially have unintended effects on ecosystems and biodiversity. For example, genetically modified crops that are designed to be resistant to herbicides can lead to the development of herbicide-resistant weeds, which in turn can be difficult to control and can impact native plant species. Additionally, the use of GMOs in agriculture may lead to increased use of pesticides and fertilizers, which can have negative impacts on soil health and water quality.
2. **Health impacts**: Some people are concerned that GMOs may have negative impacts on human health, although the scientific consensus is that GMOs are safe to eat. However, some people may be allergic to certain GMOs, and there are concerns that GMOs may have long-term health effects that are not yet fully understood.
3. **Economic impacts**: There are concerns that GMOs may have negative economic impacts on small farmers and local communities, particularly in developing countries. For example, genetically modified seeds may be more expensive than traditional seeds, making them inaccessible to some farmers.
4. **Ethical Concerns**: Some people are concerned about the ethics of genetically modifying living organisms, particularly in cases where the modifications are intended to benefit human interests rather than the well-being of the organism itself.

Overall, the controversy surrounding GMOs and their impact on sustainability is complex and multifaceted, and there is ongoing debate and research about their potential benefits and risks. It is important to carefully consider the potential impacts of GMOs in order to ensure that they are being used in a way that is sustainable and respects the values and needs of all stakeholders involved.

While the negative health effects of GMOs are debatable, there are several demonstrated potential benefits of GMOs for sustainability, including:

1. **Increased crop yields**: Some genetically modified crops have been engineered to be more resistant to pests, disease, and environmental stress, which can help to increase crop yields and improve food security.
2. **Reduced pesticide use**: By engineering crops to be more resistant to pests and disease, farmers may be able to reduce their use of pesticides, which can have negative impacts on human health and the environment.
3. **Reduced use of land and water resources**: GMOs can potentially be used to develop crops that require less water or land to grow, which can help to conserve these important resources.
4. **Improved nutrition**: Some GMOs have been developed to be more nutritious, which can help to improve the health and well-being of people who rely on these crops as a primary source of food.
5. **Improved animal welfare**: Some genetically modified crops have been developed to be more nutritious and digestible for livestock, which can help to improve animal welfare and reduce the environmental impact of animal agriculture.

It's worth noting, however, that the benefits of GMOs for sustainability are often hotly debated, and there are concerns about their potential negative impacts on the environment, human health, and socio-economic factors. It is important to carefully consider the potential benefits and risks of GMOs on a case-by-case basis and to take a precautionary approach to ensure that the use of GMOs is sustainable and respectful of all stakeholders involved. The case of the Monsanto GMO controversy is indicative of this (Elmore, 2021).

The Monsanto Company, which is now owned by Bayer, was an American agrochemical and agricultural biotechnology corporation. Monsanto was best known for its product Roundup, a glyphosate-based herbicide with documented negative effects on human health and environment risks. Monsanto once manufactured controversial products, such as the insecticide DDT, PCBs, Agent Orange, and recombinant bovine growth hormone. Later Monsanto became a major producer of genetically engineered crops. Monsanto has been criticized for its aggressive marketing of genetically modified crops, as well as its legal efforts to protect its patents and control over the use of its seeds.

One of the main concerns about the use of GMOs is their potential impact on biodiversity and the environment. Critics argue that the widespread use of genetically modified seeds can lead to the loss of traditional crops and wild plant species, which can have negative impacts on Indigenous people who rely on these resources for their livelihoods and cultural practices. Another concern is the potential health risks of consuming GMOs. Some studies have suggested that GMOs may have negative impacts on human health, although the scientific evidence is mixed. In addition to these concerns, there are also social and economic concerns associated with the use of genetically modified seeds. For example, some critics argue that the use of GMOs can lead to increased dependency on large agribusiness companies like Monsanto, which can have negative impacts on small-scale farmers and local communities.

Overall, the Monsanto GMO controversy highlights the complex social, environmental, and economic issues associated with the use of GMOs, and the need for careful consideration of the potential impacts of these technologies on all stakeholders involved. It also underscores the importance of engaging in inclusive and participatory decision-making processes to ensure that the voices and perspectives of Indigenous people and other marginalized groups are heard and respected.

Key Takeaways

1. Sustainable management involves common elements, such as balancing economic, social, and environmental factors, but each sector faces unique challenges and opportunities in implementing sustainability initiatives. Understanding the nuances of each sector is crucial for effective sustainability management.
2. Businesses can adopt sustainable practices through various means, such as joining the B Corps movement, which certifies companies that meet rigorous social and environmental performance standards.

The private sector plays a significant role in driving sustainable development by innovating and adopting responsible practices.

3. Governments at local, national, and international levels can facilitate sustainable development by creating policies and collaborating with other governments and organizations. For example, the C40 initiative fosters urban sustainability through collaboration between major cities worldwide, sharing best practices and resources.
4. The social sector, including NGOs, nonprofits, and foundations, supports sustainable development through initiatives like the SDSN (Sustainable Development Solutions Network) to promote the United Nations' Sustainable Development Goals. The academic sector also contributes by incorporating sustainability management into education and research, as demonstrated by the PRME (Principles for Responsible Management Education) initiative.
5. The healthcare sector can contribute to global health and well-being (SDG 3) by adopting sustainable practices, learning from crises like COVID-19, and fostering resilience. The technology sector, including the EdTech and high-tech industries, can drive sustainable development by creating innovative solutions, while also navigating ethical and environmental concerns, such as the Monsanto GMO controversy.

References

Elmore, B. J. (2021). *Seed money: Monsanto's past and our food future*. W. W. Norton.

Foster, C., et al. (2021). *Routledge handbook of global health rights*. Taylor & Francis.

Fowler, A. (2013). *The virtuous spiral: A guide to sustainability for NGOs in international development*. Taylor & Francis.

Hoek, M. (2018). *The trillion dollar shift*. Taylor & Francis.

IPCC. (2022). *Climate change 2022: Mitigation of climate change*. Contribution of Working Group III to the Sixth Assessment Report of the Intergovernmental Panel on Climate Change. https://www.ipcc.ch/report/sixth-assessment-report-working-group-3/. Accessed 15 March 2023.

Jagannathan, S. (2021). *Reimagining digital learning for sustainable development: How upskilling, data analytics, and educational technologies close the skills gap*. Taylor & Francis.

Jawad Sajid, M. et al. (2022). *Implications of industry 5.0 on environmental sustainability*. Business Science Reference.

Martin, E. C., & Boyd, N. M. (2021). *Sustainable public management*. Taylor & Francis.

Medine, A., & Minto-Coy, I. (2023). *Social entrepreneurship strategies and social sector sustainability: A Caribbean context*. Springer International.

Öztürk, M. (2022). *Engagement with sustainable development in higher education: Universities as transformative spaces for sustainable futures*. Springer International Publishing.

Stuss, M. M., et al. (2021). *Sustainability, technology and innovation 4.0*. Taylor & Francis.

CHAPTER 9

Sustainable Management Effective Practices

Abstract Sustainable Management Effective Practices explores the unique aspects and focus areas of sustainability management within the broader field of management. This chapter highlights effective practices and case studies from various industries, demonstrating how organizations can successfully incorporate sustainable decision-making and actions into their operations. The chapter examines topics such as stakeholder management, supply chain, marketing, human resources, financial sustainability, strategy, reporting, and alternative organizational structures.

Keywords Effective practices · Stakeholder engagement · Supply chain · Human resources · Financial sustainability · Alternative organizational structures

> *Companies that see constraints as opportunities will dominate the future.*
> —Andrew Winston, Co-author of "Green to Gold: How Smart Companies Use Environmental Strategy to Innovate, Create Value, and Build Competitive Advantage" (Winston & Esty, 2006)

Management encompasses various disciplines and areas of expertise, such as human resources, operations, marketing, strategic management, and

M. Tavanti, *Developing Sustainability in Organizations*, Sustainable Development Goals Series,
https://doi.org/10.1007/978-3-031-36907-0_9

more. While responsible management and sustainability management share similarities with general management, they differ in their emphasis on ethical decision-making, long-term planning, and stakeholder engagement. Responsible management focuses on ethical and socially responsible actions, while sustainability management specifically addresses environmental and social impacts. Sustainability management goes a step further by prioritizing environmental sustainability and engaging with a broader range of stakeholders. This chapter explores effective practices in sustainability management adopted by organizations committed to responsible and sustainable decision-making.

Sustainable Stakeholder Management

Sustainable stakeholder management is the practice of engaging with stakeholders in a manner that is responsible, ethical, and sustainable (Galati et al., 2019; O'Riordan, 2017). It involves identifying and prioritizing stakeholders, understanding their interests and concerns, and working to build positive relationships with them over the long term. The core elements of sustainable stakeholder management include:

1. **Stakeholder Identification and Prioritization**: Identifying and prioritizing key stakeholders is an essential first step in sustainable stakeholder management. Organizations need to understand who their stakeholders are, their interests, and their level of influence.
2. **Stakeholder Engagement**: Sustainable stakeholder management involves engaging with stakeholders in a meaningful way to understand their concerns and interests, and to build relationships based on trust and respect. This includes ongoing dialogue and consultation with stakeholders and may involve collaboration on sustainability initiatives.
3. **Stakeholder Communication and Transparency**: Communication and transparency are critical elements of sustainable stakeholder management. Organizations need to be transparent in their communication with stakeholders about their sustainability performance, including their successes and challenges.
4. **Stakeholder Collaboration**: Sustainable stakeholder management involves collaboration with stakeholders to identify and implement sustainability initiatives. This can involve joint problem-solving, co-creation of initiatives, and sharing of knowledge and expertise.

5. **Stakeholder Monitoring and Evaluation**: Sustainable stakeholder management involves monitoring and evaluating the effectiveness of engagement with stakeholders, as well as the impact of sustainability initiatives. This enables organizations to identify areas for improvement and to continually refine their stakeholder engagement and sustainability strategies.
6. **Integration of Stakeholder Interests into Business Decisions**: Sustainable stakeholder management involves integrating stakeholder interests into business decisions. This means considering the social and environmental impacts of business decisions, and balancing the interests of different stakeholders to ensure sustainable outcomes.

There are several leading sustainability companies that have invested in sustainable stakeholder management and have developed effective practices. For example, Patagonia engages with stakeholders including employees, customers, suppliers, and environmental and social justice organizations to ensure that it operates in a responsible and sustainable manner. Starbucks engages with stakeholders including coffee farmers, customers, and local communities to ensure that it operates in a responsible and sustainable manner. It has developed a sustainable coffee sourcing program and works with suppliers to reduce its environmental impact. The Body Shop engages with stakeholders including customers, employees, and suppliers to ensure that it operates in a responsible and sustainable manner. Some companies post but never reply to their customers, but the Body Shop uses social media to actively engage with real, prompt, and honest responses.

There are also some useful studies in the area of sustainable stakeholder management that enlist a number of innovative and effective practices. For example, Galati et al. (2019) in the edited volume entitled *Stakeholder Engagement and Sustainability* mention several stakeholder engagement practices that can be used by organizations to achieve sustainability goals. Some of these practices include:

1. **Co-creation**: Co-creation involves collaborating with stakeholders to develop sustainable solutions. This approach ensures that the

solutions developed meet the needs and expectations of stakeholders. The book highlights the importance of involving stakeholders in the entire design process, from problem identification to solution implementation.

2. **Participatory decision-making**: Participatory decision-making involves involving stakeholders in the decision-making process. This approach ensures that the decisions made are transparent and equitable. The book emphasizes the importance of providing stakeholders with the necessary information and resources to make informed decisions.
3. **Partnerships**: Partnerships involve collaborating with stakeholders to achieve shared sustainability goals. The book highlights the importance of developing long-term partnerships that are based on trust and mutual benefit.
4. **Multi-stakeholder dialogues**: Multi-stakeholder dialogues involve bringing together stakeholders from different backgrounds and perspectives to discuss sustainability issues. The book emphasizes the importance of creating a safe and respectful space for stakeholders to share their perspectives and ideas.
5. **Social media engagement**: Social media can be used as a tool to engage stakeholders and promote sustainability. The book highlights the importance of using social media to facilitate communication, build relationships, and share sustainability initiatives.

Similarly, Manetti and Bellucci (2018) in *Stakeholder Engagement and Sustainability Reporting* provide empirical evidence of stakeholder engagement practices and processes presented in the company's sustainability reporting. The sustainability reporting in themselves, as we will review in Part IV, is important processes for effectively engaging stakeholders. Here are a few examples of effective practices and innovative strategies that companies can adopt:

1. **Collaborative storytelling**: This involves working with stakeholders to co-create narratives that communicate a company's sustainability performance. Collaborative storytelling can help build trust and understanding with stakeholders while also promoting transparency and accountability.

2. **Virtual reality (VR) and augmented reality (AR)**: These technologies can be used to create immersive experiences that allow stakeholders to explore a company's sustainability practices. This approach can help engage stakeholders by providing a more interactive and dynamic experience.
3. **Materiality analysis**: This involves identifying the sustainability issues that are most relevant to a company and its stakeholders. By prioritizing these issues, companies can focus their reporting efforts on the topics that matter most to their stakeholders.
4. **Open data platforms**: These platforms allow stakeholders to access and analyze a company's sustainability data in real time. By making this data more accessible and transparent, companies can increase trust and engagement with their stakeholders.
5. **Crowdsourcing**: This involves leveraging the knowledge and expertise of stakeholders to identify sustainability challenges and solutions. Crowdsourcing can help engage stakeholders by empowering them to contribute to a company's sustainability efforts.
6. **Digital reporting tools**: These tools can help companies create more interactive and engaging sustainability reports. For example, companies can use infographics, videos, and interactive charts to communicate their sustainability performance in a more compelling way.

These are just a few examples of innovative practices that companies can use to enhance stakeholder engagement in sustainability reporting. By embracing these practices, companies can build trust, promote transparency, and demonstrate their commitment to sustainability. Overall, stakeholder engagement is an essential component and measurement of the company's commitment to sustainability. It provides insights into how organizations can share values with the local–global community by demonstrating the innovative and impactful relations to achieve shared sustainability goals. By focusing on these core effective strategies and core elements of sustainable stakeholder management, organizations can build strong and mutually beneficial relationships with stakeholders, enhance their sustainability performance, and contribute to the long-term well-being of society and the planet.

Case 9.1 FPIC and Engagement of Indigenous Communities

Companies engaging with Indigenous communities need to have a particular regard for their rights because Indigenous peoples often have a unique relationship with their land, natural resources, and cultural heritage. These relationships are often deeply tied to their identity and way of life, and are essential for their continued survival as distinct peoples.

Furthermore, Indigenous peoples often face unique challenges and vulnerabilities, including historical and ongoing discrimination, marginalization, and displacement. These challenges can impact their ability to fully participate in decision-making processes related to their lands and resources, and can lead to negative social, environmental, and human rights impacts.

Therefore, it is important for companies engaging with Indigenous communities to respect and uphold their rights, including the right to self-determination, the right to free, prior and informed consent, the right to cultural integrity, and the right to benefit-sharing. This requires meaningful consultation and engagement with Indigenous communities throughout the project cycle, and taking into account their traditional knowledge and values.

Respecting the rights of Indigenous communities can help ensure that they are able to participate in decision-making processes related to their lands and resources, and can lead to more sustainable outcomes for all stakeholders. It can also help companies build trust and long-term relationships with these communities, which is essential for achieving social license to operate and maintaining a positive reputation.

The Free, Prior, and Informed Consent (FPIC) is a principle that recognizes the right of Indigenous peoples to give or withhold their consent to any project or activity that may affect their lands, resources, territories, and other aspects of their cultural heritage. It is an internationally recognized standard that requires companies to consult and engage with Indigenous communities in a meaningful way and obtain their consent before carrying out any project or activity on their lands.

FPIC is important for sustainable development projects that involve Indigenous communities because it provides a framework for respectful engagement and collaboration between companies and these communities. FPIC recognizes that Indigenous communities have unique knowledge and values related to their lands and resources, and that their participation in decision-making processes is essential for the success of any project or activity.

The FPIC process involves several steps that companies must follow in order to engage with Indigenous communities in a respectful and collaborative way. The steps of the FPIC process can vary depending on the project and the community involved, but generally include the following:

1. **Identification of affected communities**: Companies must identify all potentially affected Indigenous communities and engage with them in a transparent and inclusive way.
2. **Information sharing**: Companies must provide accurate and timely information about the proposed project, including its potential impacts and benefits, to the Indigenous communities. This includes ensuring that the information is provided in a language and format that is accessible and understandable to the communities.
3. **Consultation**: Companies must engage in meaningful and respectful consultation with the Indigenous communities to understand their concerns and aspirations related to the project. This involves creating a safe and inclusive space for dialogue, and taking into account the traditional knowledge and values of the communities.
4. **Negotiation**: Companies must work with the Indigenous communities to negotiate the terms of the project, including the scope, duration, and conditions for implementation. This includes identifying and addressing any potential impacts on the community's lands, resources, territories, and other aspects of their cultural heritage.
5. **Consent**: Companies must obtain the free, prior, and informed consent of the Indigenous communities before implementing the project. This means that the community has given their full consent without coercion, has been fully informed of the project, and has had sufficient time to consider the information and negotiate the terms.
6. **Implementation**: Companies must implement the project in accordance with the terms agreed upon in the FPIC process. This

includes ongoing consultation and engagement with the Indigenous communities, as well as monitoring and evaluation of the project's impacts.

These steps of the FPIC process are essential for ensuring that companies engage with Indigenous communities in a respectful, transparent, and collaborative way, and that they respect the community's rights to self-determination, cultural integrity, and benefit-sharing. Furthermore, FPIC helps to ensure that sustainable development projects are aligned with the priorities and needs of Indigenous communities. By obtaining their consent, companies can demonstrate that they have taken into account the concerns and aspirations of these communities and have developed a project that is socially, culturally, and environmentally responsible.

Moreover, obtaining FPIC can help companies to manage risks and avoid negative impacts on Indigenous communities. By engaging in a transparent and collaborative process with these communities, companies can identify potential risks and challenges, and develop appropriate mitigation measures to avoid or minimize negative impacts. In other words, FPIC is an essential process to be acknowledged, respected, and properly implemented in sustainable development projects that involve Indigenous communities. These steps are necessary to engage Indigenous communities respectfully, align with community priorities, assess the risk management, and guarantee the protection of Indigenous human rights and cultural heritage.

Sustainable Supply Chain

Supply chains are critical for evaluating a company's managerial practices in terms of ethics and social responsibility. According to The Association for Supply Chain Management (APICS), supply chain is "where the rubber hits the road when it comes to ethics, whether that has to do with an organization's sustainability and carbon footprint efforts or how it treats its suppliers and the communities in which it does business" (APICS, 2018). APICS recognizes the importance of sustainability in supply chain management and has developed resources and initiatives to support sustainable practices in the field. APICS recommends that companies adopt a holistic approach to sustainable supply chain management that takes into account social, environmental, and economic factors. Specifically, APICS recommends:

1. **Incorporating Sustainability into Strategy**: APICS recommends that companies incorporate sustainability into their overall business strategy. This includes setting sustainability goals, tracking performance, and reporting on progress.
2. **Engaging with Suppliers**: APICS emphasizes the importance of engaging with suppliers to ensure that they are meeting sustainability standards. This includes setting expectations, monitoring performance, and providing support and resources to help suppliers improve their sustainability practices.
3. **Reducing Environmental Impact**: APICS recommends that companies take steps to reduce their environmental impact through measures such as energy efficiency, waste reduction, and sustainable sourcing.
4. **Ensuring Ethical Practices**: APICS emphasizes the importance of ensuring ethical practices in supply chain management, including issues such as labor practices, human rights, and fair trade.
5. **Adopting Circular Economy Practices**: APICS recognizes the potential benefits of adopting circular economy practices, such as product life extension, recycling, and the use of renewable energy sources.

Overall, APICS recognizes that sustainable supply chain management is an important consideration for companies in today's business environment. It provides resources and guidance to help companies adopt sustainable practices, and advocates for the importance of sustainability in the field of supply chain management. The Supply Chain and Sustainability Center at Loyola University Chicago goes even further and recognizes the growing importance of investing in the intersection of supply chain management and sustainability. Key findings of their research include the importance of stakeholder engagement, the benefits of sustainable practices, the role of technology, the necessity for collaboration, and the need for transparency. The center's research emphasizes that sustainable supply chain practices benefit companies, consumers, and the environment, with collaboration, transparency, and stakeholder engagement being critical to success. Additionally, they suggest integrating sustainable supply chain management more thoroughly into management studies and education.

Specialized studies and publications are emerging to address sustainable supply chain management practices. For example, Corbett et al. (2016) suggest a number of innovative approaches to sustainable supply chain management including closed-loop supply chain management, collaborative supply chain management, green logistics, sustainable procurement, and product-service systems. Sroufe and Melnyk (2017) provide insights and tools for companies to develop similar strategies, emphasizing collaboration, systemic thinking, and a focus on the entire product life cycle. Advanced technologies, such as IoT, blockchain, and AI, can significantly improve sustainability practices, promoting transparency, traceability, and sustainability in supply chain operations. Blockchain technology can improve supply chain traceability and streamline the certification process, reducing the administrative burden and improving credibility.

Case 9.2 Fair Trade Certification and Child Labor

The terms "Fair Trade" and "Fairtrade" are often used interchangeably, but there is a significant difference the two and they are a subject of conflicting values and practices. "Fair Trade" is a social movement and a market-based approach that aims to help producers in developing countries achieve better trading conditions and promote sustainable farming. The Fair Trade movement advocates for higher payment to exporters, as well as improved social and environmental standards. It focuses on products exported from developing to developed countries, most notably handcrafts,coffee, cocoa, wine, sugar, fresh fruits, chocolate, flowers, and gold. However, the term "Fairtrade" usually refers to a certification by a Fairtrade labeling organization, like Fairtrade International. Fairtrade International, which is a member of the World Fair Trade Organization (WFTO), sets the Fairtrade standards, and supports producers to gain and maintain certification and develop market opportunities. The Fairtrade mark or logo on a product ensures that the product meets specific economic, environmental, and social standards. These standards are agreed upon through research and consultation with Fairtrade stakeholders, including the producers themselves. We generally use "Fair

Trade" when we are talking broadly about the movement or the practices aimed at ensuring equitable trade deals for producers in developing countries. We use "Fairtrade" when we are referring to the certification or standards set by Fairtrade International or another Fairtrade labeling organization. Clarifying this distinction is important as not all fair trade goods are Fairtrade-certified, but all Fairtrade goods are, by definition, part of the Fair Trade movement. It's also important to note that other organizations certify Fair Trade goods, so a Fair Trade item might not necessarily be Fairtrade-certified. In general, Fair Trade is a certification system that aims to ensure that producers in developing countries receive fair prices for their products, while also promoting environmental sustainability and social responsibility. The certification is given to products that meet specific standards in terms of production, trade, and working conditions. The Fair Trade certification ensures sustainability by requiring that producers implement sustainable farming practices, such as using natural fertilizers, protecting water resources, and avoiding the use of harmful chemicals. Additionally, the certification promotes the use of renewable energy, the protection of biodiversity, and the conservation of natural habitats. Fair Trade also requires that producers adhere to specific social standards, such as paying fair wages, providing safe working conditions, and prohibiting child labor. By ensuring fair prices and working conditions, Fair Trade seeks to provide producers with the resources they need to invest in their communities and improve their standard of living.

The Fair Trade certification process involves independent auditors who verify that producers meet the certification standards. Producers must also pay a fee to participate in the certification process, which helps to support the Fair Trade organization and its efforts to promote sustainability and social responsibility.

The principles of Fair Trade are based on the values of fairness, transparency, accountability, and respect. The Fair Trade movement has developed 10 principles, which are as follows:

1. **Creating opportunities for economically disadvantaged producers**: Fair Trade aims to provide opportunities for small-scale producers, particularly in developing countries, to sell their products at a fair price.
2. **Transparency and accountability**: Fair Trade aims to be transparent and accountable in its transactions, to ensure that producers

receive a fair price for their products and that consumers know the origin and story of the products they buy.

3. **Fair trading practices**: Fair Trade seeks to establish relationships between producers and buyers that are based on trust, mutual respect, and long-term commitment.
4. **Payment of a fair price**: Fair Trade requires that producers receive a fair price for their products, which covers the cost of sustainable production and provides a fair wage for the workers.
5. **No child labor or forced labor**: Fair Trade prohibits the use of child labor or forced labor in the production of Fair Trade products.
6. **Non-discrimination, gender equity, and freedom of association**: Fair Trade promotes equality and non-discrimination, gender equity, and the freedom of association for producers and workers.
7. **Ensuring good working conditions**: Fair Trade requires that producers provide good working conditions, including safe and healthy working environments, and access to training and resources to improve their skills and productivity.
8. **Providing capacity building**: Fair Trade provides capacity building support to producers to help them improve their management and production practices, and access new markets.
9. **Promoting fair trade**: Fair Trade seeks to raise awareness and promote the values of fair trade, to increase demand for Fair Trade products, and to create a more sustainable and just economy.
10. **Respect for the environment**: Fair Trade promotes environmentally sustainable production practices and encourages producers to minimize their impact on the environment by reducing waste, conserving resources, and using renewable energy sources.

Fair Trade certification requires that producers comply with the Fairtrade Standards, which prohibit the use of child labor or forced labor in the production of Fairtrade products. The Fairtrade Standards specify that producers must meet certain criteria in order to ensure that no child labor or forced labor is used in the production process.

For example, in order to comply with the Fairtrade Standards, producers must provide a safe and healthy working environment for workers, including measures to prevent accidents and illnesses. They need to ensure that all workers are above the minimum legal working age and that no child labor is used. Fairtrade Standards prohibit the use of child labor under the age of 15, or under the age of 14 where the national law allows. They need to provide fair wages to all workers that meet or exceed legal minimum wages, as well as provide additional benefits to workers, such as healthcare and education. They also need to ensure that workers are not subject to any kind of forced labor, including debt bondage, indentured labor, or slavery. The respect of labor rights includes providing workers with the right to freedom of association and collective bargaining. To ensure that these standards are met, Fairtrade works with independent certification bodies to carry out regular audits of producers and their supply chains. These audits check for compliance with the Fairtrade Standards and include interviews with workers and on-site inspections to ensure that the standards are being followed. If a producer is found to be in breach of the Fairtrade Standards, they will be required to take corrective action, and if they fail to do so, they may lose their Fairtrade certification. This process helps to ensure that no child labor or forced labor is used in the production of Fairtrade products.

The Fairtrade certification is awarded by independent organizations that are licensed by Fairtrade International. These organizations, known as Fairtrade Certification Bodies, are responsible for carrying out audits of producers and supply chains to ensure that they meet the Fairtrade Standards. There are several Fairtrade Certification Bodies around the world, including FLOCERT, a global Fairtrade Certification Body that is based in Germany. It provides certification and verification services for Fairtrade products and supply chains around the world. Fairtrade America: Fairtrade America is the Fairtrade Certification Body for North America, including the United States and Canada. Fairtrade International: Fairtrade International is the international organization that sets the Fairtrade Standards and provides support to Fairtrade Certification Bodies around the world.

These and other fair trade organizations work closely with producers and supply chains to ensure that they meet the Fairtrade Standards and are eligible for Fairtrade certification. They also provide support to producers and supply chains to help them improve their practices and achieve Fairtrade certification. The Fairtrade certification is closely related to the concept of a sustainable supply chain, which is a supply chain that is designed to meet the needs of the present without compromising the ability of future generations to meet their own needs. Fairtrade certification helps to create a more sustainable supply chain by providing a framework for fair and equitable trade relationships between producers and buyers. This framework is based on the Fairtrade Standards, which are designed to promote social, economic, and environmental sustainability.

Some of the ways in which Fairtrade certification promotes sustainability in the supply chain include:

1. **Promoting environmental sustainability**: Fairtrade Standards require producers to adopt environmentally sustainable practices, such as reducing the use of harmful chemicals and conserving natural resources. By doing so, producers can help to protect the environment for future generations.
2. **Supporting economic sustainability**: Fairtrade Standards require that producers receive a fair price for their products, which enables them to cover the cost of sustainable production and invest in their businesses for the long term. This helps to ensure the economic sustainability of the producer communities.
3. **Promoting social sustainability**: Fairtrade Standards require that producers provide safe and healthy working conditions for workers, pay fair wages, and respect workers' rights to freedom of association and collective bargaining. By doing so, producers can help to promote social sustainability and improve the well-being of their communities.
4. **Supporting small-scale producers**: Fairtrade certification is particularly important for small-scale producers in developing countries, who often lack the resources and market access to compete in the global marketplace. By providing fair prices and access to new markets, Fairtrade certification can help to support the economic and social sustainability of small-scale producer communities.

In summary, Fairtrade certification helps to create a more sustainable supply chain by promoting environmental, economic, and social sustainability. By doing so, Fairtrade certification can help to create a more just and equitable global economy, which benefits producers, workers, and consumers alike.

Sustainability and Social Marketing

Sustainability marketing is a strategy used by companies and organizations to promote products, services, or practices that are environmentally and socially sustainable. The popularity of social marketing and sustainability marketing is evident in academia as these topics are increasingly integrated in the curricula (Hewege et al., 2021). Today, it is common to see companies and organizations that integrate sustainability and environmental concepts into their social marketing strategies (Quoquab & Mohammad, 2023). In general, the goal of sustainability marketing is to communicate a company's commitment to sustainability to consumers and other stakeholders, and to encourage them to choose products or services that have a positive environmental and social impact. Sustainability marketing typically involves the following elements:

1. **Product design and development**: Companies may design and develop products that are environmentally and socially sustainable, using materials and production processes that minimize their impact on the environment and respect workers' rights.
2. **Communication and promotion**: Companies may use marketing communications to promote their sustainable products or services, highlighting their positive impact on the environment and society. This may include advertising, public relations, social media, and other channels.
3. **Transparency and accountability**: Companies may be transparent about their sustainability practices and performance, sharing information about their environmental and social impact and their efforts to improve. This can help build trust with consumers and other stakeholders.
4. **Collaboration and partnerships**: Companies may collaborate with other organizations, such as nonprofits, governments, or suppliers, to advance sustainability goals and address social and environmental issues.

Sustainability marketing is an important tool for companies to differentiate themselves and appeal to environmentally conscious consumers. It is crucial that companies' sustainability claims are truthful and verifiable. Social marketing uses marketing techniques to promote social good and encourage positive behaviors among individuals and communities, focusing on specific issues or behaviors. Sustainability marketing promotes environmentally and socially sustainable products or services. Both types of marketing use marketing techniques, audience understanding, and effective communication to promote positive change and improve the well-being of individuals and communities. Here are a few examples of successful sustainable social marketing campaigns over the years:

1. **The Truth campaign**: The Truth campaign is a social marketing campaign aimed at reducing tobacco use among young people. The campaign uses a variety of media, including TV, social media, and public events, to communicate the dangers of smoking and promote a tobacco-free lifestyle.
2. **The Dove "Real Beauty" campaign**: The Dove "Real Beauty" campaign is a sustainability marketing campaign that promotes body positivity and self-esteem. The campaign uses images of real women of all shapes, sizes, and ages to challenge traditional beauty standards and promote self-acceptance.
3. **The Nike "Reuse-A-Shoe" campaign**: The Nike "Reuse-A-Shoe" campaign is a sustainability marketing campaign that encourages people to recycle their old sneakers. The campaign collects old sneakers and grinds them down to create material for sports surfaces and other products.
4. **The Coca-Cola "PlantBottle" campaign**: The Coca-Cola "PlantBottle" campaign is a sustainability marketing campaign that promotes the use of plant-based packaging for its drinks. The campaign highlights the environmental benefits of using renewable resources to reduce waste.
5. **Patagonia's "Don't Buy This Jacket" campaign**: In 2011, outdoor clothing company Patagonia launched a campaign to encourage consumers to buy less and reuse and repair their existing clothing instead of buying new items. The campaign aimed to promote more responsible consumption and reduce the negative environmental impacts of the fashion industry.
6. **P&G's "Like a Girl" campaign**: In 2014, P&G launched the "Like a Girl" campaign, which aimed to empower young girls and challenge gender stereotypes. The campaign included a powerful video that highlighted the negative connotations of the phrase "like a girl" and encouraged girls to embrace their strengths and abilities.

7. **The "Great Tastes of America" campaign by McDonald's**: In 2019, McDonald's UK launched a campaign to promote regional flavors and highlight the company's commitment to using locally sourced ingredients. The campaign included a series of ads and social media posts that showcased local produce and ingredients and highlighted the economic benefits of supporting local farmers and suppliers.
8. **REI's "Opt Outside" campaign**: In 2015, outdoor retailer REI launched a campaign that encouraged its employees and customers to spend time outdoors on Black Friday instead of shopping. The campaign aimed to promote a more balanced and healthy lifestyle and highlight the benefits of spending time in nature.
9. **The World Wildlife Fund's "Earth Hour" campaign**: This campaign encourages people to turn off their lights for one hour to raise awareness about climate change and the importance of energy conservation.
10. **The American Heart Association's "Life is Why" campaign**: This campaign aims to reduce heart disease and stroke by promoting healthy lifestyles. The campaign uses social media, events, and partnerships to encourage people to make small changes to their daily routines that can have a big impact on their health.
11. **The Always "Like a Girl" campaign**: This social marketing campaign aims to empower girls and challenge gender stereotypes. The campaign uses video and social media to encourage girls to pursue their dreams and be confident in their abilities.
12. **The Chipotle "Food with Integrity" campaign**: This sustainability marketing campaign promotes the use of sustainable and ethically sourced ingredients in Chipotle's food. The campaign encourages consumers to make more informed choices about what they eat and how it is produced.

These are just a few examples of marketing campaigns that promote positive social or environmental outcomes. Each campaign is designed to raise awareness, inspire action, and encourage positive changes in behavior and attitudes. These social and sustainability marketing campaigns are designed to produce positive changes in society and the environment. The specific messages aim at behavior changes and perception changes that can improve the well-being of individuals, communities, or the planet.

Case 9.3 Ben & Jerry's Values-Based Marketing

Ben & Jerry's values-based marketing approach centers around their commitment to social justice and environmental sustainability. They believe that businesses have a responsibility to not only make a profit but also to be a force for good in the world.

Some of the key elements of Ben & Jerry's values-based marketing approach include:

1. **Mission-driven branding**: Ben & Jerry's brand messaging emphasizes their commitment to social justice and sustainability. Their mission statement is "to make the best possible ice cream in the best possible way," and they strive to embody this mission in everything they do.
2. **Engaging with social issues**: Ben & Jerry's is known for taking a stand on a wide range of social issues, from climate change to racial justice to LGBTQ+ rights. They use their marketing channels to raise awareness about these issues and encourage their customers to take action.
3. **Using sustainable and ethical ingredients**: Ben & Jerry's sources its ingredients from suppliers who meet their high standards for sustainability and ethical practices. They also prioritize using non-GMO and fair trade ingredients.
4. **Partnering with advocacy organizations**: Ben & Jerry's works closely with advocacy organizations to support their causes and amplify their messages. For example, they have partnered with organizations like the NAACP and the Climate Reality Project to advance their social and environmental missions.

Overall, Ben & Jerry's values-based marketing approach is a key part of their brand identity and has helped them build a loyal following of customers who share their commitment to social justice and sustainability. Ben & Jerry's has also taken an innovative approach to marketing sustainability. They have integrated and prioritized sustainability values into every aspect of their business, from sourcing ingredients to packaging to marketing their products. Here are a few examples of their innovative marketing approaches to sustainability:

1. **Climate justice**: Ben & Jerry's has made a commitment to reducing their carbon footprint and helping to combat climate change. They have implemented a number of sustainability initiatives, such as using renewable energy sources and reducing waste in their production processes. They have also partnered with organizations like the Climate Reality Project to raise awareness about the urgent need for climate action.
2. **Ethical sourcing**: Ben & Jerry's sources their ingredients from suppliers who meet their high standards for sustainability and ethical practices. For example, they work with fair trade certified suppliers to ensure that farmers are paid a fair price for their crops, and they prioritize using non-GMO ingredients to promote biodiversity.
3. **Sustainable packaging**: Ben & Jerry's has taken an innovative approach to reducing their environmental impact by using sustainable packaging materials. For example, they have developed a compostable pint container made from sugarcane, which reduces waste and is fully compostable.
4. **Engaging customers**: Ben & Jerry's engages with their customers on sustainability issues through their marketing campaigns and social media channels. For example, they launched a "Save Our Swirled" campaign to raise awareness about the impacts of climate change and encourage customers to take action.

Overall, Ben & Jerry's innovative approach to marketing sustainability has helped to position them as a leader in the food industry and build a loyal following of customers who share their commitment to social and environmental responsibility.

Sustainable Human Resource Management

Sustainable Human Resource Management (SHRM) is an approach to managing human resources that integrates environmental, social, and economic sustainability into the policies, practices, and strategies of an organization (Mariappanadar, 2019). The primary goal of SHRM is to balance the needs of the organization with the needs of its employees, society, and the environment in a way that creates long-term value for all stakeholders. SHRM is a growing approach in HRM. This is because there is a growing recognition that organizations have a responsibility to promote sustainability, not only to protect the environment but also to create long-term value for all stakeholders, including employees, customers, and society as a whole. There are several reasons why SHRM is becoming increasingly popular. First, implementing SHRM practices can lead to increased productivity, reduced turnover, and enhanced reputation, which can translate into a competitive advantage and financial benefits for the organization. Second, SHRM practices can improve employees' well-being, work-life balance, and job satisfaction, which can lead to increased motivation, engagement, and retention. Third, SHRM can generally improve the company's social responsibility. More specifically, SHRM practices can contribute to addressing social and environmental challenges, such as climate change, poverty, and inequality, which align with the values and expectations of employees, customers, and society. Fourth, SHRM can sometimes be a good response to the growing sustainability expectations of the regulatory environment. Increasingly, governments and regulatory bodies are imposing environmental and social regulations that require organizations to implement sustainable practices, which can be achieved through SHRM practices. Overall, SHRM is becoming a popular approach in HRM because it aligns with the values and expectations of stakeholders, contributes to addressing social and environmental challenges, and provides business benefits to organizations.

SHRM involves several key principles, including:

1. **Environmental Sustainability**: Incorporating environmentally sustainable practices into HR policies, such as reducing waste, promoting energy efficiency, and implementing green procurement.
2. **Social Sustainability**: Ensuring that HR policies promote diversity, equity, and inclusion, and that employees are treated fairly and with respect.
3. **Economic Sustainability**: Ensuring that HR policies support the long-term financial health of the organization, while also providing

employees with fair compensation, benefits, and opportunities for growth and development.

4. **Stakeholder Engagement**: Engaging with stakeholders such as employees, customers, suppliers, and communities to understand their needs and perspectives, and incorporating their feedback into HR policies and practices.

In other words, SHRM is a holistic approach to managing human resources that recognizes the interconnectedness of economic, social, and environmental sustainability, and seeks to create value for all stakeholders over the long term.

There are numerous examples of companies, nonprofits, and public administrations that have successfully employed SHRM practices. Here are a few examples from well-known companies championing sustainability.

1. **Patagonia**: The company offers on-site childcare, paid time off for environmental activism, and flexible work arrangements to promote work-life balance.
2. **IKEA**: The company offers training and development opportunities to its employees, promoting diversity and inclusion, and using renewable energy sources in its operations.
3. **Unilever**: The company offers flexible work arrangements, promoting gender equality, and reducing its environmental impact through sustainable sourcing and production methods.
4. **Interface**: Its "Mission Zero" sustainability program includes the company's commitment to offer training and development opportunities to its employees for promoting diversity and inclusion.
5. **Starbucks**: The company offers health benefits to its employees and actively promotes diversity and inclusion along with using sustainable materials in its stores and products.

Here are a few examples of effective and innovative SHRM practices implemented by nonprofits:

6. **The Nature Conservancy**: As a leading global environmental nonprofit, it has implemented several SHRM practices, including offering flexible work arrangements, promoting work-life balance,

and providing professional development opportunities for its employees. The organization also has a commitment to diversity and inclusion, and it promotes sustainable practices in its operations and conservation efforts.

7. **Amnesty International**: As a well-known human rights nonprofit it has implemented several SHRM practices, including offering a competitive benefits package, promoting diversity and inclusion, and providing training and development opportunities for its employees. The organization also has a commitment to reducing its environmental impact through sustainable practices in its offices and events.
8. **Charity: Water**: A very innovative and impactful nonprofit that has provided clean drinking water to millions of people in developing countries. The organization has implemented several SHRM practices, including offering a flexible work environment, promoting work-life balance, and providing professional development opportunities for its employees. The organization also has a commitment to transparency and accountability in its operations and fundraising efforts.
9. **Teach for America**: Also another well-known nonprofit that aims to close the educational achievement gap in the United States. The organization has implemented several SHRM practices, including offering a competitive benefits package, promoting diversity and inclusion, and providing training and development opportunities for its employees. Like Amnesty and other leading nonprofits, the organization also has policies for reducing environmental impact in their offices and events.

Governments are also implementing SHRM in their own public administrations practices to promote sustainability, efficiency, and equity. Here are some examples of effective and innovative SHRM practices implemented by public administrations:

10. **City of San Francisco**: The City of San Francisco has implemented several SHRM practices, including offering a comprehensive wellness program, promoting diversity and inclusion, and providing training and development opportunities for its employees. The city also has a commitment to reducing its environmental impact

through sustainable practices in its operations, including green building design and sustainable transportation.

11. **City of Portland**: The City of Portland has also implemented several SHRM practices, including offering flexible work arrangements, promoting work-life balance, and providing training and development opportunities for its employees. The city also has a commitment to reducing its environmental impact through sustainable practices in its operations, including green procurement and waste reduction.
12. **Government of Canada**: The Government of Canada offers a competitive benefits package, promoting diversity and inclusion, and providing training and development opportunities for its employees. The government also has a commitment to reducing its environmental impact through sustainable practices in its operations and procurement, including sustainable building design and green energy usage.
13. **New Zealand Government**: The New Zealand government has implemented several SHRM practices, including offering flexible work arrangements, promoting work-life balance, and providing training and development opportunities for its employees. The government also has a commitment to reducing its environmental impact through sustainable practices in its operations and procurement, including reducing greenhouse gas emissions and promoting sustainable transportation.

Overall, these private sector companies, nonprofit organizations, and public administrations examples demonstrate how SHRM practices can be effectively integrated into their policies and practices. The SHRM provides a framework of reference and a values-based system for promoting sustainability, efficiency, inclusion, and equity practices for creating long-term value for all stakeholders, including employees, citizens, and the environment.

Case 9.4 DEI Reporting as Sustainability Practice

DEI (Diversity, Equity, and Inclusion) reporting is a practice in which companies publicly share data on their efforts to create a more diverse, equitable, and inclusive workplace. The goal of DEI reporting is to increase transparency and accountability around these issues, as well as to track progress and identify areas for improvement. DEI reporting typically includes data on a range of metrics, such as:

1. **Representation**: This includes information on the demographic makeup of a company's workforce, such as race, gender, ethnicity, age, and sexual orientation.
2. **Pay equity**: This involves analyzing pay data to identify any disparities based on demographic factors, such as gender or race.
3. **Inclusion and belonging**: This can include employee surveys to measure how included and valued employees feel in the workplace.
4. **DEI initiatives**: This includes information on the various initiatives and programs a company has implemented to promote diversity, equity, and inclusion in the workplace, such as mentoring programs or employee resource groups.

Companies may choose to report their DEI data internally, to employees and leadership, or externally, to stakeholders such as investors, customers, and the public. Some companies also choose to publish their DEI reports on their website or in other public forums to increase transparency and accountability. DEI reporting is increasingly becoming a standard practice for companies that are committed to creating a more diverse, equitable, and inclusive workplace, and can help to drive meaningful change and progress towards these goals. DEI reporting is clearly reflecting the values of sustainability management, and it demonstrates the company's commitment to social responsibility and accountability. Sustainability management focuses on the environmental, social, and economic impacts of a company's operations, and seeks to promote sustainable practices that benefit all stakeholders, including employees, customers, and the broader community. DEI reporting is one aspect of social sustainability, which involves creating a more diverse, equitable, and inclusive workplace culture. Therefore, DEI reporting can be considered a key component of sustainability management because it helps to promote social sustainability by:

1. **Enhancing employee engagement**: When companies promote diversity, equity, and inclusion in the workplace, it can lead to increased employee engagement and retention. This can help to

promote a sustainable, long-term business model that benefits all stakeholders.

2. **Improving reputation and brand value**: Companies that prioritize diversity, equity, and inclusion are often viewed more favorably by customers, investors, and other stakeholders. This can help to improve a company's reputation and brand value over the long term, which is an important aspect of sustainable business practices.
3. **Supporting the UN Sustainable Development Goals**: The UN-SDGs include a goal to promote gender equality (SDG 5) and another to reduce inequalities within and among countries (SDG 10). DEI reporting can help companies to demonstrate their commitment to these goals and contribute to broader global efforts to promote sustainability.

DEI reporting is an important tool for organizations who want to express, measure, and monitor their social sustainability practices related to SHRM. The DEI reports can demonstrate the organization's commitment to responsible business practices that benefit all stakeholders. There are many inspiring and innovative examples of companies providing DEI reporting. Here are a few examples:

1. **Intel**: Intel is committed to creating a more diverse and inclusive workplace, and has been providing annual diversity and inclusion reports since 2015. Their reports include data on employee representation, hiring and retention rates, and other key metrics related to diversity and inclusion.
2. **Salesforce**: Salesforce has been a leader in providing DEI reporting, with their annual "Equality" reports providing detailed data on their efforts to create a more diverse and inclusive workplace. Their reports include data on employee representation, pay equity, and their efforts to address systemic inequalities through programs, such as their Racial Equality and Justice Task Force.
3. **Etsy**: Etsy has been recognized for their innovative approach to DEI reporting, with their annual reports incorporating storytelling and data visualization to communicate their progress and challenges. Their reports include data on employee representation, pay equity, and the diversity of their marketplace sellers.

4. **Gap Inc.**: Gap Inc. has been providing DEI reporting since 2003, and their annual reports include data on employee representation, pay equity, and their efforts to promote diversity and inclusion throughout their supply chain. They also publish regular updates on their progress towards their diversity and inclusion goals.
5. **Microsoft**: Microsoft has been providing DEI reporting since 2016, and their annual reports include data on employee representation, pay equity, and their efforts to promote diversity and inclusion in their products and services. They also provide regular updates on their progress towards their diversity and inclusion goals.

DEI reporting is becoming standard across industries. It is also common to see them integrated into the company's sustainability reporting. The inclusion of DEI reporting in sustainability reporting can help organizations to demonstrate the company's overall commitments, performance, and measured impactful contributions to creating a more equitable and just society. This integration is due to the increasing focus on the social dimension of sustainability, including issues related to diversity, equity, and inclusion. As a result, many organizations have started to include DEI metrics and targets in their sustainability reports. As mentioned above, these metrics usually include things like the percentage of women or people from underrepresented groups in leadership positions, employee engagement and satisfaction scores for these groups, and the number of initiatives aimed at promoting diversity and inclusion in the workplace. These measurements and effective organizational practices are often compared across organizations, sectors, and countries generating a more comprehensive picture of sustainability progress.

Financial Sustainability Management

Sustainable finance, sustainability finance, and ESG finance are related concepts, but they have different meanings and scopes. Sustainable finance refers to financial services and products that are designed to support sustainable development by integrating ESG factors into financial decision-making. Sustainable finance encompasses a wide range of activities, including green bonds, impact investing, and socially responsible investing. Sustainability finance is a broader term that encompasses all financial activities that contribute to sustainable development. Sustainability finance includes sustainable finance, as well as other activities such as microfinance, community development finance, and impact investment funds. ESG finance, on the other hand, is a specific approach to sustainable finance that focuses on integrating environmental, social, and governance (ESG) factors into financial decision-making. ESG finance seeks to evaluate the non-financial risks and opportunities associated with a company or investment, such as its carbon footprint, labor practices, and board diversity.

Financial Sustainability Management (FSM) is a management approach that aims to ensure the long-term financial viability of an organization. Sustainable finance, sustainability finance, and ESG finance are related but distinct concepts. Sustainable finance involves financial services and products supporting sustainable development by integrating ESG factors. Sustainability finance is a broader term covering all financial activities contributing to sustainable development, including microfinance and community development finance. ESG finance is a specific approach focusing on integrating environmental, social, and governance factors into financial decision-making, evaluating non-financial risks and opportunities associated with a company or investment. FSM involves a set of strategies and practices that enable an organization to maintain its financial health over the long term, while also pursuing its mission and objectives.

In contrast, traditional finance management typically focuses on short-term financial goals, such as maximizing profits or minimizing costs in the current period. While traditional finance management is important for the day-to-day operations of an organization, FSM takes a more holistic approach, considering the financial sustainability of the organization over the long term. FSM involves a range of activities, including financial planning, risk management, resource allocation, and performance monitoring. It also involves stakeholder engagement, as the long-term financial sustainability of an organization is often dependent on the support of key stakeholders, such as investors, donors, and customers. Compared to traditional finance management, FSM is more forward-looking and proactive, focusing on the long-term health and viability of the organization. It also takes into account a wider range of factors, such as environmental and social impacts, that can affect an organization's financial sustainability over time. In other words, FSM is a critical component of sustainable business practices, as it helps organizations to achieve their mission and objectives over the long term, while also ensuring that they remain financially viable and resilient in the face of economic and social challenges.

The core dimensions of finance that closely relate to sustainability management are the following:

1. **Investment**: Sustainable finance involves the allocation of financial resources towards investments that generate long-term social, environmental, and economic benefits. This includes investments in renewable energy, sustainable agriculture, clean technology, and other sectors that contribute to the transition towards a more sustainable economy.
2. **Risk Management**: Sustainable finance also involves the identification and management of ESG risks that can affect the financial performance of an organization. This includes risks related to climate change, human rights, supply chain management, and other ESG factors that can impact an organization's operations, reputation, and financial performance.
3. **Reporting**: Sustainable finance requires transparent and accurate reporting of financial and non-financial information. This includes the disclosure of ESG risks, as well as the impact of an organization's activities on the environment and society. Sustainability reporting frameworks such as the GRI and SASB are commonly used to report on sustainability-related information.
4. **Stakeholder Engagement**: Sustainable finance involves engagement with stakeholders, including investors, customers, employees, and communities, to understand their concerns and interests related to sustainability. This engagement can inform an organization's strategy and decision-making, as well as improve transparency and accountability.
5. **Governance**: Sustainable finance requires effective governance structures and practices that ensure accountability and promote long-term sustainability. This includes having a clear strategy for sustainability, integrating sustainability into decision-making processes, and establishing accountability mechanisms to ensure compliance with sustainability goals and objectives.

Overall, these dimensions of finance related to sustainability management are interconnected and require a holistic approach to effectively manage sustainability risks and opportunities, while also generating long-term value for organizations and society. They are core elements in ESG finance, which incorporates environmental, social, and governance factors into investment decisions using strategies like screening, integration, and engagement. It has gained importance as investors recognize ESG-related risks and opportunities, and as a means to align investment strategies with social and environmental goals. The growth in ESG investing has led to the development of various ESG investment products, such as mutual funds and ETFs. BlackRock, a leading asset manager, is heavily invested in ESG finance, offering ESG-focused products and incorporating ESG factors into its risk management and engagement practices.

There are several major indexes on ESG investing that are used to track the performance of companies with strong ESG practices. Here are some examples:

1. **MSCI ESG Indexes**: MSCI is a leading provider of indexes for ESG investing. The MSCI ESG indexes are designed to capture companies with strong ESG performance relative to their industry peers. The MSCI World ESG Index, for example, includes large and mid-cap companies from 23 developed markets that have high ESG ratings.
2. **Dow Jones Sustainability Indexes (DJSI)**: The DJSI is a family of indexes that measures the performance of companies with strong sustainability practices. The indexes are created by S&P Dow Jones Indices in collaboration with RobecoSAM, an ESG data provider. The DJSI World Index, for example, includes companies with high scores in areas such as environmental management, social responsibility, and corporate governance.
3. **FTSE4Good Index Series**: The FTSE4Good Index Series is designed to measure the performance of companies with strong ESG practices. The indexes are created by FTSE Russell, a global index provider. The FTSE4Good Global Index, for example, includes companies from developed and emerging markets that meet ESG criteria based on a range of indicators.
4. **S&P 500 ESG Index**: The S&P 500 ESG Index is a subset of the S&P 500 Index, which includes 500 large-cap US companies. The ESG index uses ESG data to exclude companies with low ESG ratings, while also maintaining a similar risk and return profile as the broader S&P 500 Index.

These indexes are used by investors and asset managers as a benchmark for ESG investing, and many financial products, including ESG-focused mutual funds and ETFs, are designed to track these indexes.

Sustainability finance is quite important for achieving the SDGs as it provides the necessary financial resources to support sustainable development activities. Achieving the SDGs requires significant investment in areas such as renewable energy, clean water and sanitation, sustainable agriculture, and affordable housing, among others. Sustainability finance plays a crucial role in mobilizing the necessary investment capital to support these activities. By integrating ESG factors into financial decision-making, sustainability finance can help redirect investment flows towards sustainable projects and companies that are aligned with the SDGs. Sustainability finance can also help reduce the risk of investments in unsustainable activities and provide a more holistic view of the long-term financial performance of companies and projects. Here are some examples of how sustainability finance is supporting the achievement of the SDGs:

1. **Green Bonds**: Green bonds are fixed-income securities that are specifically issued to fund environmentally sustainable projects. Green bonds can be used to finance a wide range of sustainable projects, such as renewable energy infrastructure, clean transportation, and energy-efficient buildings. In 2021, the global market for green bonds surpassed $1 trillion, highlighting the growing demand for sustainable investment opportunities.
2. **Impact Investing**: Impact investing refers to investments made with the intention of generating measurable social and environmental impact alongside a financial return. Impact investors seek to support sustainable development activities that are aligned with the SDGs, such as affordable housing, sustainable agriculture, and access to healthcare and education.
3. **Socially Responsible Investing (SRI)**: SRI is an investment strategy that integrates ESG factors into investment decisions. SRI aims to support sustainable development by investing in companies that have strong ESG performance and avoiding companies that engage in unsustainable activities.
4. **Blended Finance**: Blended finance involves combining public and private financing to support sustainable development activities. Blended finance structures can help reduce the risk of investments in sustainable projects, making them more attractive to private

investors. For example, the Global Environment Facility's Sustainable Cities Program uses blended finance to support sustainable urban development projects in cities around the world.

Overall, sustainability finance can play a crucial role in supporting the achievement of the SDGs by mobilizing the necessary financial resources to support sustainable development activities. Sustainable finance will likely grow in the future as regulatory frameworks evolve in these directions. The Sustainable Finance Disclosure Regulation (SFDR), for example, is one of those developments. It was a European Union (EU) regulation that was adopted in 2019 and came into effect in March 2021. It is part of a broader EU initiative to create a sustainable finance framework that supports the transition to a low-carbon and more sustainable economy. The SFDR aims to increase transparency and improve the flow of information on sustainable finance by requiring financial market participants, including asset managers, investment advisers, and pension funds, to disclose information on the ESG risks of their investments. The SFDR is a significant development in the area of sustainable finance, as it requires financial market participants to provide more in-depth, transparent, and standardized information. This will help investors make more informed decisions and encourage greater transparency and accountability in the financial sector. By integrating ESG factors into financial decision-making, sustainability finance can help redirect investment flows towards sustainable projects and companies that are aligned with the SDGs.

Case 9.5 KIVA and Microfinance

Kiva is a nonprofit organization that aims to alleviate poverty by providing microfinance loans to people in underserved communities around the world. Microfinance is the provision of financial services, such as small loans, savings accounts, and insurance, to people who typically do not have access to traditional banking services. Kiva's platform allows individuals or groups to lend as little as $25 to entrepreneurs in need. Kiva partners with local microfinance institutions (MFIs) in various countries to identify qualified borrowers and manage the loans. Kiva lenders' funds are pooled together to provide the loans to the borrowers, and once the loans are repaid, the lenders can choose to withdraw their funds or relend them to other borrowers. Kiva's mission is to connect people through lending to alleviate poverty, and it has facilitated over $1.7 billion in loans to date, supporting more than 4 million borrowers in over 100 countries. Through Kiva's platform, lenders can directly impact the lives of people in need, help them grow their businesses, and improve their economic opportunities.

Kiva is related but different from other MFIs like the Grameen Bank. Grameen Bank was founded in Bangladesh in 1983 by Muhammad Yunus. It operates on the principle of "social business" and provides small loans to people who are too poor to qualify for traditional bank loans. Grameen Bank focuses on providing loans to women, who are often excluded from the formal financial sector. The bank has a system of group lending, where borrowers are organized into groups of five, and each group member is responsible for the other members' loans. Grameen Bank has had a significant impact on poverty reduction in Bangladesh and has inspired the development of microfinance institutions around the world. Kiva, on the other hand, is a nonprofit organization that operates as a crowdfunding platform. It partners with local MFIs, Kiva's platform allows lenders to directly impact the lives of people in need and support sustainable economic development. While both organizations aim to alleviate poverty through microfinance, Kiva's model focuses on leveraging the power of crowdfunding to provide loans to entrepreneurs in need, while Grameen Bank has a more traditional microfinance model with a focus on group lending and women's empowerment.

Microfinance is an umbrella term that includes different related practices used around the world to provide financial services to underserved communities. Here are some of the most common types:

1. **Group-based lending**: This is a common microfinance practice where borrowers are organized into groups, and each member is responsible for the other members' loans. Group-based lending helps to build social capital, encourage repayment, and reduce transaction costs for microfinance institutions.
2. **Individual lending**: In individual lending, microfinance institutions provide loans to individual borrowers based on their creditworthiness and ability to repay. This approach is typically used for larger loans or for borrowers who have a track record of successful business operations.

3. **Microsavings**: Microsavings programs allow low-income individuals to save small amounts of money on a regular basis. Microsavings programs can help individuals build assets, provide a safety net during emergencies, and improve financial stability.
4. **Microinsurance**: Microinsurance provides insurance coverage to low-income individuals who are typically excluded from traditional insurance markets. Microinsurance can provide protection against risks, such as illness, crop failure, or natural disasters.
5. **Remittances**: Remittances involve the transfer of money from individuals working in other countries back to their families in their home countries. Microfinance institutions can facilitate remittances and provide other financial services to migrant workers.
6. **Islamic microfinance**: Islamic microfinance is based on Islamic finance principles and prohibits the charging of interest. Instead, Islamic microfinance institutions use profit-sharing and partnership models to provide financial services to low-income individuals.

These microfinance practices can be used in combination to provide a range of financial services to underserved communities, promoting economic development, and reducing poverty. The impact of microfinance can be significant and far-reaching, helping to alleviate poverty, empower individuals, and promote sustainable economic development. Specifically, microfinance plays an important role in sustainable development and achieving the SDGs for several reasons:

1. **Reducing poverty**: Microfinance helps to reduce poverty by providing financial services to people who are excluded from the formal financial sector. It helps people to start and grow small businesses, generate income, and improve their living standards.
2. **Promoting gender equality**: Women are often disproportionately affected by poverty and have limited access to financial services. Microfinance programs specifically targeting women can help to promote gender equality and empower women to become entrepreneurs and leaders in their communities.
3. **Supporting economic growth**: Microfinance provides access to credit and other financial services that can help to stimulate economic growth and job creation. This can help to create more opportunities for people and reduce dependency on aid.

4. **Improving health and education**: Microfinance programs can also help to improve access to healthcare and education by providing financing for health and education-related expenses.
5. **Fostering innovation**: Microfinance institutions often use innovative approaches to deliver financial services to underserved populations. This can help to promote innovation and entrepreneurship in communities, leading to more sustainable development.

Overall, microfinance provides some innovative and impactful mechanisms for poverty alleviation, women empowerment, social entrepreneurship, and sustainable development. It plays a critical role in achieving the SDGs by empowering people, promoting economic growth, and fostering sustainable opportunities for people traditionally excluded from accessing loans from traditional offerings of commercial financial institutions.

Sustainability Strategy and Negotiation

A sustainability strategy in management is a plan that outlines an organization's approach to integrating ESG factors into its operations and decision-making processes. The goal of a sustainability strategy is to create long-term value for the organization while also contributing to sustainable development. A sustainability strategy typically involves the following steps:

1. **Assessment**: The first step in developing a sustainability strategy is to assess the organization's current sustainability performance. This involves identifying the organization's environmental, social, and governance risks and opportunities, as well as its impact on the natural environment and society.
2. **Goal Setting**: Based on the assessment, the organization sets goals and targets for improving its sustainability performance. These goals may include reducing greenhouse gas emissions, increasing energy efficiency, improving working conditions, and enhancing the sustainability of the supply chain.
3. **Integration**: The organization integrates sustainability into its core business processes, including decision-making, risk management, and reporting. This involves embedding sustainability considerations into the organization's culture, values, and operations.

4. **Implementation**: The organization implements initiatives and projects to achieve its sustainability goals. This may include investing in renewable energy, reducing waste and water use, implementing responsible sourcing practices, and engaging stakeholders on sustainability issues.
5. **Monitoring and Reporting**: The organization monitors and reports on its sustainability performance, including progress towards its sustainability goals and targets. This information is used to improve sustainability practices, identify areas for improvement, and communicate with stakeholders.

A sustainability strategy in management helps organizations to manage sustainability risks, identify opportunities for growth and innovation, and build trust with stakeholders. By integrating sustainability into their operations, organizations can create long-term value for themselves and society as a whole.

Negotiation in sustainability management involves the process of reaching an agreement between different stakeholders, such as businesses, governments, NGOs, and communities, to achieve sustainable outcomes. This can involve negotiating on issues related to environmental protection, social responsibility, and economic development.

Negotiation in sustainability management typically involves the following steps:

1. **Identifying stakeholders**: The first step in negotiation is identifying the stakeholders who will be impacted by the decision. This can include employees, customers, suppliers, governments, NGOs, and communities.
2. **Defining the issue**: The second step is to define the issue that needs to be addressed. This can include environmental impacts, social issues, or economic challenges.
3. **Identifying common interests**: The third step is to identify the common interests among the stakeholders. This can involve identifying shared values, goals, and objectives.
4. **Exploring options**: The fourth step is to explore options for resolving the issue. This can involve brainstorming and evaluating different solutions that meet the needs and interests of all stakeholders.

5. **Negotiating an agreement**: The final step is to negotiate an agreement that addresses the needs and interests of all stakeholders. This can involve making compromises and finding common ground to reach a mutually beneficial solution.

Negotiation in sustainability management is crucial as it enables stakeholders to collaborate and address complex challenges while balancing environmental, social, and economic concerns. Strategies and negotiation are interconnected, with strategies providing the framework for negotiating sustainable outcomes. Examples of sustainability strategies include sustainable supply chain, renewable energy, stakeholder engagement, circular economy, and sustainable finance strategies. By implementing these strategies and engaging in effective negotiation, organizations can build trust, manage risks, and contribute to a sustainable future.

Case 9.6 The COP and Paris Agreement Negotiations

The COP in the Paris Agreement negotiations refers to the Conference of the Parties to the UNFCCC that took place in Paris, France in 2015. The goal of the conference was to negotiate an agreement to address climate change and to keep global temperature rise well below 2 °C above pre-industrial levels, with an aim to limit the temperature increase to 1.5 °C.

The Paris Agreement, which was adopted on December 12, 2015, is an international treaty that sets out a framework for global action to combat climate change. It includes commitments from all participating countries to reduce their greenhouse gas emissions and to strengthen their efforts over time. The Paris Agreement also includes provisions for adapting to the impacts of climate change and for providing financial and technological support to developing countries.

The COP in the Paris Agreement negotiations was significant because it marked a major milestone in international efforts to address climate change. The agreement was the first to include commitments from both developed and developing countries, and it signaled a shift towards a more collaborative and cooperative approach to addressing climate change. The agreement has been ratified by 190 countries, including the United States, China, and India, and it represents a critical step forward in the global effort to combat climate change.

The negotiations leading to the adoption of the Paris Agreement involved a range of strategies and approaches to help bridge differences and reach consensus among the parties. Here are some of the strategies that were used:

1. **Transparency and inclusivity**: The negotiations were conducted in an open and transparent manner, with all parties given an opportunity to participate and provide input. This helped to build trust and foster a sense of ownership among the parties.
2. **Flexibility and compromise**: The Paris Agreement was designed to accommodate a range of different national circumstances and priorities. Parties were encouraged to take voluntary and ambitious actions to reduce their emissions, and a variety of approaches were allowed to achieve this goal. This flexibility allowed for compromise and helped to build consensus among the parties.
3. **Leadership and engagement**: Leaders from around the world played an important role in advocating for strong action on climate change and rallying support for the Paris Agreement. Civil society groups, businesses, and other stakeholders also played an important role in mobilizing support and pressuring governments to take action.
4. **Bridging initiatives**: A number of initiatives were launched during the negotiations to help bridge differences and build consensus among the parties. For example, the High Ambition Coalition was formed to advocate for a more ambitious and comprehensive agreement, while the Climate Vulnerable Forum helped to highlight the unique challenges facing vulnerable countries.
5. **Technical and scientific support**: The negotiations were supported by a range of technical and scientific experts who provided analysis and advice on key issues. This helped to ensure that the negotiations were grounded in sound science and evidence.

Overall, the Paris Agreement negotiations involved a range of strategies and approaches that helped to build trust, foster compromise, and build consensus among the parties. These strategies helped to lay the foundation for a strong and ambitious global agreement on climate change.

Sustainability Reporting and SDG Mapping

Sustainability reporting and SDG mapping are vital for organizations to showcase their sustainability performance and contributions to the SDGs. The growing popularity of sustainability reporting is due to stakeholder expectations, regulatory environments, investor demands, reputation management, and benchmarking for performance improvement. These reports help companies respond to stakeholder demands, address sustainability challenges, and comply with increasing sustainability regulations. In other words, social, economic, and environmental reports (SEERs), known as sustainability reporting, are increasingly becoming an essential element in companies who adequately respond to stakeholders' demand, and lead by example to respond to sustainability challenges and anticipate the ever growing regulations for sustainability practices. Besides fast growing voluntary engagement in sustainability reporting, regulations in many countries are also contributing to it. For example, in the European Union, companies with more than 500 employees are required to report on ESG issues. Similarly, in the United States, the Securities and Exchange Commission (SEC) has issued guidance requiring companies to disclose material climate-related risks. As we will consider in more details in Part 4, there are some current and emerging best practices in sustainability reporting and SDG mapping:

1. **Materiality assessment**: Organizations are increasingly conducting materiality assessments to identify the sustainability issues that are most important to their stakeholders and their business. This helps to focus reporting and SDG mapping efforts on the issues that matter most and demonstrate progress in addressing them.
2. **Integrated reporting**: Integrated reporting combines financial and non-financial information in a single report, providing a comprehensive view of an organization's performance. This helps to demonstrate the links between sustainability and financial performance and to communicate the organization's long-term value creation strategy.
3. **SDG alignment**: Many organizations are mapping their sustainability strategies and performance to the SDGs, identifying the goals that are most relevant to their business and setting targets

to contribute to them. This helps to demonstrate the organization's commitment to sustainable development and its contribution to global sustainability goals.

4. **Data quality and consistency**: To ensure the credibility of sustainability reporting and SDG mapping, organizations need to ensure that their data is of high quality and consistent over time. This requires robust data management systems, clear data definitions, and standardized reporting methodologies.
5. **Stakeholder engagement**: Engaging with stakeholders is a key best practice in sustainability reporting and SDG mapping. This helps to identify the issues that are most important to stakeholders, build trust, and demonstrate the organization's commitment to sustainability.
6. **Continuous improvement**: Sustainability reporting and SDG mapping should be viewed as an ongoing process of improvement. Organizations should regularly review their reporting and mapping methodologies, seek feedback from stakeholders, and make changes as needed to ensure that their reporting is transparent, credible, and relevant.

Overall, these best practices help organizations to communicate their sustainability performance and contribution to the SDGs in a credible and transparent way, and to demonstrate their commitment to sustainable development.

There are several standardized frameworks that organizations can use for sustainability reporting. These frameworks provide a common language and structure for sustainability reporting, making it easier for stakeholders to compare the sustainability performance of different organizations. Some of the most widely used frameworks include:

1. **Global Reporting Initiative (GRI)**: The GRI is one of the most widely used frameworks for sustainability reporting. It provides a comprehensive set of sustainability indicators, organized into three categories: economic, environmental, and social. The GRI also provides guidance on how to report on these indicators and how to conduct a materiality assessment to identify the sustainability issues that are most important to an organization.

2. **Sustainability Accounting Standards Board (SASB)**: The SASB is a framework for sustainability reporting that is focused on financially material sustainability issues. The SASB has developed a set of industry-specific sustainability standards, organized into five categories: environment, social capital, human capital, business model and innovation, and leadership and governance.
3. **Task Force on Climate-related Financial Disclosures (TCFD)**: The TCFD is a framework for disclosing climate-related financial risks and opportunities. The TCFD provides guidance on how to disclose climate-related risks and opportunities in four areas: governance, strategy, risk management, and metrics and targets.
4. **Carbon Disclosure Project (CDP)**: CDP is a nonprofit organization that runs a global disclosure system for companies, cities, states, and regions to report on their environmental impacts, risks, and opportunities. The CDP was founded in 2000 and has become one of the most widely recognized sustainability reporting initiatives, with over 10,000 organizations reporting to the CDP in 2020. CDP provides a questionnaire that asks organizations to report on their carbon emissions, water usage, forest protection, and other environmental issues.
5. **Integrated Reporting (IR)**: IR is a framework that enables organizations to communicate their overall value creation story, including their sustainability performance. IR encourages organizations to integrate financial and non-financial information in a single report, demonstrating the links between sustainability and financial performance.
6. **The UNGC Communication on Progress (UNGC COP)**: The UNGC COP is a sustainability reporting framework for companies that have committed to the UNGC. It is a requirement for companies that have joined the UNGC, and it is designed to provide stakeholders with information about the company's progress towards meeting the UNGC's ten principles in the areas of human rights, labor, environment, and anti-corruption. The UNGC COP asks companies to report on their sustainability performance and to provide information on their efforts to integrate the UNGC's principles into their operations and strategies. The UNGC COP provides a standardized framework for sustainability reporting, which includes a set of core indicators that companies are expected to report on, such as greenhouse gas emissions,

energy consumption, and employee diversity. The UNGC COP also includes guidance on how to report on the UNGC's principles and how to engage stakeholders in sustainability reporting.

7. **ISO 26000—Social Responsibility**: ISO 26000 is a voluntary international standard that provides guidance on social responsibility, including sustainability reporting. It was developed by the International Organization for Standardization (ISO) and was published in 2010. ISO 26000 is not a certification standard, meaning that organizations cannot be certified as compliant with ISO 26000. Rather, it is a guidance document that provides recommendations on how organizations can behave in a socially responsible manner. ISO 26000 covers a wide range of topics related to social responsibility, including human rights, labor practices, environmental responsibility, fair operating practices, consumer issues, and community involvement and development. In terms of sustainability reporting, ISO 26000 provides guidance on how organizations can report on their social responsibility performance and communicate with stakeholders. The standard recommends that organizations be transparent about their social responsibility performance and that they report on their progress towards meeting their social responsibility goals. It also recommends that organizations engage with their stakeholders in sustainability reporting and that they use a variety of communication channels, such as sustainability reports, websites, and social media, to share their sustainability performance and progress.
8. **SDG Action Manager**: The SDG Action Manager tool is closely related to sustainability reporting, as it is designed to help organizations track and report on their progress towards the SDGs. The SDG Action Manager tool is a free, user-friendly platform developed by the UN Global Compact and B Lab that helps organizations to assess their current sustainability performance, set goals, and track progress towards the SDGs. It provides a range of features and resources to support sustainability reporting, including: (1) An SDG assessment tool to help organizations identify their priorities and gaps in relation to the SDGs; (2) a dashboard that enables organizations to track their progress towards the SDGs and generate reports for internal and external stakeholders; and (3) guidance on best practices for sustainability reporting and aligning reporting with the SDGs. The SDG Action Manager tool is a simple platform

that allows those small and medium enterprises (SME) who do not have the capacity to engage in the more demanding GRI reporting to effectively track and report on their sustainability performance and progress towards the SDGs. This allows them to engage in an effective level of sustainability reporting that improves transparency, accountability, and stakeholder engagement.

Selecting the best tool for sustainability reporting can be a challenging task for large companies, SMEs, and other organizations. Organizations should take into account their own capacity and make a cost–benefit analysis along with other considerations such as purpose and what they want to achieve, compatibility with existing systems and reportings, the user-friendliness and effectiveness in the communication, the reporting requirements and expectations for the sector, including regulatory bodies. They should also consider other factors, such as data security, reputation, maintenance, and upfront costs. By considering these factors, organizations can select a tool for sustainability reporting that meets their specific needs, provides good value for money, and helps them to achieve their sustainability goals.

Case 9.7 BIA the Benefit Impact Assessment

B Lab is a nonprofit organization which works to promote responsible business practices and advance a global movement of companies using business as a force for good. The organization was founded in 2006 and is based in the United States.

One of B Lab's key initiatives is the B Impact Assessment (BIA), a tool that is used to assess a company's overall social and environmental performance. The BIA evaluates a company's performance across five key areas including governance, workers, community, environment, and customers.

1. **Governance**: This section evaluates a company's overall governance structure, including its mission and purpose, transparency, accountability, and stakeholder engagement.
2. **Workers**: This section evaluates a company's treatment of its workers, including its employment practices, compensation and benefits, training and development, and worker engagement.
3. **Community**: This section evaluates a company's impact on the communities in which it operates, including its relationships with suppliers and customers, its community engagement initiatives, and its contributions to community development.

4. **Environment**: This section evaluates a company's environmental impact, including its energy use, greenhouse gas emissions, waste management practices, and overall environmental stewardship.
5. **Customers**: This section evaluates a company's impact on its customers, including its product and service quality, customer engagement, and social and environmental impact.

Within each section, the BIA evaluates a company's performance across a range of specific indicators. These indicators are updated regularly to ensure that they remain relevant and up-to-date with changing best practices in sustainable business. The maximum score for the BIA is 200 points. Within each section, there are a set of questions and indicators that are used to evaluate a company's performance. Companies can earn points based on their responses to these questions and indicators, with the maximum score for each section being as follows: Governance: 50 points, Workers: 52 points, Community: 44 points, Environment: 56 points, and Customers: 18 points. The maximum total score for the BIA is, therefore, 220 points ($50 + 52 + 44 + 56 + 18 = 220$), but the final score is based on a scale of 0 to 200 points. A score of 80 points or higher is required to become a Certified B Corporation, which is a designation given to businesses that meet high standards of social and environmental performance, accountability, and transparency.

There are many companies that have scored high on the BIA and have been certified as B Corporations. B Corporations are businesses that meet high standards of social and environmental performance, accountability, and transparency. Here are a few examples of companies that have scored high on the BIA and are Certified B Corporations:

1. **Patagonia**: Patagonia is a clothing company that is known for its commitment to sustainability and environmental responsibility. The company has scored a 100 on the BIA and has been certified as a B Corporation since 2012.
2. **Ben & Jerry's**: Ben & Jerry's is an ice cream company that is known for its social and environmental activism. The company has scored a 98 on the BIA and has been a certified B Corporation since 2012.
3. **Allbirds**: Allbirds is a shoe company that is committed to sustainability and uses eco-friendly materials in its products. The company

has scored a 95 on the BIA and has been a certified B Corporation since 2018.

4. **New Belgium Brewing**: New Belgium Brewing is a craft beer company that is committed to sustainability and social responsibility. The company has scored a 94 on the BIA and has been a certified B Corporation since 2013.
5. **Eileen Fisher**: Eileen Fisher is a clothing company that is committed to sustainability and ethical labor practices. The company has scored a 92 on the BIA and has been a certified B Corporation since 2015.

It's important to note that the BIA is a comprehensive assessment that evaluates a company's overall social and environmental performance, and that companies can score well in some areas but not others. Nonetheless, these companies are examples of businesses that have demonstrated a strong commitment to sustainability and social responsibility, as evaluated by the B Impact Assessment.

BIA is not just a score but a reflection of the company's commitment to sustainability values. Therefore, high performing organizations integrate the tool within their sustainability strategies and authentic sustainability practices. To make the BIA scoring an integral component of the organizational sustainability performance, it is important to:

1. **Getting buy-in from senior leadership**: Companies should ensure that senior leadership is committed to the BIA process and that it is integrated into overall business strategy and decision-making.
2. **Engaging employees**: Companies should engage employees in the BIA process to build buy-in, gather information, and identify opportunities for improvement.
3. **Integrating BIA results into decision-making**: Companies should use the BIA results to identify areas for improvement and to inform decision-making across the business.
4. **Tracking progress over time**: Companies should track their progress over time by taking the BIA regularly and using the results to set and achieve sustainability goals.
5. **Sharing results with stakeholders**: Companies should share BIA results with stakeholders, including customers, investors, and other external audiences, to build trust and demonstrate their commitment to sustainability.

By following these best practices, companies can use the BIA to improve their social and environmental performance, build trust with stakeholders, and create long-term value for their business and society. Overall, the BIA is an important tool for companies that want to assess and improve their social and environmental performance and demonstrate their commitment to responsible business practices. By providing a framework for evaluating and certifying companies based on their social and environmental impact, B Lab is helping to drive a global movement of businesses that prioritize sustainability and social responsibility.

Alternative Organizational Structures

Seeking a new form of organizational structure is important for responsible management and sustainability management for several reasons. First, traditional organizational structures are often focused on maximizing profit at the expense of social and environmental concerns. This can lead to negative impacts on communities, workers, and the environment. A new form of organizational structure that prioritizes sustainability and social responsibility can help to address these issues. Second, many current organizational structures are hierarchical and centralized, with decision-making power concentrated at the top. This can result in a lack of employee engagement and participation, as well as limited input from stakeholders. A new form of organizational structure that is more democratic and participatory can help to increase engagement and input from stakeholders. Third, sustainable development requires a long-term perspective, and traditional organizational structures often prioritize short-term gains. A new form of organizational structure that prioritizes sustainability can help to ensure that decisions are made with a long-term perspective in mind. Fourth, a new form of organizational structure that prioritizes sustainability can help to create more resilient and adaptive organizations that are better able to respond to changes in the environment, market conditions, and social issues.

Finally, we need to consider that many consumers and investors are increasingly concerned about sustainability and social responsibility, and are looking for organizations that prioritize these issues. Adopting a new form of organizational structure that prioritizes sustainability can help organizations to attract and retain customers and investors who share these values. In other words, seeking a new form of organizational structure is important for responsible management and sustainability management because it can help to address current organizational shortcomings, promote stakeholder engagement and input, foster a long-term perspective, create more resilient organizations, and attract customers and investors who prioritize sustainability and social responsibility.

There are several alternative forms of organizations which reflect sustainability and social inclusion values. Some of these forms are particularly important for social/sustainability innovation as well as for generating social/sustainability impact as we will review in Part 3 and Part 4. In general, there are some new or emerging forms of organizations that reflect the following typologies:

1. **Cooperative**: A cooperative is an organization that is owned and democratically controlled by its members. Members pool resources and make decisions together, which helps to ensure that everyone's needs and interests are taken into account. Cooperatives can be organized around a variety of purposes, including agriculture, housing, and energy. For example, Organic Valley is a cooperative of more than 1800 family farms that produce organic dairy, eggs, and other products. The cooperative is committed to sustainable agriculture and has a mission of supporting family farms, building local food systems, and promoting environmental stewardship. Another example is The Co-operative Group, a UK-based cooperative that operates a range of businesses, including food retail, funeral care, and insurance. The cooperative has a strong commitment to sustainability and has set ambitious goals for reducing its carbon footprint and promoting sustainable products.
2. **Social enterprise**: A social enterprise is an organization that has a social or environmental mission as its primary objective. These organizations use business practices to achieve their goals, but instead of maximizing profit, they aim to generate social or environmental impact. Social enterprises can take many different forms, including nonprofits, for-profits, and cooperatives. There are many social enterprises that focus on sustainable development and the SDGs. Here are a few examples: (1) The Ocean Cleanup is a nonprofit social enterprise that is developing advanced technologies to rid the world's oceans of plastic pollution. The organization is committed to achieving SDG 14, which aims to conserve and sustainably use the oceans, seas, and marine resources. (2) Toast Ale is a UK-based

social enterprise that makes beer from surplus bread. The organization is committed to reducing food waste and has a goal of achieving SDG 12, which aims to ensure sustainable consumption and production patterns. (3) SunCulture is a Kenyan social enterprise that develops and sells solar-powered irrigation systems to smallholder farmers. The organization is committed to achieving SDG 2, which aims to end hunger, achieve food security and improved nutrition, and promote sustainable agriculture. (4) D.light is a social enterprise that develops and sells solar-powered lighting and energy solutions to people living off-grid in developing countries. The organization is committed to achieving SDG 7, which aims to ensure access to affordable, reliable, sustainable, and modern energy for all. (5) Pachama is a social enterprise that uses satellite imagery and machine learning to measure and verify carbon offsets from forest conservation and reforestation projects. The organization is committed to achieving SDG 13, which aims to take urgent action to combat climate change and its impacts. Social enterprises can be effective models for achieving sustainable development and the SDGs because they prioritize social and environmental impact over profit, and often develop innovative solutions to complex sustainability challenges.

3. **Benefit corporation**: A benefit corporation is a type of corporation that has a legally binding social or environmental mission. Benefit Corporations are required to consider the impact of their decisions on stakeholders, including employees, customers, suppliers, and the environment. This legal structure is designed to ensure that the corporation's mission is prioritized, even if it conflicts with the pursuit of profit. For example, B Lab—the organization that administers the B Corp certification program is itself a Benefit Corporation, and its work in promoting and supporting companies that prioritize social and environmental impact aligns with several SDGs, including SDG 8, (Decent Work and Economic Growth), SDG 9 (Industry, Innovation, and Infrastructure), and SDG 17 (Partnerships for the Goals). For example, Dudley Neighbors Inc. (DNI) is a community land trust based in Roxbury, Massachusetts works to create and preserve affordable housing, while promoting community development, and fostering social equity. DNI provides affordable housing to low-income residents of the community,

helping to reduce poverty and increase access to safe and affordable housing and contributing to SDG 1 (No Poverty). DNI's work in promoting affordable housing and community development helps to create more livable and sustainable cities and communities promoting SDG 11 (Sustainable Cities and Communities). DNI also contributes to SDG 16 (Peace, Justice, and Strong Institutions) by promoting social equity and community development helps to build more inclusive and equitable societies, and to promote peace and justice.

4. **Community land trust**: A community land trust is a nonprofit organization that acquires and holds land for the benefit of a community. The land is owned collectively, and the trust ensures that it is used in a way that benefits the community, such as for affordable housing or community gardens. This model helps to ensure that land remains in community hands, even as property values rise. For example, Oakland Community Land Trust, based in Oakland, California acquires and develops land for affordable housing, and also helps to build community wealth and resilience. Through its work, the Oakland Community Land Trust contributes to several SDGs, including SDG 1 (No Poverty), SDG 8 (Decent Work and Economic Growth), and SDG 11 (Sustainable Cities and Communities).
5. **Worker-owned cooperative**: A worker-owned cooperative is a type of cooperative in which the workers own and democratically control the organization. This model gives workers greater control over their work and can help to ensure that they are fairly compensated. It also encourages collaboration and can help to reduce income inequality. For example, Arizmendi Association of Cooperatives is a network of worker-owned cooperatives based in the San Francisco Bay Area. The association includes several bakeries and a pizzeria, all of which are owned and operated by their employees. Through its work, the Arizmendi Association contributes to several SDGs, including SDG 1 (No Poverty), SDG 2 (Zero Hunger), and SDG 12 (Responsible Consumption and Production).
6. **Limited Liability Company with Low Profit (L3C)**: An L3C is a type of business entity that combines features of both for-profit and not-for-profit organizations. L3Cs are designed to have a primary social or environmental purpose, and are structured to operate with a low-profit margin. L3Cs are recognized in several US states and

are often used by social entrepreneurs and impact investors to pursue socially beneficial activities while also generating a financial return. For example, Greyston Bakery is an L3C based in Yonkers, New York. The bakery produces baked goods, including brownies and cookies, and operates under the principle of Open Hiring, which means it hires people without regard to their past work history or background. Greyston Bakery also provides job training and support services to its employees, many of whom have faced barriers to employment. Through its work, Greyston Bakery contributes to several SDGs, including SDG 1 (No Poverty), SDG 5 (Gender Equality), and SDG 8 (Decent Work and Economic Growth).

7. **Community Interest Companies (CICs)**: CICs are a type of social enterprise in the UK that are designed to pursue social or environmental goals, while also operating as a sustainable and profitable business. CICs are regulated by the government and are required to report on their social and environmental impact. They are also able to issue shares and seek investment, but any profits must be reinvested into the business or used for the benefit of the community. An example is The Bristol Pound, a CIC based in Bristol, UK, which is a local currency designed to encourage spending in local businesses and support the local economy. The currency can only be used with participating businesses in Bristol, which helps to keep money circulating in the local economy. The Bristol Pound also supports community initiatives and promotes sustainability through its work. Through its focus on supporting local businesses and promoting sustainable economic practices, The Bristol Pound contributes to several SDGs, including SDG 8 (Decent Work and Economic Growth), SDG 10 (Reduced Inequalities), and SDG 12 (Responsible Consumption and Production).

There are several other types of organizations whose goal is to create different forms of governance and legal structures to better fit their sustainability mission. Many countries have developed legislation to address these hybrid types of organizations whose focus is to generate social impact while also providing sustainable and socially inclusive solutions.

Case 9.8 Nativa and Italian Società Benefit

Nativa Srl SB is a social enterprise based in Italy that played a significant role in the development of the Società Benefit (SB) legal status in Italy. In 2012, Nativa proposed the idea of creating a new legal form for companies that operate with a social and environmental purpose to the Italian government. The proposed legal form was designed to provide more clarity and accountability around the social and environmental impact of businesses, and to encourage more companies to pursue socially responsible business practices.

Nativa's proposal for the Società Benefit legal status was influential in the development of the legislation that was eventually passed in Italy in 2016 (law 208/2015). The SB legal status was designed to be a flexible and adaptable form of business that can be applied to a wide range of organizations, from small enterprises to larger corporations. Nativa's advocacy and thought leadership around the need for a new legal form for socially and environmentally responsible businesses played an important role in the development of the Società Benefit legal status in Italy.

The SB is, therefore, a relatively new legal form of organization in Italy. It provided a framework for companies to operate with a social and environmental purpose. The SB legal form is intended to provide greater clarity and accountability around the social and environmental impact of businesses, while also allowing companies to generate a profit. It is a flexible and adaptable legal form that can be applied to a wide range of organizations, from small enterprises to larger corporations. Since its introduction, the SB legal status has gained popularity in Italy, with many businesses choosing to adopt this form as a way to demonstrate their commitment to social and environmental impact. The SB legal form is also seen as a way to differentiate a company from its competitors and to attract customers and investors who value social and environmental responsibility.

As of now, SBs in Italy do not enjoy any fiscal benefit, tax relief, or other financial advantages that are specifically designated for them. This is because the Società Benefit legal status in Italy is relatively new and the government is still working on developing policies and regulations to support this type of business. However, it is worth noting that some of the social and environmental objectives of Benefit Corporations may overlap with those of other programs or initiatives that offer financial benefits or incentives. For example, a Benefit Corporation that invests in renewable energy or reduces its carbon footprint may be eligible for subsidies or tax credits related to renewable energy or sustainability.

Additionally, the SB legal status is designed to provide greater transparency and accountability around a company's social and environmental impact, which may help to build trust with customers and investors and lead to greater financial opportunities in the long term.

The SB legal status in Italy has a set of legal elements and obligations that companies must meet in order to qualify for this status. These elements and obligations include:

1. **Purpose and Articles of Association**: The company's articles of association must include the social and/or environmental purpose of the company, which should be specific, clear, and measurable. The articles of association must also include provisions for the management and distribution of profits, which should be aligned with the social and environmental purpose of the company.
2. **Independent Certification**: The company must obtain independent certification of its social and environmental impact on an annual basis. The certification must be conducted by a third-party organization that is recognized by the Italian government. The certifying organization must be included in the Register of the Italian Revenue Agency, and be recognized by Accredia, the Italian National Accreditation Body, or by another accreditation body recognized at the European level. Accredia is responsible for accrediting certification bodies and ensuring their compliance with international standards.
3. **Reporting**: The company must prepare an annual report that includes information on its social and environmental impact, as well as its financial performance. The report must be made publicly available on the company's website or through other channels.
4. **Governance**: The company must have a governance structure that is transparent and accountable, and that is aligned with its social and environmental purpose. This may include having a board of directors that includes representatives of stakeholders such as employees, customers, and the local community.
5. **Accountability**: The company must be accountable for its social and environmental impact, and must have mechanisms in place to monitor and evaluate its impact on an ongoing basis.
6. **Non-distribution Constraint**: The company must have a non-distribution constraint in its articles of association, which means

that profits cannot be distributed to shareholders if doing so would compromise the company's social and environmental purpose.

Overall, the Società Benefit legal status in Italy is designed to promote socially and environmentally responsible business practices while also generating a profit. Companies that meet the legal elements and obligations of the SB legal status are recognized for their commitment to social and environmental impact, which may help to build trust with customers and investors and lead to greater financial opportunities in the long term.

Key Takeaways

1. Sustainability management goes beyond general management by emphasizing environmental and social impact, stakeholder engagement, and long-term planning.
2. Sustainable stakeholder management involves engaging with diverse stakeholders, including environmental and social interest groups, to ensure responsible decision-making.
3. Incorporating sustainability into supply chain management, marketing, and human resources practices can lead to more ethical and socially responsible actions within an organization.
4. Financial sustainability management ensures the long-term viability of an organization while considering the interests of multiple stakeholders.
5. Sustainability reporting and mapping, such as the Benefit Impact Assessment (BIA), can help organizations assess and improve their sustainability performance and contribution to the SDGs.

References

APICS. (2018, November 14). In this issue of SCMR: The ethical supply chain. Retrieved February 22, 2023, from Scmr.com website: https://www.scmr.com/article/the_ethical_supply_chain

Corbett, C. J., et al. (2016). *Sustainable supply chains: A research-based textbook on operations and strategy*. Springer International.

Galati, A., et al. (2019). *Stakeholder engagement and sustainability*. Taylor & Francis.

Hewege, C., et al. (2021). *Social and sustainability marketing: A casebook for reaching your socially responsible consumers through marketing science*. Taylor & Francis.

Manetti, G., & Bellucci, M. (2018). *Stakeholder engagement and sustainability reporting*. Taylor & Francis.

Mariappanadar, S. (2019). *Sustainable human resource management: Strategies, practices and challenges*. Macmillan Education UK.

O'Riordan, L. (2017). *Managing sustainable stakeholder relationships: Corporate approaches to responsible management*. Springer International.

Quoquab, F., & Mohammad, J. (2023). *Sustainability and social marketing issues in Asia*. Emerald.

Sroufe, R. P., & Melnyk, S. A. (2017). *Developing sustainable supply chains to drive value: Management issues, insights, concepts, and tools—Implementation*. Business Expert Press.

Winston, A., & Esty, D. C. (2006). *Green to gold: How smart companies use environmental strategy to innovate, create value, and build competitive advantage*. Yale University Press.

CHAPTER 10

The Future of Sustainability Management

Abstract This chapter examines the future of sustainability management by exploring the main trends shaping the field. It also discusses the limitations and downsides of sustainability management, focusing on critiques of stakeholder governance, the triple bottom line, and the shared value model. Future trends include an increased focus on stakeholder engagement, greater integration of sustainability into business operations, growing demand for accountability and transparency, exponential growth in the use of technology and data analytics, increased emphasis on social and circular economy practices, a greater focus on social sustainability, and an increased level of collaborations and partnerships across multiple sectors. As the world faces complex and multifaceted sustainability challenges, companies and organizations will need to adapt and embrace these trends to ensure long-term value creation and success.

Keyword Limitations · Downsides · Stakeholder governance · ESG trends · Corporate self-regulation

> *Don't tell me what you value. Show me your budget and I will tell you what you value.*
>
> —U.S. President Joe Biden

M. Tavanti, *Developing Sustainability in Organizations*, Sustainable Development Goals Series,
https://doi.org/10.1007/978-3-031-36907-0_10

The Main Sustainability Management Trends

Aligning actions with values, specifically in the context of sustainability management and ESG, will become an imperative. A company's true values and priorities will be reflected not in what they say but in what they prioritize and practice. They will demonstrate values in how they allocate resources and through concrete actions, such as investing in sustainable practices, technologies, and initiatives. A company's budget allocations towards ESG initiatives serve as tangible proof of their dedication to sustainability, social responsibility, and ethical governance. In essence, the future of sustainability management will be in the hands of those companies and organizations that will "walk the talk" and back up their sustainability claims with real investments and actions. In other words, the future is for companies and organizations to integrate sustainability into their DNA. The future of sustainability management is likely to continue evolving along trends and developments that include the following:

Trend 1: An increased focus on stakeholder engagement: One reason is that there is growing recognition that companies cannot achieve sustainability goals in isolation, but rather require the cooperation and support of a range of stakeholders. Additionally, stakeholder engagement can help companies identify and mitigate risks, build trust and loyalty, and generate innovation. Companies will likely follow the examples of sustainability champions like Unilever, Patagonia, and Danone who engage stakeholders in its decision-making processes through regular dialogue, surveys, and social media platforms to ensure that their interests are taken into account. This trend will likely provide transparency on the environmental and social impacts of its products. In addition, companies will be under pressure to demonstrate their commitment to sustainability and social responsibility and demonstrate sustainability performances through ESG factors; there will be greater emphasis on stakeholder engagement, support, and cooperation. The emphasis on stakeholder engagement will intersect with the company's growing focus on long-term value creation society as a whole. They will prioritize building trust, loyalty, and relationships with stakeholders in order to create sustainable value over the long term.

Trend 2: A greater integration of sustainability into business operations: Sustainability is increasingly being seen as a key driver of business success, rather than a cost or a constraint. As a result, companies are investing more in sustainability initiatives and sustainability will be integrated into all aspects of business operations. This trend will likely be pushed by other growing factors such as the increased pressure on companies to comply with ESG regulations and standards, both at the national and international levels. As a result, companies are recognizing the need to integrate sustainability into their operations in order to remain compliant and avoid potential legal and reputational risks.

Trend 3: A growing demand for stakeholder accountability and transparency: This will likely have several implications for companies, including an increased pressure to disclose information on their ESG risks, impacts, and performance. Companies will likely need to adopt robust reporting frameworks that enable them to measure and report on their ESG performance in a transparent and consistent manner. This will help companies to demonstrate their commitment to sustainability and social responsibility, and to build trust and credibility with stakeholders. At the same time, more transparent and participatory mechanisms will likely create greater scrutiny from stakeholders including customers, employees, investors, and communities. This will require companies to engage more actively with stakeholders, and to respond to their concerns and feedback in a timely and transparent manner. This will create a focus on continuous improvement, having the companies setting ambitious targets, measuring their progress, and reporting on their performance in a transparent and accountable manner.

Trend 4: An exponential growth in the use of technology, data analytics, and AI: The growth in the use of technology and data analytics is likely to have a transformative impact on sustainability management by enabling companies to collect and analyze data more efficiently, engage with stakeholders more effectively, and develop more sustainable business models. AI is likely to have a transformative impact on sustainability management by enabling companies to collect and analyze data more efficiently, identify and respond to ESG risks more effectively, design more sustainable products, and optimize their operations more efficiently. However, it is important for companies to ensure that their use of AI is ethical, transparent, and aligned with their sustainability goals and values.

Trend 5: An increased emphasis and policies promoting social and circular economy practices: Social economy and circular economy are likely to play an increasingly prominent role in the future, driven by growing awareness of social and environmental issues, economic benefits, policy support, and corporate responsibility. This trend is expected to continue as more stakeholders recognize the importance of sustainable and socially responsible economic models. This trend will also grow for the development of policy and the expansion of the regulatory environment in these directions. Currently, many governments around the world are developing policies and initiatives to support a social and circular economy. For example, the European Union (2020) has launched a *Circular Economy Action Plan*, which aims to promote the transition to a circular economy by reducing waste and promoting resource efficiency.

Trend 6: A greater focus on social sustainability including fairer labor practices, human rights, and community engagement: As consumers, investors, and other stakeholders are increasingly demanding that companies take social sustainability issues seriously, it will lead to an increased pressure on companies to address issues such as fair labor practices, human rights, and community engagement. Companies are recognizing that their reputation and brand image are closely linked to their social sustainability performance. Poor labor practices or human rights violations can lead to negative publicity, boycotts, and other reputational damage, while strong social sustainability performance can enhance a company's reputation and brand image. These good sustainability practices will likely be recognized as beneficial for business while complying with government regulations. Fairer labor practices will likely improve employee morale and productivity, while community engagement will likely enhance a company's social license to operate.

Trend 7: An increased level and typologies of collaborations and partnerships across multiple sectors. This will likely be driven by the need to solve sustainability challenges and other "wicked problems." As sustainability challenges are complex and multifaceted, and cannot be addressed by any one organization or sector alone, collaboration and partnerships across multiple sectors will be necessary to tackle these challenges effectively. The benefits of collaboration and partnerships for sustainability management can outweigh the challenges if managed effectively. Companies that are successful in collaborating and partnering across multiple sectors can achieve greater impact, innovation, and sustainability performance than those that operate alone.

Monitoring Future Trends

Other trends with possible challenges and solutions for sustainability management will likely emerge as we progress through time. Some useful instruments that can be checked regularly to see these trends include The McKinsey Global Surveys (2023). McKinsey has been conducting the Global Survey since the early 1990s and has surveyed thousands of executives and business leaders from around the world over the years. The survey is one of the most comprehensive sources of data and insights on global business trends and challenges. McKinsey has been increasingly focusing on sustainability and ESG topics in its research and consulting work, reflecting the growing importance of these issues to businesses and investors. For example, the 2020 McKinsey Global Survey on the business response to COVID-19 included questions on companies' ESG priorities during the pandemic and their plans to address sustainability issues in the recovery phase. In addition, the 2021 McKinsey Global Survey on the future of work included questions on how companies are incorporating ESG considerations into their workforce strategies. The McKinsey Global Survey can provide valuable insights into emerging sustainability trends and best practices, as well as the challenges and opportunities that companies face in addressing ESG issues.

In addition to the McKinsey Global Survey, several other studies and reports monitor future trends for ESG and sustainability management including:

1. **World Economic Forum Global Risks Report**: This annual report identifies and analyzes global risks, including environmental, social, and governance risks that can impact businesses, governments, and societies. It provides insights into emerging trends and potential future challenges in sustainability management (WEF, 2021).

2. **KPMG Survey of Sustainability Reporting**: This survey provides an overview of corporate sustainability reporting practices, trends, and emerging issues. It covers a wide range of topics, including ESG integration, climate change, and social impacts (Threlfall et al., 2020).
3. **Deloitte Global ESG Monitor**: This report evaluates the ESG reporting practices of companies worldwide, analyzing trends, and providing insights into how businesses can improve their ESG performance and reporting (Deloitte, 2022).
4. **S&P Global ESG Research and Insights**: S&P Global provides a range of research and insights on ESG topics, covering trends, risks, and opportunities in sustainability management (S&P Global, 2023).

These studies and reports offer valuable insights into the future trends and challenges in ESG and sustainability management, helping businesses, investors, and policymakers make informed decisions and implement effective strategies.

Limits and Downsides of Sustainability Management

There are several studies that have highlighted the possible downfalls of sustainability management. These critiques include the fact that stakeholder governance, which involves the active engagement and participation of stakeholders in decision-making and governance processes, may not always lead to the desired outcomes or benefits for stakeholders or society as a whole. The TBL notion, although important, has the risk of promoting "greenwashing" the unstructured sustainability reporting activities that may present a more sustainable image than deserves to be true. The popular notion of "creating shared values" is important in sustainability management, but it also has several limits such as the power imbalances between different stakeholders impeding full participation in the decision-making process, lack of oversight and accountability, and lack of cultural alignment of different groups limiting its effectiveness.

The Limits of Stakeholder Governance

Bebchuk and Tallarita (2020), for example, argue that stakeholder governance, which prioritizes the interests of all stakeholders, including employees, customers, suppliers, and the community, over those of shareholders, may not be effective in promoting sustainability goals. They highlight several limits of sustainability management under stakeholder governance:

1. **Difficulty in aligning stakeholder interests**: Stakeholders may have divergent interests that are difficult to align, making it challenging to develop a coherent sustainability strategy that satisfies all parties.
2. **Lack of accountability**: Stakeholder governance can result in diffuse accountability, as decision-making is shared among multiple stakeholders, which can lead to a lack of responsibility and accountability for sustainability outcomes.
3. **Reduced efficiency**: The focus on stakeholder interests may lead to suboptimal decision-making, as companies may prioritize the interests of less significant stakeholders at the expense of shareholder value or overall efficiency.
4. **Potential for conflicts of interest**: Stakeholder governance may create conflicts of interest between different groups of stakeholders, particularly if there are conflicting interests between stakeholders and shareholders.
5. **Limited incentives for sustainability**: Stakeholder governance may not provide sufficient incentives for companies to pursue sustainability goals, as stakeholders may not be willing to bear the costs associated with sustainability initiatives.

While stakeholder governance may be attractive in theory, it may not be effective in practice for achieving sustainability goals. A better approach may be to focus on enhancing shareholder rights and promoting long-term value creation, which can be aligned with sustainability objectives.

The Limits of Sustainability Management

Bakan (2020) argues that there are limits to sustainability management, particularly when it is practiced by corporations that prioritize profit over social and environmental concerns. He highlights several limitations of sustainability management:

1. **Greenwashing**: Companies may engage in "greenwashing" by making superficial or false claims about their sustainability practices to improve their public image without making substantive changes.
2. **Insufficient regulation**: Current regulatory frameworks may not be sufficient to ensure that companies are accountable for their social and environmental impacts. This may lead to companies engaging in unsustainable practices or exploiting workers, communities, and natural resources.
3. **Systemic challenges**: Sustainability management may not be effective in addressing the underlying systemic challenges that contribute to social and environmental problems, such as income inequality, unsustainable consumption patterns, and economic growth imperatives.
4. **Limited scope**: Sustainability management may focus narrowly on environmental concerns, overlooking the broader social, political, and economic implications of corporate activities.
5. **Inadequate stakeholder engagemen**t: Companies may not engage meaningfully with stakeholders, such as workers, communities, and civil society organizations, in their sustainability efforts, which can limit the effectiveness and legitimacy of those efforts.

Bakan argues that these limitations are inherent in the corporate form, which prioritizes profit over social and environmental concerns. He calls for a fundamental transformation of the corporate form to prioritize the well-being of society and the environment over shareholder interests, through changes to legal frameworks, ownership structures, and governance mechanisms.

The Limits of Triple Bottom Line

Elkington (2018) himself, as mentioned in Chapter 6, has been critical about the TBL concept in which he created. He pointed out its limited scope, inadequate accountability, and insufficient focus on equity. He calls for rethinking the TBL framework and developing new metrics that better capture the complete spectrum of sustainability challenges, offer stronger accountability, and prioritize equity and social justice. New frameworks should measure outcomes instead of outputs, involve a wider range of stakeholders, and incorporate planetary boundaries and social foundations principles. For instance, Elkington (1998) acknowledged that the TBL concept could be seen as a "triple win" for companies, society, and the environment, but also noted that the framework did not fully address issues such as resource depletion, poverty, and inequality. Here are a few of the key criticisms that Elkington has raised:

1. **Incomplete coverage**: Elkington has argued that the TBL approach doesn't go far enough in addressing sustainability challenges. He has proposed expanding the framework to include additional bottom lines, such as cultural and political impacts.
2. **Lack of clarity**: Elkington has also noted that the TBL approach can be vague and lacks clear criteria for measuring performance. He has suggested that more specific targets and indicators would be helpful in guiding organizations' sustainability efforts.
3. **Risk of greenwashing**: Elkington has warned that the TBL approach could be co-opted by companies seeking to greenwash their activities. He has suggested that companies should be held to high standards of transparency and accountability to ensure that their sustainability claims are legitimate.
4. **Focus on metrics**: Elkington has also noted that the TBL approach can create a narrow focus on metrics and targets, potentially obscuring other important sustainability issues. He has suggested that organizations should take a more holistic approach to sustainability, considering the broader social and environmental context in which they operate.

Elkington (2012) has proposed new frameworks such as the "Zeronauts" concept, which focuses on creating a world where zero emissions, zero waste, and zero poverty are the norm. He has also suggested additional frameworks, such as the "triple top line" and the "circles of sustainability," to address some of the limitations of the TBL approach. He has called for a shift towards a regenerative economic system that goes beyond the

TBL framework and seeks to create positive social and environmental impacts. Despite these criticisms and more evolved concepts, Elkington remains an advocate of the TBL approach and has continued to promote its use as a tool for promoting sustainable business practices through more integrated accounting systems. Other scholars and practitioners have suggested the term "quadruple bottom line" (QBL) to address the limitations of the TBL and have added "Purpose," "Progress," or "Governance/Ethics" as a fourth dimension. Wayne Visser (2005) has advocated for adding Governance/Ethics as the fourth bottom line to consider an organization's ethical standards, transparency, and governance practices. It includes issues, such as corporate governance, board diversity, and ethical leadership.

The Limits of Creating Shared Values

De los Reyes and Scholz (2019) argue that the shared value model, which suggests that companies can create economic value by addressing social and environmental issues, has several limitations:

1. **Limited scope**: The shared value model may not address the full range of social and environmental issues facing society. De los Reyes and Scholz suggest that companies may focus on issues that are closely linked to their core business and are relatively easy to address, while neglecting more complex issues, such as poverty, inequality, and human rights abuses.
2. **Insufficient systemic change**: The shared value model may not lead to the systemic changes needed to address social and environmental problems. De los Reyes and Scholz argue that the shared value model often assumes that market mechanisms and corporate self-regulation will be sufficient to address sustainability challenges, without considering the need for regulatory and policy interventions to address market failures and ensure accountability for corporate behavior.
3. **Limited impact**: The shared value model may not generate the desired social and environmental outcomes, particularly in cases where companies prioritize their own economic interests over the well-being of society and the planet. De los Reyes and Scholz suggest that companies may use the shared value model as a

marketing tool to improve their reputation, without making meaningful changes to their business practices.

In addition, the CSV model should be complemented by a broader societal case for sustainability, which acknowledges the limitations of market mechanisms and corporate self-regulation and calls for a more comprehensive approach to addressing social and environmental problems. Such an approach should involve collaboration across sectors and stakeholders, and should prioritize the well-being of people and the planet over narrow economic interests.

These are just a few of the many critical analyses that the business case for sustainability management has several limitations. While the sustainability business case can be a powerful tool for engaging companies in sustainability, it should be complemented by a broader societal case for sustainability that acknowledges the limitations of market mechanisms and corporate self-regulation, and calls for a more comprehensive approach to addressing social and environmental problems. This approach should involve collaboration across sectors and stakeholders, and should prioritize the well-being of people and the planet over narrow economic interests. It should also play greater emphasis on the importance of investing in sustainability innovation and creating more integrated and standardized metrics for sustainability impact.

Key Takeaways

1. Stakeholder engagement will play a crucial role in achieving sustainability goals, as companies prioritize building trust, loyalty, and long-term relationships with stakeholders.
2. Sustainability will increasingly be integrated into all aspects of business operations, driven by the need to comply with EESG regulations and standards, and to avoid potential legal and reputational risks.
3. Companies will face growing demand for transparency and accountability, requiring the adoption of robust reporting frameworks and active engagement with stakeholders to address concerns and demonstrate commitment to sustainability.

4. The use of technology, data analytics, and AI will transform sustainability management by enabling more efficient data collection and analysis, enhanced stakeholder engagement, and the development of sustainable business models.
5. Companies need to recognize the limits of ESG, CSR, CSV, and other sustainability management trends as they look to better integrate regulations, align stakeholder interests, and prioritize equity and social justice.

References

Bakan, J. (2020). *The new corporation: How "good" corporations are bad for democracy*. Vintage Books.

Bebchuk, L. A., & Tallarita, R. (2020). The illusory promise of stakeholder governance. *Cornell Law Review, 106*, 91–178.

Deloitte. (2022). *Sustainability action report: Survey findings on ESG disclosure and preparedness*. https://www2.deloitte.com/content/dam/Deloitte/us/Documents/audit/us-survey-findings-on-esg-disclosure-and-preparedness.pdf. Accessed 15 March 2023.

De los Reyes, G., & Scholz, M. (2019, June). The limits of the business case for sustainability: Don't count on 'creating shared value' to extinguish corporate destruction. *Journal of Cleaner Production, 221*, 785–794.

Elkington, J. (1998). *Cannibals with forks: The triple bottom line of 21st century business*. New Society Publishers.

Elkington, J. (2012). *The Zeronauts: Breaking the sustainability barrier*. Routledge.

Elkington, J. (2018). 25 years ago I coined the phrase 'triple bottom line.' Here's why it's time to rethink it. *Harvard Business Review*. https://hbr.org/2018/06/25-years-ago-i-coined-the-phrase-triple-bottom-line-heres-why-im-giving-up-on-it

European Commission. (2020). *A new circular economy action plan for a cleaner and more competitive Europe*. https://ec.europa.eu/environment/circular-economy/

McKinsey Global Surveys. (2023). Retrieved March 10, 2023, from McKinsey & Company website: https://www.mckinsey.com/featured-insights/mckinsey-global-surveys

S&P Global. (2023). https://www.spglobal.com/esg/. Accessed 15 March 2023.

Threlfall, R., et al. (2020). *The time has come* [online]. KPMG. https://kpmg.com/xx/en/home/insights/2020/11/the-time-has-come-survey-of-sustainability-reporting.html. Accessed 15 March 2023.

Visser, W. (2005). *The age of responsibility: CSR 2.0 and the new DNA of business.* Wiley.

WEF. (2021). *Global risks report 2021* [online]. World Economic Forum. https://www.weforum.org/reports/the-global-risks-report-2021/. Accessed 15 March 2023.

PART III

Sustainability Innovation

This part discusses sustainability innovation and its importance for organizations and shared value outcomes. It differentiates between "sustainability innovation," which focuses on promoting long-term sustainability, and "sustainable innovation," which emphasizes the responsible process of innovation itself. Understanding and implementing innovation is crucial to promoting sustainability and achieving the SDGs. A focus on social, inclusive, and transformative innovation can help address global challenges like climate change, resource depletion, and social inequality.

The growing focus on social and sustainability innovation reflects a shift toward harnessing innovation to address social and environmental challenges through collaboration and participation from multiple stakeholders. Embracing a more inclusive, community-led, and human-centered approach to innovation can help build a sustainable and equitable future. This part delves into the fascinating world of sustainability innovation, exploring the diverse strategies, technologies, and methodologies that are revolutionizing the way we approach sustainable development. This section is designed to provide readers with a comprehensive understanding of the latest trends and best practices in the field, while also inspiring and empowering them to become active participants in driving sustainable change.

First, we provide a solid foundation for understanding what sustainability innovation is, its importance in today's world, and the various dimensions of sustainable development. We also discuss the key concepts and principles that underlie sustainability innovation and shed light on its role in solving complex global challenges (Chapter 11).

Second, we consider how entrepreneurship plays a critical role in driving sustainability innovations forward. We also examine the entrepreneurial mindset and the unique opportunities and challenges that come with launching and scaling sustainable ventures. We highlight successful case studies and share valuable insights on how to create and nurture an ecosystem that fosters sustainability-oriented entrepreneurship (Chapter 12).

Third, we explore the transformative potential of technology in achieving the SDGs. We discuss cutting-edge technologies, such as artificial intelligence, blockchain, and renewable energy, and their applications in addressing various sustainability challenges. We also examine the importance of collaboration between different sectors and stakeholders in harnessing the full potential of technological innovations for sustainable development (Chapter 13).

The final chapter of this section introduces design thinking as a powerful methodology for creating sustainable solutions to complex problems. We delve into the core principles of design thinking, focusing on empathy, experimentation, and iteration and illustrate its application in developing innovative and user-centric sustainability solutions. By the end of this chapter, readers will be equipped with the knowledge and tools necessary to apply design thinking in their own sustainability projects and initiatives (Chapter 14).

CHAPTER 11

Understanding Sustainability Innovation

Abstract This chapter explores sustainability innovation, which aims to create value for organizations while addressing environmental and social challenges. Unlike corporate innovation, sustainability innovation focuses on developing new products, services, technologies, processes, and business models that improve environmental and social performance. Embracing innovation helps businesses stay competitive, adapt to change, reduce costs, and engage employees. Sustainability innovation is crucial for creating environmentally and socially responsible businesses and promoting a sustainable future. Companies can engage in various types of innovation simultaneously to achieve growth, competitive advantage, and sustainability.

Keyword Sustainability innovation · Corporate innovation · Incremental improvements · Radical breakthroughs · Co-creations

M. Tavanti, *Developing Sustainability in Organizations*, Sustainable Development Goals Series,
https://doi.org/10.1007/978-3-031-36907-0_11

"The part that I believe in is where you accelerate the innovation. To me, it's not so much who you don't invest in but who you do invest in." "Innovations that are guided by smallholder farmers, adapted to local circumstances, and sustainable for the economy and environment will be necessary to ensure food security in the future."

—Bill Gates, Co-Founder of Microsoft

The Need for Sustainability Innovation

Today's global challenges, such as climate change, inequality, and environmental degradation, are complex and interconnected, requiring systemic solutions that go beyond traditional innovation frameworks. COP26, or the 26th Conference of the Parties to the United Nations Framework Convention on Climate Change, held in November 2021, placed a strong emphasis on sustainability-oriented innovation as a critical tool for addressing the climate crisis. The conference brought together world leaders, businesses, and civil society organizations to discuss and negotiate ways to accelerate action on climate change. The conference recognized the crucial role that innovation can play in achieving the goals of the Paris Agreement and the UN SDGs. Specifically, the conference highlighted the need for innovation in areas such as renewable energy, clean transportation, circular economy, sustainable agriculture, and carbon capture and storage technologies (Sustainable Innovation Forum, COP 26, 2021). During the conference, numerous commitments and initiatives were announced aimed at accelerating sustainability-oriented innovation, including:

1. **Race to Decarbonized Solutions**: The launch of the "Race to Zero Breakthroughs: Industrial Decarbonization" initiative, which aims to accelerate the development and deployment of low-carbon industrial technologies.
2. **Mission Innovation Challenge**: The announcement of a new "Mission Innovation Challenge" to accelerate the development of affordable, accessible, and scalable low-carbon hydrogen solutions.
3. **Green Innovation Alliance**: The launch of the "Green Innovation Alliance," a partnership between governments, businesses, and research institutions aimed at promoting green innovation.

Overall, the conference demonstrated a strong commitment to innovation as a critical tool for achieving sustainability goals and addressing the urgent challenges of climate change. These initiatives have the value to foster collaborations among diverse actors and sectors. They can also map a pathway for creating ecosystems for creative solutions for innovators, enterprises, and companies committed to sustainability.

Social, Sustainability, and Open Innovation

Traditional innovation frameworks typically focus on incremental improvements to existing products or services, or the development of new products or services that meet market demand (Kuratko et al., 2018). However, these approaches often overlook the broader social and environmental impacts of business activities and fail to address systemic challenges that require transformational change.

To address these challenges, new approaches to innovation are needed that are more systemic, collaborative, and inclusive. This includes approaches such as sustainable innovation, social innovation, and open innovation, which involve a range of stakeholders, including businesses, government, civil society, and academia, working together to co-create solutions that address the root causes of global challenges. Social innovation (Schmidpeter & Osburg, 2021) and sustainability innovation share multiple values as they both aim to create positive social and environmental impact.

1. **Social Innovation**: Social innovation involves developing new solutions to address social challenges and improve social outcomes, such as poverty, inequality, healthcare, and education. Social innovation focuses on creating value for society and improving the quality of life for individuals and communities. At the same time, social innovation addresses "wicked" problems such as systemic socio-economic exclusions through the development of new products, services, and models that empower marginalized communities and foster social inclusion.
2. **Sustainability Innovation**: Sustainability innovation, on the other hand, involves developing new solutions to address environmental challenges and improve environmental outcomes, such as climate change, resource depletion, and pollution. Sustainability innovation

focuses on creating value for the environment and improving the long-term sustainability of our planet.

Both social innovation and sustainability innovation are concerned with creating positive impact and value for society and the environment, and they often overlap in their goals and objectives. For example, sustainable solutions may help to alleviate poverty and improve social equity, while social innovations may help to reduce resource consumption and promote environmental sustainability. Sustainable innovation involves the development of products, services, and business models that not only meet customer needs and generate profits, but also have a positive social and environmental impact. In addition, social and sustainability innovations often require collaboration and partnerships between different stakeholders, such as governments, businesses, nonprofits, and communities. By working together, these stakeholders can create innovative solutions that address both social and environmental challenges and promote a more sustainable and equitable world.

3. **Open Innovation**: Open innovation involves collaborating with external stakeholders, such as customers, suppliers, and partners, to co-create solutions that meet diverse needs and perspectives. While this form of innovation clearly responds to social and sustainability challenges, its focus is different. Open innovation is primarily concerned with improving organizational performance and competitiveness, while social innovation and sustainability innovation are primarily concerned with creating positive social and environmental impact. However, open innovation can also be used to support social and sustainability innovation by enabling collaboration between organizations and stakeholders with different perspectives, expertise, and resources. By leveraging open innovation approaches, social and sustainability innovators can access new ideas, technologies, and funding sources and accelerate the development and scaling of innovative solutions that address social and environmental challenges.

Overall, the complex, rapidly changing, and interconnected challenges facing the world today require us to move beyond traditional innovation frameworks and adopt new approaches that are more collaborative, inclusive, and systemic and that prioritize stakeholder engagement through open solutions and that produce sustainability and social impact for shared value results.

Agile and Disruptive Innovations and Sustainability

There are other typologies of innovation that can be used and adapted for sustainability innovation outcomes. This is the case of *agile innovation* (Ma et al., 2014); an approach that emphasizes flexibility, adaptability, and rapid iteration in response to changing conditions and continuous learning. In the context of sustainability innovation, agile principles can be used to develop and implement sustainable solutions more effectively and efficiently.

Disruptive innovation (Akkucuk, 2021) can also be used in sustainability innovation. Disruptive innovation refers to the introduction of new products, services, technologies, or business models that significantly alter existing markets or industries, often displacing established competitors. In the context of sustainability innovation, disruptive innovations can create more sustainable solutions that address environmental and social challenges more effectively than current offerings. Disruptive sustainability innovations can:

1. **Drive** an effort towards more sustainable practices and technologies, such as renewable energy, circular economy, or alternative materials that reduce environmental impact and resource consumption.
2. **Encourage** the development of new markets and industries that prioritize sustainability and generate new economic opportunities.
3. **Displace** less sustainable products, services, or processes, leading to positive environmental and social outcomes.
4. **Create** new business models that promote shared value, where both the organization and society benefit from sustainable practices.
5. **Increase** awareness and adoption of sustainable solutions among consumers, businesses, and policymakers, leading to broader systemic change.

Disruptive sustainability innovations can play a significant role in transforming markets and industries towards a more sustainable future. By developing and implementing disruptive solutions, organizations can not only create competitive advantages but also contribute to addressing pressing environmental and social challenges.

There are many examples of disruptive innovations that promote sustainability values while transforming industries and creating new opportunities. Here are a few examples:

1. **Renewable energy**: The rise of renewable energy sources like solar and wind power is disrupting the energy sector and creating a more sustainable future. These sources of energy are becoming increasingly cost-competitive with traditional fossil fuels and are rapidly expanding around the world.
2. **Electric vehicles**: The growing popularity of electric vehicles (EVs) is disrupting the automotive industry and reducing dependence on fossil fuels. EVs offer a more sustainable and efficient mode of transportation, and as battery technology improves, their range and performance are rapidly approaching parity with traditional gasoline-powered cars.
3. **Circular economy**: The circular economy is a disruptive approach to production and consumption that seeks to minimize waste and maximize resource efficiency. By keeping materials and products in use for as long as possible, the circular economy can help reduce the environmental impact of resource extraction and waste disposal.
4. **Precision agriculture**: Precision agriculture uses technology to optimize farming practices, reducing waste, and improving yields. By using data analytics, sensors, and other technologies, farmers can more precisely manage inputs like water, fertilizer, and pesticides, reducing waste and environmental impact.
5. **Vertical farming**: Vertical farming is a disruptive approach to agriculture that grows crops in indoor facilities, using technology to optimize growing conditions and reduce waste. By eliminating the need for large amounts of land, water, and pesticides, vertical farming has the potential to transform the way we grow food and reduce the environmental impact of agriculture.

These are just a few examples of disruptive innovations for sustainability. As we consider in Chapter 13, there are many more emerging technologies and approaches that are transforming industries and creating a more sustainable future. Unfortunately, not all disruptive innovations can have sustainable effects, particularly if their environmental and social impacts are not fully considered. Here are a few examples:

1. **Cryptocurrencies**: While cryptocurrencies like Bitcoin are disrupting traditional financial systems and enabling new forms of payment and investment, their energy consumption is a major concern. The high computational power required to process Bitcoin transactions consumes a significant amount of energy, much of which comes from non-renewable sources.
2. **E-commerce**: Online shopping and home delivery have disrupted traditional retail and logistics systems, but they have also led to an increase in packaging waste, unsustainable amounts of e-returns and carbon emissions, and traffic congestion from transportation.
3. **Single-use plastics**: The invention of single-use plastics like straws and food packaging has disrupted traditional packaging systems, but the environmental impacts of these products have been devastating. Single-use plastics are not easily recyclable and often end up in landfills or the ocean, where they can harm wildlife and ecosystems.
4. **Large-scale agriculture**: Industrial agriculture has disrupted traditional farming systems and enabled large-scale production of food, but it has also led to environmental degradation, soil erosion, and water pollution. The use of pesticides and fertilizers can also have negative impacts on human health and wildlife.

It is important to note that disruptive innovations themselves are not inherently good or bad for sustainability; it depends on how they are implemented and managed. It is essential to consider the potential environmental impacts of disruptive innovations and work to mitigate them through sustainable practices and policies. That is why to generate sustainable outcomes in innovations we need to consider the mindsets and representation of the innovators involved. We also need to consider the ecosystems that drive innovation and the regulatory policies that promote them.

Sustainability Innovation Ecosystems

To thrive, sustainable innovation needs an ecosystem that supports it. Similar to other ecosystems for innovation, the sustainable innovation ecosystems refer to networks of interconnected individuals, organizations, and institutions that collaborate to promote sustainable innovation and create long-term value for society and the environment. These ecosystems are designed to support the development and diffusion of sustainable innovations, which are innovations that address societal and environmental challenges while also creating economic value.

Sustainable innovation ecosystems can include a range of stakeholders, such as universities, research institutions, startups, established companies, government agencies, investors, and NGOs. These stakeholders can collaborate to share knowledge, resources, and expertise to develop and implement sustainable innovations which address critical sustainability challenges, such as climate change, resource depletion, and biodiversity loss. Typologies of sustainable innovation ecosystems include:

1. **Technology clusters** that bring together tech startups, established firms, venture capitalists, and academic institutions to promote innovation in a specific geographic area. For example, the United Nations Office for Project Services (UNOPS) has a *Sustainable Development Cluster* coordinating global innovation centers in Antigua and Barbuda, Japan and Sweden which support entrepreneurs, programmers, and developers in the creation of sustainable innovations contributing to the SDGs.
2. **Accelerator and incubator** programs that provide mentorship, funding, and resources to startups and entrepreneurs. For example, the Santa Clara University's *Miller Center for Social Entrepreneurship* has been a pioneer in accelerating entrepreneurship to end global poverty and protect the planet since 1997. In the last 20 years, it has accelerated over 1300 social enterprises worldwide contributing to the common goals for development and sustainability.
3. **Open innovation platforms** that connect organizations with external talent to solve complex problems or develop new ideas. For example, the United Nations Development Programme (UNDP) and "la Caixa" Foundation have joined forces to promote *Open Innovation Platforms* designed to promote collaboration and innovation among different actors in society. These platforms are open to anyone who wants to participate, including entrepreneurs, researchers, academics, and social organizations. They represent a different approach to project-based development and address deep systems challenges necessary to achieve the SDGs. *Innonatives* are another example. It is the world's first open innovation platform for sustainable solutions. It combines crowdsourcing, crowd-voting, crowd-funding to start innovation challenges, share ideas, comment

and vote, contribute to solutions for sustainability and collaborate with creative people around the world.

4. **Public–private partnerships** that bring together government, industry, and academia to address social challenges, such as climate change or public health. The approach in sustainability is that People is first in public–private partnership (PfPPP). *The Chesapeake Forest Project* is an example of a PPP that aims to promote sustainable development and support the achievement of the SDGs. It is a collaborative effort between the US Forest Service, the Maryland Department of Natural Resources, and The Conservation Fund; a nonprofit organization that focuses on conservation and sustainable development. The project aims to protect and restore forested land in the Chesapeake Bay watershed, which is an important ecological and economic resource in the region. *The Centre Hospitalier Sud Francilien* in France is another example. It is a hospital facility in the southern suburbs of Paris that was built and is operated under a PPP agreement between the French government and a private consortium of companies. The PPP model used for the Centre Hospitalier Sud Francilien project allowed the French government to leverage private sector expertise and resources to deliver a complex infrastructure project with multiple social and environmental benefits.

Sustainable innovation ecosystems address complex and multifaceted ("wicked") problems by providing sustainable innovation ideas and solutions the necessary strength to make an impact and substantially contribute to the common goals. The strength provided on the "ecosystems" is usually at three levels:

1. **Integration**: Integration in sustainable development involves combining different parts, elements, or perspectives to form a coherent and coordinated whole, addressing complex systemic challenges. It emphasizes connectedness across economic, social, and environmental dimensions, requiring design, collaboration, and operations aligned with shared goals and values. Attention to marginalized and vulnerable groups is vital to ensure no one is left behind. Successful integration can elevate development pathways and recovery from crises, leading to efficiency gains. By

uniting stakeholders, perspectives, and resources, integration fosters innovative solutions and accelerates progress towards SDGs.

2. **Acceleration**: Acceleration in sustainable development refers to achieving faster progress towards sustainability outcomes by identifying and leveraging "accelerators"—context-dependent factors that significantly impact complex systems. These accelerators allow for addressing interconnections and trade-offs across the SDGs. By focusing on key accelerators, progress can be made towards multiple SDGs simultaneously, while addressing potential unintended consequences. Examples include investing in renewable energy infrastructure or promoting gender equality. The concept of acceleration highlights the importance of targeting influential factors to drive progress and achieve broader impact across SDGs, addressing trade-offs, and reaching those left behind.
3. **Scale**: Scale in sustainability innovation ecosystems involves achieving collective action on a broad scale by engaging various stakeholders to address complex sustainability problems. This can be done through scaling up, scaling out, and scaling deep. Scaling up expands the reach and impact of initiatives, scaling out replicates successful initiatives in new contexts, and scaling deep fosters deeper behavioral changes. A comprehensive approach to sustainability innovation includes both the "software" (cultural and social dimensions) and "hardware" (technologies, tools, and infrastructure) aspects. Achieving scale requires collaboration among government, civil society, private sector, and communities, supported by global and regional networks.

An ecosystem for sustainable innovation shares similarities with other innovation ecosystems, including collaborative networks, knowledge sharing, and value creation. However, there are important differences. Sustainable innovation ecosystems focus on addressing environmental and societal challenges while creating economic value, integrating sustainability goals into core objectives. They involve stakeholders with a sustainability focus, such as environmental NGOs, sustainability-focused startups, and academic institutions with sustainability research expertise. Additionally, sustainable innovation ecosystems may face extra regulatory challenges due to the need to comply with sustainability regulations and standards. The main distinction is their focus on sustainability, promoting innovations addressing sustainability challenges and fostering more inclusive solutions.

Community-Led Sustainable Innovation Ecosystems

Community-led innovation ecosystems are crucial for achieving sustainable development goals and promoting inclusive, participatory development. These ecosystems empower local communities to identify and prioritize their needs, providing resources, tools, and support to develop and implement innovative solutions. By centering local communities and stakeholders, these initiatives are more relevant, effective, and sustainable. Community-led approaches also foster collaboration among different actors and leverage unique local knowledge. They prioritize equity and social justice, ensuring marginalized and vulnerable groups are included in sustainability initiatives. The UNDP has studied the power of community-led approaches in sustainable development and innovation, showcasing the potential of grassroots initiatives in driving progress towards the SDGs. Some of these studies include *The Power of Local Action: Learning from Communities on the Frontlines of Sustainable Development* (UNDP, 2015) and *Community-Based Climate Solutions for Sustainable Development* (UNDP, 2022) that showcase local innovation and community-led approaches to sustainable development highlighting the potential of grassroots initiatives in driving progress towards the SDGs.

Examples of community-led innovation ecosystems include:

1. **SDG Platforms**: These are digital platforms or networks that connect individuals, organizations, and communities to facilitate collaboration and innovation towards achieving the SDGs. They can build an ecosystem for sustainability innovation by connecting stakeholders and co-creating solutions. SDG platforms can connect stakeholders from diverse sectors, such as governments, civil society, academia, and the private sector, to exchange ideas, share knowledge, and collaborate on initiatives for sustainable development. SDG platforms can facilitate co-creation of solutions by bringing together different perspectives and expertise to address complex sustainability challenges. This can lead to innovative solutions that are more effective, efficient, and sustainable. SDG platforms are also useful for scaling up impact, monitoring progress, and fostering accountability. They can connect innovators with resources and funding, enabling replication and dissemination of successful solutions. They can track progress towards the SDGs, allowing stakeholders to monitor and evaluate the effectiveness of their initiatives

and adjust their approaches as needed. They can promote transparency and accountability by providing a platform for stakeholders to share information on their sustainability efforts and progress towards achieving the SDGs.

2. **Fab Labs**: These are community-based digital fabrication workshops that provide access to tools, technologies, and training to support innovation and entrepreneurship. Fab Labs are often used to develop locally relevant solutions to challenges in areas such as healthcare, agriculture, and education. For example, Fab Lab (2020) in Uganda developed a 3D-printed infant incubator that is affordable and easy to transport, which can help improve neonatal health outcomes and contributed to SDG 3—Good Health and Well-being.
3. **Social Innovation Labs**: These are collaborative platforms that bring together diverse stakeholders to co-create and test innovative solutions to complex social challenges. Social Innovation Labs often involve local communities as active participants in the design and implementation of solutions (Hassan, 2014). Social Innovation Labs provide a structured process for co-creation, experimentation, and iteration of new solutions and approaches to societal problems. They often involve stakeholders from government, civil society, academia, business, and local communities and use a variety of methods and tools, such as design thinking and systems thinking, to facilitate collaboration and innovation. Social Innovation Labs can play an important role in addressing complex and interconnected social and environmental challenges and in contributing to several of the SDGs by fostering collaboration, experimentation, and innovation.
4. **Community Innovation Centers**: These are community-based spaces that provide access to resources, training, and mentorship to support entrepreneurship and innovation. Community Innovation Centers (CoICs) often focus on supporting marginalized communities or groups, such as women or youth, who may face barriers to accessing traditional sources of support for entrepreneurship. CoICs are designed to promote innovation and collaboration among individuals and groups from diverse backgrounds, with the aim of addressing social, economic, and environmental challenges in the local community. For example, CoICs like those hosted by the International Development Innovation Network (IDIN) are physical spaces worldwide designed to foster creativity, collaboration,

and innovation within local communities (IDIN, 2022). They typically provide access to resources, tools, training, and mentorship for community members to develop and implement solutions to local challenges. They play an important role in promoting innovation, entrepreneurship, and collaboration among diverse groups and in contributing to several of the SDGs by addressing social, economic, and environmental challenges in the local community.

5. **Incubators and Accelerators**: These are programs that support the growth and development of startups and social enterprises. Incubators and accelerators can play an important role in building community-led innovation ecosystems by providing mentorship, training, and access to funding to support the development of locally relevant solutions. There are many incubators and accelerators that contribute to community-led sustainability innovation ecosystems. For example, Climate-KIC (2020) is a European innovation initiative focused on climate change mitigation and adaptation. They support startups and entrepreneurs working on sustainable solutions through various programs and incubators. Climate-KIC contributes to the SDGs by promoting innovation in areas such as renewable energy, sustainable transport, and circular economy.

   Spring Activator is a Canadian accelerator that supports startups and entrepreneurs focused on social and environmental impact. They offer mentorship, resources, and funding to help these businesses grow and contribute to the SDGs. Spring Activator supports innovations in areas such as sustainable food systems, clean energy, and waste reduction. *Clean Energy Trust,* as another example, is a US-based accelerator that supports startups working on clean energy and sustainability solutions. They provide funding, mentorship, and resources to help these businesses grow and contribute to the SDGs. Clean Energy Trust supports innovations in areas such as renewable energy, energy efficiency, and sustainable transportation.

   Social Alpha is an Indian incubator that supports startups working on social and environmental challenges. They offer mentorship, resources, and funding to help these businesses grow and contribute to the SDGs. Social Alpha supports innovations in areas such as affordable healthcare, sustainable agriculture, and clean energy. *The Yield Lab is* another example; it is a global accelerator that supports startups working on sustainable agriculture and food systems. They provide funding, mentorship, and resources to help these businesses grow and contribute to the SDGs. The Yield Lab supports innovations in areas such as regenerative agriculture, food waste reduction, and sustainable packaging.

6. **Information Hub Libraries**: Public and specialty libraries can serve as repositories for knowledge and information on sustainability, green technologies, and other innovative solutions. By providing access to these resources, they encourage community members to learn about sustainable practices and innovations. Libraries can promote sustainable innovation by organizing educational events, facilitating collaboration and networking, supporting local innovators with resources and connections, raising public awareness and engagement through events, offering digital resources for remote learning, ensuring inclusivity in their initiatives, and leading by example through sustainable practices.

   These efforts help foster eco-friendly practices and drive positive change within communities. For example, The New York Public Library has incorporated the SDGs into its programming, providing resources, and hosting events related to sustainability, climate change, and social justice. They have also partnered with the Earth Institute at Columbia University to host panel discussions and workshops on various SDGs. Elsevier (2022) outlines seven ways libraries can support and promote the UN SDGs: raising awareness, mapping existing activities to SDGs, developing relevant collections, collaborating with faculty and researchers, supporting teaching and learning, engaging with local and global communities, and reflecting on their own practices. These recommendations emphasize the role of libraries in fostering community-led sustainability ecosystems through awareness, research support, collaboration, and sustainable practices.

Overall, building community-led innovation ecosystems is essential to promoting inclusive and participatory development that ensure development efforts are both relevant and effective. By empowering local communities to identify and address their own development needs, it is possible to create sustainable solutions that are better aligned with the needs and perspectives of local communities.

Regulatory Policies for Sustainability Innovation

Regulatory policies for sustainability contribute to promoting sustainability innovation because they provide a framework for businesses, organizations, and individuals to understand their environmental and social responsibilities and create incentives for them to invest in sustainable practices and innovations. Green, social, and inclusive regulatory policies can set clear guidelines and expectations for businesses and individuals, which can help them understand what actions they need to take to comply with sustainability standards. This clarity can help drive innovation by providing a clear direction for sustainable development. They can create financial and non-financial incentives for businesses and individuals to invest in sustainable practices and technologies. This can include tax incentives, grants, subsidies, and other rewards that encourage innovation in sustainability. They can encourage competition among businesses to improve their sustainability performance, which can lead to innovation in sustainable technologies and practices. This competition can help drive down costs, increase efficiency, and improve overall sustainability outcomes. Regulatory policies can also encourage collaboration between businesses, governments, and other stakeholders to work together to achieve sustainability goals. Collaboration can help drive innovation by combining different perspectives, resources, and expertise. Finally, they can help drive market demand for sustainable products and services, which can create opportunities for businesses to innovate in sustainability. This demand can create a business case for investing in sustainable technologies and practices, which can lead to further innovation. Here are some examples of sustainability related regulatory policies that can stimulate sustainability innovation:

1. **Carbon pricing**: Carbon pricing is a regulatory policy that puts a price on carbon emissions in order to incentivize companies to reduce their carbon footprint and GHG emissions. This policy can encourage investment in renewable energy and other sustainable practices. Emissions trading systems (ETSs) and carbon taxes are the two main types of carbon pricing mechanisms. Both can be effective ways to reduce greenhouse gas emissions and promote sustainable innovation practices. The *Regional Greenhouse Gas Initiative* (RGGI) is the first mandatory cap-and-trade program in the United States to limit carbon dioxide emissions from the power sector

(Chauvin, 2013). In partnership with other progressive states, California's program was the first multi-sector cap-and-trade program in North America. Coincidentally, California is the state with the greatest number of all-electric vehicles (EVs), approximately 39% of EVs nationwide.

2. **Extended Producer Responsibility (EPR)**: EPR is a policy that holds producers responsible for the waste generated by their products throughout their life cycle. This policy can incentivize companies to design products that are more easily recyclable or compostable, and to invest in more sustainable manufacturing practices. Under EPR regulations, companies must mitigate the environmental impacts of their products throughout the entire product life cycle. Starting in 2022, if you sell in France and/or Germany, companies must become EPR compliant by registering their packaging products, reporting, and paying their fees. The *German Packaging Act* (VerpackG), which came into effect in 2019 and incorporates the principle of EPR, has significantly promoted sustainable and reusable packaging to reduce the amount of waste generated by packaging materials.
3. **Ban on single-use plastics**: Many countries have implemented bans or restrictions on single-use plastics, such as straws, bags, and utensils. These policies can help reduce waste and promote the use of more sustainable alternatives. The *National Development and Reform Commission in China* issued a phased policy in 2020 which bans single-use plastic bags and straws across all cities starting in 2022, while markets selling fresh produce will be exempt until 2025. This Chinese government's policy is fostering the development of innovative new technologies for biodegradable packaging materials and can lead to increased investment in research and development, which can then drive down the cost and improve the performance of these materials. This can help make biodegradable plastics more competitive with traditional plastics in the packaging industry. Some major e-commerce actors, like Alibaba, have started to use incentives like price discounts and shopping coupons to encourage consumers to choose green packaging for their online orders.
4. **Product labeling**: Product labeling policies require companies to disclose information about the environmental and social impact of their products. This can help consumers make more informed purchasing decisions and incentivize companies to improve their

sustainability performance. Sustainability labels can encourage companies to invest in sustainable innovations, such as using renewable materials or improving their production processes to reduce their environmental impact. Companies that adopt sustainable practices can use sustainability labels as a way to differentiate themselves from their competitors and appeal to consumers who are concerned about the environment. The OECD (2013) has a long history of influencing national and international sustainability related labels through what is called the *Environmental Labeling and Information Schemes* (ELIS) developed in the late 1990s. NGOs and other civil society organizations have driven much of the rapid development of ELIS, with voluntary sustainability standards (VSS) such as those of Rainforest Alliance and Fair Trade labeling. These holistic product labeling of rigorous certifications has contributed to integrate environmental, social, and economic dimensions of sustainability.

5. **Green public procurement**: Green public procurement policies require public entities to purchase products and services that meet certain sustainability standards. This can create a market demand for sustainable products and services and encourage companies to innovate in sustainability. The European Commission (EC, 2014) has implemented a *Green and Sustainable Public Procurement* (GPP and SPP) since 2014 that regulates public authorities to purchase goods, services, and works with a reduced environmental impact throughout their life cycle. Other international organizations such as the United Nations have also implemented similar policies following the criteria of ISO 20400:2017. The UN sustainable procurement is in response to the UNEP's findings and recommendations that make it increasingly evident that the world cannot achieve sustainable economic growth without significant innovation to both the supply and demand sides of the market.
6. **Circular economy regulations**: Circular economy regulations can promote a more circular use of resources by requiring companies to design products that are easily repairable, reusable, or recyclable. These policies can help reduce waste and promote sustainable production and consumption patterns. The *Circular Economy Action Plan* (CEAP) is a key part of the European Green Deal, which is a comprehensive plan to make the European Union (EU) climate-neutral by 2050 (EC, 2020). The CEAP outlines a set of

measures to accelerate the transition to a circular economy in the EU. The transition to a circular economy is expected to create new opportunities for innovation, sustainable growth, and job creation. It will also help to reduce the EU's dependence on scarce and imported resources and contribute to the achievement of the EU's climate and environmental goals, such as the 2050 climate neutrality target and the halt of biodiversity loss.

7. **Social economy policies**: Social economy policies support the development of socially responsible businesses that prioritize social and environmental impact over profits. These policies can promote the creation of jobs and support marginalized communities. The *Economic Commission for Latin America and the Caribbean* (ECLAC, 2023), in recent years, has focused on promoting social economy policies and sustainability innovation as a means of achieving inclusive and sustainable development in the region. ECLAC has emphasized the potential of social economy policies to create decent work, reduce poverty and inequality, and promote sustainable development. The commission has also highlighted the need for sustainability innovation to address the urgent environmental challenges facing the region, including climate change, biodiversity loss, and water scarcity.

Overall, these policies and others like them promote sustainability, circular economy, and social economy by incentivizing businesses and individuals to invest in more sustainable practices and innovations, and by creating a regulatory environment that supports these goals.

Assessing Sustainability Innovation

Assessing innovation, particularly in the context of sustainability, can be done through various frameworks and models, such as the Sustainability Innovation Cube and the Transformative Innovation Framework (Hansen et al., 2009). These tools help evaluate the effectiveness, impact, and scalability of innovations, especially those aimed at addressing complex social and environmental challenges.

1. **Sustainability Innovation Cube (SIC)**: This model assesses sustainability innovation from three dimensions—economic, environmental, and social. It helps evaluate the performance of an innovation in terms of its potential for value creation, ecological impact reduction, and contribution to social well-being. By examining an innovation's performance across these three dimensions, stakeholders can better understand the holistic impact of a given innovation and make more informed decisions regarding its implementation and scaling.
2. **Transformative Innovation Framework (TIF)**: This framework aims to understand and assess innovation in terms of its potential to drive transformative change towards a more sustainable and equitable society. Transformative innovation goes beyond incremental improvements and focuses on radical shifts in socio-technical systems. The Transformative Innovation Framework evaluates the innovation process, outcomes, and potential impact on existing systems, with the goal of identifying and supporting innovations that can drive systemic change.

Both the Sustainability Innovation Cube and the Transformative Innovation Framework can be useful tools for assessing innovation in the context of sustainability. However, it is essential to recognize that no single framework can capture all aspects of innovation assessment. The choice of a framework depends on the specific objectives, context, and stakeholders involved. It is often beneficial to use a combination of frameworks or develop a tailored approach to assess the innovation's impact comprehensively and effectively.

Key Takeaways

1. Sustainability innovation focuses on creating value for organizations while addressing environmental and social challenges, distinguishing it from corporate innovation.
2. Sustainable products, services, technologies, processes, and business models can improve environmental and social performance, reduce negative impacts, and create economic value.
3. Innovations in sustainability can range from incremental improvements to existing products and processes to radical breakthroughs that create entirely new markets and industries.

4. Sustainable innovation solutions often emerge from collaborative relationships and co-creations with partners and stakeholders, helping to identify urgent needs, new opportunities, and sustainable solutions.
5. Embracing multiple types of innovation can help businesses achieve growth, competitive advantage, employee engagement, and contribute to a more sustainable future.

References

Akkucuk, U. (2021). *Disruptive technologies and eco-innovation for sustainable development*. IGI Global.

Chauvin, S. (2013). *The regional greenhouse gas initiative: Lessons and related cap-and-trade considerations*. Nova Science Publishers.

Climate-KIC. (2020). *What is EIT Climate-KIC?—Climate-KIC* [online] https://www.climate-kic.org/who-we-are/what-is-climate-kic/#:~:text=EIT%20Climate%2DKIC%20is%20a,and%20adapt%20to%20climate%20change. Accessed 16 March 2023.

EC. (2014). *Sustainable GPP—Environment—European Commission* [online] https://ec.europa.eu/environment/gpp/versus_en.htm. Accessed 16 March 2023.

EC. (2020). *Circular economy action plan* [online]. https://environment.ec.europa.eu/strategy/circular-economy-action-plan_en. Accessed 16 March 2023.

ECLAC (2023). *Economic Commission for Latin America and the Caribbean* [online]. Cepal.org. https://www.cepal.org/en. Accessed 16 March 2023.

Elsevier. (2022). 7 ways that libraries can support and promote the UN SDGs at their institutions. *Elsevier Connect*. https://www.elsevier.com/connect/library-connect/7-ways-that-libraries-can-support-and-promote-the-un-sdgs-at-their-institutions

FabLabs. (2020). Welcome|FabLabs—The Fab Lab Network [online]. https://www.fablabs.io/. Accessed 16 March 2023.

Hassan, Z. (2014). *The social labs revolution: A new approach to solving our most complex challenges*. Berrett-Koehler Publishers.

Hansen, E. G., et al. (2009). Sustainability innovation cube—A framework to evaluate sustainability-oriented innovations. *International Journal of Innovation Management, 13*(04), 683–713.

IDIN. (2022). *Innovation centers|International development innovation network* [online]. https://www.idin.org/innovationcenters. Accessed 16 March 2023.

Kuratko, D. F., Hornsby, J. S., & Goldsby, M. G. (2018). *Corporate innovation: Disruptive thinking in organizations*. Taylor & Francis.

Ma, M., et al. (2014). *Agile innovation: The revolutionary approach to accelerate success, inspire engagement, and ignite creativity*. Wiley.

OECD. (2013). *Environmental Labelling and Information Schemes (ELIS)—* OECD [online]. https://www.oecd.org/env/labelling-and-information-schemes.htm. Accessed 16 March 2023.

Schmidpeter, R., & Osburg, T. (2021). *Social Innovation: Solutions for a sustainable future*. Springer.

Sustainable Innovation Forum, COP26. (2021). Sustainable Innovation Forum 2021|COP26|Climate Action Event [online]. https://events.climateaction.org/2021/sustainable-innovation-forum/. Accessed 16 March 2023.

UNDP. (2015). *The power of local action: Learning from communities on the frontlines of sustainable development* [online]. https://www.undp.org/publications/power-local-action-learning-communities-frontlines-sustainable-development. Accessed 16 March 2023.

UNDP. (2022). *Community-based climate solutions for sustainable development* [online]. https://sgp.undp.org/innovation-library/item/2284-community-based-climate-solutions-for-sustainable-development.html. Accessed 16 March 2023.

CHAPTER 12

Entrepreneurship for Sustainability Innovations

Abstract This chapter delves into the realm of entrepreneurship for social innovation, with a focus on sustainability-oriented organizations. It discusses various types of social enterprise organizations, including Benefit corporations, L3Cs, CICs, and cooperatives, exploring their unique characteristics and their role in fostering sustainable innovation. The chapter then shifts its attention to intrapreneurship, which refers to innovation within large organizations, and provides insights into what drives intrapreneurship, the traits of intrapreneurs, and the distinguishing features of social-sustainable intrapreneurs. Finally, the chapter concludes by examining sustainable frugal innovation; an approach that emphasizes resource optimization, affordability, and inclusivity in addressing social and environmental challenges. Through these discussions, the chapter aims to provide a comprehensive understanding of how entrepreneurship and intrapreneurship contribute to social innovation and sustainable development.

Keyword Social enterprises · Intrapreneurship · Sustainability-oriented organizations · Ecopreneurship · Frugal Innovation

M. Tavanti, *Developing Sustainability in Organizations*, Sustainable Development Goals Series,
https://doi.org/10.1007/978-3-031-36907-0_12

I'm encouraging young people to become social business entrepreneurs and contribute to the world, rather than just making money. Making money is no fun. Contributing to and changing the world is a lot more fun.
—Muhammad Yunus, Founder of the Grameen Bank

Sustainability innovation needs entrepreneurship because it requires a mindset and approach that is different from traditional business models (Asgary & Maccari, 2019). It focuses on creating organizational products and programmatic solutions through business models that address social and environmental challenges, while also generating economic value. This requires a willingness to take risks, experiment with new ideas, and challenge existing assumptions about how business is done. There are different approaches to entrepreneurship that differ across industries and organizations. We also need new approaches to entrepreneurship as the diversity of cultural and geographical contexts demand. In this chapter, we offer a more in-depth look at entrepreneurship practices for sustainability innovation practices applicable to large corporations and industries, SMEs, as well as grassroots organizations and nonprofit enterprises. We also need to consider how more established and specialized fields such as social entrepreneurship play a role in sustainability entrepreneurship across CSR approaches in government-public sectors and academic institutions.

Although commonly used interchangeably, social entrepreneurship, ecopreneurship, sustainability-oriented innovation (SOI), and sustainability entrepreneurship do not indicate the same organizational practices. They are all related concepts that aim to combine economic, social, and environmental objectives but with some key differences between them.

1. **Social entrepreneurship** refers to the use of entrepreneurial skills and approaches to address social challenges. Social entrepreneurs create businesses or organizations that aim to have a positive social impact, while also generating revenue. They often focus on marginalized communities, social justice issues, or other social problems.
2. **Ecopreneurship** refers to entrepreneurship that is focused specifically on addressing environmental challenges. Eco-entrepreneurs create businesses or organizations that aim to reduce environmental impact or promote sustainable development. They often focus on innovations related to renewable energy, waste reduction, or sustainable agriculture.

3. **Sustainability-oriented innovation (SOI)** refers to the development of new products, services, or business models that promote sustainability. SOI can be applied in a variety of fields, including energy, transportation, food systems, and more. It aims to create economic value while also addressing social and environmental challenges.
4. **Sustainability entrepreneurship** refers to entrepreneurship that is focused on creating sustainable businesses that balance economic, social, and environmental objectives. Sustainability entrepreneurs create businesses or organizations that are designed to operate in a way that is environmentally responsible, socially equitable, and economically viable. They aim to create long-term value for all stakeholders, including employees, customers, investors, and the environment.

In practice, numerous innovative programs and organizations that define themselves as "social enterprise" often aim, like sustainability entrepreneurship, to address social and environmental challenges and create positive impact. As the practices advance and the clarifications become more sophisticated, we need to consider social entrepreneurship as a practice that focuses on addressing social challenges and improving the well-being of individuals and communities, while sustainability entrepreneurship an organizational practice that focuses on addressing environmental and social challenges and improving the well-being of individuals, communities and the planet. Therefore, social entrepreneurship is a type of entrepreneurship that focuses on creating innovative solutions to address social problems, while sustainability entrepreneurship is a type of innovation that focuses on creating innovative solutions to address environmental and social problems. Social entrepreneurship can be considered a subset of sustainability innovation, as it is focused on creating solutions that are both economically and socially sustainable.

To better understand the field of sustainability entrepreneurship, we need to distinguish it from the wider practices of sustainability innovation. While closely related, sustainability innovation and sustainability entrepreneurship have some key differences:

1. **Sustainability innovation**, as stated earlier, refers to the development of new products, services, technologies, or business models that promote sustainability. The focus is on creating innovative solutions that address social and environmental challenges while generating economic value. Sustainability innovation can occur in a wide range of contexts and can involve a variety of stakeholders, such as businesses, governments, nonprofits, and academic institutions.
2. **Sustainability entrepreneurship**, on the other hand, refers to the creation of new businesses or organizations that are specifically designed to address social and environmental challenges. Sustainability entrepreneurs are focused on creating businesses that are socially and environmentally responsible, while also generating economic value. These entrepreneurs aim to build sustainable businesses that can operate over the long term, and they often have a strong sense of social and environmental mission.

In other words, sustainability entrepreneurship is a specific form of entrepreneurship that is focused on sustainability, while sustainability innovation is a broader concept that encompasses a range of activities aimed at promoting sustainability. Sustainability entrepreneurs use sustainability innovation to create sustainable businesses, while sustainability innovation can be used by a variety of stakeholders for a variety of purposes beyond entrepreneurship.

Social Enterprises for Sustainability Innovation

Social enterprises are these businesses that are primarily focused on achieving a social impact and/or an environmental impact, while also generating revenue to sustain their operations. Their legal configurations vary across different state and national legislations but they are often classified as hybrid types as they combine aspects of traditional for-profit and nonprofit organizations. Social enterprises are typically structured as businesses with an income generating model to sustain their operations whose mission and priorities are clearly social and/or environmental. Here are some examples of hybrid legal classifications that social enterprises and other socially and environmentally conscious corporations may adopt:

1. **Benefit Corporations (B Corps)**: These are a specific legal entity in some US States with similar adaptations in other national legal systems. The legislations may differ on some details but they generally agree to legally require companies to balance the interests of their stakeholders, including employees, customers, the environment, and the broader community, in addition to generating profits. The first benefit corporation law was enacted in Maryland in April 2010, making it the first US state to create a legal framework for benefit corporations. The law, called the Maryland Benefit Corporation Act, was the result of a collaborative effort between social entrepreneurs, lawyers, and policymakers who saw a need for a new type of corporation that would prioritize social and environmental objectives alongside financial goals. The Maryland Benefit Corporation Act established a new type of corporation that is legally required to pursue a general public benefit, defined as a positive impact on society and the environment.

   The 2011 California Benefit Corporation law similarly allows corporations to pursue both profit and social or environmental objectives, while also providing legal protection to directors and officers who make decisions that prioritize these objectives. Under this law, benefit corporations are required to consider the impact of their decisions on their shareholders, employees, customers, community, and the environment, and they must also file an annual report with the California Secretary of State that assesses their overall social and environmental performance.

   Similarly, Società Benefit (SBs) in Italy, as we have seen in the case study, also provides a legal framework for corporations to pursue social and environmental goals in addition to their financial objectives. However, there are some key differences in the legal structure as the Società Benefit is a legal form that can be adopted by any type of business entity in Italy, including corporations, cooperatives, and partnerships. Benefit Corporation legal entities are not to be confused with B Corps certifications given by the nonprofit B Lab to corporations that score 80/200 in the Benefit Impact Assessment. Although the Benefit Corporation legal status is preferred, B Lab's certification is available to companies of any legal structure, including traditional corporations, LLCs, and cooperatives. Examples of Benefit Corporations in the United States include Allbirds, Ben & Jerry's, Change.org, Danone, Etzy, King

Arthur Flour, New Belgium Brewing Company, and Patagonia. An example of SB in Italy is Terra! Onlus, a nonprofit organization that promotes sustainable development and environmental protection in the Veneto region of Italy that became a Società Benefit in 2018.

2. **Social Purpose Corporations (SPCs)**: There are several legislations that regulate and classify diverse organizational structures with financial interests with shared social and/or environmental purposes. California, Florida, New York, and Oregon have similar legislations regulating SPCs that have a social and/or environmental mission as part of their business operations and are accountable to a broader set of stakeholders beyond just shareholders. The main difference between Benefit Corporations and Social Purpose Corporations is the way they prioritize their social and environmental missions.

   Benefit Corporations are required to balance the interests of their stakeholders, while Social Purpose Corporations are required to have a social and/or environmental mission as part of their business operations. Another difference is the level of legal recognition of the two classifications. Benefit Corporations are recognized in more states and have been around for longer than Social Purpose Corporations, which are a more recent legal innovation.

   Another organizational form that is similar is *Flexible Purpose Corporations* (FPCs). In California, FPCs are required to have a "special purpose" in their articles of incorporation, which can include social or environmental objectives. The FPCs and SPCs laws in California are similar as they both prioritize social and environmental objectives alongside financial goals. However, they differ as FPCs provide more flexibility in their mission and reporting requirements, while SPCs have more specific requirements for their social or environmental mission and additional liability protection. Many SPCs and FPCs are also B Corp-certified organizations. Examples of SPCs include Method Products, a cleaning products company that is committed to sustainability and reducing its environmental impact, and Revolution Foods, a company that provides healthy school meals to students. An example of FPCs is Lygos, a biotechnology company that is committed to developing sustainable and renewable chemicals. Its flexible purpose allows it to pursue both financial goals and social and environmental goals related to sustainability.

3. **Low-Profit Limited Liability Company (L3C)**: An L3C is a hybrid legal classification that combines aspects of a for-profit LLC and a nonprofit organization. L3Cs are designed to have a primary social or environmental purpose, while also generating revenue. As of 2021, the following states in the United States have passed legislation to recognize L3Cs as a legal business entity: Illinois, Louisiana, Maine, Michigan, North Carolina, Rhode Island, Utah, Vermont, and Wyoming. In the UK, the legal entity that is most similar to the L3C is the Community Interest Company (CIC). CICs are designed to support social enterprises and other community-focused organizations by providing a legal structure that allows them to operate with a social mission while still generating revenue. CICs are required to have a community purpose and must use their profits and assets for the benefit of the community they serve. They also must file an annual report that details their social and environmental impact, and they must have a community interest statement that outlines their social purpose. In other countries, there are similar "hybrid" organizational structures to L3Cs and CIC as in the case of the Community Contribution Companies in Canada. Examples of L3Cs include HUB Seattle and the Montpelier Beanfield Centre. Examples of CICs are Big Issue, a well-known magazine sold by homeless and vulnerably housed individuals in the UK, and The Bristol Bike Project, a bicycle repair and recycling social enterprise that aims to promote sustainable transport and support marginalized communities.
4. **Cooperatives and Social Cooperatives**: A cooperative is a business that is owned and democratically controlled by its members, who share in the profits and decision-making. Cooperatives can be organized as for-profit or nonprofit entities and can have a social or environmental mission. Examples of cooperatives include REI and the Mondragon Corporation. In Italy, for example, there are also general cooperatives (*cooperativa*) as a type of legal entity that is owned and controlled by its members, can engage in any type of business activity, including for-profit and nonprofit activities, and share in the profits and decision-making of the organization.

   There are also social cooperatives (*cooperativa sociale*) that is a specific type of cooperative that is focused on providing social services or promoting social inclusion. Social cooperatives are recognized as a distinct legal form under Italian law and are subject to additional regulations and requirements. A social cooperative is specifically focused on providing social services or promoting social inclusion and must have at least 30% of their members be workers or volunteers who provide the social services or activities. They can also be eligible for certain tax benefits and exemptions that are not available to traditional cooperatives.

While both cooperatives and social cooperatives distribute profits to their members, social cooperatives are required to reinvest a portion of their profits back into the organization's social mission. In Italy, there are two types of social cooperatives: Type A and Type B. Type A social cooperatives are focused on providing social services and activities to disadvantaged or marginalized people, including those with disabilities, mental health issues, or substance abuse problems. These cooperatives may provide a wide range of services, including healthcare, education and training, housing, and employment support. Type B social cooperatives, on the other hand, are focused on creating employment opportunities for disadvantaged or marginalized people. These cooperatives may operate in a variety of industries and sectors, such as agriculture, manufacturing, and services, and may provide training and support to help workers develop new skills and gain valuable work experience.

These are just a few examples of the legal classifications that social enterprises may adopt. The specific legal structure of a social enterprise may vary depending on the organization's mission, goals, and location. Figure 12.1 represents a simplified configuration of social enterprises and social entrepreneurship for social/environmental benefits. The organizational identities and areas of social and sustainability investments affect a spectrum of organizations going from for-profit corporations with integrated CSR practices to nonprofit organizations with income generating activities.

Innovative Enterprise Contributions to Society

Social enterprises and sustainability enterprises can contribute to society in a variety of ways, often through innovative programs that address social and environmental challenges. Some of the main areas in which these enterprises can have a positive impact include:

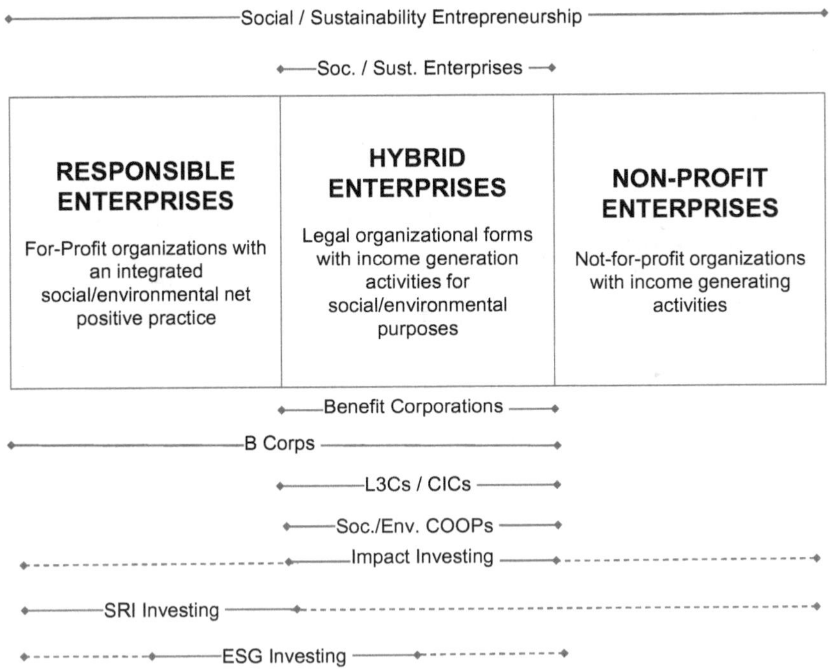

Fig. 12.1 Spectrum of social/sustainability enterprises

1. **Environment**: Many social and sustainability enterprises are focused on promoting environmental sustainability and reducing the impact of human activities on the planet. They may develop and implement innovative technologies and practices to reduce waste, conserve resources, and promote renewable energy. One innovative example of a social enterprise contributing to the environment is *The Ocean Cleanup*. As a nonprofit organization, Ocean Cleanup has developed advanced technologies to rid the world's oceans of plastic pollution. It has attracted significant support from investors, philanthropists, and other organizations, and the group has already made significant progress in removing plastic waste from the ocean.
2. **Sustainable Agriculture**: Social enterprises focused on sustainable agriculture aim to promote environmentally friendly farming practices and create market opportunities for small-scale farmers. One

example is *Alter Eco*, a fair trade organic chocolate company that sources its ingredients from small-scale farmers who use sustainable farming methods.

3. **Renewable Energy**: Social enterprises focused on renewable energy seek to promote the use of clean energy sources like wind, solar, and hydropower. An example is *Off Grid Electric*; a company that provides solar power systems to homes and businesses in rural areas of Africa.
4. **Waste Reduction and Recycling**: Social enterprises focused on waste reduction and recycling aim to create circular economies where waste is minimized and resources are conserved. An example is *TerraCycle*, a company that collects hard-to-recycle waste materials and repurposes them into new products.
5. **Ethical Fashion**: Social enterprises focused on ethical fashion aim to create a more sustainable and equitable fashion industry by promoting fair labor practices and using environmentally friendly materials. An inspiring and impactful example is the *Ethical Fashion Initiative* (EFI), an international initiative promoting fair labor practices, empowering women, and reducing poverty through the fashion industry. The EFI Production Centers in several countries in Africa, Asia, and the Caribbean connect social enterprises with international brands making a significant socially inclusive and environmentally friendly impact.
6. **Sustainable Tourism**: Social enterprises focused on sustainable tourism aim to promote responsible travel practices that minimize negative environmental and social impacts. An example is *G Adventures*, a company that offers sustainable and culturally immersive travel experiences while supporting local communities and conservation efforts.
7. **Education and training**: Social and sustainability enterprises may offer training and education programs to help individuals and communities develop new skills and improve their economic prospects. These programs may be focused on vocational training, entrepreneurship, financial literacy, or other areas that can improve people's lives. One inspiring example of a social enterprise contributing to education and training for sustainability innovation is *Barefoot College*. Barefoot College is a nonprofit organization based in India that provides education and training

to rural and underprivileged communities in developing countries. The organization's goal is to empower these communities to become self-sufficient and sustainable and to promote the use of renewable energy and green technologies.

One of Barefoot College's flagship programs is the Solar Engineering Program, which trains women from rural communities to become solar engineers. The program selects illiterate or semi-literate women from remote and marginalized areas and provides them with six months of training in solar technology, electronics, and computer skills. The women then return to their communities and install solar lighting systems, water heaters, and other sustainable technologies. The program has trained over 1,200 women from 91 countries and has installed more than 95,000 solar lighting systems in rural areas around the world.

8. **Healthcare**: Some social enterprises are focused on improving access to healthcare and addressing health disparities in underserved communities. They may provide healthcare services directly, or work to develop new technologies and programs that improve healthcare delivery and outcomes. An inspiring example of this is *We Care Solar*. This is a social enterprise and nonprofit organization that designs and distributes solar-powered lighting and electricity systems to improve maternal and child health in developing countries. Its signature product is the Solar Suitcase, a portable, solar-powered system that provides lighting, electricity, and mobile communication charging for healthcare facilities. The Solar Suitcase includes solar panels, battery, LED lights, and medical devices, such as fetal heart rate monitors and pulse oximeters. The Solar Suitcase has been distributed to over 30 countries and has impacted over 2 million lives.
9. **Poverty alleviation**: Many social enterprises work to address poverty and economic inequality, often by creating new opportunities for marginalized communities. They may offer job training, microfinance programs, or other forms of support to help people improve their economic prospects and become more self-sufficient. One inspiring example of a social enterprise contributing to poverty alleviation through sustainability innovation is *Ecofiltro*. This is a social enterprise based in Guatemala that produces and distributes water filters to rural and underserved communities in Latin America. The organization's goal is to provide clean drinking

water to people living in poverty, while promoting sustainable solutions for water treatment and reducing the use of plastic bottles. Their water filters use natural materials, such as clay and sawdust, to remove bacteria, viruses, and other contaminants from water. The filters are easy to use, affordable, and have a lifespan of up to five years. By providing clean drinking water, Ecofiltro is helping to reduce the prevalence of waterborne diseases, improve health outcomes, and alleviate poverty. The organization provides education and training on sustainable development practices and has impacted over 1 million people in Latin America.

10. **Social justice**: Social enterprises aim to promote social justice and address systemic inequalities. They advocate for policy changes, provide legal services, or raise awareness of social issues. A social enterprise example that is making a significant contribution to the global effort to achieve social justice and sustainability is *The Empowerment Plan*. It is a Detroit-based nonprofit that produces specialized coats that transform into sleeping bags for the unhoused. They also have an employment and education program. This approach helps break the cycle of homelessness and poverty, empowering people to take control of their lives. The Empowerment Plan's coats have been distributed across 40 states and four Canadian provinces. Their job training program has helped many individuals secure stable employment and improve their lives.

Overall, social and sustainability enterprises can contribute to society and the environment in a variety of ways. Their diverse organizational structures and their embedded social/environmental missions with sound and innovative business plans can make a difference to address complex social and environmental challenges.

Intrapreneurship for Sustainability-Oriented Organizations

Intrapreneurship refers to the practice of entrepreneurship within an established organization or company. It involves individuals or teams within a company who take the initiative to develop innovative ideas and bring them to life, often by taking calculated risks and pushing the boundaries of traditional business practices. Intrapreneurs typically have a high degree of autonomy and are empowered by their organization to pursue new ideas and opportunities. Intrapreneurship practices are particularly apt for promoting sustainability-oriented innovations (SOIs) in well-established organizations and large corporations. In the Harvard Business Review's article *Driving Sustainability-Oriented Innovation*, Geradts and Bocken (2018), define SOI as "the development and commercialization of products, services, technologies, and business models that create environmental and social value while also generating economic value." Adopting and integrating an SOI approach can help businesses create new markets, reduce costs, enhance brand reputation, and mitigate risks. In addition, businesses need to adopt a strategic approach to SOI, which involves integrating sustainability into the company's overall strategy, engaging with stakeholders, and developing a culture of innovation (Ossmane et al., 2023). In well-established organizations, the practice of SOI is often visible in the creation of new initiatives, departments, programs, or projects. Here are some examples of intrapreneurship for SOI that can be created across sectors and industries:

1. **Creation of a sustainability department**: A dedicated sustainability department is responsible for leading the organization's sustainability efforts, including identifying and implementing sustainability innovations. This department may report to the CEO or another senior executive and may have a cross-functional role, working with other departments such as R&D, marketing, and operations.
2. **Establishment of a sustainability steering committee**: A sustainability steering committee is a group of senior executives who are responsible for setting the organization's sustainability strategy and goals. The committee may also be responsible for overseeing the implementation of sustainability innovations and ensuring that they align with the overall strategy.
3. **Founding of an innovation lab or center**: An innovation lab or center is a dedicated team or facility that is responsible for identifying, developing, and testing new products, services, and business models. This can be focused on sustainability innovation and may have a cross-functional role, working with other departments such as R&D, marketing, and operations.
4. **Formation of a sustainability task force**: A sustainability task force is a group of employees from different departments and functions who are responsible for identifying, developing, and implementing

sustainability innovations. This group may be temporary or permanent and may report to a sustainability department or steering committee.

5. **Embedded sustainability teams**: An embedded sustainability team is a group of employees who are responsible for promoting sustainability within their respective functions or departments. They may focus on sustainability innovation and be responsible for identifying, developing, and implementing new sustainable products, services, and business models within their specific functions.
6. **Sustainability/Social entrepreneurship unit**: A sustainability or social entrepreneurship unit is a team that focuses on developing new business models and ventures that create social and environmental impact. They may be responsible for identifying and pursuing new sustainability innovations within the organization.

Beside corporations and social enterprises, government agencies can also experiment with these approaches and integration strategies. In addition, government agencies have a critical role to allocate funding, set policy goals, and regulate businesses to promote sustainable practices. The Environmental Protection Agency (EPA), for example, develops and enforces regulations related to air and water quality, hazardous waste, and other environmental issues, and they also provide funding and technical assistance to support environmental sustainability initiatives. The *Sustainable Communities Program* is another example. It is a partnership between several federal agencies, including the EPA, HUD (housing), and DOT (transportation), that is aimed at promoting sustainable development at the local level. They provide funding and technical assistance to support sustainable community planning and development initiatives, and they also support programs that promote equitable and sustainable transportation.

Academic institutions can also adopt these approaches and promote an integration of sustainability in their curricula, operations, research, and engagement activities. Universities and research institutions may conduct research on critical social and environmental challenges, train the next generation of social entrepreneurs and sustainability professionals, or provide incubation services for new ventures. Harvard University, for example, hosts several research centers and institutes focused on sustainability, including the Harvard Kennedy School's *Corporate Social Responsibility Initiative* and the *Harvard Center for Green Buildings and Cities*. The university also offers courses and programs in social entrepreneurship and sustainable business through the Harvard Business School. University of Oxford is another example. It hosts several research centers and institutes focused on sustainability, including the *Environmental Change Institute* and the *Oxford Martin School*. The university also offers courses and programs in social entrepreneurship and sustainable business through the *Saïd Business School.*

What is Intrapreneurship Innovation?

The term "intrapreneurship" was first coined by Gifford Pinchot III in his book *Intrapreneuring: Why You Don't Have to Leave the Corporation to Become an Entrepreneur* (1985). However, the concept of intrapreneurship was discussed in various forms prior to this, with the earliest known reference dating back to 1976, when the term was used by a writer in The Economist magazine. Since then, the concept of intrapreneurship has gained widespread recognition and has become an important concept in the fields of entrepreneurship and innovation management.

Intrapreneurship allows established organizations to foster innovation and adapt to changing markets by identifying new business models, products, or services. This approach can generate new revenue streams, increase efficiency, and improve customer satisfaction. Intrapreneurs also drive cultural change, promoting creativity and experimentation.

A supportive organizational culture, resources, and risk-taking are essential for intrapreneurship. Successful companies can enjoy increased competitiveness, higher employee engagement, and a reputation for innovation. Intrapreneurship for sustainability involves using entrepreneurial approaches to address social and environmental challenges while creating economic value, leading to innovative and sustainable solutions.

What Drives Intrapreneurship?

Intrapreneurship is driven by both internal and external factors. Internally, companies can promote an entrepreneurial culture by offering incentives, resources, and support for employees to pursue new opportunities. This fosters a culture of innovation that empowers employees to contribute to the company's success and promotes personal and professional growth.

Externally, factors like market changes, new competitors, technological advancements, and shifts in consumer preferences create opportunities for intrapreneurs to develop innovative solutions. Fast-paced, uncertain, and dynamic environments can encourage employees to take risks and experiment with new ideas, particularly in industries where innovation and agility are crucial for success.

Organizations should pay attention to both internal and external factors to foster intrapreneurship, creating a culture that supports and rewards innovation while providing employees with resources and autonomy to explore new ideas. This will drive growth and innovation within the organization.

Who Are Intrapreneurs?

An intrapreneur is an employee within an organization who takes an entrepreneurial approach to their work, generating new ideas and initiatives that create value for the company. Intrapreneurs have the ability to identify new opportunities and leverage the resources available to them within the organization to bring their ideas to fruition. They are typically innovative, proactive, and willing to take risks to achieve their goals. Intrapreneurs are important to organizations because they help drive innovation, increase efficiency, and generate new revenue streams, while also contributing to a culture of creativity and entrepreneurship within the company. There are many examples of individuals who have demonstrated intrapreneurial qualities and have been instrumental in driving sustainability initiatives within their organizations. Here are a few notable examples:

1. **Cynthia Cummis, Director of Private Sector Climate Mitigation at the World Resources Institute**: Cummis has worked with companies to reduce their greenhouse gas emissions and promote sustainable business practices. She has been instrumental in developing the Science Based Targets Initiative, which helps companies set emissions reduction targets in line with the goals of the Paris Agreement.
2. **Hannah Jones, former Chief Sustainability Officer at Nike**: Jones was responsible for driving Nike's sustainability initiatives, including the company's commitment to using sustainable materials and reducing its carbon footprint. She also oversaw the creation of Nike's circular innovation program, which aims to create closed-loop manufacturing systems.

3. **Andrew Winston, sustainability consultant and author**: Winston works with companies to help them develop sustainability strategies and implement sustainable business practices. He is the author of several books on sustainability, including "Green to Gold" and "The Big Pivot."
4. **Ellen MacArthur, founder of the Ellen MacArthur Foundation:** MacArthur is a former professional sailor who founded the Ellen MacArthur Foundation, which works to promote a circular economy. The foundation works with businesses, governments, and other organizations to develop strategies for reducing waste and creating more sustainable production systems.

Social and sustainable intrapreneurs can be particularly effective in driving innovation and change within their organizations by creating new business models that address social or environmental challenges. For example, social purpose business models may prioritize social or environmental impact over traditional financial metrics, while corporate social innovation may focus on creating sustainable solutions to societal problems. By pushing their organizations out of their comfort zones, social intrapreneurs can help their companies identify new opportunities for growth and innovation while also creating value for society. They can challenge traditional ways of thinking and operating, and bring new perspectives and approaches to problem-solving. This can lead to more sustainable and responsible business practices, as well as new revenue streams and competitive advantages.

What Distinguishes Social-Sustainable Intrapreneurs?

Social entrepreneurs and social-sustainable intrapreneurs are similar in that they both seek to create positive social or environmental impact. However, they may differ in their approach, ownership, resources, scope, risk, and impact:

1. **Ownership**: Social entrepreneurs typically start their own businesses or organizations to address a social or environmental issue, whereas social-sustainable intrapreneurs work within existing organizations to create change.

2. **Resources**: Social entrepreneurs often have to rely on their own resources to get their ventures off the ground, whereas social-sustainable intrapreneurs may have access to the resources of their organizations, such as funding, personnel, and infrastructure.
3. **Scope**: Social entrepreneurs tend to focus on creating new ventures that are entirely dedicated to addressing a specific social or environmental issue, while social-sustainable intrapreneurs may work on projects or initiatives that are integrated into the larger operations of their organizations.
4. **Risk**: Social entrepreneurs typically face greater financial risk than social intrapreneurs, as they are often responsible for securing funding and generating revenue to support their ventures. Social-sustainable intrapreneurs, on the other hand, may have more stability and security as they work within established organizations.
5. **Impact**: Both social entrepreneurs and social intrapreneurs aim to create positive social or environmental impact, but their approaches may differ. Social entrepreneurs may focus on developing innovative solutions to specific issues, while social-sustainable intrapreneurs may seek to integrate sustainability and social responsibility into the overall strategy of their organizations.

Frugal Innovation for Sustainability

The context in which innovation is promoted and implemented matters. That is why we need to embrace context-effective approaches such as frugal innovation. This approach in innovation refers to the process of creating high-quality products or services with limited resources. Frugal innovation is becoming increasingly popular in today's business world, as companies seek to create more sustainable and efficient solutions. It is a concept that involves designing and developing high-quality; affordable products and services that are optimized to meet the specific needs of customers in low-income and emerging markets. The goal of frugal innovation is to create solutions that are not only affordable but also effective and efficient, while minimizing unnecessary complexity and waste.

The concept of frugal innovation was first introduced by two scholars, N. Radjou and J. Prabhu (2015) in their book titled *Frugal Innovation: How to Do More with Less*. The authors argued that frugal innovation is not just about making products cheaper, but also about creating innovative solutions that are affordable, sustainable, and accessible to everyone. The concept emerged from the observation that many companies were struggling to sell their high-priced products and services in emerging markets, where consumers have limited purchasing power. To succeed in these markets, companies needed to think differently and come up with innovative solutions that are affordable and adapted to the local context. Moreover, the authors also noted that frugal innovation is not just relevant for emerging markets, but also for developed countries facing economic and environmental challenges. Frugal innovation can help companies and organizations to create sustainable and efficient solutions that reduce waste and optimize resources.

One of the key value contributions of frugal innovation is that it promotes a more inclusive approach to innovation (Brem & Agarwal, 2021). By working with limited resources, frugal innovators are often forced to think outside the box and develop solutions that are accessible to a broader range of people, including those with lower incomes. This can lead to the creation of products and services that are more affordable, efficient, and sustainable than traditional alternatives. Additionally, frugal innovation often involves a more collaborative approach, with input and feedback from a variety of stakeholders, including citizens. This can help to ensure that solutions are tailored to the specific needs and context of the communities they serve, leading to more effective and impactful outcomes. In other words, the value contribution of frugal innovation lies in its ability to create innovative solutions that are accessible, sustainable, and inclusive and that reflect the needs and perspectives of a broader range of stakeholders.

Today, frugal innovation is widely recognized as a powerful approach to innovation that can help companies and organizations to create high-quality, affordable, and sustainable solutions that benefit everyone (Bhatti et al., 2018). Specifically, frugal innovation has some key elements that define it and identify its process. It focuses on affordability, simplicity, sustainability, co-creation, and agility, with the goal of creating products and services that are accessible and beneficial to a wide range of people, particularly those with limited resources. The key elements of frugal innovation include:

1. **Affordability**: Frugal innovation focuses on creating products and services that are affordable and accessible to people with low incomes. This involves using low-cost materials, simplifying the design, and minimizing waste.
2. **Simplicity**: Frugal innovation emphasizes simplicity in design, production, and operation. The products or services are designed to be easy to use, maintain, and repair, with a minimum number of components and features.
3. **Sustainability**: Frugal innovation aims to create products and services that are environmentally sustainable, socially responsible, and economically viable. This involves using renewable materials, minimizing waste and energy consumption, and creating jobs and economic opportunities for local communities.
4. **Co-creation**: Frugal innovation involves collaboration and co-creation with end-users, customers, and local communities. This helps to ensure that the products or services meet the needs of the users and are culturally appropriate.
5. **Agility**: Frugal innovation is characterized by an agile and adaptive approach to design, production, and distribution. The products or services are developed quickly and iteratively, based on feedback from users and customers.

Overall, frugal innovation has had a positive impact on sustainable development by promoting affordability, sustainability, and inclusivity. By providing affordable and accessible solutions to social and environmental challenges, frugal innovation has helped to reduce poverty, promote economic growth, and protect the environment. Here are some examples of frugal innovation:

1. **Tata Nano**: The Tata Nano is a low-cost car designed and manufactured by Tata Motors in India. The car was created to meet the transportation needs of the growing middle class in India, while keeping the price tag under $2,000. The Tata Nano contributes to several SDGs including SDG 1 (no poverty) for making personal transportation more affordable and accessible for low-income households in India, helping to reduce poverty and increase mobility. It also contributes to SDG 7 (affordable and clean energy) by designing a fuel-efficient vehicle with a high mileage per liter of

petrol, reducing the consumption of fossil fuels and lower carbon emissions. It contributes to SDG 9 (industry, innovation, and infrastructure) by creating innovative engineering and manufacturing solutions for a safe and affordable car and for automotive industry and infrastructure development in India. It also contributes to SDG 11 (sustainable cities and communities) by making Tata Nano a popular choice for city driving, helping to reduce congestion and improve urban mobility in India. Finally, Tata Nano contributes to SDG 12 (responsible consumption and production) by designing a lightweight car made with fewer materials than traditional cars, reducing waste, and promoting responsible consumption and production.

2. **M-Pesa**: M-Pesa is a mobile payment system developed in Kenya. The system allows users to transfer money and make payments using their mobile phones (Lee & Dang, 2017). M-Pesa has revolutionized the way people in Kenya and other emerging markets conduct financial transactions. M-Pesa was first introduced in 2007 by the telecommunications company Safaricom. The service was created in response to the lack of access to formal financial services in Kenya, particularly among low-income households and those in rural areas.

   M-Pesa contributes to several SDGs including SDG 1—no poverty. M-Pesa has helped to reduce poverty in Kenya by providing a secure and accessible way for low-income households to save and transfer money. This has helped to increase financial inclusion and reduce the financial exclusion of those who do not have access to traditional banking services. It contributes to SDG 3—good health and well-being. M-Pesa has enabled people in remote areas of Kenya to access healthcare services and pay for medical expenses using their mobile phones. This has helped to improve health outcomes and reduce the financial burden of healthcare on low-income households. It contributes to SDG 8—decent work and economic growth. M-Pesa has created employment opportunities for people in Kenya, particularly in the mobile money agent network. The service has also helped to stimulate economic growth by providing a secure and efficient way for businesses to make payments and conduct transactions. It contributes to SDG 10—reduced inequalities. M-Pesa has helped to reduce inequalities in Kenya by providing a level playing field for people to access financial services, regardless of their socio-economic status, geographic location, or gender. Finally, it also contributes to

SDG 16—peace, justice and strong institutions. M-Pesa has helped to promote transparency and accountability in financial transactions, reducing the risk of corruption and money laundering.

3. **Solar Bottle Lights**: In areas without electricity, simple technology can make a big difference. Solar Bottle Lights, also known as Liter of Light, is a social innovation project that aims to provide sustainable and affordable lighting solutions to communities that lack access to electricity. It consists of a simple plastic bottle filled with water and bleach, which refracts sunlight and illuminates the room during the day. The project was created by Illac Diaz, a social entrepreneur and founder of MyShelter Foundation, a nonprofit organization based in the Philippines. The bleach is added to prevent the formation of algae. It is then installed in a hole created in the roofs of houses. Sunlight passes through the water-filled bottles and refracts into the house, providing a free source of natural light during the day. Solar Bottle Lights contributes to several of the SDGs, including SDG 7—affordable and clean energy, with a simple but affordable and accessible to all communities that lack access to electricity. It also contributes to SDG 11—sustainable cities and communities, by providing a low-cost and eco-friendly lighting solution that reduces the reliance on fossil fuels and grid-based electricity. It contributes to SDG 13—climate action by promoting the use of renewable energy sources and reducing the reliance on non-renewable sources of energy. Finally, it also contributes to SDG 17—partnerships for the goals as Solar Bottle Lights is a collaborative project that involves partnerships between local communities, nonprofit organizations, and businesses to provide sustainable and affordable lighting solutions to those who need it most.
4. **D.light Solar Lanterns**: D.light provides solar-powered lanterns that are affordable, durable, and highly efficient. The lanterns are designed to provide a safe, bright, and long-lasting light source for people living off the grid. D.light Solar Lanterns is a social enterprise that contributes to SDG 1 (no poverty) and SDG 7 (affordable and clean energy). It also contributes to SDG 4 (quality education) by providing lighting for studying after dark. It also contributes to SDG 5 (gender equality) by providing lighting that improves the safety and security of women and girls. By reducing the need for kerosene lamps and candles, D.light's products help reduce the risk of fire and burns, which disproportionately affect women and girls.

5. **Aravind Eye Care System**: Aravind Eye Care System is a nonprofit organization and a network of eye hospitals in India that provides affordable and high-quality eye care to millions of people. Aravind Eye Care System provides an essential service to low-income communities and contributes to several SDGs such as SDG 3 (good health and well-being). Aravind Eye Care System contributes to the goal of ensuring healthy lives and promoting well-being for low-income communities. It contributes to SDG 10 (reduced inequalities) by addressing vision problems in marginalized communities, and therefore, reducing inequalities in access to healthcare and promoting social inclusion. It contributes to SDG 1 (no poverty) by improving eye health. Aravind Eye Care System can help to increase economic opportunities and reduce poverty. It contributes to SDG 4 (quality education), by addressing vision problems in students by giving eye exams and corrective glasses to students resulting in improved academic performance and reduced absenteeism. It also contributes to SDG 5 (gender equality) by addressing gender disparities in eye care. Women are more likely to suffer from eye problems due to factors such as poverty, lack of access to healthcare, and cultural norms. By providing eye care services that are accessible and affordable to women, Aravind Eye Care System helps to promote gender equality.

Frugal innovation shares characteristics and solutions similar to inclusive innovation, sustainable innovation, social innovation, and open innovation. Inclusive innovation refers to the creation of new products, services, or processes that are designed to benefit a wide range of people, including those who are typically marginalized or excluded from traditional innovation processes. Inclusive innovation aims to create solutions that address societal challenges and promote social and economic inclusion. As we have seen earlier, sustainability innovation focuses on creating solutions that are environmentally sustainable and reduce the negative impact of human activities on the planet.

Social innovation, on the other hand, aims to create solutions that address social challenges and improve a person's well-being. Additionally, open innovation involves collaborating with a wide range of external partners, including customers, suppliers, and other organizations, to develop new ideas and solutions. Frugal innovation focuses on creating high-quality products or services with low cost and inclusive features. While each of these innovation approaches has a unique focus, they are all interconnected and can overlap in their goals and outcomes. For example, inclusive innovation can also be sustainable, social, open, or frugal, depending on the specific context and approach. Similarly, sustainability innovation can be inclusive, social, open, or frugal if it is designed to benefit a wide range of stakeholders, promote social and economic inclusion, involve collaboration with external partners, or create high-quality solutions with limited resources. Overall, these innovation approaches are complementary and can be combined to create more holistic and impactful solutions that address a range of societal challenges.

Key Takeaways

1. Social enterprise organizations, including Benefit corporations and B Corps, L3Cs, CICs, and cooperatives, play a critical role in promoting social innovation and sustainability.
2. Intrapreneurship is a form of innovation within large organizations that drives sustainability and adapts to changing market conditions by identifying new business models, products, or services.
3. Intrapreneurs in sustainability-oriented organizations possess unique traits that enable them to navigate the complexities of social and environmental challenges while creating economic value.
4. Social-sustainable intrapreneurs are distinguished by their focus on addressing social and environmental issues, fostering cultural change, and promoting creativity and experimentation within their organizations.
5. Sustainable frugal innovation is a powerful approach that emphasizes affordability, inclusivity, and resource optimization in solving social and environmental problems, contributing to sustainable development goals.

References

Asgary, N. H., & Maccari, E. A. (2019). *Entrepreneurship, innovation and sustainable growth: Opportunities and challenges*. Taylor & Francis.

Bhatti, Y., Basu, R., Barron, D., & Ventresca, M. J. (2018). *Frugal innovation: Models, means, methods*. Cambridge University Press.

Brem, A., & Agarwal, N. (2021). *Frugal innovation and its implementation: Leveraging constraints to drive innovations on a global scale*. Springer International Publishing.

Geradts, T., & Bocken, N. (2018). *Driving sustainability-oriented innovation*. Harvard Business Review. Retrieved March 10, 2023, from https://store.hbr.org/product/driving-sustainability-oriented-innovation/SMR724

Lee, D. K. C., & Dang, R. H. (2017). *Handbook of blockchain, digital finance, and inclusion, volume 1: Cryptocurrency, FinTech, InsurTech, and regulation*. Elsevier Science.

Ossmane, E., et al. (2023). *Solving societal challenges through sustainability-oriented innovation*. Engineering Science Reference.

Pinchot, G. (1985). *Intrapreneuring: Why you don't have to leave the corporation to become an entrepreneur*. Harper & Row.

Radjou, N., & Prabhu, J. (2015). *Frugal innovation: How to do more with less*. Profile Books.

CHAPTER 13

Technology Innovations for the SDGs

Abstract This chapter explores the transformative potential of various cutting-edge technologies in driving progress towards the SDGs. It delves into ten key technologies, including mobile technology, artificial intelligence, blockchain, biotechnology, renewable energy, the Internet of Things, virtual and augmented reality, autonomous driving, carbon capture and storage, and energy storage. It examines how these innovations can contribute to addressing global challenges in areas such as poverty, climate change, and inequality. The chapter also discusses the importance of fostering supportive ecosystems for technology innovations, encouraging collaboration among stakeholders, and sharing knowledge to accelerate progress. Additionally, it highlights technology advancements from the Global South, emphasizing the role of inclusive innovation in promoting sustainable development across the world.

Keywords Technology innovations · Mobile technology · Artificial Intelligence · Global south · Inclusive innovation · Ecosystems for technology

M. Tavanti, *Developing Sustainability in Organizations*, Sustainable Development Goals Series,
https://doi.org/10.1007/978-3-031-36907-0_13

> *Digital technologies sustain life, work, health and learning for billions of people. [...] Yet 3.7 billion people – nearly half the world's population – remain unconnected to the Internet; and of these, the majority are women. [...] Let us commit to work together to [...] ensure that digital technologies are a force for good that help us to achieve the SDGs and leave no one behind.*
> —António Guterres, Secretary-General of the United Nations

Innovative Technology for Sustainability

Technological advancements for sustainability innovation are crucial to achieving sustainable development and the SDGs. Research on various aspects of sustainable development, such as environmental sustainability, social and economic inclusion, and governance, can generate new knowledge and insights that inform policy and practice. It is vital to align research and innovation agendas with inclusive development principles and avoid harmful development practices that may increase the marginalization of underrepresented groups. This requires adopting a participatory and co-creation approach, engaging with diverse stakeholders, including marginalized groups, throughout the research process. Promoting innovation and best practices for inclusive development through research can advance sustainable development and contribute to achieving the SDGs. It can also help address complex, interrelated challenges such as climate change, poverty, and inequality, creating a more sustainable and equitable future for all. The following are some examples of innovative technological solutions that can benefit the advancement of the SDGs and address urgent societal and planetary challenges.

Mobile Technology and SDGs

Mobile technology has revolutionized access to information, goods, and services in many parts of the world. It can be used to improve healthcare, education, and economic opportunities and can help to reduce poverty and inequality (SDG 1, 3, 4, 8, and 10). One inspiring example of how mobile technology can help with SDG 3 (Good Health and Well-being) is through the use of mHealth (mobile health) applications. mHealth applications can help to improve access to healthcare, particularly in remote or underserved areas where traditional healthcare services may not be readily available.

These applications can be used for a range of purposes, such as: (1) Providing information and education about health and wellness; (2) Enabling remote consultations with healthcare providers; (3) Monitoring and tracking health data, such as blood pressure, blood sugar levels, and medication adherence, and (4) Delivering personalized health interventions, such as exercise programs or nutrition plans. For example, in Kenya, the mobile health service M-TIBA was developed to help individuals save, send, and receive funds for healthcare services via their mobile phones. This has enabled people to access healthcare services they may not have been able to afford before and has helped to reduce the financial burden of healthcare.

Another example is the mobile app called mDiabetes, developed in India to support diabetes management. The app provides personalized guidance on diabetes management, including diet, exercise, and medication adherence. It also allows individuals to track their blood sugar levels and receive reminders for important health screenings. By improving access to healthcare and enabling individuals to take a more active role in their own health and wellness, mobile technology can play an important role in achieving SDG 3.

Artificial Intelligence and SDGs

Artificial Intelligence (AI) has the potential to transform many aspects of our lives, from healthcare to transportation to energy management. It can help to improve efficiency, reduce costs, and promote sustainability by optimizing resource use and reducing waste (SDG 7, 9, 11, 12, and 13). For example, AI can contribute to SDG 13 which aims to take urgent action to combat climate change and its impacts, through climate modeling and prediction. Climate modeling involves using mathematical models to simulate the Earth's climate system and make predictions about future climate trends. AI can be used to improve the accuracy and speed of these models, enabling more detailed and accurate predictions about the impacts of climate change.

Microsoft has developed an AI-based tool called "AI for Earth" that uses machine learning algorithms to analyze satellite imagery and provide insights into environmental issues such as deforestation, climate change, and water scarcity. This tool can be used by researchers and policymakers to better understand the impacts of climate change and develop more effective strategies for mitigating them. Another example is the use of AI in energy management systems. AI algorithms can analyze data from sensors and other sources to optimize energy use, reducing carbon emissions and improving energy efficiency.

For instance, Google has used AI to reduce energy consumption in its data centers, resulting in a 15% reduction in energy use. Future AI applications and new developments will play a significant role in achieving SDG 13 through modeling's that predict the impacts of climate change and by integrating algorithms that can significantly reduce carbon emissions and improve energy efficiency. Also, another example and possible application of AI is Natural Language Processing (NLP) for Education. The AI-powered language translation, speech recognition, and personalized learning tools can help overcome language barriers and provide customized educational content, improving access to quality education (SDG 4). These developments would need appropriate policies and regulations for equitable, inclusive, and ethical use of AI (Huang & Zhang, 2021).

Blockchain and SDGs

Blockchain technology can be used to promote transparency and accountability in areas such as supply chain management and financial transactions. It can help to reduce corruption and improve access to finance, which are critical for sustainable development (SDG 8, 9, and 16). For example, blockchain technology can help to achieve the SDG 16 (Peace, Justice, and Strong Institutions) which aims to promote peaceful and inclusive societies, provide access to justice for all, and build effective, accountable, and inclusive institutions at all levels.

Blockchain technology can improve transparency, accountability, and security in governance systems. For instance, "Blockchain for Social Impact" initiative launched by ConsenSys, a blockchain technology company, supports social impact projects around the world that use blockchain technology to address social and environmental challenges. One project supported by this initiative is the "BitGive" platform, which uses blockchain technology to provide transparency and accountability in charitable giving. Donors can track the use of their donations in real-time, ensuring that their contributions are being used effectively and efficiently.

Another project is the "Ujo" platform, which uses blockchain technology to provide greater transparency and accountability in the music industry. Musicians can use the platform to distribute their music and receive payments directly from their fans, without the need for intermediaries. The use of blockchain technology ensures that payments are secure and transparent, and that artists receive fair compensation for their work. By adapting, improving and expanding these systems, blockchain technology can contribute to building more effective, accountable, and inclusive institutions, which is the key goal of SDG 16.

Biotechnology and SDGs

Biotechnology has the potential to revolutionize medicine, agriculture, and energy production. It can be used to develop new therapies, improve crop yields, and produce sustainable biofuels (SDG 2, 3, 7, and 12). Genetically modified (GM) crops, if developed and deployed carefully, can be instrumental to SDG 2 which aims to end hunger, achieve food security and improved nutrition, and promote sustainable agriculture. It is known that the use of GM crops is a complex issue with varying perspectives and potential risks and benefits. However, there are several arguments showing how GM crops can be good for humanity and the SDGs without resulting in harmful outcomes. One is that GM crops can be designed to produce higher yields, resist pests and diseases, and tolerate environmental stresses such as drought and heat.

Some GM crops are designed to be resistant to pests and diseases, reducing the need for harmful chemical pesticides and fertilizers. GM crops can be designed to produce higher levels of key nutrients, such as vitamin A, iron, and zinc. An example is the development of "Golden Rice," which is genetically modified to produce high levels of vitamin A. This has the potential to reduce vitamin A deficiency in populations that rely on rice as a staple food, improving nutrition and reducing the incidence of blindness and other health problems associated with vitamin A deficiency.

There are also potential risks associated with GM crops, such as the potential for unintended consequences on non-target organisms, the emergence of herbicide-resistant weeds, and the potential for GM traits to spread to wild relatives. It is therefore important to carefully assess the potential risks and benefits of GM crops on a case-by-case basis, and to implement appropriate regulations and safety measures to ensure that they are safe and beneficial for humanity and the SDGs.

Renewable energy and SDGs

Renewable energy technologies, such as solar, wind, and hydropower, are becoming increasingly affordable and widespread. They can help to reduce greenhouse gas emissions and mitigate the impacts of climate change and provide access to clean, sustainable energy for all (SDG 7, 13). While still needing more research and development, nuclear fusion has the potential to be a game-changer in the quest for sustainable and renewable energy as targeted in SDG 7 (affordable and clean energy).

The recent advancements in generating energy through nuclear fusion have the potential to significantly contribute to achieving renewable energy in the same process that powers the sun and other stars. Unlike nuclear fission, which involves splitting atoms and can result in the release of harmful radiation, nuclear fusion does not produce any harmful byproducts or greenhouse gasses. Nuclear fusion has the potential to be more energy efficient than traditional sources of energy as a single fusion reaction can release several times more energy than a traditional chemical reaction. The fuel source for nuclear fusion, hydrogen, is abundant and can be extracted from seawater. This makes it a more sustainable and renewable source of energy compared to fossil fuels, which are finite and non-renewable. Although nuclear fusion is not currently economically viable, research and development are ongoing and could lead to the development of cost-effective fusion reactors in the near future.

Internet of Things and SDGs

Internet of Things (IoT) technology can be used to monitor and optimize resource use in areas such as energy, water, and transportation. It can help to reduce waste and improve efficiency, while also promoting sustainability and reducing the impact of human activities on the environment (SDG 6, 7, 9, 11, and 12). For example, IoT can benefit SDG 11 (sustainable cities and communities) through the development of smart cities that use sensors and devices to collect and analyze data to improve the efficiency and sustainability of urban infrastructure and services. IoT sensors can be used to monitor traffic flow and optimize traffic patterns, reducing congestion and improving air quality.

Smart parking systems use sensors to guide drivers to available parking spots, reducing traffic and emissions. IoT sensors can be used to monitor energy consumption in buildings and adjust heating, cooling, and lighting systems to optimize energy use and reduce waste. These can also be used to monitor garbage bins and waste containers, optimizing waste collection routes and reducing unnecessary pickups. They can also be very helpful to monitor public spaces for potential safety hazards, such as fires or natural disasters, and alert emergency responders and residents. Finally, they can also be used to monitor water usage and detect leaks, optimizing water consumption and reducing waste. Smart cities can improve the quality of life for residents and reduce the environmental impact of urban areas. By using IoT devices and sensors to collect and analyze data, smart cities can identify areas for improvement and make data-driven decisions to create more sustainable and efficient communities.

VR and AR Technologies for SDGs

Virtual Reality (VR) and Augmented Reality (AR) technologies have the potential to transform the way we address the SDGs by creating new opportunities for education, communication, and problem-solving. For example, VR simulations can be used to teach students about the effects of climate change on ecosystems, while AR can be used to provide interactive experiences that help people learn about sustainable agriculture practices. For SDG 3, telemedicine applications that use VR and AR technologies can allow doctors to provide virtual consultations and surgeries to patients who live in remote areas. VR and AR technologies can be used to help individuals understand the impact of their daily choices on the environment.

For example, VR simulations can show individuals the effects of their carbon footprint on the planet, while AR can provide information about sustainable products and packaging. In disaster response, VR and AR technologies can be used to simulate disaster scenarios and train responders on how to handle emergency situations. VR simulations can be used to train firefighters on how to navigate burning buildings, while AR can provide real-time information about hazards and evacuation routes during a natural disaster. For SDG 1, poverty reduction, VR and AR technologies can be used to create job training programs and improve access to financial services for individuals living in poverty. For example, VR simulations can provide training on how to use tools and equipment for manufacturing jobs, while AR can be used to provide financial literacy training and access to banking services.

Autonomous Driving and SDGs

Autonomous driving technologies have the potential to contribute to sustainability innovation and the SDGs by reducing carbon emissions by optimizing vehicle efficiency, reducing congestion, and promoting more sustainable driving behaviors. They can also have the potential to significantly reduce the number of road accidents and fatalities, which can have a positive impact on public health and well-being (SDG 3: Good Health and Well-Being). Autonomous vehicles can help improve access to transportation for individuals who are unable to drive, such as elderly or disabled people. This can contribute to achieving (SDG 10: Reduced Inequalities).

Autonomous driving technologies can help reduce congestion, improve traffic flow, and free up space currently used for parking, which can contribute to more sustainable urban environments (SDG 11: Sustainable Cities and Communities). These technologies can optimize the use of vehicles by coordinating ride-sharing and delivery services, reducing the number of vehicles on the road, and reducing the need for parking spaces (SDG 12: Responsible Consumption and Production). Autonomous driving technologies can substantially contribute to a more sustainable and efficient transportation system, which can have positive impacts on the environment, public health, and economic development, all of which are essential to achieving the SDGs.

Carbon Capture and Storage and SDGs

Carbon capture and storage (CCS) technologies are a suite of technologies that capture carbon dioxide (CO_2) emissions from various sources, such as power plants, industrial processes, and transportation, and store them in deep geological formations, such as depleted oil and gas reservoirs, or saline aquifers, or in other long-term storage facilities. CCS is a critical tool for reducing greenhouse gas emissions and mitigating climate change by preventing the release of CO_2 into the atmosphere. CCS technologies clearly contribute to SDG 7 (Affordable and Clean Energy) as they can be used to capture CO_2 emissions from fossil fuel power plants, thereby reducing the carbon footprint of electricity generation and facilitating a transition to a low-carbon energy system. CCS technologies can contribute to SDG 9 (Industry, Innovation, and Infrastructure) when integrated with industrial processes to capture emissions from energy-intensive sectors such as cement, steel, and chemical production. They obviously contribute to SDG 13 (Climate Action) by reducing greenhouse gas emissions and mitigating the impacts of climate change.

Some innovative practices in CCS include (1) Direct air capture (DAC) which involves capturing CO_2 directly from the air using large-scale facilities, rather than from point sources like power plants or factories; (2) Carbon mineralization, which involves converting CO_2 into stable, solid minerals that can be safely stored for thousands of years, such as carbonate rocks or concrete; (3) Bioenergy with carbon capture and storage (BECCS) which involves generating energy from biomass, such as wood chips or agricultural waste, and capturing and storing the CO_2 emissions generated during the process; and (4) Integrated CCS and renewable energy sources like wind and solar that can help to balance the variability of these sources and ensure a more stable and reliable energy system.

Energy Storage and SDGs

Energy storage technologies refer to devices and systems that can store energy for later use. These technologies can play an important role in sustainability by enabling a more reliable and efficient use of renewable energy sources, such as wind and solar power. Batteries, for example, are the most common form of energy storage technology. They can store energy from renewable sources during periods of low demand and release it during periods of high demand. This can help balance the supply and demand of energy, reduce peak demand on the grid, and increase the use of renewable energy sources.

Pumped hydro storage is another example. This storage involves using excess energy to pump water to a higher elevation. When the energy is needed, the water is released, and the potential energy is converted back into electrical energy. This technology can provide large-scale energy storage and is particularly useful for balancing the grid during times of high demand. Flywheels are another technology example. They store energy by spinning a heavy rotor at high speeds. When the energy is needed, the rotor is slowed down, and the kinetic energy is converted back into electrical energy. Flywheels are particularly useful for providing short bursts of power and can help stabilize the grid during times of high demand.

Thermal storage is also a solution as it involves storing heat or cold energy in a substance, such as water or phase-changing materials. When the energy is needed, the stored heat or cold is used to generate electricity or provide heating and cooling. Thermal storage is particularly useful for reducing energy consumption in buildings and industrial processes. These examples of energy storage technologies can have a significant impact on sustainability by increasing the use of renewable energy sources, reducing greenhouse gas emissions, and improving the reliability and efficiency of the energy grid.

Overall, technological solutions can play a critical role in achieving the SDGs by improving access to resources, promoting efficiency and sustainability, and reducing the impact of human activities on the environment. New technologies have the potential to bring significant benefits to sustainability innovations. Quantum computing, for example, has the potential to solve complex environmental problems, such as predicting and mitigating the effects of climate change. It can also be used to optimize energy systems, reduce waste, and enhance supply chain efficiency. 5G technology can enable smart cities, which can significantly reduce carbon emissions by optimizing traffic flow, reducing energy consumption, and improving waste management. It can also support remote monitoring and control of industrial processes, reducing energy waste, and improving productivity. 3D printing can help reduce waste by allowing manufacturers to produce only what is needed, reducing excess inventory and shipping costs. It can also enable the production of more sustainable materials and products, such as recycled plastics and biodegradable materials.

Many other technological innovations, like smart grid technologies, precision agriculture, sustainable bioplastics, and water efficient irrigation systems, among others can play a critical role in addressing urgent and future sustainability challenges. Overall, these new technologies have the potential to revolutionize sustainability innovations by enabling more precise, efficient, and sustainable solutions to environmental problems. These technology driven innovations can promote a more sustainable and resilient future and enhance the well-being of people and communities around the world.

Ecosystems for Technology Innovations

The invention, development, and deployment of technological innovations do not happen in a vacuum. They require ecosystems that promote innovation and creativity along with collaborations and constructive competitions. Ecosystems for technology innovations are crucial for sustainable development, requiring conditions such as supportive policies, collaboration, access to financing, education, infrastructure, and consumer demand. Governments, businesses, researchers, and other stakeholders should work together to create an environment that promotes innovation, facilitates knowledge sharing, and provides resources necessary for sustainable technologies. By fostering such an ecosystem, we can advance both environmental and societal benefits.

There are several examples of ecosystems that have fostered sustainable technological innovations:

1. **Silicon Valley, California**: Silicon Valley has a thriving ecosystem for sustainable technology innovation, with numerous startups and established companies working on technologies such as electric vehicles, solar power, and energy storage. The region benefits from a supportive policy environment, access to financing, and a culture of innovation and entrepreneurship.
2. **Copenhagen, Denmark**: Copenhagen has developed a reputation as a leader in sustainable urban planning and transportation. The city has invested heavily in cycling infrastructure, renewable energy, and green roofs and has developed partnerships with businesses, universities, and research institutions to promote sustainable innovation.
3. **The Netherlands**: The Netherlands has established itself as a hub for sustainable agriculture and food systems innovation, with companies and research institutions developing technologies such as vertical farming, precision agriculture, and sustainable packaging.
4. **Israel**: Israel has developed a thriving ecosystem for sustainable water technologies, with startups and established companies developing technologies such as desalination, water treatment, and smart water management.
5. **Singapore**: Singapore has positioned itself as a leader in sustainable urban development and has invested heavily in technologies such as green buildings, energy-efficient transportation, and smart

grids. The city-state benefits from a supportive policy environment, a strong research and development sector, and access to financing.

These ecosystems demonstrate that creating the right conditions can foster innovation and support sustainable development. By building on these successes, we can accelerate the transition to a more sustainable future.

Technology Advancements from the Global South

Some could perceive the Global South as simply recipient of technological innovations from the Global North, but this is not the case (Soman et al., 2014). The contextual needs, innate creativity, and capacity for frugal innovations by the people, organizations, and nations of the Global South have been driving several technology innovations that contribute substantially to achieving the SDGs. Before we mention a few examples, we need to clarify that the term "Global South" includes developing countries as well as countries that have achieved a high level of economic development but continue to face challenges related to social and environmental sustainability. The Global South encompasses a broader set of countries and highlights the complex and interconnected nature of economic, social, and environmental issues that face these countries. Here are some sustainability innovations from the Global South:

1. **Off-grid Renewable Energy Solutions**: In the Global South, where access to electricity is limited, off-grid renewable energy solutions, such as solar panels and micro-hydropower systems, have emerged as a sustainable alternative to traditional fossil fuel-based energy sources (Louie, 2018). This has helped improve access to electricity, especially in rural areas, contributing to achieving SDG 7: Affordable and Clean Energy.
2. **Mobile Payment Systems**: Mobile payment systems have revolutionized financial services in the Global South, allowing for greater financial inclusion and improved access to banking services (Malala, 2017). This has contributed to achieving SDG 1: No Poverty and SDG 8: Decent Work and Economic Growth.

3. **Affordable Medical Devices**: In the Global South, innovative medical technologies, such as low-cost prosthetics and medical imaging devices, have been developed to improve access to health-care services, especially in low-income communities (Chaturvedi, 2016). This has contributed to achieving SDG 3: Good Health and Well-being.
4. **Water Management Technologies**: In regions where access to clean water is limited, water management technologies, such as rainwater harvesting and drip irrigation systems, have been developed to help conserve water resources and improve access to clean water (Chen, 2016). This has contributed to achieving SDG 6: Clean Water and Sanitation.
5. **Agroforestry**: Agroforestry is a sustainable land use system that combines trees and crops to improve soil health and biodiversity, while also providing food and income (Shukla et al., 2021). This has contributed to achieving SDG 2: Zero Hunger and SDG 15: Life on Land.
6. **Jute-Based Biodegradable Products**: In Bangladesh, for example, a social enterprise called Jute Lab has developed a range of biodegradable products made from jute fiber, a locally grown crop. These products include shopping bags, tableware, and packaging materials that are sustainable alternatives to plastic products. This innovation addresses the problem of plastic waste and contributes to achieving SDG 12 (Responsible Consumption and Production).
7. **Agroecology**: In Brazil, for example, a movement called Agroecology has emerged as a sustainable alternative to industrial agriculture. Agroecology involves the use of ecological principles to design and manage agricultural systems that are diverse, resilient, and socially just. This innovation promotes sustainable food production and contributes to achieving SDGs 2 (Zero Hunger) and 15 (Life on Land).
8. **Renewable Energy**: In India, for example, the government has launched several initiatives to promote the use of renewable energy, including solar and wind power. The country has set a target of achieving 175 GW of renewable energy capacity by 2022. This innovation addresses the challenge of energy access and contributes to achieving SDG 7 (Affordable and Clean Energy).

9. **Green Building Design**: In South Africa, for example, a company called Ecolution Consulting has developed a green building certification system called Green Star SA. This system promotes sustainable building design and construction practices that reduce energy and water consumption and improve indoor air quality. This innovation contributes to achieving SDG 11 (Sustainable Cities and Communities).
10. **Community-Based Natural Resource Management**: In Namibia, for example, a community-based natural resource management system has been developed to promote sustainable use of natural resources, including wildlife, forests, and water. This system involves local communities in decision-making processes related to natural resource management and provides them with incentives to conserve these resources. This innovation contributes to achieving SDGs 14 (Life Below Water) and 15 (Life on Land).

Overall, the Global South has been driving several sustainability innovations that offer solutions to global challenges. These include the challenges of balancing technological disruptions with core values like dignity, freedom, democracy, and free choice (Ghezzi et al., 2021). Even the amplitude of challenges, like digital gaps in the Global South (Gladkova & Ragnedda, 2020), could serve as reminders of the persisting gaps elsewhere. In addition, the Global South has offered solutions to the Global North for global challenges related to climate change, poverty, and inequality. Microfinance, for example, is a social innovation mechanism that emerged from the Global South that has been adopted by the Global North to address its own challenges related to poverty and marginalization.

Since the early 1980s, microfinance has been instrumental to low-income individuals and small businesses to access capitals through small loans and other financial services. It has helped millions of people improve their livelihoods and reduce poverty. In recent years, microfinance institutions have been established in several developed countries, including the United States, Canada, and the United Kingdom, to provide small loans and financial services to low-income individuals and communities. However, the adoption of microfinance in the Global North has also raised concerns about the potential for exploitation and the commodification of poverty along with the higher concern on profit-making than poverty reduction. It has also received some criticism that microfinance in the Global North may contribute to the marginalization of low-income communities by providing them with access to high-interest loans rather than addressing the underlying causes of poverty. In other words, social mechanisms for poverty alleviation, like sustainability technical innovations, may come from different contexts and will probably need the critical participation of all to make sure they continue to produce net positive impact.

Key Takeaways

1. Advanced technologies can significantly contribute to the achievement of the SDGs by addressing global challenges such as poverty, climate change, and inequality.
2. Mobile technology, artificial intelligence, blockchain, biotechnology, renewable energy, the Internet of Things, virtual and augmented reality, autonomous driving, carbon capture and storage, and energy storage are some of the key technology innovations discussed in the chapter.
3. Fostering supportive ecosystems for technology innovations, which include collaboration among stakeholders and sharing knowledge, is crucial for accelerating progress towards the SDGs.
4. The chapter highlights the role of technology advancements from the Global South, emphasizing the importance of inclusive innovation in promoting sustainable development worldwide.
5. Integrating technology innovations into sustainable development strategies can enhance their effectiveness and help create a more equitable, resilient, and sustainable future for all.

References

Chaturvedi, J. (2016). *Inventing medical devices: A perspective from India*. Notion Press.

Chen, D. (2016). *Sustainable water management and technologies, two-volume set*. Taylor & Francis.

Ghezzi, C., Werthner, H., Prem, E., & Lee, E. A. (2021). *Perspectives on digital humanism*. Springer International Publishing.

Gladkova, A., & Ragnedda, M. (2020). *Digital inequalities in the global south*. Springer International Publishing.

Huang, R., & Zhang, H. (2021). *AI and education: A guidance for policymakers.* UNESCO Publishing.

Louie, H. (2018). *Off-grid electrical systems in developing countries*. Springer International Publishing.

Malala, J. (2017). *Law and regulation of mobile payment systems: Issues arising 'post' financial inclusion in Kenya*. Taylor & Francis.

Shukla, G., et al. (2021). *Agroforestry: Small landholder's tool for climate change resiliency and mitigation*. IntechOpen.

Soman, D., et al. (2014). *Innovating for the global south: Towards an inclusive innovation agenda*. University of Toronto Press.

CHAPTER 14

Design Thinking for Sustainable Innovation

Abstract This chapter delves into Design Thinking (DT) as a powerful methodology for fostering sustainable innovation. It discusses the Double-Diamond model and core stages of DT in the context of sustainability design, highlighting its human-centered, empathetic, and collaborative nature. By examining organizational examples, the chapter demonstrates the practical application of DT in sustainability designs. Additionally, the chapter explores the integration of DT with other frameworks, such as the Ignatian Pedagogical Paradigm, Cradle to Cradle, and Appreciative Inquiry Model, showcasing the versatility of DT. Lastly, the chapter emphasizes the importance of inclusion and diverse stakeholder engagement in the DT process for achieving truly sustainable innovation.

Keywords Design thinking · Double-Diamond model · Collaborative approach · Ignatian pedagogical paradigm · Cradle to cradle · Appreciative inquiry

> *"Sustainability can't be like some sort of a moral obligation or some sort of a philosophy. It has to be a design challenge."*
> —Tim Brown, CEO and President of the design consultancy IDEO

M. Tavanti, *Developing Sustainability in Organizations*, Sustainable Development Goals Series, https://doi.org/10.1007/978-3-031-36907-0_14

Design Thinking Models for Sustainability Innovations

Design Thinking (DT) is a human-centered problem-solving methodology that emphasizes empathy, creativity, and iterative prototyping. The model, in different variations and adaptations, has been used to create many social innovation designs, business design models, and sustainability innovation solutions (Beausoleil, 2022). The DT Double-Diamond model and the DT's Core Stages can be connected to other frameworks and models, such as the Ignatian Pedagogical Principles, Appreciative Inquiry 5D model, and the Cradle to Cradle model, to develop innovative and sustainable solutions to complex challenges. Figure 14.1 illustrates the pathways and comparable steps of the DT models integrated with values emerging from other paradigms and practices. The four-stage of the Double-Diamond process that consists of Discover, Define, Develop, and Deliver encourages a broad exploration of ideas before narrowing down to specific solutions. The DT five stages parallel the Ignatian pedagogical principles consisting of five steps: Context, Experience, Reflection, Action, and Evaluation. These steps can be integrated with DT stages to enrich the learning process, fostering personal growth, and social responsibility. The Appreciative Inquiry 5D model which includes Define, Discover, Dream, Design, and Destiny focuses on an organization's strengths and successes. It complements DT by creating a positive and engaging environment for problem-solving. The Cradle to Cradle model emphasizes the design of products and systems that are regenerative and restorative, considering the entire life cycle of materials. Integrating this model with DT ensures a focus on sustainability and environmental responsibility. DT for sustainability-oriented innovations (SOIs) involves applying the principles and tools of DT to address sustainability challenges through innovative solutions, engaging diverse stakeholders, and co-creating solutions with a multi-disciplinary team. In my own professional and academic practice guiding social enterprise and social innovation students to use this combined DT model, the starting point of preliminary research is complementary to the experience and discovery stage. In addition, formalizing the process of comparing your own "dreamt" and "drafted" innovation with similar existing innovations and enterprises can be very helpful in between the Define and Develop stages. The three checkpoints for developing real (wicked) problems awareness, developing

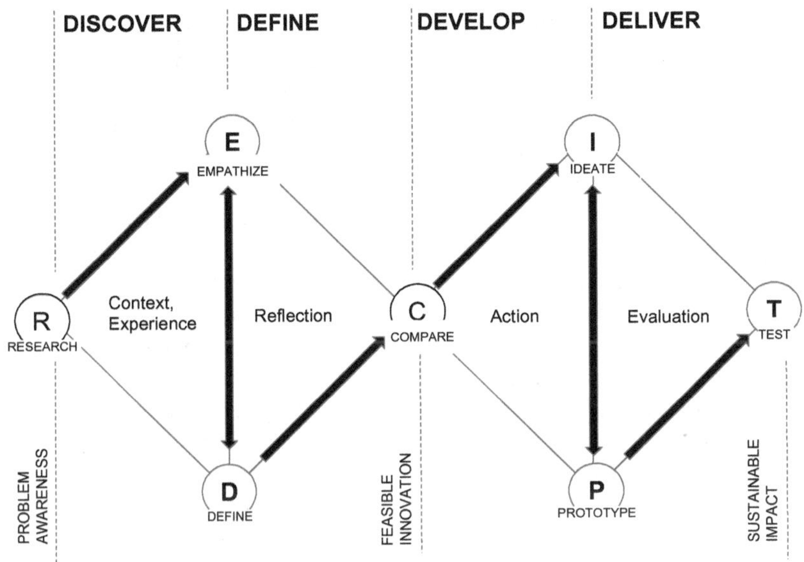

Fig. 14.1 Integrated DT model for sustainability innovations

a feasible innovation idea, and developing innovative solutions for sustainability impact are proven useful marks in the DT process for sustainability. By combining DT with these complementary models and principles, it is possible to develop more sustainable, equitable, and effective solutions that address complex social, environmental, and economic challenges.

The DT Double-Diamond Model

While the design thinking process can be approached in many different ways, it generally involves a series of steps that are meant to help teams create innovative solutions to complex problems. One commonly used framework is the "Double Diamond" model (Dekker, 2020), which consists of four stages: Discover, Define, Develop, and Deliver.

1. **Discover**: In the "Discover" stage, the team seeks to understand the problem space and the needs of the people for which they are designing. This involves researching the problem, conducting interviews, and gathering data to develop a deep understanding of the

challenge at hand. By engaging with the community and gathering insights, the team can identify the root causes of a problem, as well as the needs, values, and behaviors of the people impacted by it. This understanding can help ensure that the solutions developed are truly sustainable and designed to meet the needs of the target group.

2. **Define**: In the "Define" stage, the team works to synthesize their research and insights into a clear problem statement that will guide their design efforts. This involves identifying the key stakeholders and their needs, as well as defining the constraints and opportunities that will influence the design. This stage is critical for sustainability design and social innovation, as it allows the team to identify the key stakeholders and their needs, as well as defining the constraints and opportunities that will influence the design. By identifying these factors, the team can ensure that the solution developed is both effective and sustainable.
3. **Develop**: In the "Develop" stage, the team generates and tests a range of possible solutions. This involves brainstorming, prototyping, and testing different ideas in order to identify the most promising options. This stage is important for sustainability design and social innovation because it allows the team to explore a wide range of potential solutions, including those that may be unconventional or outside of the box thinking. By testing and refining these solutions, the team can identify the most promising options and ensure that the solution developed is both effective and sustainable.
4. **Deliver:** In the "Deliver" stage, the team finalizes the design and creates a plan for implementation. This involves refining the solution based on feedback and testing, creating a detailed plan for how the solution will be implemented, and communicating the plan to stakeholders. This final stage in the DT double-diamond model is also critical for sustainability design and social innovation because it ensures that the solution developed is not only effective and sustainable but also feasible to implement. By creating a detailed plan on how the solution will be implemented and communicating this plan to stakeholders, the team can ensure that the solution is embraced and adopted by the community.

Throughout the design thinking process, the team may ask a range of questions to guide their efforts, such as "What is the problem we are trying to solve?", "What are the needs of the people we are designing for?", "What are the constraints and opportunities we need to consider?", and "How can we test and refine our solutions to ensure they meet the needs of our stakeholders?" Overall, the Double-Diamond model of design thinking can benefit sustainability design and social innovation by providing a structured approach to problem-solving that focuses on creating solutions that are both effective and sustainable. By engaging with the community, gathering insights, and testing and refining solutions, the team can ensure that the solutions developed meet the needs of the people they are designed for and are sustainable in the long term.

The DT Core Stages for Sustainability Design

Design thinking is important for sustainability innovation because it offers a human-centered, empathetic, iterative, and collaborative approach to problem-solving, fostering the development of effective, innovative, and inclusive solutions which address complex sustainability challenges. The DT 5 core stages expand on the Double-Diamond model by adding a fifth stage, "Empathize," and providing more detailed guidance on how to approach each stage. These DT core stages have important implications and applications for sustainability innovation. They are also a very helpful framework for integrating DT into sustainability innovation curricula, programs in accelerators and incubators, competition challenges, or intense ideation processes like design sprints (4–5 days) or hackathons (48–72 hours) (Wrigley & Mosely, 2022). Let's consider the DT stages with some examples of their relevance and possible applications for SOI needs.

1. **Empathize:** Empathizing is a crucial stage in the design thinking process for sustainability innovation, as it allows designers and innovators to understand the needs, wants, and motivations of those affected by sustainability issues. By comprehending the impact of these issues on people's lives, innovators can identify and prioritize pressing concerns, develop tailored solutions, and foster collaboration and partnerships with communities, organizations, and stakeholders. Empathizing helps create practical, affordable, and culturally appropriate solutions for renewable energy, sustainable food systems, and waste reduction, ultimately influencing subsequent stages of the design thinking process and ensuring relevant and valuable outcomes.

2. **Define:** The Define stage in the design thinking process involves specifying and outlining the problem or challenge using insights and data gathered during the Empathize stage. This stage is critical for sustainability innovation, as it ensures the design team addresses a genuine sustainability issue while considering the context and stakeholders involved. For example, in developing a sustainable packaging solution, the team must define the problem as reducing plastic waste while maintaining product protection and meeting consumer needs. The Define stage guarantees alignment among team members and allows them to proceed to the Ideate stage, where they can generate potential solutions that are both effective and sustainable.
3. **Ideate:** The Ideate stage of the design thinking process involves generating a variety of potential solutions to the defined problem using creative techniques like brainstorming and mind mapping. This stage is crucial for sustainability innovations, as it encourages participants to think creatively, challenge assumptions, and develop novel solutions to complex sustainability challenges. By fostering a culture of experimentation and risk-taking, the Ideate stage enables transformative and impactful innovations. Moreover, it allows the integration of diverse perspectives and expertise, leading to a more comprehensive understanding of the challenge and more effective, sustainable solutions.
4. **Prototype:** The Prototype stage in the design thinking process involves transforming ideas into tangible models for testing and evaluation. This stage is vital for sustainability innovations, as it enables rapid testing and iteration, helping to identify potential flaws and opportunities for improvement. Creating prototypes allows designers to gather valuable feedback from users and stakeholders, informing further development and refinement. Additionally, prototypes can effectively communicate ideas, engage stakeholders in the design process, and build momentum and support for sustainability innovations. In summary, prototyping helps transform abstract concepts into testable solutions, leading to more effective and impactful sustainability innovations.
5. **Test:** The Test stage in the design thinking process involves evaluating prototypes with stakeholders to gather feedback and refine solutions. This stage is crucial for sustainability innovations, as it enables designers to identify potential flaws, challenges, and opportunities for improvement in a real-world context. Testing helps

refine and improve solutions, increasing the likelihood of successful implementation and adoption. Additionally, the test stage builds confidence and support for sustainability innovations by demonstrating their effectiveness and impact. In summary, testing prototypes in real-world contexts helps designers achieve their sustainability goals by refining solutions and securing support for further development and implementation.

These five core stages can help to design sustainability innovation solutions by providing a structured approach that emphasizes empathy, collaboration, and iteration. By engaging with the people impacted by the problem and empathizing with their needs, the team can ensure that the solutions developed are truly sustainable and meet the needs of the community. By generating a range of possible solutions, prototyping, and testing, the team can ensure that the solution developed is effective and sustainable. Additionally, the iterative nature of the design thinking process allows the team to continue refining and improving the solution based on feedback from stakeholders, ensuring that it remains effective and sustainable over time. Overall, the DT five core stages can be a powerful tool for designing sustainability innovation solutions that truly meet the needs of the community and are sustainable over the long term.

DT Organizational Examples of Sustainability Designs

By applying design thinking to sustainability challenges, companies and organizations can develop more sustainable and equitable solutions that meet the needs of diverse stakeholders. Moreover, design thinking can help to foster a culture of innovation and creativity that supports ongoing sustainability efforts. There are numerous examples of social innovation solutions generated through the DT process. Many of them contribute directly to the sustainability agenda of the SDGs. Here are a few examples:

1. **TOMS Shoes:** TOMS Shoes is a company that has used design thinking to create a sustainable business model that addresses the issue of poverty and lack of shoes in developing countries. They

have implemented a "One for One" model where for every pair of shoes purchased, a pair is donated to a child in need.

2. **Warby Parker:** Warby Parker is an eyeglass company that has used design thinking to create a sustainable business model which addresses the issue of lack of access to affordable eyeglasses in developing countries. They have implemented a "Buy a Pair, Give a Pair" model where for every pair of glasses purchased, a pair is donated to a person in need.
3. **The Pesticide Project:** The Pesticide Project is an organization that has used design thinking to create sustainable solutions for farmers in developing countries to reduce their dependence on chemical pesticides and improve their livelihoods. They have developed a training program that teaches farmers about sustainable farming practices, and also provides them with access to non-toxic pest control options.
4. **IDEO.org:** IDEO.org is a nonprofit organization that uses design thinking to create sustainable solutions for social issues in developing countries. They have worked on projects such as designing a clean cookstove that is affordable and accessible for families in the developing world and developing a mobile-based financial service for small farmers in Africa.
5. **Grameen Bank:** Grameen Bank, founded by Muhammad Yunus, is a pioneer in the field of microfinance. They have used design thinking to create sustainable solutions for poverty in developing countries. They developed a new banking model which provides small loans to poor people, particularly women, to start or expand small businesses.
6. **Sanergy:** Sanergy is a social enterprise that was created to address the lack of access to safe and hygienic sanitation facilities in urban slums. The company uses a franchise model to provide affordable, high-quality sanitation facilities to communities in need. By providing these facilities, Sanergy is helping to improve health and reduce poverty, while also promoting sustainable development.
7. **Lumkani:** Lumkani is a social enterprise that has developed a low-cost, early-warning fire detection system designed for informal settlements in South Africa. The device uses temperature sensors to detect fires early and sends out alerts to people in the surrounding area. By detecting fires early, Lumkani is helping to reduce the risk

of fire-related deaths and property damage, while also promoting sustainable development.

8. **Hello Tractor:** Hello Tractor is a social enterprise that has developed a low-cost, tractor-sharing platform designed for smallholder farmers in Africa. The platform allows farmers to rent tractors on demand, helping to increase crop yields and improve productivity. By improving agricultural productivity, Hello Tractor is helping to reduce poverty and promote sustainable development.
9. **BioLite:** BioLite is a social enterprise that produces clean energy products for off-grid households. Using design thinking, the company developed a range of affordable and sustainable products, including stoves that use wood and other biomass fuels to generate electricity. By providing access to clean and sustainable energy, BioLite contributes to SDG 7 (Affordable and Clean Energy) and SDG 13 (Climate Action).
10. **Solar Sister:** Solar Sister is a social enterprise that uses a design thinking process to empower women entrepreneurs in rural Africa to distribute clean energy solutions. The company provides training, support, and financing to help women start and grow their own clean energy businesses, helping to increase access to renewable energy and promote economic development. Solar Sister's work aligns with several SDGs, including SDG 5 (Gender Equality), SDG 7 (Affordable and Clean Energy), and SDG 8 (Decent Work and Economic Growth).

These are just a few examples of social enterprises that have been created using a design thinking process and are aligned with the SDGs. By using design thinking principles to create sustainable and impactful business models, these enterprises are helping to address some of the world's most pressing social and environmental challenges.

While DT has shown promise as an approach for developing innovative solutions to sustainability challenges, it is important to note that it is not a panacea. DT should be used in combination with other approaches and frameworks to ensure that sustainability considerations are fully integrated into decision-making processes. Additionally, DT should be used in a way that is culturally and contextually appropriate to ensure that solutions are relevant and effective for local communities and contexts.

The DT and Ignatian Pedagogical Paradigm

The DT process can be adapted to specific contexts, such as incorporating the Ignatian Pedagogical Paradigm (IPP), a Jesuit educational framework emphasizing holistic learning, reflection, action, and evaluation (Go & Atienza, 2019; Mesa, 2017). The IPP is relevant to sustainability as it encourages critical examination of our relationship with the environment and our responsibility to care for it. The five stages of the IPP are context, experience, reflection, action, and evaluation. The IPP also encourages learners to take action on environmental issues, such as promoting conservation efforts or advocating for policy changes that support sustainability. The IPP's emphasis on reflection and evaluation encourages learners to consider the impact of their actions on the environment and to seek ways to minimize their ecological footprint. In other words, the IPP provides a useful framework for education that promotes critical thinking, reflection, and action on issues related to sustainability, which is crucial in promoting a sustainable future. The five elements of the IPP provide a framework for a holistic and reflective approach to education that promotes critical thinking, action, and social justice. The five stages of DT and the five stages of IPP share similarities and can be compared and integrated as follows.

1. **Context and Empathize:** The first stage of DT involves understanding the needs, perspectives, and experiences of the user or target audience. This is similar to the Context stage of the IPP, which involves becoming aware of the context and needs of the learners. Both stages emphasize the importance of empathizing with the user/learner and understanding their unique experiences and perspectives.
2. **Experience and Define:** The second stage of DT involves creating a direct and meaningful experience for the user and defining the problem or challenge that needs to be addressed. This is similar to the Experience stage of the IPP, which also involves engaging learners in a meaningful experience that challenges them to think critically. Both stages emphasize the importance of experiential learning and defining the problem or challenge that needs to be addressed.

3. **Reflection and Ideate:** The third stage of DT involves reflecting on the experience and generating ideas for potential solutions. This is similar to the Reflection stage of the IPP, which also involves reflecting on the experience and analyzing its meaning and significance. Both stages emphasize the importance of reflection and generating new ideas based on the insights gained.
4. **Action and Prototype:** The fourth stage of DT involves taking action and prototyping potential solutions. This is similar to the Action stage of the IPP, which involves taking responsible action based on the insights gained from reflection. Both stages emphasize the importance of taking action and testing potential solutions.
5. **Evaluation and Test**: The fifth and final stage of DT involves evaluating the effectiveness of the solution and testing it with the user. This is similar to the Evaluation stage of the IPP, which involves evaluating the learning process and outcomes and using this evaluation to inform future learning and action. Both stages emphasize the importance of evaluation and testing to ensure that the solution meets the needs of the user/learner.

Overall, both the five stages of Design Thinking and the five stages of the Ignatian Pedagogical Paradigm provide a framework for a holistic and reflective approach to problem-solving and education that emphasizes empathy, experiential learning, critical reflection, action, and evaluation. Integrating the IPP into DT can provide a valuable framework for promoting sustainability through education that fosters critical thinking, reflection, and action on sustainability issues.

The DT and the Appreciative Inquiry Model

The Appreciative Inquiry Approach (AIA) is a model developed in the 1980s by David Cooperrider and Suresh Srivastva at Case Western Reserve University. It has since been used by many organizations around the world to facilitate positive change and innovation (Cooperrider & Whitney, 2005). The AIA is a strengths-based approach that focuses on identifying and building on the positive aspects of an organization or situation, rather than focusing on the negative aspects. It can be a useful tool for fostering sustainability innovation in organizations (Woodman, 1989). For example, organizations can use the AIA to identify and amplify existing sustainability successes within the organization. By focusing on what is already working well, organizations can build on these successes and identify opportunities for further innovation and improvement. As the AIA emphasizes collaboration and co-creation with stakeholders, it can be useful for effectively involving a diverse group of stakeholders in the sustainability innovation process so that organizations can gain new perspectives, ideas, and solutions. The AIA can also be used to create a shared vision for sustainability within the organization. By engaging stakeholders in a positive and collaborative process, organizations can create a shared understanding of what sustainability means and what it looks like in practice. This shared vision can then guide the organization's sustainability innovation efforts. The main value of the AIA is that it is using positive language to inspire action and change. Organizations can use positive language to communicate their sustainability goals and inspire employees and stakeholders to take action towards achieving those goals.

By applying the AIA, organizations can foster a culture of innovation and sustainability that drives positive social and environmental outcomes while also creating value for the organization. For example, Fairmount Minerals, a mining company, used the AIA to develop a sustainability strategy that focused on creating positive social and environmental outcomes. Through the AIA and its process, employees and stakeholders identified ways to reduce waste and energy consumption, increase community engagement, and create new products that were more sustainable.

World Vision, an international development organization, used the AIA as a model to develop a sustainability strategy that focused on building resilient communities. Through the AIA, World Vision engaged with community members to identify their strengths and assets, and worked with them to co-create solutions that would increase their resilience to climate change and other challenges. McDonald's too used the AIA to develop a sustainability strategy that focused on reducing waste and greenhouse gas emissions. Through the AIA and process, McDonald's engaged with suppliers and employees to identify ways to reduce waste and energy consumption throughout their supply chain, while also improving the nutritional value of their menu offerings.

The AIA originally included a 4-stage process (or 4-D cycle of Discover, Dream, Design, and Deliver) resembling the DT Double-Diamond model. Later the AIA model was modified to include 5 stages and called the 5D model of AIA. While it is a different methodology than DT in its core 5 stages, it shares some common elements and can be complementary in their application.

1. **Define:** This phase involves setting the focus of the inquiry by defining the topic or area of interest. The topic should be affirmative and framed positively, concentrating on what is working well and what the organization wants to develop further. Similar to the DT Empathize stage, the Define phase in Appreciative Inquiry establishes the topic or area of interest for the inquiry with a focus on the positive aspects of the organization.
2. **Discover:** The stage of the AIA involves discovering the positive aspects of the organization or situation. This involves identifying the organization's strengths, successes, and values, and understanding what is working well. This stage often involves interviews, focus groups, and other data-gathering methods to identify positive examples. This is similar to the DT Empathize stage where insights about users' needs and experiences are collected. Both methodologies emphasize understanding the current situation and learning from it.
3. **Dream:** In this stage of the AIA, participants use the insights from the Discover stage to imagine what the organization or situation could look like in future. This involves creating a shared vision of what is possible and what success would look like. Participants are encouraged to think big and be creative in their ideas. Similarly, the DT Ideate phase is about generating a wide range of ideas to address the defined problem.
4. **Design:** This stage of the AIA involves designing concrete actions and initiatives that can help bring the dream to life. Participants identify specific actions and projects that can move the organization towards its shared vision of success. This stage often involves prioritizing actions, creating implementation plans, and assigning responsibilities. In DT, the Prototype stage is about creating a physical or digital representation of one or more ideas to make them more concrete and testable.
5. **Deliver (or Destiny):** In the final stage of the AIA, participants take action to implement the initiatives and projects that were identified in the Design stage. This stage involves monitoring progress, adapting plans as needed, and celebrating successes along the way. In DT, the Test phase is about assessing the effectiveness of the prototypes and iterating on the design based on user feedback.

Overall, the AIA is a model that provides a positive and collaborative approach to problem-solving and innovation, focusing on what is working well and building on strengths. By applying the AIA in its model and process, organizations can create a shared vision for the future, identify concrete actions to achieve that vision, and work collaboratively to bring their sustainability goals to life. DT and AIA are two different models but they clearly share some similarities in their steps and approaches for problem-solving and sustainability innovation. The connection between the two models is their shared emphasis on creativity, collaboration, and holistic thinking. Both models involve a deep understanding of the problem or situation, collaboration with stakeholders, and a focus on creating holistic solutions that address the needs of all stakeholders. In particular, both models emphasize the importance of empathy and understanding the needs of users or stakeholders. Design thinking relies on empathizing with users to create user-centered solutions, while appreciative inquiry seeks to understand and appreciate the perspectives of all stakeholders to create solutions that benefit everyone. Additionally, both models emphasize the importance of iteration and continuous improvement. In design thinking, prototypes are tested and refined based on user feedback, while in appreciative inquiry, the design and delivery stages involve continuous learning and improvement. Used in combination with one another, the DT and AIA models can be useful tools that provide practical steps for creating more effective and holistic solutions to complex problems.

The DT and Cradle to Cradle Framework

Design thinking, when combined with the Cradle to Cradle (C2C) framework, can be an extremely powerful approach for eco-design innovations, ultimately driving us towards a circular economy and increasing resource efficiencies (Matsumoto, 2016). The DT-C2C can generate eco-design innovations that not only address environmental and social challenges but also cater to the needs and desires of end-users. C2C is a framework that promotes the creation of products and systems that are not only environmentally sustainable but also economically and socially beneficial. This powerful combination encourages innovation, collaboration, and continuous improvement, ultimately driving us towards a more circular and resource-efficient society. The C2C concept was first developed by architect William McDonough and chemist Michael Braungart (2002), in the book *Cradle to Cradle: Remaking the Way We Make Things*. At its core, C2C is based on the idea that waste is a human invention and that in nature, there is no waste, only nutrients. The framework encourages the creation of products and systems that mimic natural systems by designing them with the end of their life cycle in mind, and ensuring that all materials and resources are either returned to the Earth as nutrients (biological cycle) or kept in closed-loop technical cycles (technical cycle) to be reused in the production of new products.

The C2C framework has five main criteria for evaluating the environmental and social impact of a product or system:

1. **Material health:** ensuring that all materials used are safe for humans and the environment.
2. **Material reutilization**: designing products and systems for disassembly and reuse.
3. **Renewable energy and carbon management**: using renewable energy and reducing greenhouse gas emissions.
4. **Water stewardship:** minimizing water use and ensuring clean water discharge.
5. **Social fairness:** ensuring that the product or system is socially responsible and promotes social justice.

These principles guide the design of products, systems, and supply chains that minimize environmental impact and maximize positive social impact. C2C is focused on creating products and systems that are designed to be regenerative, restorative, and circular, with a goal of eliminating waste and pollution. It has been applied to a wide range of products, from building materials to textiles and consumer goods, and has gained popularity in the sustainability field as a way to create products that are truly sustainable and restorative to the environment.

The C2C design framework and the DT process share some similarities in that they both prioritize sustainability and a holistic approach to problem-solving. The C2C framework and the design thinking process can be complementary. Design thinking can be used to help designers and companies develop C2C products and systems by providing a structured approach to ideation, prototyping, and testing. For example, designers can use the design thinking process to identify user needs, generate ideas for C2C products or systems, and rapidly prototype and test those ideas in a real-world context. By using design thinking to support C2C design, designers can create products and systems that are not only sustainable but also meet the needs and desires of users.

Overall, the C2C framework and the DT process are complementary approaches to sustainability innovation. The C2C framework provides a set of principles for sustainable design, while design thinking provides a structured approach to ideation, prototyping, and testing that can be used to support the development of C2C products and systems. By combining these approaches, designers can create products and systems that are not only sustainable but also meet the needs and desires of users.

The DT and Inclusion for Sustainability Innovation

There are numerous opportunities for advancing sustainability innovation solutions by including critical stakeholders. For example, people with disabilities and forced migrants are two important groups that can create new opportunities for creative solutions affecting many in our global-local communities. Considering and including people with disabilities and forced migrants is a moral imperative and a fulfillment of the 2030 Sustainability Agenda (Quirico, 2022). It is also an opportunity to make the sustainable innovation process and products more relevant and impactful. Including stakeholders like people with disabilities and forced migrants and refugees in the social innovation and sustainable development process can create opportunities for several reasons.

First, they bring diverse perspectives. People with disabilities and refugees bring unique perspectives and experiences to the table that can help identify problems and potential solutions that may not have been considered otherwise. By including these stakeholders, social innovators can better understand the needs and challenges of marginalized communities, which can lead to more effective and inclusive solutions. Second, they can reinforce the co-creation process. By involving people with disabilities and refugees in the design process, social innovators can create solutions that are more relevant and impactful. Third, they can provide better marketing solutions and increase social impact. Including marginalized communities in the social innovation and sustainable development process can help address social inequalities and promote social inclusion. By creating solutions that are accessible and inclusive, social innovators can contribute to a more equitable society.

Research and innovation can play a critical role in achieving sustainable development, but it is also true that policies governing research and innovation often prioritize economic growth and output, which can reinforce economic inequality and marginalize certain groups, including persons with disabilities. The DT process is an opportunity for co-creating inclusive solutions to these systemic problems. To design solutions for people with disabilities and refugees, it is important to keep their unique challenges and needs in mind throughout the design thinking process.

By following this process, designers can create solutions that are tailored to the needs of these communities and ultimately improve their quality of life. The systematic exclusion of our society and economic systems is a challenge that needs to be addressed through a more inclusive and participatory approach to research and innovation. Unfortunately, there is a significant evidence gap regarding development approaches that ensure the equal participation of persons with disabilities around the world. For example, in many countries, assistive devices and technologies are not readily available or affordable, which can limit the ability of persons with disabilities to participate fully in society. Moreover, widespread prejudice towards persons with disabilities can lead to their exclusion from important areas of life, such as education, employment, and community participation.

The UN Office of the High Commissioner for Human Rights (OHCHR, 2020) in its *Policy Guidelines for Inclusive Sustainable Development Goals: Research and Innovation* highlights how persons with disabilities continue to be excluded from sustainable development initiatives, including research and innovation. Despite the fact that persons with disabilities make up 15% of the world's population, they often face significant barriers to accessing education, healthcare, employment, and other basic services. This exclusion can be exacerbated by a lack of funding and support for disability-inclusive initiatives, including research and innovation. The brief reports that only 2% of aid projects were targeted to persons with disabilities between 2014 and 2018, and only 2% of private funding on human rights was directed to persons with disabilities.

To address these challenges, it is important to prioritize disability-inclusive initiatives across all areas of sustainable development, including research and innovation. This requires adopting a more inclusive and participatory approach to research and innovation that actively involves persons with disabilities and other marginalized groups in the process.

More inclusive solutions can also involve measures such as funding and support for disability-led research and innovation, the development of accessible and affordable assistive technologies, and the promotion of disability-inclusive policies and practices across all sectors. For example, this can involve measures such as providing access to assistive devices and technologies, promoting awareness and understanding of disability issues, and addressing the root causes of prejudice and discrimination towards persons with disabilities. By adopting a more inclusive and participatory approach to research and innovation, and prioritizing policies and initiatives that promote the inclusion of persons with disabilities, we can help to ensure that the benefits of sustainable development can fulfill the *Leave No One Behind* (LNOB) central promise of the sustainability agenda (Kharas, 2019).

Key Takeaways

1. Design thinking (DT) is a problem-solving methodology to create sustainable and equitable products, services, and systems by emphasizing empathy, creativity, and iterative prototyping. DT can help address complex sustainability challenges by incorporating a user-oriented and collaborative approach.
2. The DT Double-Diamond Model process of discovery, definition, development, and delivery demonstrates how DT can be applied to sustainability design, helping to identify, understand, and address the diverse needs and perspectives of stakeholders.
3. The DT core stages of empathizing with users, defining the problem, ideating potential solutions, prototyping, and testing can create innovative solutions that meet sustainability goals while involving diverse stakeholders in the process.
4. The DT method can be integrated with other frameworks, such as the Ignatian Pedagogical Paradigm, Cradle to Cradle, and Appreciative Inquiry Model to enhance its effectiveness in driving sustainable innovation.
5. DT emphasizes the importance of co-creation, collaboration, and diverse stakeholder inclusion for a better understanding of their needs and perspectives, ultimately leading to more effective and sustainable solutions that address complex challenges.

References

Beausoleil, A. M. (2022). *Business design thinking and doing: Frameworks, strategies and techniques for sustainable innovation*. Springer International Publishing.

Cooperrider, D., & Whitney, D. D. (2005). *Appreciative inquiry: A positive revolution in change*. Berrett-Koehler Publishers.

Dekker, T. D. (2020). *Design thinking*. Taylor & Francis.

Go, J. C., & Atienza, R. J. (2019). *Learning by refraction: A practitioner's guide to 21st century Ignatian pedagogy*. Ateneo de Manila University Press.

High Commissioner for Human Rights (OHCHR). (2020). *Policy guidelines for inclusive sustainable development goals: Research and innovation*. Available at https://www.ohchr.org/sites/default/files/thematic-brief-research-and-innovation.pdf. Accessed on March 18, 2023.

Kharas, H., et al. (2019). *Leave no one behind: Time for specifics on the sustainable development goals*. Brookings Institution Press.

Matsumoto, M. (2016). *Sustainability through innovation in product life cycle design*. Springer Nature Singapore.

Mesa, J. (2017). *Ignatian pedagogy: Classic and contemporary texts on Jesuit education from St. Ignatius to today*. Loyola Press.

Quirico, O. (2022). *Inclusive sustainability: Harmonising disability law and policy*. Springer Nature Singapore.

Woodman, B. R. (Ed.). (1989). Appreciative inquiry and sustainable value creation. In*Research in organizational change and development* (Vol. 1, pp. 129–169). JAI Press.

Wrigley, C., & Mosely, G. (2022). *Design thinking pedagogy: Facilitating innovation and impact in tertiary education*. Taylor & Francis.

PART IV

Sustainability Impact

In the fourth and final part of this book, we turn our attention to the critical aspect of sustainability: impact. We explore the challenges, dimensions, and assessment of sustainability impact, while envisioning the future of sustainable development. Our goal in this section is to provide readers with a comprehensive understanding of the importance of evaluating and maximizing the positive impact of sustainability initiatives, ensuring long-lasting and meaningful change for our planet and its inhabitants.

First, we discuss the various challenges associated with achieving meaningful and lasting impact in the realm of global sustainability. We explore the complexities of addressing complex challenges as well as the importance of addressing interconnected issues, such as social, economic, and environmental dimensions, to create lasting change (Chapter 15). Second, we delve into the multidimensional nature of sustainability impact, examining the social, economic, and environmental aspects that must be considered when designing and implementing sustainable solutions. We discuss the importance of a holistic approach and highlight the potential synergies and trade-offs that can emerge between different dimensions of sustainability. We also propose an integrated model of mapping sustainability into organizations (Chapter 16).

Third, we focus on the crucial task of assessing and measuring the impact of sustainability initiatives. We present various methodologies, tools, and indicators used to evaluate the effectiveness of sustainability efforts and to guide decision-making processes. We also discuss the challenges and limitations associated with impact assessment and offer insights on best practices for robust and accurate evaluation (Chapter 17). In our concluding chapter, we envision the future of sustainable impact, exploring emerging trends, technologies, and strategies that hold the potential to shape the way we approach sustainability in the coming years. We discuss the importance of collaboration, innovation, and continuous learning in driving impactful change and offer inspiration and guidance for individuals and organizations seeking to make a meaningful difference in the world (Chapter 18). By delving into the critical aspect of sustainability impact, this final section of the book equips readers with the knowledge and tools necessary to design, implement, and evaluate effective and impactful sustainability initiatives, paving the way for a more sustainable and just future.

CHAPTER 15

The Impact Challenge for Global Sustainability

Abstract This chapter delves into the challenges of achieving lasting and meaningful impact in the field of global sustainability. In the context of our increasingly Volatile, Uncertain, Complex, Ambiguous, and Unsustainable (VUCA(S)) world, we examine the obstacles faced by individuals, organizations, and governments as they work towards creating a sustainable future. The chapter discusses how the VUCA(S) context can exacerbate the complexities of implementing and scaling sustainability initiatives. We address the resistance to change as a significant impact challenge. Resistance can emerge from various sources, including organizational inertia, individual reluctance, and social or cultural factors. Finally, we examine wicked problems as a unique category of impact challenges in global sustainability. These complex, multifaceted, and often interrelated issues, such as climate change and social inequality, require innovative and collaborative solutions. The chapter highlights the need for interdisciplinary approaches, systems thinking, and stakeholder engagement to address wicked problems and achieve meaningful impact in the realm of sustainability.

Keywords Global sustainability · Impact challenge · VUCA(S) world · Resistance to change · Wicked problems · Systems thinking

M. Tavanti, *Developing Sustainability in Organizations*, Sustainable Development Goals Series,
https://doi.org/10.1007/978-3-031-36907-0_15

"The world is reaching the tipping point beyond which climate change may become irreversible. If this happens, we risk denying present and future generations the right to a healthy and sustainable planet – the whole of humanity stands to lose."

— (Kofi Annan, Former UN Secretary-General)

We Live in a VUCA(S) World

VUCA is an acronym that stands for Volatility, Uncertainty, Complexity, and Ambiguity. It is a concept that was first used by the US Army War College to describe the changing nature of the global security environment. Today, it is used more broadly to describe the increasingly complex and unpredictable business environment in which organizations operate. The term is used to highlight the challenges that organizations face in navigating rapidly changing market conditions, evolving customer needs, and disruptive technologies, among other factors. By understanding and adapting to the VUCA environment, organizations can develop the agility and resilience they need to succeed in today's fast-paced and unpredictable business landscape (Krämer, 2015).

Some organizations and scholars have expanded the VUCA acronym to include an "S" for "unsustainable," creating the acronym VUCA(S). This expansion recognizes the additional challenge posed by the unsustainability of many of our current social, economic, and environmental systems. The addition of the "S" highlights the urgent need for organizations to consider their impact on the planet and society as they navigate the volatile, uncertain, complex, and ambiguous business environment. To succeed in this environment, businesses and organizations must be agile, adaptable, and collaborative, and they must leverage digital technologies in a way that supports sustainability goals. This requires a systems-thinking approach with competent leaders, managers, and agencies that take into account the complexity and uncertainty of the VUCA(S) world (Ducheyne, 2017).

1. **Volatility:** The rapid pace of technological change and shifting market conditions can make it difficult for organizations to keep up with emerging sustainability trends and innovations. This also includes positive discoveries and sustainability innovations that could

help implement long-term investment plans over existing solutions. The fast-paced and ever-changing nature of a VUCA(S) world requires businesses and organizations to be agile and adaptable. Digital technologies enable companies to quickly respond to changing market conditions, customer demands, and supply chain disruptions. At the same time, sustainability challenges such as climate change, resource depletion, and social inequality require long-term planning and collaboration among multiple stakeholders.

2. **Uncertainty:** Climate change and other environmental threats create significant uncertainty around the future availability of resources, the impacts of extreme weather events, and the viability of traditional business models. Political uncertainties or other uncertainties due to conflict could also add another layer of challenges to plan and implement sustainability solutions. In a VUCA(S) world, the future is difficult to predict. This can create challenges for businesses and organizations trying to make strategic decisions about digitalization and sustainability. Digital technologies can provide real-time data and analytics that help organizations make informed decisions, but they also require investment and expertise. Sustainability challenges, such as the transition to a low-carbon economy, may require significant changes in business models and operations that are difficult to predict and plan.
3. **Complexity:** Sustainability challenges are often complex, involving interconnected systems and actors across multiple sectors and geographies. For example, addressing the issue of ocean plastic pollution requires action from governments, corporations, consumers, and NGOs, each with their own set of interests and priorities. The complexity also requires mindsets and skill sets for working across organizational boundaries, the sector's diversity, and national interests that are not easily found in leaders, managers, and innovators. Digitalization and sustainability challenges are both complex issues that require a systems-thinking approach. A VUCA(S) world adds another layer of complexity, as businesses and organizations must navigate multiple stakeholders with diverse interests and priorities. Digital technologies can help organizations manage this complexity by providing tools for collaboration, communication, and data analysis. Sustainability challenges, such as the circular economy and sustainable supply chains, require

collaboration among multiple stakeholders, including governments, NGOs, and consumers.

4. **Ambiguity:** Many sustainability challenges are characterized by ambiguity, with multiple competing interpretations and definitions of the problem. This can make it difficult to develop clear and actionable solutions. Ambiguity can also foster a conflict of interest that can emerge from implementing sustainability strategies in organizations that have to balance economic, social, and environmental pressures. In a VUCA(S) world, information is often incomplete or ambiguous, making it difficult to make informed decisions. Digital technologies can provide access to a wealth of information, but they also require careful interpretation and analysis. Sustainability challenges, such as the measurement and reporting of environmental and social impacts, can be ambiguous and require clear standards and frameworks for assessment.
5. **Unsustainability**: Unsustainable practices and systems create additional challenges for sustainability efforts, by exacerbating environmental degradation, social inequality, and economic instability. For example, unsustainable agricultural practices can lead to soil depletion, water pollution, and loss of biodiversity, while also contributing to food insecurity and poverty. Short-term solutions that do not account for sustainability impact could have long-term consequences that could affect many and unforeseeable consequences for future generations.

In "*The Ages of Globalization*," Jeffrey Sachs (2020) discusses the challenges of the Digital Age, focusing on inequality, environmental crisis, and fragility of peace. He emphasizes the need for technology to promote equity, environmental sustainability, and peaceful coexistence. The VUCA(S) world framework underlines the interconnectedness of these challenges, but as the world continues to evolve, some have argued for the need of a new framework. Some have suggested that given the current global challenges we face, the VUCA acronym may even stand for Violent, Unsustainable, Corrupt, and Anxiety-ridden (Mathur, 2022). Another author, Jamais Cascio (2023), introduced the BANI (Brittle, Anxious, Non-linear, and Incomprehensible) framework emphasizing the fragility and non-linear nature of the challenges faced in the modern world. The BANI framework acknowledges that systems can be fragile, and disruptions can lead to disproportionate consequences. It highlights the anxiety and stress caused by an unstable environment and recognizes that situations can often be too complex to fully comprehend. By shifting the focus from uncertainty to fragility and non-linearity, BANI provides an updated perspective on the challenges faced in today's rapidly changing world. Either with the BANI or the VUCA(S) framework, the challenges persist, and to address today's sustainability issues, societies must embrace agility, resilience, and a commitment to equitable outcomes, overcoming resistance from those maintaining the status quo (Tindall et al., 2022).

Resistance to Change as Impact Challenges

The resistance to change is not something new. It was very evident in the American industrial practice of adding lead to gasoline and the effort to stop using it. The use of lead in gasoline was considered normal in the past because it was believed to improve the performance of automobile engines by preventing engine knock or "pinging." In the early twentieth century, when gasoline engines were first becoming popular, engine knock was a common problem that limited the performance of engines. Adding lead to gasoline was seen as a solution to this problem, and it became widely adopted by the automotive industry. In the 1960s, American geochemist Clair Cameron Patterson studied the effects of lead in gasoline. He discovered that lead was a dangerous toxin and that the use of lead in gasoline posed a significant health risk to humans. Patterson's research also showed that lead contamination was not only a public health problem but also an environmental issue. His work showed that lead was accumulating in the environment, including in human bodies, and that it was causing serious health problems, particularly in children. He faced serious retaliation from the lead and gas industries who tried to discredit his findings (Desmond, 2017). In the end, Clair Cameron Patterson's research led to the creation of the Clean Air Act in 1970 and the eventual removal of lead from gasoline in the United States in 1996.

The resistance to change away from leaded gasoline was largely driven by economic factors. The lead industry had invested heavily in the production of lead additives for gasoline, and was resistant to changes that could impact their profits. The oil companies, which were major customers of the lead industry, were also resistant to change because they had significant investments in infrastructure that was designed to handle leaded gasoline. Additionally, there was skepticism about the health risks associated with leaded gasoline, despite the mounting evidence presented by researchers like Patterson. The lead industry and its supporters argued that the health risks were overstated and that there was insufficient evidence to justify a change away from leaded gasoline. It took several decades of research, public pressure, and regulatory action before the use of lead in gasoline was finally phased out. Today, we know that lead is a potent neurotoxin that can cause a wide range of health problems, especially in children.

We see a similar corporate and political opposition to change towards ESG investments and regulatory frameworks for environmental, social, and governance responsibility. Some conservative groups view ESG investing as a threat to their political or economic interests and have been actively opposing the integration of ESG metrics in addition to traditional financial metrics. Conservative leaders and parties have raised concerns about the potential impacts of ESG on the fossil fuel industry and on the ability of money managers to prioritize profits for their clients. Some conservatives have also expressed skepticism about the motivations behind ESG investing, suggesting that it may be driven by political or ideological concerns rather than sound financial principles (Aronoff, 2023).

The Securities and Exchange Commission (SEC) has been actively involved in developing regulations and guidelines related to ESG investing. In recent years, the SEC has taken a number of steps to promote greater transparency and disclosure of ESG-related risks and opportunities for investors. One of the key developments in this area was the SEC's issuance of interpretive guidance in 2010 on climate change disclosure. The guidance clarified that companies must consider the potential impact of climate change on their businesses and disclose material risks to investors. This guidance has been seen as an important step towards integrating ESG considerations into financial reporting and analysis. More recently, the SEC has proposed new rules that would require companies to disclose information about their human capital management practices, including issues related to diversity, equity, and inclusion. The SEC has also proposed rules that would require companies to disclose their exposure to climate-related risks and the potential impact of those risks on their businesses.

While some stakeholders have welcomed these proposals as a step towards greater transparency and accountability, others have expressed concerns about the costs and burdens of complying with new regulations. The SEC has indicated that it is committed to strike a balance between promoting ESG disclosure and avoid unnecessary regulatory burdens on companies. Overall, the SEC's efforts to develop regulations and guidelines related to ESG reflect a growing recognition that environmental, social, and governance factors are important considerations for investors and businesses alike. As such, it is likely that the SEC will continue to play an important role in shaping the future of ESG investing and reporting. Ultimately, the debate over ESG is likely to continue as investors, regulators, and policymakers grapple with the challenges and opportunities of integrating social and environmental considerations into financial decision-making. As with any complex issue, it is important to weigh the evidence and consider multiple perspectives in order to arrive at informed and effective solutions.

Wicked Problems as Impact Challenges

The Harvard Business Review article *Wicked-Problem Solvers: Lessons from Successful Cross-Industry Teams* by Amy C. Edmondson (2016) presents how cross-industry teams can come together to solve complex, "wicked" problems that cannot be solved by any one organization or sector alone. The study highlights that leaders of cross-industry teams must balance the need for clarity of purpose with the potential for shifting goals, which can be a common feature of complex, "wicked" problems encountered in the sustainability impact challenges. These wicked problems cannot be solved by any one organization or sector alone. They also require a capacity to operate across multiple stakeholders, communities, and nations. Impactful leadership for wicked sustainability challenges needs to use a balanced approach with a variety of strategies. For instance, from removing barriers (enabling) to channeling vision and energy (motivational) and from focusing on systems of interactions (technical) to focusing on emotions and communication (psychological). This study demonstrates the need to balance an adaptable vision while also fostering an inclusive, collaborative, and empowering ecosystem.

Sustainability: A Wicked Problem Needing New Perspectives by Carl Brønn and Peggy Simcic Brønn (2018) deepens the understanding of impact challenges tackling wicked sustainability problems. The authors offer some perspectives that highlight the challenges and needed considerations for leaders and organizations to foster impactful solutions. First, they argue that sustainability is a wicked problem, meaning that it is complex, interconnected, and difficult to solve due to the numerous social, economic, and environmental factors involved. Second, they argue traditional problem-solving approaches are inadequate for tackling wicked problems like sustainability. These approaches tend to focus on identifying and solving individual problems, rather than addressing the underlying systemic issues that contribute to sustainability challenges. Third, they argue that new perspectives and approaches are needed to address sustainability challenges. They suggest that a more holistic and integrated approach is necessary, one that considers the interconnectedness of social, economic, and environmental factors and recognizes the complexity of sustainability challenges. Fourth, they argue that collaboration is essential for addressing sustainability challenges. They suggest that collaborative approaches that bring together diverse stakeholders and perspectives are more likely to lead to innovative and effective solutions. Fifth, they argue that leadership is crucial for addressing sustainability challenges. They suggest that leaders need to take a long-term perspective, have the ability to take risks and experiment with new approaches, and are able to inspire and motivate others to take action. In other words, impactful solutions for the complex challenges of sustainability and their wicked problems require new perspectives and approaches that include embracing collaboration, adopting a more holistic approach, and demonstrating strong leadership.

Therefore, sustainability impact challenges present wicked problems requiring new leadership mindsets and skill sets. On the one hand, leaders need to have a clear and compelling vision for the team's mission and goals. This clarity can help to align team members from different industries and backgrounds and ensure that everyone is working towards the same objective. In the context of wicked problems, goals may need to evolve over time as new information is uncovered, unexpected challenges arise, or the team learns more about the problem they are trying to solve. To navigate this tension, sustainability impactful leaders need to be able to communicate the team's purpose and goals effectively while also remaining flexible and adaptable in the face of uncertainty. This requires strong communication skills, an ability to balance competing priorities, and a willingness to engage in ongoing study and reflection. Managing this tension between clarity of purpose and potentially shifting goals in sustainability challenges requires leaders, managers, and innovators to pivot towards principle-based leadership, stakeholder-inclusive practices, and effective, accountable, and transparent communication skills. Sustainability leaders who have tackled these challenges demonstrate the need for adaptability, flexibility, open-mindedness, perseverance, and humility, while also being fiercely determined and focused on achieving their sustainability vision.

Adaptive Strategies for Impact Challenges

Adaptive strategies are crucial for overcoming impact challenges in the realm of sustainability. They have been used by many organizations to find adaptive solutions to climate-related systemic challenges (Ganpat & Isaac, 2016). These strategies involve flexibility, resilience, and continuous learning, allowing individuals and organizations to adjust their approaches as circumstances change or new information becomes available. Adaptive strategies help organizations navigate the complexities and uncertainties of the VUCA(S) world and address wicked problems more effectively. Effective communication is an example of adaptive strategies. Open and transparent communication with stakeholders, including employees, customers, partners, and communities, can foster trust, collaboration, and better decision-making. By keeping stakeholders informed and involving them in the process, organizations can ensure their sustainability initiatives are well-understood and supported. Also, actively involving relevant stakeholders in the planning, implementation, and evaluation of sustainability initiatives helps ensure that these efforts are well-informed, context-sensitive, and more likely to succeed. Stakeholder engagement helps identify potential barriers, opportunities, and synergies that can enhance the impact of sustainability efforts. Change management can also be an impactful and adaptive strategy. By embedding change management principles into sustainability initiatives, organizations can minimize resistance, address unforeseen challenges, and maximize the positive impact of their efforts. This may involve considering multiple possible future scenarios which can help organizations identify potential risks and opportunities and develop contingency plans. This forward-looking approach enables organizations to better anticipate and adapt to changes in the external environment, ensuring their sustainability initiatives remain effective and relevant.

The United Nations Environment Programme (UNEP) has employed various adaptive strategies, such as collaborating with governments, businesses, and civil society to develop and implement policies and practices that promote sustainability. UNEP also supports continuous learning and capacity building, enabling countries to adapt and improve their sustainability efforts over time. The Ellen MacArthur Foundation, as we have mentioned earlier, focuses on accelerating the transition to a circular economy, which is a systemic response to the wicked problem of resource depletion and waste generation. By working with businesses, governments, and academia, the foundation develops and promotes circular economy principles, practices, and policies that address interconnected environmental and social challenges. The Global Footprint Network is another inspiring example of an organization that has successfully employed adaptive strategies to address complex and systemic sustainability challenges. This organization works to measure and communicate the ecological impact of human activities by calculating the Ecological Footprint. This consists of the complex interdependencies between resource use, waste generation, and ecosystem health. By providing data and insights, the Global Footprint Network enables businesses, governments, and individuals to make informed decisions and develop systemic solutions for a more sustainable future. These are just a few examples of organizations that demonstrate how adaptive and systemic approaches can be applied to address wicked problems in sustainability by considering the complex interdependencies between environmental, social, and economic factors, and by promoting holistic, integrated solutions.

Key Takeaways

1. **VUCA(S) world:** The volatile, uncertain, complex, ambiguous, and unsustainable nature of today's world presents unique challenges for global sustainability efforts. Adapting to this context requires resilience and flexibility in addressing sustainability issues.
2. **Resistance to change:** Achieving impactful global sustainability can be hindered by resistance from various sources, such as organizational inertia, individual reluctance, and social or cultural factors. Overcoming resistance is vital to ensuring the successful implementation of sustainability initiatives.
3. **Wicked problems:** Complex, multifaceted, and interrelated issues, such as climate change and social inequality, are considered wicked problems that pose significant impact challenges in global sustainability. These problems require innovative and collaborative solutions.
4. **Adaptive strategies:** To overcome impact challenges, adaptive strategies are necessary, including effective communication, stakeholder engagement, and change management. These strategies help to facilitate the acceptance and implementation of sustainability efforts.

References

Aronoff, K. (2023). The Right Has It In for Woke Investors. The Only Problem? They Don't Exist [Online]. *The New Republic*. Available at https://newrepublic.com/article/170229/right-woke-investors-problem-dont-exist. Accessed 18 March 2023.

Brønn, C., & Brønn, P. C. (2018). Sustainability: A wicked problem needing new perspectives. In H. Borland et al. (Eds.), *Business strategies for sustainability* (Chapter 1). United Kingdom: Taylor & Francis.

Cascio, J. (2023). Jamais Cascio | Speaker | TED [Online]. Ted.com. Available at https://www.ted.com/speakers/jamais_cascio. Accessed 17 March 2023.

Desmond, K. (2017). *Planet savers: 301 extraordinary environmentalists*. Taylor & Francis.

Ducheyne, D. (2017). *Sustainable leadership: How to lead in a VUCA world*. Die Keure Publishing.

Edmondson, A. C. (2016). Wicked-problem solvers: Lessons from successful cross-industry teams. *Harvard Business Review, 94*(6), 52–59.

Krämer, A. (2015). *Managing in a VUCA world*. Springer International Publishing.

Mathur, A. (2022). The demands of ethical learning and character development in our changing times. In A. Bose et al. (Eds.), *Learning without Burden: Where are we a quarter century after the Yash Pal Committee Report* (Chapter 9). Taylor & Francis.

Sachs, J. (2020). *The ages of globalization: Geography, technology, and institutions*. Columbia University Press.

Tindall, T. B., et al. (2022). *Handbook of anti-environmentalism*. Edward Elgar Publishing.

Wayne Ganpat, W., & Isaac, W. P. (2016). *Environmental sustainability and climate change adaptation strategies*. IGI Global.

CHAPTER 16

The Dimensions of Sustainability Impact

Abstract This chapter delves into the dimensions of sustainability impact and presents an integrated model to comprehensively assess and implement sustainability initiatives within organizations. It highlights the role of well-being dimensions in sustainability and emphasizes the importance of collective impact for achieving sustainable goals. The chapter also discusses the integration of sustainability impact within organizations and presents a process for mapping and integrating the SDGs. Lastly, it explores the connection between sustainability impact and collective well-being, demonstrating how addressing various dimensions of sustainability can lead to positive outcomes for both individuals and the environment.

Keywords Well-being dimensions · Collective impact · Organizational integration · Collective well-being

> *"You cannot get through a single day without having an impact on the world around you. What you do makes a difference, and you have to decide what kind of difference you want to make."*
>
> —Dr. Jane Goodall, Ethologist, Conservationist, Humanitarian

M. Tavanti, *Developing Sustainability in Organizations*, Sustainable Development Goals Series,
https://doi.org/10.1007/978-3-031-36907-0_16

Integrated Model for Sustainability Impact

What are the dimensions we need to consider in order to foster sustainable impact as solutions to world challenges? Sustainability impact is the assessment of the positive or negative effects of human activities on the environment, social systems, and economic systems, both in the present and for future generations. The notion of *positive sustainable impact* in society and organizations is helpful to clarify that we need a multifaceted approach that addresses interconnections and trade-offs of environmental, social, and economic sustainability aspects through a systematic approach and consideration of needs and benefits across contexts, communities, and regions. Positive sustainability impact is a state of collective well-being where human activities are in harmony with the environment, society, and the economy, resulting in long-term benefits for all. We need to further study international and cross-cultural perspectives on the connections of well-being with sustainability in organizational leadership (Di Fabio, 2022). There are several dimensions of positive sustainability impact that are essential for achieving this state:

1. **Environmental dimension:** This refers to the positive impact of human activities on the natural environment. It includes reducing greenhouse gas emissions, conserving biodiversity and ecosystems, and promoting sustainable use of natural resources.
2. **Social dimension:** This refers to the positive impact of human activities on social systems. It includes promoting social equity, improving access to education, healthcare, and basic services, and ensuring that communities are resilient and able to adapt to environmental and social challenges.
3. **Economic dimension:** This refers to the positive impact of human activities on the economy. It includes promoting sustainable economic growth, creating jobs and opportunities for people, and ensuring that economic activities do not harm the environment or society.
4. **Governance dimension:** This refers to the positive impact of governance structures on sustainability. It includes promoting transparency, accountability, and participation in decision-making processes, ensuring that policies and regulations are designed to promote sustainability, and fostering cooperation and collaboration among stakeholders.

5. **Health dimension:** This refers to the positive impact of human activities on the health and well-being of individuals and communities. It includes promoting healthy lifestyles, improving access to healthcare and medical resources, and reducing exposure to harmful pollutants and toxins.
6. **Cultural dimension:** This refers to the positive impact of human activities on cultural diversity, heritage, and identity. It includes promoting respect for cultural differences, preserving cultural artifacts and traditions, and supporting the participation of diverse communities in decision-making processes.
7. **Technological dimension:** This refers to the positive impact of technology on sustainability. It includes promoting the development and adoption of sustainable technologies, such as renewable energy, energy-efficient buildings, and smart transportation systems.
8. **Ethical dimension:** This refers to the positive impact of human activities on ethical principles and values, such as justice, equity, and human rights. It includes promoting ethical business practices, fair trade, and social responsibility.
9. **Resilience dimension:** This refers to the positive impact of human activities on the ability of communities and ecosystems to adapt to changing environmental and social conditions. It includes promoting sustainable management of natural resources, disaster preparedness and response, and social safety nets.

Overall, these dimensions of positive sustainability impact are interconnected and mutually reinforcing. Achieving positive sustainability impact requires a comprehensive and integrated approach that considers these dimensions in combination with the environmental, social, economic, and governance dimensions. Positive sustainability impact requires a balance between these dimensions that support sustainable development. Achieving positive sustainability impact is essential for ensuring that human activities contribute to the well-being of current and future generations.

Well-Being Dimensions in Sustainability

Well-being and sustainability are interconnected concepts, and when addressing them, it is essential to consider multiple dimensions. There are several major publications that identify and measure the sustainability impact in relation to well-being. These span various disciplines and approaches including the *Sustainable Development Goals Report* (UN, 2022), the *Human Development Report* presenting the Human Development Index (HDI) overall well-being of nations based on income, education, and life expectancy in relation to inequality, climate change, and the SDGs (UNDP, 2022), the *Beyond GDP: Measuring What Counts for Economic and Social Performance* (OECD, 2018), by the Organization for Economic Co-operation and Development (OECD, 2018), the *World Happiness Report* (SDS, 2022), the *Planetary Health: Safeguarding Human Health in the Anthropocene Epoch* (Lancet, 2015), and *The Economics of Ecosystems and Biodiversity* (UNEP, 2022). These publications and annual reports represent a diverse range of perspectives and approaches to understanding the multiple dimensions of well-being in relation to sustainability. They provide valuable insights into the challenges and opportunities associated with promoting human well-being in the context of sustainable development. But what are these well-being dimensions? There is no one comprehensive list. The official definition of well-being from the World Health Organization (WHO) shows these multiple dimensions in relation to purpose and in connection to sustainability: *"Well-being encompasses quality of life and the ability of people and societies to contribute to the world with a sense of meaning and purpose. Focusing on well-being supports the tracking of the equitable distribution of resources, overall thriving and sustainability"* (WHO, 2023). This definition emphasizes the multidimensional nature of well-being, recognizing both subjective experiences and objective life circumstances. It highlights the importance of various factors, including emotional and cognitive aspects, social relationships, basic needs, resilience, and access to resources and opportunities in contributing to overall well-being.

We identify five core and five correlated dimensions to understanding well-being in its relation to sustainability impact. The core dimensions include:

1. **Social well-being:** This dimension focuses on the quality of relationships, social cohesion, and equity among individuals and communities. In the context of sustainability, it involves promoting social inclusion, reducing inequalities, and ensuring access to basic needs such as education, healthcare, and social support.
2. **Economic well-being:** Economic well-being refers to the material aspects of life, including income, employment, financial security, and economic opportunities. Sustainable economic well-being involves creating a stable and prosperous economy that fosters equitable wealth distribution, provides decent work opportunities, and promotes responsible consumption and production.
3. **Environmental well-being:** Environmental well-being is centered around maintaining the health and integrity of ecosystems, biodiversity, and natural resources. In the context of sustainability, this dimension involves minimizing environmental degradation, reducing waste and pollution, addressing climate change, and preserving ecosystems and biodiversity for future generations.
4. **Physical well-being:** Physical well-being is related to personal health and the conditions in which people live and work. Sustainable physical well-being involves ensuring access to clean air, water, and sanitation, providing safe and healthy living and working environments, and promoting healthy lifestyles that reduce the burden of non-communicable diseases.
5. **Psychological well-being:** This dimension refers to mental health, emotional stability, and personal growth. Sustainable psychological well-being involves fostering resilience, reducing stress, promoting mental health awareness and support, and encouraging personal growth and self-awareness.

The correlated dimensions which are no less important and connected to the core dimension include:

6. **Cultural well-being:** Cultural well-being encompasses aspects such as cultural diversity, heritage, and identity. In the context of sustainability, this dimension involves preserving and promoting cultural diversity, respecting the rights and traditions of Indigenous communities, and fostering intercultural understanding and appreciation.

7. **Political well-being:** Political well-being involves the ability to participate in and influence political processes and decision-making. It includes aspects such as political rights, freedom of expression, and access to information. Political well-being can contribute to sustainable development by empowering individuals and communities to advocate for policies and actions that promote social, economic, and environmental sustainability.
8. **Spiritual well-being:** Spiritual well-being relates to a sense of purpose, meaning, and connection to something greater than oneself. It may involve religious beliefs, personal values, or a general sense of spirituality. This dimension can contribute to overall well-being by providing individuals with a sense of direction, inner peace, and resilience in the face of adversity.
9. **Intellectual well-being:** Intellectual well-being refers to the ability to engage in critical thinking, problem-solving, and continuous learning. It involves cognitive development, curiosity, and the pursuit of knowledge. Intellectual well-being contributes to personal growth and adaptability, which can be essential in navigating the complexities of modern life and sustainability challenges.
10. **Emotional well-being:** Emotional well-being encompasses the ability to understand, express, and manage emotions effectively. This dimension includes emotional intelligence, self-awareness, and emotional regulation. Emotional well-being is crucial for building resilience, maintaining healthy relationships, and coping with stress and adversity.

Addressing these dimensions of well-being in relation to sustainability dimensions requires a holistic and integrated approach that considers the complex interdependencies between environmental, social, economic, and individual factors. These multifaceted dimensions of well-being express the values-based integrated understanding of human life in the context of personal and interpersonal, organizational and institutional, economic and social, and environmental and natural relations that make up our sustainable, flourishing, and thriving existence. This comprehensive list of well-being dimensions provides a more nuanced understanding of the factors that contribute to overall well-being beyond simply the social, environmental, and economic dimensions generally associated with sustainability. They are indicative of the more inclusive and holistic approach in which we should target sustainability impact, realistically address gaps, and measure its progress towards human development.

Collective Impact for Sustainability

Understanding sustainability impact with its multidimensional well-being dimensions requires comprehensive and multifaceted frameworks. The notion of *collective impact* is one of these helpful frameworks. It recognizes that we need a collaborative approach to problem-solving and social change for complex social problems, such as poverty, inequality, and environmental degradation. This approach requires coordinated efforts and collaboration across sectors and disciplines to achieve lasting and meaningful impact. It involves multiple organizations and stakeholders working together towards a shared goal.

Collective impact requires a shared agenda and shared vision of what multiple stakeholders want to achieve. It also requires that stakeholders agree on a set of shared measurements and collaborative activities to reinforce each other's work to maximize impact. The sustainability impact approach uses these dimensions along with regular and open communication among stakeholders, and coordinating bureaucratic structures and champions to facilitate the impact process, provide coordination and support, and ensure accountability.

Collective impact can play a crucial role in achieving sustainability impact, as it enables stakeholders to work together towards a shared vision of sustainable development. By bringing together different actors, collective impact initiatives can help identify and address complex environmental and social challenges, such as climate change, biodiversity loss, and poverty that require coordinated action and collaboration across sectors. For example, a collective impact initiative focused on sustainable agriculture might bring together farmers, scientists, food processors, retailers, consumers, and environmental organizations to work towards a shared vision of sustainable food production and consumption. Through this collaborative effort, they could identify and address environmental and social issues associated with food production, such as water use, soil health, and labor conditions, while also promoting economic development and social equity in the agricultural sector. In other words, we need an integrated model for sustainable impact that includes key and essential elements such as:

1. **Strong leadership and governance:** Effective leadership and governance are necessary to set ambitious sustainability goals, establish policies and regulations that support sustainable development, and create a productive environment for sustainable practices.
2. **Collaboration and stakeholder engagement:** Achieving a sustainable society requires the active participation and engagement of different stakeholders, such as government, business, civil society, and communities. Collaboration and stakeholder engagement are necessary to align goals and priorities, share knowledge and expertise, and create collective action.
3. **Sustainable business practices:** Businesses play a critical role in shaping the economy and have a significant impact on society and the environment. Adopting sustainable business practices such as reducing resource consumption, improving energy efficiency, and investing in renewable energy can help promote sustainable development.
4. **Investment in sustainable infrastructure:** Developing sustainable infrastructure such as clean energy systems, public transportation, and green buildings is essential for promoting sustainable development and creating a more resilient society.
5. **Education and awareness:** Sustainability impact requires education and awareness-raising promoting sustainable behavior and decision-making. This includes educating the public about the importance of sustainability and the actions they can take to promote it, as well as training professionals and workers in sustainable practices.
6. **Innovation and research:** Sustainability impact requires constant innovation and research to develop new technologies, products, and systems that are more sustainable, efficient and resilient.
7. **Monitoring and evaluation:** Sustainability impact should be measured and evaluated regularly; this helps to track progress, identify areas for improvement, and make adjustments as necessary.

These are important solutions and priorities for promoting an integrated and collective impact of sustainability. In addition, the dimensions of positive collective impact are to be considered in relation to a holistic and integrated approach for understanding the multifaceted nature of sustainability and well-being. Promoting a positive sustainability impact requires a holistic and integrated approach because sustainability is a complex and multifaceted concept that involves interdependent economic, social, and environmental factors. A holistic approach recognizes the interconnectedness of these factors and considers their interdependence when measuring sustainability impact. An integrated approach is necessary because sustainability impacts are often cross-cutting and can affect multiple sectors and stakeholders. An integrated approach brings together diverse perspectives and expertise from different disciplines, sectors, and stakeholders to develop a comprehensive understanding of sustainability impact.

Sustainability Impact and Organizational Integration

Integrating sustainability goals (such as the SDGs) with the organization's priorities can promote sustainability impact at various levels. Through a properly managed process expressed in Fig. 16.1, organizations can align their operations, strategies, and values with global sustainability objectives. By integrating the SDGs into their business practices, organizations can contribute to the global effort to address social, economic, and environmental challenges. By embedding sustainability principles into their core values and operations, organizations can create value not only for their stakeholders but also for society as a whole. This holistic approach to business allows organizations to consider the well-being of people, planet, and profit simultaneously. The stages one through five reflect the recommendations of the SDG Compass (2015), a guide developed by the GRI and the WBCSD to help organizations integrate sustainability impact by aligning organizational priorities, strategies, operations, and reporting with the SDGs (Fig. 16.2).

Leadership commitment, education and training, and continuous improvement are strategically important for organizations. These five stages are critical in the organizations' integration of the SDGs.

1. **Understanding the SDGs:** This step involves raising awareness and understanding the SDGs, their targets, and their relevance to the organization. It is crucial for organizations to comprehend the global context, recognize their role in achieving the SDGs, and identify areas where they can make the most significant impact.
2. **Defining priorities**: Organizations should assess their impacts (both positive and negative) on the SDGs and identify priority areas for action. By understanding which SDGs are most relevant to

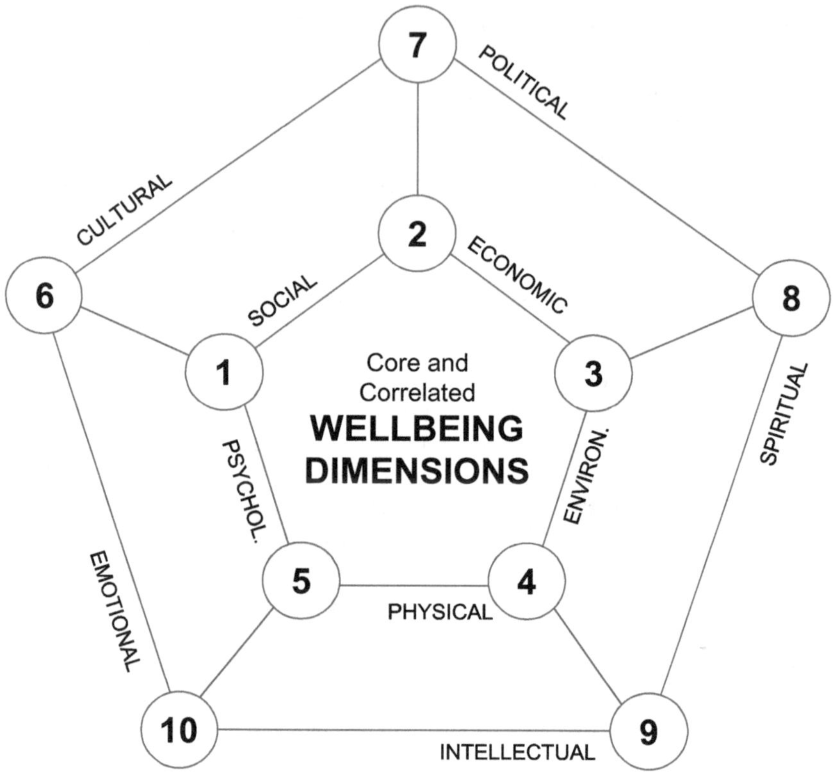

Fig. 16.1 Core-correlated dimensions of well-being in sustainability

their operations and stakeholders, businesses can focus their efforts and resources on areas where they can make the most meaningful contributions.

3. **Setting goals:** After identifying priorities, organizations should set Specific, Measurable, Achievable, Relevant, and Time-bound (SMART) goals that align with the SDGs. Setting clear objectives helps organizations develop targeted strategies and action plans to achieve their sustainability goals and contribute to the SDGs.
4. **Integrating:** Organizations should integrate the SDGs and their sustainability goals into their core business operations, decision-making processes, and company culture. This integration involves

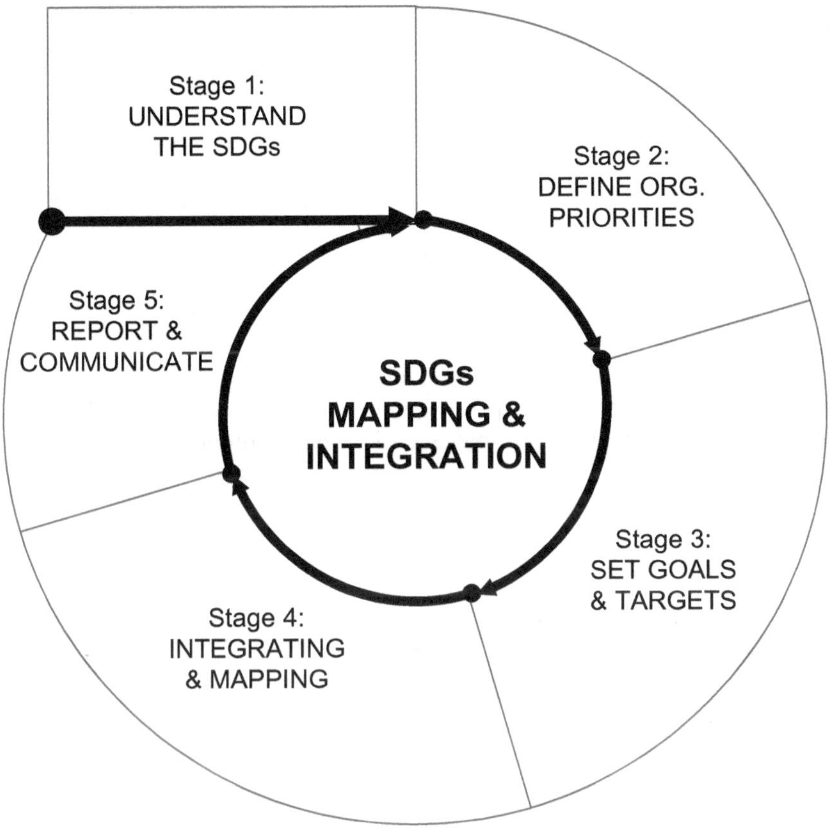

Fig. 16.2 Process for mapping and integrating SDGs

embedding sustainability across all levels of the organization, from senior management to frontline employees, and aligning it with the organization's values, strategies, and performance management systems.

5. **Reporting and communicating:** Organizations should regularly report on their progress towards achieving their sustainability goals and contributing to the SDGs. Transparent and consistent reporting helps businesses demonstrate their commitment to sustainability, maintain stakeholder trust, and identify areas for improvement.

By following these steps, organizations can align their operations with the SDGs, contribute to global sustainability efforts, enhance their competitive advantage, and contribute to positive sustainability impact with measurable and coherent practices.

Sustainability Impact for Collective Well-Being

The successful integration of sustainability goals within organizations fosters the sense of collective well-being which reflects many of the well-being dimensions mentioned above. Collective well-being is a comprehensive concept that takes into account the overall welfare of individuals, organizations, communities, society, and the environment, encompassing various interconnected dimensions such as physical and mental health, social connectedness, economic security, environmental sustainability, education, cultural diversity, and good governance. These dimensions are interdependent, and their mutual reinforcement is vital for achieving sustainable outcomes. By adopting a holistic approach which considers these multiple dimensions, organizations can better understand the complexities of positive sustainability impact and work towards creating more resilient and sustainable communities. This integrated approach ensures that the well-being of individuals and the planet are prioritized, ultimately contributing to a brighter and more sustainable future for all.

Collective well-being is a notion that refers to the overall well-being of a group of people or a community and encompasses a range of dimensions that are interconnected and interdependent. Some of the dimensions of collective well-being include:

1. **Physical health:** This dimension refers to the physical well-being of individuals and communities, including access to healthcare services, nutrition, exercise, and safe living conditions.
2. **Mental health:** This dimension refers to the mental and emotional well-being of individuals and communities, including access to mental healthcare services, stress management, and social support.
3. **Social connectedness:** This dimension refers to the sense of belonging and connectedness that individuals and communities feel towards each other. It includes social networks, social cohesion, and community participation.

4. **Economic security**: This dimension refers to the economic well-being of individuals and communities, including access to employment, adequate income, and social safety nets.
5. **Environmental sustainability**: This dimension refers to the health and well-being of the natural environment and its ability to support human life. It includes the sustainable use of natural resources, protection of biodiversity, and addressing climate change.
6. **Education and learning:** This dimension refers to the access to education and opportunities for lifelong learning. It includes access to quality education, skill-building, and training.
7. **Cultural diversity and expression:** This dimension refers to the preservation and promotion of cultural diversity, heritage, and identity. It includes respect for cultural differences, protection of cultural artifacts and traditions, and support for cultural expression.
8. **Good governance:** This dimension refers to the effective and transparent management of public resources, including policies and institutions that promote democracy, human rights, and the rule of law.

These dimensions of collective well-being are interdependent and mutually reinforcing. Achieving collective well-being requires a comprehensive and integrated approach that considers all of these dimensions together. The dimensions of positive sustainability impact can benefit from other models such as collective well-being and collective impact by providing complementary perspectives and approaches that can help to achieve more comprehensive and sustainable outcomes. By prioritizing these integrated dimensions, we can work towards creating more resilient and sustainable communities that promote the overall well-being of individuals and the planet.

Key Takeaways

1. An integrated model for sustainability impact combines various dimensions of well-being, including physical, mental, social, economic, environmental, and cultural aspects, to provide a comprehensive approach for achieving sustainable outcomes.

2. The well-being dimensions in sustainability emphasize the importance of considering the welfare of individuals and communities when implementing sustainable initiatives, ensuring a more holistic and balanced approach.
3. Collective impact for sustainability highlights the need for collaboration and cooperation between various stakeholders, including businesses, governments, and civil society, to effectively address and overcome sustainability challenges.
4. Integrating sustainability impact within organizations requires a systematic approach that aligns organizational strategies, policies, and practices with the SDGs, ensuring that sustainability becomes an integral part of decision-making processes.
5. Focusing on sustainability impact for collective well-being ensures that sustainable initiatives contribute to the overall welfare of individuals, communities, and the environment, ultimately leading to more resilient and sustainable societies.

References

Di Fabio, A. (2022). *Cross-cultural Perspectives on Well-Being and Sustainability in Organizations*. Springer International Publishing.

Lancet. (2015). Safeguarding human health in the Anthropocene epoch: report of The Rockefeller Foundation–Lancet Commission on planetary health. *The Lancet, 386*(10007), 1973–2028. Available at https://www.thelancet.com/journals/lancet/article/PIIS0140-6736(15)60901-1/fulltext. Accessed 19 March 2023.

OECD. (2018). *Beyond GDP: Measuring what counts for economic and social performance*. Available at https://www.oecd.org/social/beyond-gdp-9789264307292-en.htm. Accessed 19 March 2023.

SDS. (2022). *World Happiness Report 2022*. Available at https://worldhappiness.report/. Accessed 19 March 2023.

UN. (2022). *The Sustainable Development Goals Report 2022*. Un.org. Available at https://unstats.un.org/sdgs/report/2022/. Accessed 19 March 2023.

UNDP. (2022). *Human Development Reports*. Available at: https://hdr.undp.org/. Accessed 19 March 2023.

UNEP. (2022). *The economics of ecosystems and biodiversity*. Available at https://teebweb.org/. Accessed 19 March 2023.

WHO. (2023). *Promoting well-being*. Available at https://www.who.int/activities/promoting-well-being#:~:text=Well%2Dbeing%20encompasses%20quality%20of,resources%2C%20overall%20thriving%20and%20sustainability. Accessed 19 March 2023.

CHAPTER 17

Assessing and Measuring Sustainability Impact

Abstract This chapter provides a comprehensive overview of the various tools and frameworks available for assessing and measuring sustainability impact. The complexity of sustainability measurement and standards can be overwhelming for companies and organizations entering this domain. To address this challenge, the chapter systematically categorizes these tools and frameworks into basic, standard, and advanced classifications. By providing a systematic overview of the various sustainability impact measurement tools and frameworks, this chapter equips companies and organizations with the knowledge and resources needed to initiate or enhance their sustainability measurement and accounting processes.

Keywords Life Cycle Assessment · Environmental Management Systems · Social Impact Assessment · Global Reporting Initiative · Sustainability Accounting · ISO Standards

> Measure what is measurable And make measurable what is not so.
>
> —Galileo Galilei a member of the *Academia dei Lincei* located in Villa Farnesina Where in 1968 They established *the Club of Rome*

M. Tavanti, *Developing Sustainability in Organizations*, Sustainable Development Goals Series,
https://doi.org/10.1007/978-3-031-36907-0_17

The phrase "you cannot change what you cannot measure," often attributed to management consultant Peter Drucker, underscores the importance of quantifying and assessing various aspects of sustainability in order to drive meaningful change. Sustainable impact measurements require comprehensive, accurate, and transparent metrics that can effectively capture the progress and performance of sustainability initiatives.

Here is a summary of tools and frameworks from basic, standard, and advanced classifications to introduce the concepts of sustainability impact measurements.

The Basics of Sustainability Impact Measurements

The Basics of Sustainability Impact Measurements section introduces fundamental metrics and tools such as Carbon footprint and GHG measurements, LCA and SLCA Social Life Cycle Assessments, TBL Triple Bottom Line Accounting, DJSI World Index and ESG Metrics, Environmental Management Systems (EMS), and Social Impact Assessment (SIA).

1. **Carbon footprint and GHG measurements**: Carbon footprint is a measure of the total greenhouse gas (GHG) emissions caused by an individual, organization, product, or event. It is expressed in units of carbon dioxide equivalents (CO2e), which is a standardized unit used to compare the impact of different greenhouse gasses based on their global warming potential. The measurement may occur with online tools that estimate the carbon footprint of an individual or organization based on their activities or operations. Carbon calculators typically use data on energy consumption, transportation, waste, and other factors to estimate carbon emissions. Sometimes, the Life Cycle Assessment (LCA) software allows organizations to evaluate the environmental impacts of a product or service over its entire life cycle, including carbon emissions. LCA software can help identify opportunities for reducing emissions and improving the environmental performance of a product or service. Other GHG inventory software is used to track and report on an organization's GHG emissions. It can help organizations measure and manage their emissions, set reduction targets, and report on progress.

Many organizations incorporate these basic measurements in their sustainability reporting software to track and report on their sustainability performance that includes carbon emissions. This software can help organizations gather and analyze data, track progress towards sustainability goals, and report on their sustainability performance to stakeholders. In some cases, organizations may work with expert consultants who have specialized knowledge and experience in carbon footprint measurement. These consultants can help organizations identify opportunities for emissions reductions and provide guidance on best practices for sustainability reporting.

In addition to carbon footprint, there are other GHG measurements that are commonly used to assess and manage climate change risks. Other tools often used for GHG emission measurements include Greenhouse Gas Inventory that includes emissions from direct sources (e.g., combustion of fuels) and indirect sources (e.g., electricity consumption). It is used to identify areas where emissions can be reduced and track progress over time. Carbon offsetting is a common practice used with these measurements. The organization may opt to invest in projects that reduce GHG emissions to offset one's own emissions. For example, an organization may purchase carbon credits from a renewable energy project to offset their emissions from operations. Science-based Targets (SBTs) are also commonly associated with these measurements as the GHG reduction targets are aligned with the latest climate science and designed to limit global warming to a maximum of 1.5°C above pre-industrial levels. SBTs are used by organizations to set ambitious emissions reduction goals and demonstrate leadership in addressing climate change.

2. **LCA and SLCA Social Life Cycle Assessments:** Life Cycle Assessment (LCA) is a method for evaluating the environmental impacts of a product or service throughout its entire life cycle, from the extraction of raw materials to the disposal of the product at the end of its life. Social Life Cycle Assessment (SLCA) is an extension of LCA which considers the social impacts of a product or service throughout its life cycle, such as labor rights, human rights, health and safety, and community impacts. While LCA and SLCA are both tools used to assess the sustainability impact of products or services, they focus on different aspects of sustainability and use different methodologies.

LCA focuses on environmental impacts, while SLCA assesses social impacts. LCA assesses the environmental impacts of a product or service over its entire life cycle, from raw material extraction to end-of-life disposal. In contrast, SLCA assesses the social impacts of a product or service across its entire life cycle, including impacts on workers, communities, and society as a whole. LCA and SLCA use different methodologies to assess sustainability impacts. LCA typically uses a set of standardized metrics to evaluate environmental impacts such as greenhouse gas emissions, energy use, and water consumption. In contrast, SLCA uses social impact categories such as human rights, labor rights, and community health and safety. LCA and SLCA both require data on the product or service being assessed, as well as information on the supply chain and other relevant factors.

However, the data requirements for SLCA may be more complex and varied than those for LCA, as social impacts can be harder to measure and quantify than environmental impacts. LCA is typically used to identify environmental "hotspots" in a product's life cycle and to help companies reduce their environmental impact. SLCA, on the other hand, is used to assess the social impact of a product or service and to help companies identify and address social risks and opportunities.

3. **TBL Triple Bottom Line Accounting:** The Triple Bottom Line (TBL) is a framework that incorporates social, environmental, and financial performance into an organization's accounting practices. It is a method of evaluating a company's overall performance based on three dimensions: economic, social, and environmental. The TBL framework was first introduced by John Elkington in 1994 as a way to measure sustainable business practices. The three dimensions of the TBL framework are commonly referred to as the "three Ps": people, planet, and profit. The economic dimension of the TBL framework evaluates a company's financial performance, including revenues, profits, and return on investment. The social dimension assesses a company's impact on people, including its employees, customers, suppliers, and the communities where it operates. This includes issues such as labor practices, human rights, and social justice. The environmental dimension evaluates a company's impact on the planet, including its use of natural resources, waste management, and its carbon footprint.

The TBL framework encourages companies to take a more holistic approach to account and to consider the broader impact of their operations on society and the environment. It is often used as a tool to help companies identify areas for improvement and to set sustainability goals. To better understand TBL, we need to compare it with the Global Reporting Initiative (GRI) sustainability reporting. While the TBL and GRI frameworks are both useful tools for measuring and reporting on sustainability performance, the TBL is by nature more flexible and simple, and the GRI is a much more robust and standardized framework which provides a more comprehensive set of guidelines for sustainability reporting.

4. **DJSI World Index and ESG Metrics:** The Dow Jones Sustainability World Index (DJSI World) was created by S&P Dow Jones Indices and SAM (Sustainable Asset Management) in 1999. It is a benchmark index that tracks the financial performance of leading sustainability-driven companies worldwide. SAM conducts an annual Corporate Sustainability Assessment (CSA) to evaluate companies' sustainability performance based on a range of environmental, social, and governance (ESG) factors.

   The CSA evaluates companies on various criteria, including corporate governance, climate change mitigation, environmental performance, labor practices, human rights, and stakeholder engagement. The companies that rank among the top 10% of their industry in the CSA are included in the DJSI World Index. This index is widely regarded as one of the most respected and credible sustainability benchmarks globally and is used by investors and asset managers to identify sustainable investment opportunities. The companies that have consistently ranked among the top 10 companies in the DJSI World Index in recent years include: Alphabet Inc. (parent company of Google), Cisco Systems Inc., Enel SpA, Ford Motor Company, ING Group, Johnson & Johnson, Kao Corp, Neste Oyj, Nestle SA, and Roche Holding AG. It's important to note that the composition of the DJSI World Index changes annually as companies are evaluated based on their sustainability performance in the previous year's CSA.

5. **Environmental Management Systems (EMS):** An EMS is a systematic approach to managing an organization's environmental impact. It involves developing policies, procedures, and practices

to minimize negative environmental impacts and improve sustainability performance. EMS can be based on various standards, such as the basic ISO 14001 (widely recognized international standard for EMS) or the more advanced EMAS (the EU Eco-Management and Audit Scheme, see below). EMS differs from other sustainability impact assessments in a few key ways.

First, Scope: EMS focus specifically on environmental impacts, while other sustainability impact assessments may cover a broader range of sustainability issues, including social and economic impacts. Second, EMS are typically designed to help organizations manage their own environmental impacts, whereas other sustainability impact assessments may be more focused on external stakeholders and the broader societal impacts of a product or service. Third, EMS are designed to be ongoing, with organizations continually monitoring and improving their environmental performance over time. Other sustainability impact assessments may be more focused on a one-time assessment of sustainability impacts. Fourth, while EMS are typically voluntary, many organizations choose to implement them as a way to demonstrate their commitment to environmental sustainability. Other sustainability impact assessments may be mandatory, such as those required by government regulations or industry standards. While they share some similarities with other sustainability impact assessments, EMS are unique in their scope, focus, and ongoing nature.

6. **Social Impact Assessment (SIA)**: Social impact assessment is a methodology used to evaluate the social and economic impacts of an organization's activities on stakeholders, including employees, customers, communities, and society as a whole. SIA is often used to evaluate the social impacts of a proposed project or development activity. SIA is a type of sustainability impact assessment that considers the potential social implications of a project, such as impacts on local communities, social cohesion, cultural heritage, and social equity.

   SIA typically involves a systematic process of identifying, predicting, and evaluating the potential social impacts of a project or development activity. The process typically involves engagement with stakeholders, including local communities, to understand their concerns and priorities, as well as a review of relevant policies and regulations. SIA can be used in conjunction with other sustainability impact assessments, such as environmental impact assessment (EIA) and health impact assessment (HIA), to provide a more comprehensive understanding of the potential impacts of a project or development activity. By considering the social, environmental, and economic impacts of a project, sustainability impact assessments can help organizations to make more informed decisions and identify opportunities to improve sustainability performance. Overall, SIA is an important tool for ensuring that development activities and projects are conducted in a way that takes into account the needs and priorities of local communities and stakeholders, and that supports sustainable development.

The Standards of Sustainability Impact Measurements

The Standards of Sustainability Impact Measurements section discusses more established standards and reporting frameworks, including GRI and Sustainability Reporting, SASB and Sustainability Accounting, ISO Standards and Certifications, Eco-Management and Audit Scheme (EMAS), B Corp Impact Assessment and Certification, and STARS and other sector-specific assessments.

7. **GRI and Sustainability Reporting:** The GRI was established in 1997 and has become one of the most widely recognized standards for sustainability reporting worldwide. The GRI framework provides a set of guidelines and indicators that organizations can use to report their sustainability performance. The framework covers a wide range of sustainability issues, including ESG issues, and is based on a materiality assessment that helps organizations to identify the most relevant issues to report on. The GRI is considered the standard in sustainability reporting for several reasons. First, GRI is widely recognized by stakeholders, including investors, regulators, and NGOs. This recognition helps to build trust and credibility with stakeholders and can demonstrate an organization's commitment to sustainability. Second, the GRI framework is quite comprehensive. It covers a wide range of sustainability issues, which helps organizations to report on all

aspects of their sustainability performance. Third, the GRI framework is based on a materiality assessment. This helps organizations to identify the most relevant sustainability issues to report on and to focus their reporting on the issues that are most important to their stakeholders. Fourth, the GRI framework is voluntary, which means that organizations can choose to report on their sustainability performance based on their own sustainability goals and priorities. Fifth, the GRI framework is continually evolving to reflect changing sustainability issues and stakeholder expectations. This helps organizations to stay up-to-date with the latest sustainability trends and best practices.

The GRI Standards 2021, which was released in April 2021, updates and replaces the previous GRI Standards 2016, and includes several updates and changes to the reporting requirements. The GRI Standards 2021 consists of 36 sustainability reporting standards that are organized into three universal standards and 33 topic-specific standards. The universal standards cover general reporting principles, governance, and stakeholder engagement, while the topic-specific standards cover a range of sustainability issues, such as climate change, human rights, and labor practices. The GRI Standards 2021 also includes new requirements for reporting on several sustainability issues, including biodiversity, waste, and water. In addition, it includes new guidance on how to report on social and environmental issues in supply chains, as well as how to report on the impact of COVID-19 on an organization's sustainability performance. Nike, Nestle, Microsoft, Unilever, and Patagonia demonstrate exemplary GRI reports that include the companies' sustainability strategy and performance data along with their sustainability governance, including diversity and inclusion initiatives.

8. **SASB and Sustainability Accounting:** The Sustainability Accounting Standards Board (SASB) is a nonprofit organization that has developed a framework for measuring and reporting on the sustainability performance of companies. As we illustrated in its case study, SASB's framework focuses on identifying and reporting on financial material sustainability issues that are relevant to specific industries. SASB's framework is important for sustainability accounting for several reasons. First, SASB's framework is tailored to specific industries. This makes it easier for companies

to prioritize and report on sustainability issues that are most relevant to their business. Second, SASB's framework focuses on identifying sustainability issues that are financially material to companies. This means that the issues identified by SASB have a significant impact on a company's financial performance and are important to investors and other stakeholders. Third, SASB's framework provides a standardized approach to measuring and reporting on sustainability performance. This makes it easier for investors and other stakeholders to compare sustainability performance across companies within the same industry. Fourth, SASB's framework is designed to be integrated with financial reporting, which means that sustainability performance is reported in a way that is consistent with financial reporting standards.

The SASB's framework can be used in conjunction with Social Return on Investment (SROI), another framework used to measure the sustainability performance of organizations. SROI is a methodology used to measure the social, environmental, and economic value created by an organization's activities. SROI is not industry-specific and can be applied to any type of organization or project. SROI is a more holistic approach that takes into account the full range of social, environmental, and economic impacts created by an organization's activities, and it provides a monetary value to these impacts. Overall, SASB's framework is an important tool for measuring and reporting on the sustainability performance of companies. It provides a standardized and financial approach to sustainability accounting that can help companies prioritize and report on sustainability issues that are most relevant to their business. This can help investors and other stakeholders make informed decisions about the sustainability performance of companies, which can ultimately drive positive social and environmental outcomes.

9. **ISO Standards and Certifications**: The International Organization for Standardization (ISO) is an independent, non-governmental international organization that develops and publishes standards for various industries and sectors around the world. ISO standards are developed through a consensus-based process involving experts from around the world and are intended to provide a common set of guidelines and best practices for a particular industry or sector. ISO has developed a number of standards related to sustainability, which can help organizations reduce

their environmental impact and improve their social and economic sustainability. Some of the ISO standards related to sustainability include:

ISO 14001: Environmental Management System (EMS)—This standard provides a framework for organizations to manage their environmental impacts and reduce their carbon footprint. ISO 14001 is a widely recognized international standard for EMS. It specifies the requirements for an EMS and provides guidance for organizations to manage their environmental impacts effectively. ISO 14001 requires organizations to establish a policy, identify environmental aspects and impacts, establish objectives and targets, implement and maintain programs to meet objectives, and monitor and measure their environmental performance. ISO 14001 is voluntary and can be implemented by any organization, regardless of its size or sector.
ISO 50001: Energy Management System (EnMS)—This standard provides a framework for organizations to manage their energy use and reduce their energy consumption, which can lead to cost savings and reduced greenhouse gas emissions.
ISO 26000: Social Responsibility—This standard provides guidance on social responsibility and how organizations can contribute to sustainable development. It is not a certification.
ISO 20121: Sustainable Events Management—This standard provides a framework for event organizers to manage the environmental, social, and economic impacts of their events. By implementing ISO standards related to sustainability, organizations can demonstrate their commitment to sustainability and improve their sustainability performance. Additionally, these standards can help to create a common language and understanding of sustainability issues and best practices across industries and sectors, which can contribute to more widespread adoption of sustainable practices and contribute to sustainability on an international level.

10. **Eco-Management and Audit Scheme (EMAS):** EMAS is a voluntary European Union (EU) regulation for organizations to assess, manage, and report on their environmental performance. EMAS

goes beyond the requirements of ISO 14001 and includes additional requirements, such as mandatory reporting on environmental performance, external verification, and stakeholder engagement. Organizations must also demonstrate continuous improvement in their environmental performance to maintain their EMAS registration. EMAS is available to organizations operating within the EU and is particularly popular among public authorities and larger organizations. EMAS is a more comprehensive and rigorous program that includes additional requirements and is specific to organizations operating within the EU.

EMAS is an important advancement in standardized and policy requirements for sustainability impact assessments and reporting. For instance, EMAS is based on a standardized framework that provides a common language for sustainability reporting and assessment. This allows organizations to compare their performance with others and track progress over time. In addition, EMAS is a voluntary scheme that encourages organizations to go beyond compliance with regulatory requirements and to continuously improve their sustainability performance. EMAS is open to all types of organizations, including businesses, public authorities, and nonprofit organizations. This means that organizations can choose to participate in EMAS based on their own sustainability goals and priorities. Organizations that participate in EMAS demonstrate a strong commitment to reduce their environmental impact and to promote sustainable development. Overall, EMAS is an important advancement in standardized and policy requirements for sustainability impact assessments and reporting because it provides a framework for organizations to assess and report on their environmental impact and to demonstrate their commitment to sustainability. EMAS is aligned with other EU policies and regulations related to environmental sustainability, such as the EU Emissions Trading System (ETSs), the Renewable Energy Directive, and the Energy Efficiency Directive. This alignment helps to ensure that organizations participating in EMAS are complying with relevant EU requirements and policies. By promoting transparency and continuous improvement, EMAS can help organizations reduce their environmental impact and support sustainable development.

11. **B Corp Impact Assessment and Certification**: B Corp certification is a designation which recognizes businesses that meet high standards of social and environmental performance, transparency, and accountability. To become a certified B Corp, businesses must undergo a rigorous assessment process and meet a minimum score across several impact areas, including governance, workers, community, and environment. The B Corp Impact Assessment (BIA) is a comprehensive tool used to evaluate a company's social and environmental performance. The assessment includes over 200 questions that cover a range of impact areas, including governance, workers, community, and environment. The questions are designed to evaluate a company's practices, policies, and performance across these areas.

    To become a certified B Corp, a company must meet a minimum score on the B Corp Impact Assessment and meet certain legal requirements. The legal requirements vary by country, but typically include a commitment to consider the impact of business decisions on all stakeholders, not just shareholders. B Corp certification is a voluntary designation, but it is increasingly being used as a way for businesses to demonstrate their commitment to social and environmental responsibility.

    B Corps are part of a global movement of businesses that are working to use business as a force for good and create positive social and environmental impact. B Corps assessments and certifications have had a significant impact in promoting and advancing social and environmental responsibility in the business world. Specifically, by certifying companies that meet high standards of social and environmental performance, transparency, and accountability, the B Corps movement has encouraged many businesses to prioritize sustainability and social impact in their operations.

    The BIA has set new standards of corporate accountability. The B Corps certification requires companies to meet rigorous standards of social and environmental performance, governance, and transparency. By holding companies to a higher standard of accountability, B Corps have set a new standard for what it means to be a responsible and ethical business. In addition, B Corps have been successful in attracting investors who are interested in supporting companies that prioritize social and environmental responsibility. This has helped to create a new market for impact investments and encouraged more businesses to adopt sustainable practices. At some level, B Corps have been influential in advocating for legal changes that promote social and environmental responsibility in business.

For example, the B Corp movement played a key role in the creation of Benefit Corporation legislation, which is now recognized in over 30 US states and in several other countries. Overall, the B Corp movement had a significant impact in promoting sustainable and responsible business practices and has helped to create a new paradigm for what it means to be a successful business in the twenty-first century. It has created a community of businesses that are committed to social and environmental responsibility. This community provides support, networking opportunities, and resources for businesses that are working to create a more sustainable and equitable world.

12. **STARS and other sector-specific assessments:** STARS (Sustainability Tracking, Assessment & Rating System) is a sustainability assessment framework developed by the Association for the Advancement of Sustainability in Higher Education (AASHE) for academic institutions. STARS provides a comprehensive set of sustainability metrics and benchmarks that institutions can use to evaluate their sustainability performance across a range of impact areas, including academics, engagement, operations, and planning and administration.

    Institutions can use the STARS framework to set sustainability goals, track progress, and benchmark their performance against other institutions. There are several other sector-specific sustainability assessments that are widely used by organizations in various industries. Among them is the Global Real Estate Sustainability Benchmark (GRESB), a sustainability assessment framework for real estate companies and funds. The Carbon Disclosure Project (CDP) is an annual questionnaire-based assessment of corporate greenhouse gas emissions and climate change strategy. The Higg Index is an assessment tool for the apparel and footwear industry that measures sustainability performance across a range of impact areas, including materials, water, energy, and waste. The LEED (Leadership in Energy and Environmental Design) is a green building certification program for the design, construction, and operation of buildings.

The Green Star is a sustainability rating system for the design and construction of buildings in Australia. The Fairtrade certification systems for products that meet social and environmental standards. These are just a few examples of the many sector-specific sustainability assessments and their contributions to measure sustainability impact. These tools and frameworks are continuously improving and evolving to provide organizations with accurate, realistic, and comprehensive evaluations of their sustainability performance. By benchmarking their performance against others in their industry, organizations can identify areas where they can make the most impact and drive sustainability innovation within their sector.

The Advancements of Sustainability Impact Measurement

Finally, The Advancements of Sustainability Impact Measurement section explores cutting-edge approaches to sustainability measurement, such as Integrated Reporting, SDG Mapping, and SNA for Sustainability. These advanced methods help organizations to further improve their sustainability impact measurement practices and align with global sustainability goals.

13. **Integrated Reporting (IR or <IR>):** Integrated reporting involves the integration of financial and non-financial information to provide a more comprehensive view of an organization's performance. This approach can help to identify areas where sustainability practices can be improved and can also be used to communicate sustainability performance to stakeholders. Integrated reporting is a reporting framework which aims to provide a holistic view of an organization's value creation over time. It brings together information on an organization's financial performance, sustainability performance, and other non-financial factors that impact its ability to create value over the long term. Integrated reporting is considered a more advanced method of reporting than general sustainability reporting because it takes a more comprehensive and integrated approach to measuring and reporting on the impact of an organization's activities. Unlike traditional sustainability

reporting, which tends to focus on specific sustainability metrics, integrated reporting considers how sustainability performance is linked to financial performance and overall value creation. There are several benefits to using an integrated reporting approach for impact measurement.

First, integrated reporting provides a more holistic view of an organization's impact by considering both financial and non-financial factors that contribute to value creation. Second, integrated reporting takes a long-term perspective, which means that it considers the impact of an organization's activities over time, rather than just in the short term. Third, integrated reporting requires organizations to engage with a wide range of stakeholders to understand their expectations and concerns, which can help to identify material sustainability issues and opportunities. Fourth, integrated reporting provides a more complete picture of an organization's impact, which can help to inform decision-making and support the development of more sustainable strategies.

In addition, integrated reporting often includes reporting on diversity, equity, and inclusion (DEI) issues, as these factors are considered to be material to the long-term success of organizations. This includes issues such as diversity in leadership, equal opportunities for employees, and fair treatment of customers and suppliers. Reporting on DEI issues can be included in an organization's integrated report as part of its broader sustainability performance reporting. This might involve reporting on the organization's policies and practices related to diversity, equity, and inclusion, as well as its progress in achieving diversity goals and addressing any gaps or challenges that have been identified. Overall, integrated reporting provides a platform for organizations to report on a wide range of sustainability issues, including DEI, and to demonstrate how these issues are linked to the organization's overall value creation over time. By taking a more comprehensive and integrated approach to reporting, organizations can better understand their impact on society and the environment, and identify opportunities to improve sustainability performance and create long-term value.

14. **SDG Mapping**: SDG mapping is a method used to link an organization's sustainability strategy and goals with the SDGs. Beyond the more superficial approach of coloring and organizational sustainability performance along the colorful icons of the SDG wheel (the so-called SDG-washing or rainbow-washing), a more accurate and detailed SDG mapping can offer a detailed framework for sustainability impact reporting using the 5Ps, the 17 goals, the 169 targets, and the 232 indicators. By mapping their sustainability goals and activities to the SDGs, organizations can demonstrate how their sustainability efforts contribute to the achievement of these global goals. SDG mapping is considered a more advanced approach in sustainable impact measurement for several reasons.

    First, SDG mapping gives a holistic view of the organization's sustainability impact. By linking their sustainability goals to the SDGs, organizations connect their specific performances with people, planet, prosperity, peace, and partnership framework of the SDGs. Second, the SDGs provide a globally recognized framework for sustainable development, which means that organizations can align their sustainability efforts with global priorities and demonstrate their contribution to the achievement of these goals. Third, SDG mapping encourages collaboration and partnerships between organizations and other stakeholders to achieve shared sustainability goals. Fourth, the SDGs are focused on achieving sustainable development over the long term, which means that organizations are encouraged to take a long-term perspective when setting their sustainability goals and strategies.

    There are several SDG mapping tools available that organizations can use to map their sustainability performance along the SDGs. One that emerged earlier is the SDG Compass (2015), a guide developed by the United Nations Global Compact, the Global Reporting Initiative, and the World Business Council for Sustainable Development. The five steps of the SDG Compass provide a framework for companies to align their strategies and operations with the SDGs and they include: (1) Understanding the SDGs; (2) Defining Priorities; (3) Setting Goals; (4) Integrating Sustainability; and (5) Reporting and Communicating. The responsibility of companies is also to comply with relevant legislation, respect international minimum standards, and address negative human rights as these are fundamental aspect of corporate sustainability and social responsibility, and should be integrated into each of the five steps of the SDG Compass framework.

Another commonly used tool is the SDG Action Manager. It is a tool developed by the United Nations Global Compact and B Lab that helps companies to assess their sustainability performance and identify opportunities to align their strategies with the SDGs. The tool includes a mapping feature that enables companies to identify which SDGs are most relevant to their business and to set specific targets related to each goal. Another tool is Future-Fit Business Benchmark, developed by the Future-Fit Foundation. It helps companies to assess their sustainability performance and identify opportunities to align their strategies with the SDGs. The tool includes a mapping feature that links sustainability goals and activities to specific SDGs and targets. The GRI Standards also include a mapping feature that links sustainability goals and activities to specific SDGs and targets, and provides guidance on how to report on progress towards achieving these goals.

The Corporate Reporting Dialogue (CRD), an initiative led by the International Integrated Reporting Council, brings together a number of leading corporate reporting standard setters, including the GRI and SASB. The CRD has developed a mapping tool that links sustainability goals and activities to the SDGs, which can be used by companies to align their sustainability strategies with the SDGs. There are numerous other emerging tools that, thanks to technological advances, can be quite helpful to make the organization, in its detailed and continuous performances mapped along the SDGs. These reporting tools can also be helpful to monitor the organization's SDG performance through appropriately designed dashboards. Novartis, to continue with the same example, has developed an SDG dashboard that tracks the company's progress towards achieving its sustainability goals and targets, which are mapped to the relevant SDGs. The dashboard includes a summary of progress towards each goal, as well as detailed information on the company's performance in specific areas such as climate change, access to healthcare, and ethical conduct.

15. **SNA for Sustainability**: The System of National Accounts (SNA) is a set of international guidelines and standards for the compilation of national accounts, which provides a comprehensive and consistent framework for measuring economic activity. As new social and environmental accounting criteria for those organizations specifically contributing to the social economy and circular economy will emerge, most likely, the measurement of sustainability impact will improve (Tavanti, 2019). The revised SNA (2008) guidelines already make strong recommendations for nations to account for contributions specific to well-being and sustainability. This marked a significant step forward in recognizing the importance of sustainability and well-being in measuring economic progress. Such inclusion has several implications for sustainability impact measurements at the national levels, and consequently for organizations reporting on their sustainability impact. With this inclusion, the updated SNA framework encourages countries to go beyond traditional economic indicators (such as GDP), to adopt alternative measurements to better understand and address the social and environmental challenges they face (Hoekstra, 2019).

    Alternative measurements include the Genuine Progress Indicator (GPI), Index of Human Development (HDI), Human Poverty Index (HPI), Gross Domestic Happiness (GDH), Index of Sustainable Economic Welfare (ISEW), Happy Planet Index—measure of environmental efficiency for supporting well-being, Green gross domestic product (green GDP or GGDP), Median income (average wages), Well-Being index, and Social Progress Index. The SNA current and future guidelines will surely provide more criteria for the standardization of metrics across countries for measuring well-being and sustainability. These will provide more cross-country comparability and more meaningful assessments of progress towards the SDGs and future sustainability agendas. Further the integration of environmental and social indicators into economic accounts will help countries and organizations to better understand the links between economic, social, and environmental factors and inform more holistic and sustainable policy decisions. Already, the inclusion of well-being and sustainability chapters in the SNA (2008) revision has important implications for sustainability impact measurements, promoting a more comprehensive

> and standardized approach to measure progress towards sustainable development. This can inform better policymaking, public awareness, and global cooperation to address pressing social and environmental challenges.

As the initiatives for promoting integrated approaches and standardized metrics will probably increase and ameliorate in the years to come, we anticipate a growing movement towards advanced sustainability impact practices. Investor-led initiatives like the Task Force for Climate-related Financial Disclosure (TCFD), headed by Michael Bloomberg, are pushing for more integration of EESG and the harmonization of the GRI and SASB approaches. The B Lab and its BIA will surely continue to grow in popularity and effectiveness in the measurements, generating more accessible tools than the GRI through straightforward, online, and free to use frameworks like the SDG Action Manager.

Other initiatives like the GHG Protocol will continue to become standards in measuring GHG emissions. Organizations like the World Resources Institute (WRI) and the World Business Council for Sustainable Development (WBCSD), who developed the Corporate Standard and Project Standard of the GHG Protocol, will continue to push other organizations to better understand their carbon footprint and identify areas where they can reduce their emissions. The Carbon Disclosure Project (CDP), and other nonprofit organizations, will probably continue to run their global disclosure system for companies, cities, states, and regions to report their environmental impact. Other important organizations like the Corporate Reporting Dialogue (CRD) are also to be watched as they are instrumental in bringing the GRI, SASB, and GHG Protocol together with CDP. The International Organization for Standardization (ISO), along the International Integrated Reporting Council framework (<IR >), the Climate Disclosure Standards Board (CDSB), the Natural Capital Protocol Framework, and other initiatives and organizations will surely be contributing to the future of sustainability impact measurements and reporting.

Key Takeaways

1. **Comprehensive overview:** This chapter provides a systematic overview of the various tools, metrics, and frameworks available for assessing and measuring sustainability impact, categorized into basic, standard, and advanced classifications.
2. **Starting point:** The Basics of Sustainability Impact Measurements section introduces fundamental concepts and tools, such as Carbon footprint, GHG measurements, and Triple Bottom Line Accounting, providing a starting point for organizations beginning their sustainability measurement journey.
3. **Established standards:** The Standards of Sustainability Impact Measurements section covers widely recognized standards and reporting frameworks, such as GRI, SASB, ISO Standards, and B Corp Certification, which help organizations align with best practices and improve transparency.
4. **Advanced approaches:** The Advancements of Sustainability Impact Measurement section explores cutting-edge methods, such as Integrated Reporting and SDG Mapping, which can help organizations further refine their sustainability impact measurement practices and align with global sustainability goals.
5. **Adaptability:** The chapter acknowledges that sustainability measurement tools and frameworks may sometimes overlap and should be adapted to the specific needs of large organizations, individual sectors, and geographical contexts with advanced sustainability policy requirements.

References

GRI, UNGC, WBCSD. (2016). *SDG compass: The guide for business action on the SDGs TM*. Retrieved March 14, 2023, from https://sdgcompass.org/aligning-your-business-with-the-sdgs/

Hoekstra, R. (2019). *Replacing GDP by 2030: Towards a common language for the well-being and sustainability community*. Cambridge University Press.

SDG Compass. (2015). *The guide for business action on the SDGs*. https://sdgcompass.org/. Accessed on March 10, 2023.

SNA. (2008). *SNA chapter 2: National accounts and measures of well-being and sustainability*. https://unstats.un.org/unsd/nationalaccount/aeg/2022/M21/SNA_AO_Ch2.pdf. Accessed on March 10, 2023.

Tavanti, M. (2019). Social economy enterprises: The Third/Social Economy (TSE) sector classification for advancing shared values for the common good. *Entretextos* 11/33—Economía Social y Solidaria (December 2019–March 2020), 51–64.

CHAPTER 18

The Future of Sustainable Impact

Abstract This chapter discusses the future of sustainable impact by examining the potential negative and positive impacts on our planet, as highlighted in David Attenborough's life message to us. The chapter emphasizes the crucial role of the current generation in addressing sustainability challenges and presents three major values that are expected to grow and become further integrated into sustainability impact assessments and reporting: specialty rights, diversity integrations, and political coherence. Additionally, the chapter outlines five key paradigms for our common future that can foster more sustainable, equitable, inclusive, and prosperous outcomes through shared values and global commitments.

Keywords David Attenborough · Specialty rights · Diversity integrations · Political coherence · Sustainability paradigms · Global governance

> *What humans do over the next 50 years will determine the fate of all life on the planet.*
>
> *The future of life on earth depends on our ability to take action.*
>
> —Sir David Attenborough, Renowned British broadcaster and natural historian,

M. Tavanti, *Developing Sustainability in Organizations*, Sustainable Development Goals Series,
https://doi.org/10.1007/978-3-031-36907-0_18

Negative and Positive Impacts

In the book and Netflix produced documentary *David Attenborough: A Life on Our Planet* (2020), Sir David Attenborough presents a stark warning about the future of sustainability and the impact of human activity on the planet:

1. **Biodiversity loss**: Attenborough argues that we are in the midst of a sixth mass extinction event caused by human activity. He presents evidence of the staggering loss of biodiversity, including the decline of populations of mammals, birds, fish, and insects. He suggests that this loss of biodiversity is a threat not just to other species, but to our own survival.
2. **Climate change**: Attenborough discusses the impact of climate change on the planet, including rising temperatures, melting ice caps, and rising sea levels. He emphasizes that we must take action to reduce greenhouse gas emissions if we hope to mitigate the worst effects of climate change.
3. **Unsustainable agriculture**: Attenborough argues that industrial agriculture is driving deforestation, soil degradation, and water pollution, and that we must shift towards more sustainable and regenerative farming practices.
4. **Overconsumption**: Attenborough suggests that our culture of overconsumption is driving environmental destruction, and that we must learn to live within the limits of the planet's resources. He argues that we must move away from a linear economy based on extraction and consumption towards a circular economy that values resource efficiency and waste reduction.
5. **Human population growth**: Attenborough notes that human population growth is putting increasing pressure on the planet's resources, and that we must address population growth if we hope to achieve sustainability.

Overall, Attenborough argues that we are at a critical moment in human history, and that we must take immediate action to address these environmental challenges. His modern language for sustainability recalls the pioneering and notorious messages of the *Operating Manual for Spaceship Earth* (Fuller & Snyder, 2008) that presents the Earth as a "spaceship" with limited resources that must be managed carefully to ensure the survival and well-being of its inhabitants. He also presents a list of solutions that can have a positive impact for a possible sustainable future recalling the civic responsibilities of the anthropocene (Dalbotten et al., 2014). Attenborough presents a vision of sustainable solutions that can help us to address the environmental challenges we face. Here are some of the solutions he presents:

1. **Regenerative agriculture**: Attenborough argues that we need to shift away from industrial agriculture towards more regenerative farming practices that restore soil health, reduce chemical inputs, and promote biodiversity.
2. **Renewable energy**: Attenborough emphasizes the importance of shifting towards renewable energy sources like wind, solar, and hydropower to reduce greenhouse gas emissions and mitigate the effects of climate change.
3. **Protected areas**: Attenborough suggests that we must increase the amount of land and sea that is protected from human activity to preserve biodiversity and ecosystem services.
4. **Sustainable forestry**: Attenborough argues that we must shift towards sustainable forestry practices that maintain forest health and promote biodiversity.
5. **Circular economy**: Attenborough emphasizes the importance of shifting towards a circular economy, in which resources are used efficiently, waste is minimized, and materials are reused and recycled.
6. **Sustainable fishing**: Attenborough argues that we must shift towards sustainable fishing practices that maintain healthy fish populations and promote ecosystem health.
7. **Reducing waste**: Attenborough suggests that we must reduce our reliance on single-use plastics and other materials that contribute to waste and pollution.
8. **Population control**: Attenborough notes that human population growth is putting increasing pressure on the planet's resources, and that we must address population growth if we hope to achieve sustainability.

Overall, Attenborough presents a vision of a future where humans live in harmony with nature, and where we prioritize sustainability, conservation, and regeneration over short-term economic gain. He suggests that by taking action to implement these sustainable solutions; we can create a more resilient and sustainable future for ourselves and for future generations. His message for urgent actions and the adoption of systemic changes across various sectors echoes the voice of many other leaders in the sustainability movement. His recommendations for current and future generations parallel those made by climate change advocates that care about the future of humanity in our common planet earth (Holthaus, 2020).

Sustainability at a Crossroad: The First and Last Generation

Sustainability is a multifaceted concept that can help us make a net positive difference for the well-being of current and future generations (Lawrence, 2014). Yet, it can remain just an adjective on other terms and simply included as an elective in our education and life. Perhaps President Obama was inspired by the words of the US Senator Gaylord Nelson and the founder of Earth Day in 1970 when he said, "We are the first generation to feel the effect of climate change and the last generation who can do something about it" (Obama, 2014). Failing to act may undermine the very existence of humans on this planet. Not fully understanding the scale and implications of our impact on the environment means that we have a unique responsibility to take action to prevent further damage and ensure a sustainable future. At the same time, delaying action or failing to address environmental challenges in a meaningful way risks passing a degraded and less sustainable planet on to future generations. It is an urgent call for implementing sustainable solutions before it is too late.

Sustainability is at a crossroads because we are facing a critical moment in human history. On the one hand, there is growing awareness and recognition of the urgent need to address environmental challenges, such as climate change, biodiversity loss, and resource depletion. Many individuals, businesses, and governments are taking steps to reduce their environmental impact and transition towards more sustainable practices. On the other hand, we are still seeing a significant and growing gap between the pace and scale of action needed to address these challenges and the actual progress being made. The scale of the environmental challenges we face is immense, and addressing it requires transformative changes in the way we produce and consume goods and services, as well as in our lifestyles and values. These changes are often difficult to implement and can be impeded by a variety of factors, including lack of political will, social and economic inertia, and short-term thinking.

In addition, the COVID-19 pandemic has highlighted the interconnectedness of environmental, social, and economic systems, and underscored the need for a more holistic and integrated approach to sustainability. Yet, many people and organizations are not using this crisis to learn about our interconnectedness and make resilient adjustments. Sustainability is truly at a crossroads because the decisions we make today will have a significant impact on the future of our planet and its inhabitants. It is up to individuals, businesses, and governments to come together and take action to create a more sustainable and resilient future for all.

The effects of climate change are already being felt, and the window of opportunity to prevent catastrophic and irreversible impacts is rapidly closing. This requires us to recognize that the choices and actions we take today will have profound and far-reaching consequences for future generations, and that we have a responsibility to act with urgency and foresight to mitigate and adapt to the impacts of climate change. This requires recognizing that the challenges of sustainability are complex and interconnected, and that addressing them requires collaboration and cooperation across sectors, disciplines, and borders. This underscores the critical importance of acting now, with urgency and determination, to address the challenges of sustainability and mitigate the impacts of climate change.

We predict that three major values will be growing and further integrated in sustainability impact assessments and reporting: specialty rights, diversity integrations, and political coherence.

1. **Specialty Rights**: Specialty rights, such as disability rights, Indigenous rights, and climate refugee rights, will become important components in the future of sustainability impact reporting for several reasons. Firstly, sustainability impact reporting has traditionally focused on environmental and economic impacts, but it is increasingly recognized that social impacts, including human rights, are an important part of sustainability. These specialty rights are critical to social sustainability, as they address the needs and concerns of marginalized communities and vulnerable populations. Secondly,

there is a growing awareness that climate change disproportionately affects certain communities, including Indigenous peoples and people with disabilities, who are often the most vulnerable to its impacts. Recognizing and addressing the rights of these groups in sustainability impact reporting can help to ensure that they are not further marginalized by climate change. Thirdly, sustainability impact reporting is becoming more important for investors and other stakeholders who are interested in the social and environmental performance of companies.

Companies that are able to demonstrate that they are committed to respecting and promoting human rights, including specialty rights, are likely to be viewed more favorably by investors and customers. Finally, there is a growing recognition that sustainable development cannot be achieved without addressing the needs and concerns of all communities, including those with specialty rights. Including specialty rights in sustainability impact reporting can help to ensure that all communities are included in the transition to a more sustainable future.

2. **Diversity Integrations**: Diversity integrations, including race, gender, sexual orientation, and other intersectional identities will become important components in the future of sustainability impact reporting for several reasons. Firstly, diversity and inclusion are essential components of sustainability, and recognizing and addressing issues related to race, gender, and other intersectional identities is critical to promoting social sustainability. By integrating diversity and inclusion into sustainability impact reporting, companies can demonstrate their commitment to promoting a more equitable and just society. Secondly, there is growing pressure from stakeholders, including investors, customers, and employees, for companies to address issues related to diversity and inclusion. Companies that are able to demonstrate that they are committed to promoting diversity and inclusion are likely to be viewed more favorably by these stakeholders. Thirdly, diversity and inclusion can have a positive impact on business performance, as it can lead to a more engaged and innovative workforce, and better decision-making.

   Companies that integrate diversity and inclusion into their sustainability impact reporting can demonstrate their commitment to creating a positive and inclusive work environment. Finally, there is a growing recognition that sustainable development cannot be achieved without addressing issues related to diversity and inclusion. By integrating diversity and inclusion into sustainability impact reporting, companies can help to ensure that their sustainability efforts are inclusive and benefit all members of society.

3. **Political coherence**: The future of sustainability reporting will need more political coherence expressed in issues such as ending self-serving lobbying, avoiding paying taxes, ending corruption, stopping overpay of executives, and other issues for several reasons. Firstly, political coherence is essential for creating a level playing field for companies to operate in. Companies that engage in self-serving lobbying, avoid paying taxes, or engage in corrupt practices can gain an unfair advantage over their competitors, which can undermine the sustainability of the entire industry. Secondly, political coherence is important for promoting social sustainability. Corruption and the abuse of power can lead to a range of negative social impacts, including the exploitation of workers, human rights abuses, and environmental degradation. By promoting political coherence and ending corrupt practices, companies can help to ensure that their sustainability efforts have a positive impact on society. Thirdly, political coherence can help to create a more stable and predictable regulatory environment.

   Companies that operate in an environment with unclear or inconsistent regulations may struggle to make long-term investment decisions or to plan for the future. By promoting political coherence and creating a more stable regulatory environment, companies can help to reduce uncertainty and promote sustainability. Finally, promoting political coherence is essential for building trust with stakeholders, including customers, investors, and employees. Companies that engage in self-serving lobbying, avoid paying taxes, or engage in corrupt practices may face reputational damage, which can undermine their sustainability efforts. In summary, promoting political coherence is essential for creating a level playing field, promoting social sustainability, creating a stable regulatory environment, and building trust with stakeholders. The future of sustainability reporting will need to address these issues in order to create a more sustainable and just society.

Promoting all types of human rights and increasing the effectiveness of a broader agenda for diversity and inclusion are not negotiable targets for the future of sustainability impact reporting. Political coherence should also be discerned along the international practices of companies that may choose to support regimes associated with dictators and war crimes. For example, Dutch companies like Unilever, Heineken, and Philips, who are well known for their sustainability leadership, have delayed withdrawing their operations from Russia as other companies have already done in response to the Ukraine invasion. Coherence means to consider all SDGs in the reporting of sustainability impact. Avoiding cherry-picking will provide organizations with a more complete and coherent assessment of their sustainability performance on environmental, social, and economic levels but also political and collaborative. For example, a few years ago some organizations in Chicago chose not to install Interface carpet tiles because the company's choice for their installers fell below the labor standard. Being strong in environmental "net-zero" performance requires coherence in other rights and social performances, including labor rights. An organization that adopts sustainability needs to map their performance along all of the SDGs in order to avoid SDG-washing or rainbow-washing. It is important to take a holistic approach to sustainability, promote accountability and transparency, and ensure alignment with the broader global sustainability agenda.

The Paradigms of Our Common Future

There are several paradigms that are important for our common future of sustainability. It depends on us to embrace our collective, systemic and global challenges necessary to foster a more sustainable, equitable, inclusive, and prosperous future for all. As we recognize the world is complex, interconnected, and dynamic, we need to equip ourselves and others with the capacity to think systemically and globally, acting practically and locally. We need understanding the relationships and interdependencies among social, economic, and environmental systems in order to achieve sustainability. We need to welcome, promote, incubate, and accelerate innovations and transformations in social, economic, and environmental systems to achieve sustainability. We need mindsets and competencies adequate for the current and future challenges of sustainability. These include creativity, experimentation, and learning to design new systems that are sustainable and resilient. These also include the ability to dialogue and work with diverse stakeholders. The paradigms surely include the awareness, knowledge, and competencies for appropriate integrations of digital technologies such as the Internet of Things (IoT), artificial intelligence (AI), and blockchain. These will continue to increase and will play an increasingly important role in promoting sustainability impact by improving efficiency, reducing resource consumption, and enabling new forms of collaboration and governance. Future paradigms will surely have a greater focus on social sustainability and its key aspects of sustainable development: poverty alleviation, inequality reduction, and social inclusion. More dimensions of social sustainability will surely become the norm for assessing and pursuing collective well-being such as neurodiversity and disability within the Diversity, Equity, Inclusion and Access (or IDEA).

As a way to summarize and cluster these paradigms we highlight here five elements that can surely play a role in developing sustainability in organizations through shared values and global commitments. These include consciousness interconnectedness, resilience and adaptation, stewardship and equity, regenerative generation, and global governance.

1. **Conscious Interconnectedness**: A cultural evolution is urgently needed to build global consensus for a sustainable future. Indigenous cultures often hold deep respect for the natural world, understanding that the health of the environment directly impacts their own well-being. They see humans as part of the larger ecosystem, rather than as separate or superior entities. This holistic perspective encourages a symbiotic relationship with the environment, which fosters sustainable practices and respect for the delicate balance of ecosystems (Montgomery, 2023). By embracing the concept of conscious interconnectedness, we can learn from Indigenous wisdoms and adopt a more holistic approach to sustainability. Conscious interconnectedness can be an important factor to foster a sense of shared values and goals among individuals, communities, and organizations. This can lead to greater alignment and cooperation towards achieving sustainable development goals. When people feel connected to each other and to the planet, they are more likely to work towards a common goal of sustainability. Conscious interconnectedness can foster empathy and compassion towards other people and the planet. This can lead to greater care and concern for the environment and for vulnerable populations, and a greater sense of responsibility towards creating a more sustainable future.

   Conscious interconnectedness can also encourage collective action towards sustainability. When people feel connected to each other and to the planet, they are more likely to engage in collective action, such as volunteering, advocacy, or participation in social and environmental movements. This can lead to greater impact and influence in driving sustainability efforts. Conscious interconnectedness can promote systemic thinking and understanding of the interdependence of social, economic, and environmental systems. This can lead to more effective and holistic solutions that address the root causes of sustainability challenges, rather than just their symptoms. Finally, conscious interconnectedness can also inspire innovation and creativity towards sustainable solutions. When people feel connected to each other and to the planet, they may be more open to new ideas and approaches that challenge conventional thinking and promote sustainable practices.

2. **Resilience and Adaptation**: A sustainable future will require organizations and societies to be more adaptable and resilient to changes and challenges. Some have argued that we need to adopt a "multiresilient approach" (Fathi, 2022). One that recognizes the interconnectedness of various dimensions of resilience (such as social, economic, and ecological resilience) and the need for comprehensive and integrated strategies to enhance the ability of societies to adapt to change and withstand shocks. This approach resembles one of the core messages of this book: organizations, communities, and systems need to adopt a holistic perspective on resilience and sustainability. We need to recognize and emphasize the need for integrated strategies and collective action to secure a more sustainable and resilient future for societies around the world.

   Resilience, as the ability of systems to withstand and recover from shocks and disturbances, recognizes that the world is complex, dynamic, and interconnected, and that systems are subject to unexpected events and disruptions. Resilience emphasizes the importance of adaptability, flexibility, and learning in response to changing conditions. This paradigm is important because it helps us to build systems that can withstand and recover from the challenges of sustainability, such as climate change, economic shocks, and social disruptions. Environmental challenges such as climate change, resource depletion, and natural disasters are becoming more frequent and intense. To adapt to these challenges, organizations and societies must be able to adjust their operations and practices in response to changing conditions. Social challenges such as inequality, poverty, and migration are also becoming more pressing. To address these challenges, organizations and societies must be able to respond to the changing needs and demands of diverse populations. Economic challenges such as global competition and market volatility are also affecting organizations and societies. To remain competitive and sustainable, organizations must be able to adapt to changing economic conditions and innovate in response to new challenges and opportunities. Technological change is also driving rapid and transformative shifts in society and the economy. To remain relevant and competitive, organizations must be able to adopt and adapt to new technologies and ways of working.

3. **Stewardship and Equity**: Environmental stewardship and social equity are important paradigms for our sustainable future because they help ensure that our actions are not only environmentally responsible but also socially and economically responsible (Nikolakis & de Veiga, 2023). Stewardship refers to our responsibility to protect and manage natural resources, such as land, water, and air, for future generations. This means that we must use these resources in a sustainable manner, taking into account their long-term impacts on the environment and human health.

   By practicing good stewardship, we can ensure that these resources are preserved for future generations and that we maintain the biodiversity and resilience of our ecosystems. Social equity, on the other hand, refers to the fair and just distribution of resources and opportunities within society. This means that everyone, regardless of their background or social status, should have access to the same resources and opportunities, including education, healthcare, housing, and employment. This paradigm emphasizes the importance of fairness, social equity, and justice in achieving sustainability. It recognizes that sustainability must be inclusive and equitable for all, and that social and economic systems must be designed to support human well-being and social justice.

   By promoting social equity, we can ensure that everyone has a fair chance to succeed and that no one is left behind. Combined, stewardship and equity, provide a framework for sustainable development that is both environmentally responsible and socially just. By taking a holistic approach to sustainability, we can create a future that is not only environmentally sustainable but also socially and economically sustainable, ensuring that future generations can thrive in a healthy and equitable world.

4. **Regenerative Generations**: Refers to the growing sensitivity of younger generations toward environmental causes and the practice of creating regenerative systems for self-sustaining solutions such as: regenerative agriculture, circular economy, restorative design, biomimicry and other holistic, participatory and system-thinking approaches. These new generations are a wake-up call to all to become concerned citizens and engage in stakeholder activism (Hawken, 2021). We share a responsibility to advocate for policies and practices that support environmental, social, and economic sustainability. Stakeholder activism will likely help to raise awareness and mobilize public opinion, as well as exert pressure on businesses and governments to adopt more sustainable practices. We also share the responsibility to equip these younger generations of activists with the necessary tools for problem-solving, experiential learning, and project-based learning skills for addressing complex sustainability challenges. Education and training for regenerative generations will also emphasize interdisciplinary and cross-sectoral approaches that align community engagement and impact assessment competencies.
5. **Global Governance**: The future of sustainability impact will depend on consensus building and multi-stakeholder engagement in governance for sustainable development (Negi et al., 2020). Achieving consensus on how to make needed changes, such as in energy systems, land use, and urban planning, can be challenging due to vested interests, diverse perspectives, and cultural differences. We need effective and inclusive governance structures and mechanisms to address the challenges of sustainability including policies, regulations, and institutions that promote sustainable practices and balance economic, social, and environmental goals. This will require consensus building by engaging with diverse stakeholders, including governments, civil society, business, and academia, to identify common goals and solutions. It may require compromise and negotiation to find a shared vision and approach. It will also require acknowledgment and managing vested interests, such as those of the fossil fuel industry that may pose a challenge to achieving consensus on sustainable development.

These interests may resist change and prioritize short-term profit over long-term sustainability. Ultimately, multi-stakeholder deliberations and consensus building efforts to implement good ideas would need to arise not from ideologies but data driven research analyses. These elements will be necessary to build a shared understanding and commitment to action. Global governance will be necessary to create investments and opportunities through circular and social economic policies. In spite of the resistance by some, the social and circular economy policies will gain more traction in the future for inclusive growth, reduce waste and pollution, enhance resource productivity and competitiveness, and create new economic opportunities.

In conclusion, the paradigms of our common future revolve around five key elements: Conscious Interconnectedness, Resilience and Adaptation, Stewardship and Equity, Regenerative Generations, and Global Governance. These paradigms emphasize the importance of a holistic approach to sustainability, integrating social, economic, and environmental considerations to achieve a future that is resilient, inclusive, and equitable for all. By adopting these paradigms, fostering innovation, embracing global challenges, and nurturing a shared sense of responsibility, we can collectively work towards a sustainable, prosperous, and harmonious future for generations to come.

Throughout this book, we have explored diverse facets of sustainability in the modern era, from leadership and management to innovation and impact. As we stand at a critical juncture in human history, we must urgently reassess our values, principles, and actions to ensure that we build a better future for all. Throughout the chapters, we've delved into the core concepts of sustainability leadership, management, innovation, and impact. We've examined the importance of aligning values and principles with higher purpose, fostering mindsets and ethos that support sustainability, and leveraging effective practices across sectors. Moreover, we've explored the role of entrepreneurship and technology innovations in driving progress towards the SDGs. Emphasizing the significance of design thinking and other creative approaches, we've underscored the need for adaptive and systemic solutions to the complex challenges we face. Finally, we've confronted the impact challenge for global sustainability and scrutinized the various dimensions of sustainability impact. As we strive to assess and measure our efforts, we must remember that our ultimate goal is to create a more resilient, equitable, and prosperous world for current and future generations.

In the era of sustainability, our collective actions will shape the course of history. By embracing the insights and lessons from this book, we can work together to transform our societies, economies, and environments. Let us rise to the challenge and seize the opportunity to create a truly sustainable world, one that nurtures and protects the well-being of all its inhabitants and the planet that sustains us.

Key Takeaways

1. The current generation plays a pivotal role in addressing the challenges of climate change and sustainability, being the first to feel its effects and the last with the opportunity to make a meaningful difference.
2. Specialty rights, diversity integrations, and political coherence are three major values that are anticipated to become increasingly important in sustainability impact assessments and reporting.
3. Embracing interconnectedness and recognizing the systemic nature of sustainability challenges are essential for fostering a more sustainable future.
4. Resilience, adaptation, stewardship, and equity should be at the forefront of sustainable development efforts to ensure a balanced and inclusive approach to addressing global challenges.
5. Regenerative generation and global governance are critical paradigms for creating a sustainable future, emphasizing the need for collective action, shared values, and global commitments.

References

Attenborough, D. (2020). *A life on our planet: My witness statement and a vision for the future*. Ebury Publishing.

Dalbotten, D. et al. (2014). *Future earth: Advancing civic understanding of the anthropocene*. Wiley.

Fathi, K. (2022). *Multi-Resilience—Development—Sustainability: Requirements for securing the future of societies in the 21st century*. Springer Fachmedien Wiesbaden.

Fuller, R. B., & Snyder, J. (2008). *Operating manual for spaceship earth*. Springer Singapore.

Hawken, P. (2021). *Regeneration: Ending the climate crisis in one generation*. Penguin Books.

Holthaus, E. (2020). *The future earth: A radical vision for what's possible in the age of warming*. HarperCollins.

Lawrence, P. (2014). *Justice for future generations: Climate change and international law*. Edward Elgar.

Montgomery, M. (2023). *Re-indigenizing ecological consciousness and the interconnectedness to indigenous identities*. Lexington Books.

Negi, A. et al. (2020). *Sustainability standards and global governance: Experiences of emerging economies*. Springer Nature Singapore.

Nikolakis, W., & da Veiga, R. M. (2023). *Social value, climate change and environmental stewardship: Insights from theory and practice*. Springer International Publishing.

Obama, B. (2014). *Remarks by the president at the U.N. climate change summit*. https://obamawhitehouse.archives.gov/the-press-office/2014/09/23/remarks-president-un-climate-change-summit#:~:text=As%20one%20of%20America's%20governors,begun%20to%20do%20something%20about. Accessed 19 March 2023.

Appendix 1: Essential Glossary for Developing Sustainability

Anthropocene: The Anthropocene is a proposed geological epoch that reflects the significant and pervasive impact of human activities on the Earth's geology and ecosystems. It is characterized by the dominance of human activities over natural processes, resulting in widespread and lasting changes to the planet's geology, atmosphere, biosphere, and oceans.

Blue Economy: The blue economy is a term used to describe the sustainable use of ocean resources for economic growth, improved livelihoods, and jobs while preserving the health and biodiversity of the marine environment. It includes various sectors, such as fisheries, aquaculture, maritime transportation, renewable energy, tourism, and biotechnology.

Carbon Emissions: Carbon emissions refer to the release of carbon dioxide (CO2) and other greenhouse gasses (such as methane, nitrous oxide, and fluorinated gasses) into the atmosphere as a result of human activities, such as burning fossil fuels (coal, oil, and natural gas), deforestation, and industrial processes.

Carbon Footprint: Carbon footprint is the total amount of greenhouse gasses, particularly carbon dioxide (CO2), released into the atmosphere as a result of human activities, such as transportation, energy use, food production, and other daily activities. It is often expressed in units of

M. Tavanti, *Developing Sustainability in Organizations*, Sustainable Development Goals Series,
https://doi.org/10.1007/978-3-031-36907-0

carbon dioxide equivalent ($CO2e$) and measured over a specific period, usually a year.

Carbon Neutral: Carbon neutral refers to a state in which there is no net release of greenhouse gasses, particularly carbon dioxide, into the atmosphere. It is achieved by balancing the amount of carbon emissions produced with an equal amount of carbon removal or reduction activities.

Carbon Offsetting: Carbon offsetting refers to a mechanism that allows individuals, companies, or organizations to compensate for their greenhouse gas emissions by funding projects that reduce or remove carbon dioxide or other greenhouse gas emissions from the atmosphere. The concept is based on the idea that emissions from one activity or source can be offset by investing in activities that reduce emissions or sequester carbon, such as renewable energy, energy efficiency, reforestation, and carbon capture and storage.

Carbon Positive: Carbon positive is a term used to describe a state in which there is a net removal of carbon dioxide ($CO2$) from the atmosphere, resulting in a reduction in the concentration of greenhouse gasses. This can be achieved by taking actions that sequester more carbon than is emitted, such as planting trees, restoring degraded ecosystems, and adopting regenerative agricultural practices.

Carbon Sequestration: Carbon sequestration is the process of capturing and storing atmospheric carbon dioxide ($CO2$) or other carbon compounds, such as methane, from the atmosphere or from industrial processes, and then preventing it from being released back into the atmosphere. This can be done through natural means, such as photosynthesis by plants and trees that absorb and store carbon in their biomass and in the soil, or through engineered solutions such as carbon capture and storage (CCS) technologies that capture $CO2$ emissions from power plants, industrial processes, and other sources, and store them deep underground, in geological formations or in the ocean.

Circular Economy: A circular economy is an economic system that aims to keep resources in use for as long as possible and minimize waste by designing out waste and pollution, keeping products and materials in use, and regenerating natural systems. It is a closed-loop system that contrasts with the traditional linear economy, in which products are made, used, and then disposed of as waste.

Climate Action: Climate action refers to the efforts and actions taken to mitigate or adapt to the impacts of climate change. It involves measures to reduce greenhouse gas emissions, promote sustainable development, and protect vulnerable communities and ecosystems from the impacts of a changing climate.

Climate Change: Climate change refers to long-term changes in the Earth's climate, including changes in temperature, precipitation patterns, and weather events. These changes are primarily caused by human activities, such as burning fossil fuels and deforestation, which have led to increased concentrations of greenhouse gasses, such as carbon dioxide, in the atmosphere.

Collective Impact: Collective impact is a collaborative approach to problem-solving and social change that involves multiple organizations and stakeholders working together towards a shared goal. It recognizes that complex social problems, such as poverty, inequality, and environmental degradation, require coordinated efforts and collaboration across sectors and disciplines to achieve lasting and meaningful impact.

Conscious Capitalism: Conscious capitalism is a business philosophy and approach that emphasizes the importance of social and environmental considerations alongside financial performance. It recognizes that businesses have a broader responsibility to create value for all stakeholders, including employees, customers, suppliers, communities, and the environment, rather than solely focusing on maximizing profits for shareholders.

Conscious Consumerism: Conscious consumerism is a form of consumer behavior that prioritizes social and environmental considerations when making purchasing decisions. It involves being mindful of the impact of one's consumption choices on people, animals, and the planet and making informed decisions that align with personal values and beliefs.

Corporate Social Responsibility: Corporate Social Responsibility (CSR) refers to a business approach in which a company takes responsibility for its impact on society and the environment. It involves conducting business operations in a manner that promotes social and environmental values alongside economic performance. CSR encompasses a wide range of activities and practices, including philanthropy, volunteerism, sustainability, ethical business practices, and community engagement.

Ecosystems: An ecosystem refers to a community of living organisms, including plants, animals, and microorganisms, interacting with each other and with their physical environment. An ecosystem can be as large as a forest or as small as a pond or a tree trunk. It includes all the living (biotic) and non-living (abiotic) components within an area, such as water, air, soil, sunlight, and nutrients. In management, ecosystems refer to a system of interconnected businesses, organizations, and stakeholders that collaborate to create and deliver value to customers and society. An ecosystem approach to management emphasizes the importance of collaboration, partnerships, and innovation to create value and solve complex problems.

Environmental Management Systems: Environmental management systems (EMS) are a set of policies, procedures, and practices that organizations use to manage their environmental impact and comply with relevant environmental regulations. EMS is a systematic approach to identifying, measuring, controlling, and reducing the environmental impact of an organization's operations, products, and services.

Ethical Investment: Ethical investment, also known as socially responsible investing (SRI), is an investment strategy that seeks to align financial goals with ethical and social values. Ethical investment involves investing in companies or organizations that are believed to have a positive impact on society and the environment, while avoiding those that are seen as harmful or unethical.

Fair Trade: Fair Trade is a social movement and trading partnership that aims to provide better working conditions and fairer terms of trade for producers in developing countries. Fair Trade organizations work with producers to establish fair prices for their products, improve working conditions, and provide support for community development projects.

Global Warming: Global warming refers to the long-term increase in the average temperature of the Earth's atmosphere and oceans, primarily due to the release of greenhouse gasses, such as carbon dioxide, into the atmosphere. The increase in greenhouse gasses traps more heat from the sun, leading to an overall warming effect on the planet.

Green Economy: The green economy is an economic system that prioritizes sustainability, social equity, and environmental protection. It is a system in which economic growth and development are achieved through the efficient use of natural resources, the reduction of pollution and waste, and the promotion of renewable energy and sustainable practices.

Greenhouse Gasses: Greenhouse gasses are gasses that trap heat in the Earth's atmosphere, contributing to the greenhouse effect and global warming. These gasses, including carbon dioxide (CO_2), methane (CH_4), nitrous oxide (N_2O), and fluorinated gasses, occur naturally in the Earth's atmosphere and are also released into the atmosphere through human activities such as burning fossil fuels, deforestation, and industrial processes.

Greenwashing: Greenwashing refers to the practice of making false or misleading claims about the environmental benefits of a product, service, or organization in order to appeal to environmentally conscious consumers. Greenwashing is a form of marketing or advertising that is designed to make a company or product appear more environmentally friendly than it actually is.

Integrated Reporting: Integrated reporting is a reporting framework which aims to provide a comprehensive and concise view of an organization's performance, including its financial, social, and environmental impact. The purpose of integrated reporting is to provide stakeholders with a holistic understanding of the organization's value, strategy, and risks, as well as its impact on society and the environment.

Life Cycle Assessment: Life Cycle Assessment (LCA) is a tool for evaluating the environmental impacts of a product, service, or process over its entire life cycle, from raw material extraction, through production and use, to disposal or recycling. The purpose of LCA is to identify the environmental impacts associated with the life cycle of a product or service, and to help identify opportunities for improvement in terms of resource use, energy consumption, and waste generation.

Microfinance: Microfinance refers to the provision of financial services, such as loans, savings accounts, and insurance, to individuals and small businesses who lack access to traditional banking services. Microfinance institutions typically serve low-income populations in developing countries, providing access to credit, and other financial services to help promote economic development and reduce poverty.

Natural Capital: Natural capital refers to the stock of renewable and non-renewable natural resources, such as forests, minerals, water, air, and biodiversity, that provide economic and social benefits to humans. Natural capital includes both the resources themselves and the services they provide, such as carbon sequestration, soil fertility, and pollination.

Paris Agreement: The Paris Agreement is an international treaty on climate change that was adopted by 195 countries at the United Nations Framework Convention on Climate Change (UNFCCC) in Paris in December 2015. The primary goal of the Paris Agreement is to limit global warming to well below 2 degrees Celsius above pre-industrial levels, while pursuing efforts to limit the temperature increase to 1.5 degrees Celsius.

Product Stewardship: Product stewardship is a concept that involves the responsible management of a product throughout its entire life cycle, from design and production to disposal. The goal of product stewardship is to minimize the environmental and social impacts associated with a product, and to ensure that the product's impact on the environment and society is managed throughout its life cycle.

Recyclable: Recyclable refers to materials that can be collected, processed, and reused to create new products or materials. Recycling is a key component of the circular economy and sustainable waste management, as it reduces the amount of waste that is sent to landfills, conserves natural resources, and reduces energy consumption and greenhouse gas emissions associated with extracting and processing raw materials.

Regeneration: Regeneration in the context of sustainability refers to the process of restoring, renewing, and revitalizing natural and social systems to a healthy and resilient state. Regenerative approaches prioritize the health and well-being of the planet and its inhabitants, and seek to improve the functioning of ecosystems and communities.

Remanufacturing: Remanufacturing is a process of restoring used products to their original specifications or better, using a combination of reused, repaired, and new parts. Remanufacturing involves disassembling a product, cleaning and inspecting each component, repairing or replacing any damaged parts, and reassembling the product to meet the same quality and performance standards as a new product.

Resilience: Resilience is the ability of a system or entity to withstand and recover from external stresses and disturbances, while maintaining its essential structure, function, and identity. Resilience is an important concept in the context of sustainability, as it focuses on creating systems and communities that can adapt and thrive in the face of changing conditions and uncertainties.

Restoration: Restoration in the context of sustainability refers to the process of returning ecosystems or landscapes to their original state or a desired state of health and ecological function. Restoration aims to repair the damage caused by human activities or natural disasters and to create conditions that support the long-term health and resilience of ecosystems.

Shared Value: Shared value is a business concept that refers to the creation of economic value in a way that also creates value for society and the environment. Shared value is based on the idea that business success is tied to the well-being of the community and the natural environment.

Sharing Economy: The sharing economy is an economic model that enables individuals to share or rent out their unused assets or services to others, usually facilitated through digital platforms. It allows for the efficient use of resources, reduces waste and environmental impact, and provides new income opportunities for individuals.

Social Capital: Social capital refers to the networks, relationships, and norms of trust and reciprocity that exist within a society or community, and that facilitate cooperation, collaboration, and social interaction. Social capital is an important resource for individuals and communities, and can have a significant impact on economic, social, and environmental outcomes.

Social Enterprise: A social enterprise is a business or organization that aims to achieve social or environmental objectives while also generating revenue or profits. Social enterprises use business models and strategies to address social and environmental challenges, and typically reinvest a significant portion of their profits back into their mission.

Social Impact: Social impact refers to the effect that an organization, program, or project has on social and environmental outcomes. It refers to the positive or negative changes in the lives of people and communities, and the natural environment, that can be attributed to a particular intervention.

Social Innovation: Social innovation refers to the development and implementation of new ideas, products, services, or models that address social and environmental challenges and create positive social outcomes. Social innovation involves finding new and creative solutions to complex social problems, and often involves collaboration between stakeholders from different sectors and disciplines.

Supply Chain: In the context of sustainability, a supply chain refers to the network of organizations, processes, and activities involved in the production, distribution, and delivery of goods and services in a manner that is socially, environmentally, and economically sustainable.

Sustainability: Sustainability refers to the ability to meet the needs of the present without compromising the ability of future generations to meet their own needs. It involves balancing economic, social, and environmental considerations in decision-making and taking action to ensure that resources are used in a responsible and equitable manner.

Sustainable Business: Sustainable business refers to an organization that operates in a manner that is environmentally responsible, socially equitable, and economically viable over the long term. A sustainable business recognizes that its operations have an impact on the environment, society, and the economy, and seeks to manage these impacts in a way that creates positive outcomes for all stakeholders.

Sustainable Design: Sustainable design, also known as eco-design or green design, refers to the practice of designing products, buildings, and systems in a way that minimizes negative environmental impacts while maximizing positive social and economic benefits.

Sustainable Development Goals: The Sustainable Development Goals (SDGs) are a set of 17 global goals established by the United Nations General Assembly in 2015 as part of the 2030 Agenda for Sustainable Development. The SDGs provide a framework for addressing some of the world's most pressing social, economic, and environmental challenges, including poverty, inequality, climate change, and biodiversity loss.

Sustainable Procurement: Sustainable procurement refers to the process of purchasing goods and services in a way that takes into account social, economic, and environmental considerations, and aims to support sustainable development goals.

Systems Thinking: Systems thinking is an approach to problem-solving and decision-making that views problems and situations as complex systems composed of interconnected and interdependent parts or elements. It involves understanding the relationships and interactions between these parts and how they affect the behavior and performance of the system as a whole.

Triple Bottom Line: The Triple Bottom Line (TBL) is an accounting framework that considers the economic, social, and environmental impacts of an organization's activities, often referred to as the "three Ps": profit, people, and planet.

Value Chain: A value chain is a series of activities that organizations undertake to create and deliver a product or service to their customers. The value chain concept describes the full range of activities that add value to a product or service, from the sourcing of raw materials to the delivery of the final product or service to the end customer.

Waste Stream: A waste stream refers to the flow or movement of waste materials from their point of generation to their final disposal. Waste streams can vary in composition, volume, and type, depending on the source of the waste and the way it is managed.

Zero Carbon: Zero carbon refers to the goal of achieving a net-zero carbon footprint, which means that no carbon dioxide or other greenhouse gasses are emitted or that any emissions are offset by activities that remove an equivalent amount of carbon from the atmosphere. The term "zero carbon" is often used in the context of efforts to combat climate change by reducing greenhouse gas emissions, particularly carbon dioxide emissions from fossil fuel combustion.

Zero Waste: Zero waste is a philosophy and a set of principles aimed at reducing waste generation and promoting resource conservation. The goal of zero waste is to send as little waste as possible to landfill or incineration and to instead recycle, compost, or reuse materials to the greatest extent possible.

Appendix 2: Must Know Publications in Sustainability

1. ***Silent Spring*** by Rachel Carson (1962): This book is often credited with launching the modern environmental movement. It exposed the dangers of DDT pesticide use and highlighted the need for greater environmental regulation.
2. ***The Limits to Growth*** by Donella Meadows, Dennis Meadows, Jorgen Randers, and William W. Behrens III (1972): This book used computer modeling to explore the long-term sustainability of economic growth. It argued that if current trends continued, the world would soon reach its limits to growth, and called for a transition to a more sustainable economy.
3. ***Small is Beautiful*** by E.F. Schumacher (1973): This book challenged the dominant paradigm of economic growth and development, arguing for a focus on human-scale technologies, local self-reliance, and sustainable living.
4. ***Our Common Future*** (1987): Also known as *The Brundtland Report*, this report defined sustainable development as "development that meets the needs of the present without compromising the ability of future generations to meet their own needs." It fostered the global sustainable development movement.

M. Tavanti, *Developing Sustainability in Organizations*, Sustainable Development Goals Series,
https://doi.org/10.1007/978-3-031-36907-0

5. ***Agenda 21*** (1992): A comprehensive plan of action adopted at the United Nations Conference on Environment and Development (UNCED) in Rio de Janeiro, Agenda 21 sets out a global agenda for sustainable development. It covers a range of issues, including poverty, health, education, gender equality, and environmental protection.
6. ***Natural Capitalism*** by Paul Hawken, Amory Lovins, and L. Hunter Lovins (1999): This book argued that businesses could profitably and sustainably operate by focusing on resource efficiency, eco-innovation, and stakeholder engagement.
7. ***The Earth Charter*** (2000): This document is a declaration of fundamental principles for building a just, sustainable, and peaceful global society in the twenty-first century. It sets out ethical values and principles for sustainable development, including respect for nature, social justice, and intergenerational equity.
8. ***The Millennium Declaration*** (2000–2015): This is the document that introduces the Millennium Development Goals (MDGs), a set of eight goals adopted by the UN to reduce poverty, improve health, and promote sustainable development. They included eradicating extreme poverty and hunger, achieving universal primary education, and ensuring environmental sustainability.
9. ***Cradle to Cradle: Remaking the Way We Make Things*** by William McDonough and Michael Braungart (2002): This book introduced the concept of "cradle-to-cradle" design, which aims to eliminate waste and pollution by designing products and processes that mimic natural systems.
10. ***Transforming Our World: The 2030 Agenda For Sustainable Development*** (2015–2030)—this is the document with the plan of action adopted by the United Nations General Assembly in September 2015. It is a global framework for sustainable development that aims to end poverty, protect the planet, and ensure peace and prosperity for all people. The Agenda includes 17 Sustainable Development Goals (SDGs) with 169 targets to be achieved by 2030.

Appendix 3: Must Know Initiatives for Sustainability Leadership

1. **B Corporation**: B Corporation is a certification program for companies that meet rigorous standards of social and environmental performance, accountability, and transparency. Becoming a B Corp allows companies to demonstrate their commitment to sustainability and access a community of like-minded businesses.
2. **Carbon Disclosure Project (CDP)**: CDP is an international organization that helps companies and cities disclose their environmental impacts and take action to reduce them. Joining CDP allows companies to measure and manage their greenhouse gas emissions and set targets for emissions reduction.
3. **Chief Executives for Corporate Purpose (CECP)**: CECP is a nonprofit organization that brings together CEOs and senior corporate leaders to advance the role of business in creating a sustainable and inclusive society. Founded in 1999, CECP has more than 200 members, including some of the world's largest and most influential companies.
4. **Global Reporting Initiative (GRI)**: GRI is an international organization that sets standards for sustainability reporting. Companies can use these standards to disclose their sustainability performance and communicate their sustainability commitments to stakeholders.

M. Tavanti, *Developing Sustainability in Organizations*,
Sustainable Development Goals Series,
https://doi.org/10.1007/978-3-031-36907-0

5. **Principles for Responsible Management Education (PRME)**: PRME is a United Nations-supported initiative launched in 2007, which seeks to promote responsible management education worldwide. PRME is a voluntary initiative, and its signatories commit to incorporating six principles of responsible management education into their academic activities and curriculum.
6. **Sustainability Accounting Standards Board (SASB)**: SASB is a nonprofit organization that sets industry-specific standards for sustainability disclosure. Companies can use these standards to report on their sustainability performance and compare their performance with peers.
7. **The International Integrated Reporting Council (IIRC)**: The IIRC is a global organization that promotes integrated reporting, a reporting framework that combines financial and non-financial information to provide a comprehensive view of a company's performance. By joining the IIRC, companies can learn how to integrate sustainability into their reporting and communicate their sustainability performance to stakeholders.
8. **The Natural Step**: The Natural Step is a nonprofit organization that provides sustainability consulting and training services to companies and organizations. They offer a framework for sustainability planning that helps organizations understand the connections between environmental, social, and economic systems.
9. **The World Business Council for Sustainable Development (WBCSD)**: The WBCSD is a global organization that brings together leading businesses to accelerate the transition to a sustainable world. The organization provides a platform for businesses to collaborate on sustainability initiatives, share best practices, and advocate for policies that promote sustainable business practices.
10. **United Nations Global Compact (UNGC)**: The UNGC is a voluntary initiative launched in 2000 that aims to mobilize a global movement of responsible companies and organizations to create a sustainable and inclusive global economy. Joining UNGC allows companies to demonstrate their commitment to sustainability and access resources and tools to implement sustainable practices.

Appendix 4: Must Know Tools for Sustainability Management

1. **Biodiversity Assessment**: Biodiversity assessment is a tool that measures the impact of a company's activities on biodiversity and ecosystem services. It helps companies identify their main impacts on biodiversity and develop strategies to mitigate them.
2. **Carbon Footprinting**: Carbon footprinting is a tool that measures the greenhouse gas emissions associated with a company's activities, products, or services. It helps companies identify their main sources of emissions and develop strategies to reduce them.
3. **Environmental Management Systems (EMS)**: An EMS is a framework for managing an organization's environmental impacts. It provides a systematic approach to identifying and managing environmental risks and opportunities, and helps companies improve their environmental performance.
4. **Life Cycle Assessment (LCA)**: LCA is a tool that assesses the environmental impact of a product or service throughout its entire life cycle, from raw material extraction to disposal. It provides a comprehensive view of a product's environmental impact and helps companies identify opportunities to reduce their environmental footprint.
5. **Materiality Assessment**: A materiality assessment helps companies identify the sustainability issues that are most important to their stakeholders and their business. It helps companies prioritize their

M. Tavanti, *Developing Sustainability in Organizations*,
Sustainable Development Goals Series,
https://doi.org/10.1007/978-3-031-36907-0

sustainability efforts and develop sustainability strategies that align with their business objectives.

6. **Social Impact Assessment**: Social impact assessment is a tool that measures the social impacts of a company's activities, products, or services on stakeholders, such as employees, communities, and customers. It helps companies identify their main social impacts and develop strategies to promote social sustainability.
7. **Stakeholder Engagement**: Stakeholder engagement involves communicating with and listening to stakeholders, including customers, employees, investors, and communities, to understand their expectations and concerns related to sustainability. It helps companies build trust and credibility with their stakeholders and incorporate their feedback into their sustainability strategies.
8. **Sustainability Reporting**: Sustainability reporting involves communicating a company's sustainability performance to stakeholders through various channels, such as annual reports, sustainability reports, and online platforms. It helps companies demonstrate their commitment to sustainability and accountability to their stakeholders.
9. **Sustainable Product Design**: Sustainable product design involves designing products that have a lower environmental impact and are more socially responsible throughout their life cycle. It helps companies reduce their environmental footprint and improve their sustainability performance.
10. **Sustainable Supply Chain Management**: Sustainable supply chain management involves assessing and managing the social and environmental impacts of a company's supply chain. It helps companies identify risks and opportunities related to sustainability in their supply chain and work with suppliers to improve sustainability performance.

Index

M. Tavanti, *Developing Sustainability in Organizations*, Sustainable Development Goals Series,
https://doi.org/10.1007/978-3-031-36907-0

FSC
www.fsc.org
MIX
Papier | Fördert gute Waldnutzung
FSC® C083411

Kolibri 360 GmbH
Ferdinand-Jühlke-Straße 7
99095 Erfurt, Deutschland
produktsicherheit@kolibri360.de